BLOOD, SWEAT, AND TEARS

BOOKS BY

WINSTON S. CHURCHILL

SAVROLA

THE STORY OF THE MALAKAND FIELD FORCE

THE RIVER WAR

LONDON TO LADYSMITH VIA PRETORIA

IAN HAMILTON'S MARCH

LORD RANDOLPH CHURCHILL

MY AFRICAN JOURNEY

LIBERALISM AND THE SOCIAL PROBLEM

THE WORLD CRISIS: 1911–1918

THE WORLD CRISIS, 1918–1928; THE AFTERMATH

UNKNOWN WAR; THE EASTERN FRONT

A ROVING COMMISSION; MY EARLY LIFE

AMID THESE STORMS; THOUGHTS AND ADVENTURES

MARLBOROUGH, HIS LIFE AND TIMES, 5 VOLS.

GREAT CONTEMPORARIES

WHILE ENGLAND SLEPT

STEP BY STEP: 1936–1939

BLOOD, SWEAT, AND TEARS

Photograph by Cecil Beaton

BLOOD, SWEAT, AND TEARS

by

THE RT. HON. WINSTON S. CHURCHILL
C.H., M.P.

With a Preface and Notes by
RANDOLPH S. CHURCHILL, M.P.

NEW YORK

G. P. PUTNAM'S SONS

Printed and bound in United States of America
By The Haddon Craftsmen, Inc., Camden, N. J.

CONTENTS

INTRODUCTION

TWO AND A HALF years have passed since the publication of *While England Slept,* a collection of speeches by Mr. Winston Churchill on National Defense and Foreign Policy from 1932 to 1938.

A number of people, both in this country and in the United States, have recently urged me to bring the story up to date. With the Prime Minister's permission, I have therefore collected all his speeches from May, 1938, down to the present day.

This volume sees the fulfillment of all the darkest fears to which Mr. Churchill gave utterance in the earlier volume. By the time this set of speeches begins the situation had already become so desperate that less emphasis is placed upon our laggardly rearmament than in the earlier speeches. With the danger so close upon us, and with so little time to expand our defenses, Mr. Churchill clearly thought it more useful, in the hopes of deterring the aggressor, to dwell upon such elements of strength as we possessed rather than to exhibit our weakness nakedly to the world. Reading between the lines, however, the warnings persist with even more urgency than before. As in the previous volume, these speeches will be found not only to revive many warnings, whose timeliness all can judge today, but to provide a running commentary upon the remorseless deterioration of the foreign situation.

The book begins with Mr. Churchill's warning on the folly of handing over the Treaty ports to the Irish Free State—a warning which, it is interesting to recall, was supported by only a handful of Members of Parliament. It carries us past the tremendous and mournful events at Munich to the inevitable and plainly pointed sequel in Prague. And so we are brought relentlessly stage by stage to the challenge of war which Mr. Churchill had so often urged could, by timely arrangements and adequate preparations, have been warded off.

Thereafter, as First Lord of the Admiralty and, later, as Prime Minister, his speeches naturally become more official. Despite this, and the inevitable pressure of business, I do not think that they will be found to lack the literary and dramatic quality of those which he made as a private Member. Indeed, they constitute a contemporary history of the war which is as lively as it is authoritative; and, so far as contemporary history is of value, they may be said to be the last word upon the war.

There are few public men who would care to have their speeches printed without alteration within two or three years of their delivery. But, as in *While England Slept,* I have not altered even a phrase on the grounds of political expediency, and, except for the excision of certain passages which are no longer of much general interest, and occasional compressions to allow for the difference between the spoken and the written word, these speeches are printed as they were delivered.

I acknowledge, with grateful thanks, the help of Mr. Desmond Flower in compiling these speeches.

RANDOLPH S. CHURCHILL

ICKLEFORD HOUSE
November, 1940

CONTENTS

BLOOD, SWEAT, AND TEARS

EIRE BILL

The House of Commons

May 5, 1938

1938

January 12.   Mr. de Valera and two colleagues come to London to discuss outstanding questions affecting relations between the United Kingdom and Eire.

February 4.   Dismissal of Field-Marshal von Blomberg and General von Fritsch precipitated by the former's marriage.

February 12.   Dr. Schuschnigg, Chancellor of Austria, summoned to Berchtesgaden by Herr Hitler.

February 16.   Dr. Schuschnigg accepts Herr Hitler's demands and introduces Nazi members into his Cabinet.

February 21.   Mr. Anthony Eden resigns the post of Foreign Secretary owing to Mr. Chamberlain's determination to conclude a new pact with Italy, notwithstanding the latter's continued breaches of the Non-Intervention Agreement.

March 11.   German ultimatum to Austria, followed immediately by invasion.

March 13.   Germany announces the incorporation of Austria in the Reich.

April 16.   Agreement signed between Great Britain and Italy, its operation being contingent upon the withdrawal of Italian forces from Spain.

April 24.   Herr Henlein, leader of the Nazis in the Sudetenland, formulates the "Karlsbad Program" of eight demands to be made on the Czechoslovakian Government.

April 25.   Mr. de Valera and other Eire ministers sign an agreement whereby, among other things, the United Kingdom foregoes any power or authority over the ports of Eire. The Navy cannot, therefore, in future use any of these ports as bases.

May 2.   The Anglo-Italian Agreement approved by the House of Commons.

EIRE BILL

I COULD not reconcile it with my duty to the House, as a signatory to the Treaty, the broken Treaty, if I kept silent upon this Bill. However thankless the task may be, I feel bound to record the view which I have formed as the result of long and intimate contacts with Irish affairs. When I read this Agreement in the newspapers a week ago I was filled with surprise. On the face of it, we seem to give everything away and receive nothing in return, except the payment of £10,000,000. But then I supposed there was another side to the Agreement, and that we were to be granted some facilities and rights in Southern Ireland in time of war. That, I notice, was the view taken by a part of the Press, but soon Mr. de Valera in the Dail made it clear that he was under no obligations of any kind and, as the Prime Minister confirmed this afternoon, there were no reservations on either side attached to this Agreement. On the contrary, Mr. de Valera has not even abandoned his claim for the incorporation of Ulster in the independent Republic that he has established. Indeed, he said in his speech in the Dail—I am not quoting his actual words—that the ending of Partition will remain the main purpose of his life, and he believed that it would ultimately be found to be brought nearer by this Agreement.

It is very necessary to make some review of the past in order to see the setting in which these particular proposals lie. The Prime Minister said that we must look to the intangible and imponderable as the counterpoise of the great concessions which we have made under this Agreement. Let us look at that for a moment. We are told that we have ended the age-long quarrel between England and Ireland, but that is clearly not true, because Mr. de Valera has said that he will never rest until Partition is swept away. Therefore, the real conflict has yet to come, and nothing in the nature of a final settlement has been reached upon the most difficult point of all. We have been told, and I would not underrate it, that we are to have the precious atmosphere of good will and that the people of Southern Ireland will henceforward be friendly to us and will side with us in any trouble that arises. There is nothing new in that. At the beginning of the Great War the people of Ireland showed themselves very friendly to us and threw themselves most heartily into the defense of the common cause. Ireland was represented in the fullest manner in this House. Members were in the closest touch with their constituents, and were united, I think unanimously; and the Irish Members, north and south, voted for the War, and not only for the War but for all the measures, severe as they were, necessary for sustaining it in its opening stages.

I remember well that Ireland was described at that time as the one bright spot in the world. Undoubtedly we enjoyed the friendship and comradeship of the Irish nation at that time, and undoubtedly it was signified in the most formal manner by all their representatives, but that did not prevent the dark forces of the Irish underworld from trying to strike us in the back in the most critical and dangerous period of the struggle. After the War a painful conflict followed, in which we made a Treaty with those same forces, and of that Treaty I am one of the few remaining signatories. An Irish Parliament, freely assembled, accepted the Treaty by a majority. That Treaty has been kept in the letter and the spirit by Great Britain, but the Treaty has been violated and repudiated in every detail by Mr. de Valera, quite consistently, because he had already rebelled against his colleagues who had made the Treaty in his despite. He has repudiated, practically for all purposes, the Crown. He has repudiated appeal to the Privy Council. He has repudiated the financial arrangement. He claims to have set up an independent sovereign Republic for Ireland, and he avows his determination to have all Ireland subject to that independent Republic.

His Majesty's Government, supported by the Conservative Party and the Opposition Parties, have now accepted Mr. de Valera's claim practically without challenge, except for the fact that they are not prepared to put pressure upon Ulster to make her leave the United Kingdom. No doubt they would defend Ulster with all their strength if she were violently attacked. All the rest of the contentions of Mr. de Valera are, it seems to me, tacitly or directly accepted. I think that is a fair statement of the position.

I have for a great many years walked in step and in agreement with my right hon. Friend the Prime Minister on the Irish question. I remember when I was conducting the Irish Free State Bill through this House the resolute support which he gave to that Government as a Private Member, speaking from below the Gangway, at the most painful and most difficult part of that process, immediately after Sir Henry Wilson had been murdered close by this House, in Eaton Square. In 1925 we were both Members of the same Government, when Mr. Justice Feetham's Boundary Commission gave an award which deeply disappointed the Irish Ministers. On that occasion I made, as the hon. Member for County Down [Sir D. Reid] has mentioned, a substantial modification of the financial provisions, in order to make the position easier for the men with whom we had signed the Treaty, and who were so faithfully endeavoring to give effect to the Treaty.

Respect for treaties is a very important factor, and it cannot be treated as if it were a matter of no consequence. I remember very well that the Irish Government of those days described the arrangement which resulted from that concession not only as just but generous. When Mr. de Valera came to power against these men, in 1931, the National Government, of which my right hon. Friend the Prime Minister was the mainspring—he did much the hardest part of the work—did not hesitate, when Mr. de Valera repudiated the financial provisions, to impose retaliatory duties, which were so well conceived from this particular point of view that they had the effect of recovering for us practically the whole of what was our due, forcing Mr. de Valera to pay a large proportion of his obligations to this country by the roundabout but costly method of bounties upon exports. I was in agreement with my right hon. Friend on that matter.

The British Government, in the fairest manner, offered to submit the whole question of land purchase annuities and the general financial question to arbitration. Mr. de Valera was willing to agree to arbitration, but he insisted that there should be a foreigner upon the tribunal. But the British Government, to all intents and purposes the same Government as today, would not agree to anyone being on the tribunal who was not a subject of the King Emperor. I thought, and I still think, that the position taken up by my right hon. Friend and the Government was right, and it was steadfastly approved by this House. Now all the difficulty about the tribunal has been removed, and removed by the simple process of complete surrender on our part of the whole case. We have given away our whole case in regard to the financial position, which was just and sound, and on which we relied; and we have given away our whole position on land annuities without arbitration of any kind, on account of a payment of £10,000,000, a derisory payment if it is to be regarded as a settlement of the sum in question. Practically, we have given away £100,000,000, to which we had a valid claim. As the Chancellor of the Exchequer reminded us in his Budget speech, that action has imposed upon this country in this year of onerous taxation, with great needs and burdens, over £4,000,000, which we shall have to meet this year and in the future.

What were these land annuities? They were not a tribute wrung by England from Ireland. They were the purchase price by which a peasant proprietor—a luxury which we have never been able to achieve in England—was established on Irish soil. Moreover, a large part of this £4,000,-000 or £5,000,000 which we received on this account went back to Ireland, and will go back for many years to come, in the shape of pensions which are paid by the British Exchequer, and are spent in Ireland. Therefore, I must say that I am puzzled, and I regret that the Government have abandoned our rights wholesale in this matter, and have departed entirely, without warning to Parliament, from the position which they had deliberately taken up with full assent both before the General Election and afterwards.

I confess that I was wholly unprepared to read in the newspapers that we have abandoned all our contentions about the repudiation of the Treaty, about the annuities, and, above all—and this is the subject which makes me feel compelled to speak—our contentions about the strategic ports. It is this issue of the strategic ports which makes me undertake the thankless task of bringing some of these matters very respectfully to the attention of the House. The ports in question, Queenstown, Berehaven and Lough Swilly, are to be handed over unconditionally, with no guarantees of any kind, as a gesture of our trust and good will, as the Prime Minister said, to the Government of the Irish Republic. When the Irish Treaty was being shaped in 1922 I was instructed by the Cabinet to prepare that part of the Agreement which dealt with strategic reservations. I negotiated with Mr. Michael Collins, and I was advised by Admiral Beatty, who had behind him the whole staff of the Admiralty, which had just come out of the successful conduct of the Great War. Therefore, we had high authority in prescribing the indispensable minimum of reservations for strategic security.

The Admiralty of those days assured me that without the use of these ports it would be very difficult, perhaps almost impossible, to feed this Island in time of war. Queenstown and Berehaven shelter the flotillas which keep clear the approaches to the Bristol and English Channels, and Lough Swilly is the base from which the access to the Mersey and the Clyde is covered. In a war against an enemy possessing a numerous and powerful fleet of submarines these are the essential bases from which the whole operation of hunting submarines and protecting incoming convoys is conducted. I am very sorry to have to strike a jarring note this afternoon, but all opinions should be heard and put on record. If we are denied the use of Lough Swilly and have to work from Lamlash, we should strike 200 miles from the effective radius of our flotillas, out and home; and if we are denied Berehaven and Queenstown, and have to work from Pembroke Dock, we should strike 400 miles from their effective radius out and home. These ports are, in fact, the sentinel towers of the western approaches, by which the 45,000,000 people in this Island so enormously depend on foreign food for their daily bread, and by which they can carry on their trade, which is equally important to their existence.

In 1922 the Irish delegates made no difficulty about this. They saw that it was vital to our safety that we should be able to use these ports and, therefore, the matter passed into the structure of the Treaty without any serious controversy. Now we are to give them up, unconditionally, to an Irish Government led by men—I do not want to use hard words—whose rise to power has been proportionate to the animosity with which they have acted against this country, no doubt in pursuance of their own patriotic impulses, and whose present position in power is based upon the violation of solemn Treaty engagements. I read in *The Times* that:

"The Agreement on defense...releases the Government of the United Kingdom from the articles of the Anglo-Irish Treaty of 1921 by which they assumed the onerous and delicate task of defending the fortified harbors of Cork, Berehaven and Lough Swilly in the event of war."

That is the way it is put—we are released from these burdens. I dare say you could make arrangements with many countries to release us from a great many burdens of a similar kind. I am not going to trespass on controversial grounds by reciting some of the countries who would be willing to release you from some of your difficult and delicate obligations of defending ports of the British Empire in time of war. We are to sacrifice £4,000,000 revenue because this tiresome business of defense is taken out of our hands and we are released from the necessity of defending these ports. It is quite true that the Prime Minister has read out the clauses which are to be repealed in the Irish Free State Act. It is quite true that we spoke in those clauses of the coastal defense of Ireland. That was polite. It was felt by both sides that it was better to put it that way. But these are not ports which are part of the coastal defenses of Ireland; they are the life defenses of the crowded population of England. Incidentally, the possession of these ports by a superior British Navy enables us to give protection to Ireland against invasion from overseas, protection to their shipping and trade, and general protection except from the air. But the primary purpose of holding these ports is the defense of Britain.

In all my experience nothing has surprised me more than that I should have to stand here today and plead this argument against a National Government and the Conservative Party. Well was it said that "the vicissitudes of politics are inexhaustible." We have been told that this was settled after consultation with the Chiefs of Staff. If it is true that they have recommended this course as being free from danger, that they have raised no serious objection, then I must say that they are advising contrary to the whole weight of the expert opinion placed before the Government which made the Irish Free State Treaty. We do not know, of course, how the questions were put to these experts, and it is evident that in these matters politics and defense are inextricably mingled together. Of course, if we accept the basis that we are to have a friendly Ireland and that the ports will be in trustworthy and competent hands, then the argument falls to the ground, but to say that is to beg the whole question in dispute. What grounds of experience have we for assuming that all will be well in the future? We are conceding rights, and we have no guarantees at all except the hope and assertion that these rights will be replaced by good will. Obviously, if these ports, or any part of Ireland, fell into the hands of an enemy Power, or if Southern Ireland became herself an enemy Power, then the matter would pass into the region of force, and if we possessed superior forces we should be able to rectify the situation.

I am not going to argue, although it should not be excluded, that these ports will fall into the hands of an enemy Power. There is a great deal of substance in Mr. de Valera's declaration that the Irish would resent the landing of any foreign Power upon their shores, and that their main desire would be to rid their country from such an intrusion. But it seems to me that the danger which has to be considered, and which ought not to be excluded, is that Ireland might be neutral. I have not been able to form a clear opinion of the exact juridical position of the Government of that portion of Ireland called Southern Ireland, which is now called Eire. That is a word which really has no application at the present time, and I must say, even from the point of view of the ordinary uses of English, that it is not customary to quote a term in a foreign language, a capital town, a geographical place, when there exists a perfectly well-known English equivalent. It is usual to say "Paris"—not "Paree."

But what guarantee have you that Southern Ireland, or the Irish Republic, as they claim to be—and you do not contradict them—will not declare neutrality if we are engaged in war with some powerful nation? The first step certainly which such an enemy might take would be to offer complete immunity of every kind to Southern Ireland if she would remain neutral. What answer will Mr. de Valera or his successors—the world does not end with the life of any man—what answer will Mr. de Valera give? He may say, of course, "I will stand by your side." That is what we all hope. But he may also say, "I will be neutral." There is a third course, and this is one to which I want to draw the attention of the House. He might say, "Restore the integrity of our country, give me the whole of Ireland, and then I will throw in my lot with you, and make common cause with you." That is a serious contingency ahead in the future. We can see it, because there it is, and it may be that is what he meant when he said that this Agreement would ultimately further the ending of Partition.

The Ministers of the Crown have established pleasant relations with Mr. de Valera. I understand that his view—a characteristically Irish view —is that the only way to unite the two islands is to dissolve every possible connection between them. Ministers have certainly formed the impression, and, after all, they have had the advantage of close contact with him, that if they trust him he will see them through. But he has made no promise of this kind; he has given no guarantees, and every act of his life points in the contrary direction. Under this Agreement, it seems to me more than probable—at any rate it is a contingency which we cannot exclude —that Mr. de Valera's Government will at some supreme moment of emergency demand the surrender of Ulster as an alternative to declaring neutrality. He has made no promises, and even if he had I do not think we should have conceded our rights without some protection.

You may say that he is a man of his word. You could certainly say that of Mr. Michael Collins, who died for it. You could say it of Mr. Kevin O'Higgins, who died for his word, and of Mr. Arthur Griffiths. I do not know whether he died in consequence of the Treaty, but he died because of his exertions to carry out what he had promised. And then there is Mr. Cosgrave and his colleagues. They have lost all their power in their own country in an effort to make good their undertakings to Great Britain, and they are now utterly stultified by the fact that we have abandoned every point which they regarded themselves as in honor bound to maintain unless we released them. That was the time, if you were going to make these concessions. If they were possible and agreeable to our safety, then we had the men who had actually signed the Treaty, and who were out vehemently to sustain the Treaty. This would have made their part easy. As it is, it has only set a premium on all those who come forward in Ireland to break engagements with the British Government and to overturn the men who are faithfully adhering to solemnly contracted pledges.

MR. LOGAN: Mr. Cosgrave welcomed it [the new agreement].

MR. CHURCHILL: Naturally, he did. I am sure he would. I admire very much the immediate manner in which he welcomed the great concessions which have been made to his country; but, as I say, I only wish that if they were to be made, they had been made to those who kept faith with us. None the less, the fact remains that in Irish history, Mr. Cosgrave, his party and his friends will always be considered to have taken a poorer view of Ireland's chances than Mr. de Valera, and Mr. de Valera to have been the one who gained them the great advantages they got. That is a hard burden to impose in history upon men who faithfully adhere to solemnly contracted treaties. Mr. de Valera has given no undertaking, except to fight against Partition as the main object of his life. But behind and beneath him there are other forces in Ireland. The dark forces in Ireland renew themselves from year to year. When some are conciliated, others present themselves. They are very powerful in Ireland now. No one has ever been brought to justice in Ireland since the Treaty for murdering an Englishman. There is a whole organization of secret men bound together on the old principle that England's danger is Ireland's opportunity. Even Mr. de Valera, while gaining these astonishing triumphs over what these persons regard as their hereditary foe, is only with difficulty holding these forces in check and in suspense. Let him proclaim a friendly policy towards England and you will find that they will immediately grow in force and become the party in the ascendant. Let him ask these people to expose Ireland to the great tribulations of war for the sake of England and see what they will do. It seems to me that you cannot exclude this possibility of neutrality as being one which may well come within the immediate sphere of our experience. Therefore, I say that the ports may be denied to us in the hour of need and we may be hampered in the gravest manner in protecting the British population from privation, and even starvation. Who would wish to put his head in such a noose? Is there any other country in the modern world where such a step would even have been contemplated? Let me say this —and I hope it will not give offense—can anyone remember any other House of Commons where such proposals would have gone through in this easy manner? No doubt hon. Members will speak about the Dominions. No doubt I shall be told about South Africa, Canada and Australia. The case of Ireland is not comparable with the Dominions. Southern Ireland is not a Dominion; it has never accepted that position. It is a State based upon a Treaty, which Treaty has been completely demolished. Southern Ireland, therefore, becomes a State which is an undefined and unclassified anomaly. No one knows what its juridical and international rights and status are. The Dominions are far away. We could guarantee their immunity from attack with our Fleet. The Dominions are loyal. Great as would be their loss, still I cannot feel that it would necessarily be fatal to us if, during the course of a war, there was a declaration of neutrality by one or other of the Dominions. But here the danger is at our very door. Without the use of these Treaty ports, even if their use were also withheld from an enemy, we should find the greatest difficulty in conducting our supply.

I wish it were possible, even at this stage, to postpone the passage of the Bill—I put it to the Prime Minister, if I may, even at this stage— until some further arrangements could be made about the Treaty ports, or some more general arrangement could be made about common action and defense. Would it not be far better to give up the £10,000,000, and acquire the legal right, be it only on a lease granted by treaty, to use these harbors when necessary? Surely, there should be some right retained. The garrisons, of course, are at present only small ones, little more than care and maintenance parties. It would be a serious step for a Dublin Government to attack these forts while they are in our possession and while we have the right to occupy them. It would be an easy step for a Dublin Government to deny their use to us once we have gone. The cannon are there, the mines will be there. But more important for this purpose, the juridical right will be there. We are going away, we are giving up these ports, and giving to this other Government the right as well as the power to forbid our re-entry. You had the rights. You have ceded them. You hope in their place to have good will, strong enough to endure tribulation for your sake. Suppose you have it not. It will be no use saying, "Then we will retake the ports." You will have no right to do so. To violate Irish neutrality should it be declared at the moment of a great war may put you out of court in the opinion of the world, and may vitiate the cause by which you may be involved in war. If ever we have to fight again, we shall be fighting in the name of law, of respect for the rights of small countries—Belgium, for instance—and upon the basis and within the ambit of the Covenant of the League of Nations.

When we are proceeding, as we should be in such unhappy circumstances, upon the basis of law and equity, how could we justify ourselves if we began by violating the neutrality of what the world will regard, and what we are teaching the world to regard, as the Independent Irish Republic? At the moment when the good will of the United States in matters of blockade and supply might be of the highest possible consequence, you might be forced to take violent action against all law and accepted usage, or alternatively you might be forced to sacrifice Ulster, or, in the third place, do without the use of these almost vitally important strategic ports. What is it all being done for? What are the new facts which have led to this sudden departure? To me, it is incomprehensible. To the world, to all the hungry aggressive nations, it will be taken as another sign that Britain has only to be pressed and worried long enough, and hard enough, for her to give way. If that is so, by that very fact you will bring the possibility of war nearer and you will lessen your resources for dealing with that danger. You are inviting demands from every quarter. You are casting away real and important means of security and survival for vain shadows and for ease.

THE CHOICE FOR EUROPE
The Free Trade Hall, Manchester

May 9, 1938

1938

May 3–9. Visit of Herr Hitler to Rome.

THE CHOICE FOR EUROPE

I HAVE felt it my duty to make exertions, so far as I can, to rouse the country in the face of an ever-growing danger. This is no campaign against the Government of the day, nor against the Opposition. It is not intended to promote the interests of any Party, or to influence the course of any Election. All Parties, Conservative, Liberal, Labor, Socialist, are on the platform. Church and Chapel, Protestant and Catholic, Jew and Gentile, have come together. Trade Union leaders, Co-operators, merchants, traders, industrialists, those who are reviving the strength of our Territorial forces, those who are working on A.R.P.—none have felt themselves debarred.

But what is the purpose which has brought us all together? It is the conviction that the life of Britain, her glories and message to the world, can only be achieved by national unity, and national unity can only be preserved upon a cause which is larger than the nation itself. However we may differ in political opinion, however divergent our Party interests, however diverse our callings and stations, we have this in common: We mean to defend our Island from tyranny and aggression, and so far as we can, we mean to hold out a helping hand to others who may be in even more immediate danger than at this moment we are ourselves. We repudiate all ideas of abject or slothful defeatism. We wish to make our country safe and strong—she can only be safe if she is strong—and we wish her to play her part with other Parliamentary democracies on both sides of the Atlantic Ocean in warding off from civilization, while time yet remains, the devastating and obliterating horrors of another world war. We wish to see inaugurated a reign of international law, backed, as it must be in these turbulent times, by ample and, if possible, superabundant strength.

At this moment in history the broad, toiling masses in every country have for the first time the opportunity of a fuller and less burdened life. Science is at hand to spread a more bountiful table than has ever been offered to the millions and to the tens of millions. Shorter hours of labor, greater assurances against individual misfortune: a wider if a simpler culture: a more consciously realized sense of social justice: an easier and a more equal society—these are the treasures which, after all these generations and centuries of impotence and confusion, are now·within the reach of mankind.

Are these hopes, are these prospects, are all the secrets which the genius of man has wrested from Nature, to be turned by tyranny, aggression and war only to his own destruction? Or are they to become the agencies of a broadening freedom, and of an enduring peace?

Never before has the choice of blessings or curses been so plainly, vividly, even brutally offered to mankind. The choice is open. The dreadful balance trembles. It may be that our Island and all the Commonwealths it has gathered around it may if we are worthy play an important, perhaps even a decisive part in turning the scales of human fortune from bad to good, from fear to confidence, from miseries and crimes immeasurable to blessings and gains abounding.

We make ourselves the servants of this cause, but it is no use espousing a cause without having also a method and a plan by which that cause may be made to win. I would not affront you with generalities. There must be the vision. There must be a plan, and there must be action following upon it. We express our immediate plan and policy in a single sentence: "Arm, and stand by the Covenant." In this alone lies the assurance of safety, the defense of freedom, and the hope of peace.

What is this Covenant by which we are to stand? It is the Covenant of the League of Nations. After the calamities of the Great War, many States and peoples banded themselves together to establish a system of collective security, whereby the violent aggression of one Government upon another should be curbed and prevented; and so that processes should be devised whereby the grievances of peoples or communities should be redressed fairly and sincerely without recourse to war. By the Covenant of the League, and by the Kellogg Pact, almost all countries have bound themselves to adopt these principles, to enforce them, and to submit themselves to them.

How far, alas, do man's endeavors fall short in practice of his inspirations! Great States and peoples have fallen away. Some have violated the faith they had pledged. Some are seduced by intrigue, or have yielded themselves to the cynical, short-sighted and selfish. Many are oppressed by a sense of isolation and weakness. Others are obviously frightened. The Covenant has been broken. The League has been frustrated. Over all the anxious Governments, over all the vast masses, broods the baleful shadow of disunity and failure. In our ears ring the taunts of mockery and the reproach of fiasco.

And yet we stand here today to proclaim that this was the sovereign plan: that it remains at once the wisest, the most noble, the most sane, and the most practical path upon which the men and women of every land should set their feet tonight: on which they should march forward and for which they should strive with might and main.

If the League of Nations has been mishandled and broken, we must rebuild it. If a League of peace-seeking peoples is set at nought, we must convert it into a League of armed peoples, too faithful to molest others, too strong to be molested themselves. Why should we deem this task beyond our strength at the present time?

Outside this happy Island the world is dark with storm. In the Far East a brutal onslaught has been made upon what was thought to be an enormous, unorganized people. But the Chinese, patient, intelligent, brave, though sadly lacking in weapons, have rallied in resistance to the cruel invader and aggressor; and it is by no means certain that in the end they will be trampled down. Here we must recognize the service which Russia is rendering in the Far East. Soviet Russia, without firing a shot, is holding the best troops of Japan close-gripped upon the Siberian front, and the rest of the Japanese armies may not in the end be found capable of subjugating and exploiting the four hundred millions of Chinese. At home in Japan there is not only financial and economic strain, but also a social awakening of the Japanese people, which already takes the form of serious discontent. If the Japanese nation be warned in time, they will withdraw before it is too late from a vainglorious enterprise, which if pursued might cast away all the wonderful progress they have made in fifty years.

Let us return to Europe. Two Dictators, men of unusual force and commanding ability, are saluting and embracing each other in Rome. But anyone can see the natural antagonisms of interest and perhaps of aim which divide their peoples. Anyone can see that the Italian Dictator is hard-pressed. In Abyssinia his conquest has proved a curse. The strength and resources of the industrious, amiable Italian people are draining away. Abyssinia is occupied, but not subdued. Agriculture and industry are at a standstill. A very large army is being maintained far from home at a ruinous cost. The Italian people are being overstrained and impoverished. Their standards of living have noticeably declined. They can hardly purchase across the Exchange the many commodities they need to maintain the crushing weight of the armaments they have been called upon to bear. The violent seizure of Austria by Nazi Germany exposes Italy to direct contact with a far stronger aggressive power and the German leaders already speak of a road being opened to the Mediterranean, and to what they call "the riches of Africa." Even the Fascists of Italy, the Party men, are asking themselves whether all this is to the permanent safety and advantage of their native land. Here then again, all is not well with Dictatorial power. Behind the horseman sits dull care. At this feast they might read, like Belshazzar, the handwriting on the wall.

Let us come farther to the west. The agony of the Civil War continues. Had it been only a Spanish quarrel fought out by Spaniards, we might have averted our eyes from its horrors; but the shameful intrusions of Dictator powers with organized troops and masses of munitions under the deceitful masquerade of Non-Intervention, has invested their struggles with an added bitterness and a significance which extends far outside the Spanish Peninsula. But the Republican Government is still resisting. The end may be long delayed. The sympathy of the United States has become manifest in a remarkable degree. We may still cherish the hope that our country, which has acted in entire good faith, may yet find the means of mediating between the combatants, and helping both sides to reach some settlement which will make Spain a home for all her people.

But this brings me to the best news of all. France and England, the two Parliamentary democracies of the West, have come together, openly and publicly, in a defensive alliance; they are making common cause, and are taking the necessary measures in common for their mutual safety, and for the defense of the principles of freedom and free Government for which they stand. But what is this but a first and most important step towards collective security? Do we not all feel safer because the French and British peoples, numbering 85 millions in Europe alone, have joined hands to safeguard one another from unprovoked aggression?

Why should we stop here? Why should we not invite others to join the combination, and why should we not associate this necessary action with the sanctions and authority of the Covenant of the League? Is this not moreover a policy which will unite the greatest measure of opinion here at home? It would be a great mistake if the Nation were needlessly divided by any attempt to mock and disparage the principles of international law and collective security which were common ground between all parties at the last election.

It is said that the League will embroil us in other peoples' quarrels, and we shall get no corresponding protection in return. Let us examine that objection. We are already deeply involved in Europe. Only a month ago the Prime Minister read out to the House of Commons a long list of countries in whose defense we were bound to go to war: France, Belgium, Portugal, Egypt and Iraq. He then discussed another class of countries which might become the victims of aggression, for whom we were not bound to go to war, but whose fate was a matter of great interest to us. We would not make any automatic and obligatory commitments in regard to them, but would judge an act of aggression when it occurred. Take the case of Czechoslovakia, which he mentioned. Although we have not gone as far as France in giving a pledge to Czechoslovakia, Mr. Chamberlain has gone a long way. We are the ally of France, which would certainly be involved. We may be drawn in, says the Prime Minister, by the force of circumstances, even in cases where there is no legal engagement. Finally, we are at this minute offering advice to Czechoslovakia, and if she takes that advice, and makes the concessions we think right, and finds herself attacked none the less, is it not clear that we are morally entangled? We have thus in this case, the most urgent, undertaken in the name of detachment engagements beyond what the Covenant prescribes. The Covenant does not prescribe that we should go to war for Czechoslovakia or any other country, but only that we should not be neutral in the sense of being indifferent as between an aggressor and the victim of aggression.

If the war breaks out in Europe, no one can say how far it will spread, or who will have it in their power to stand out of it. Is it not better then, on grounds of prudence alone, to gain the strength which comes from combined action? Is it not wise to try to invest the Covenant with reality, to unite as many nations as possible in its support, to gain a measure of protection for ourselves, in return for the risks we are to run for others? By this present policy of decrying the League and making the Covenant a matter of division between parties we are only having the disadvantage of both courses. It would indeed be disastrous if we were led into a fierce division here at home about foreign policy. An election fought on ordinary domestic issues is a process with which we are all familiar; but an election turning on the dread issues of defense and foreign policy might leave us a deeply divided nation, with an evenly balanced, incoherent Parliament, and this at the very moment when the danger on the Continent had reached its height. That is why I plead for national unity, and for a policy upon which alone it is to be achieved. We might be having a general election in this country, or preparing for one, with both sides rivaling each other as to who was most in favor of peace at any price. We might have this at the very moment when the war-lust of Dictator Powers had reached its culminating explosion point.

But we are told that we must not involve ourselves in a quarrel about ideologies. If this means that we are not to back Communism against Nazi-ism or vice versa, we all agree. Both doctrines are equally obnoxious to the principles of freedom. Certainly we should not back one against the other. But surely we must have an opinion between Right and Wrong? Surely we must have an opinion between Aggressor and Victim? This is no question of resisting Dictators because they are Dictators, but only if they attack other people. Have we not an ideology—if we must use this ugly word—of our own in freedom, in a liberal constitution, in democratic and Parliamentary government, in Magna Charta and the Petition of Right? Ought we not to be ready to make as many sacrifices and exertions for our own broad central theme and cause as the fanatics of either of these new creeds? Ought we not to produce in defense of Right, champions as bold, missionaries as eager, and if need be, swords as sharp as are at the disposal of the leaders of totalitarian states?

Finally, there must be a moral basis for British foreign policy. People in this country, after all we have gone through, do not mean to be drawn into another terrible war in the name of old-world alliances or diplomatic combinations. If deep causes of division are to be removed from our midst, if all our energies are to be concentrated upon the essential task of increasing our strength and security, it can only be because of lofty and unselfish ideals which command the allegiance of all classes here at home, which rouse their echoes in the breasts even of the Dictator-ridden peoples themselves, and stir the pulses of the English-speaking race in every quarter of the globe. That is why I say, "Stand by the Covenant and endeavor to revive and fortify the strength of the League."

Here is the practical plan. Britain and France are now united. Together they are an enormous force, moral and physical, and one which few would dare to challenge. I should like to see these two countries go to all the smaller states that are menaced, who are going to be devoured one by one by the Nazi tyranny, and say to them bluntly, "We are not going to help you if you are not going to help yourselves. What are you going to do about it? What are you going to contribute? Are you prepared to take special service in defense of the Covenant? If you are willing to do so, and to prove it by actions, then we will join together with you, if there are enough of you, in active military association under the authority of the League in order to protect each other and the world from another act of aggression."

You cannot expect all the states of the League to take equal obligations. Some are far away and some are in no danger. But if we could rally even ten well-armed states in Europe, all banded together to resist an aggression upon any one of them, all banded together to counter-attack the aggressor upon a combined plan, then we should be so strong that the immediate danger would be warded off, and a breathing space be gained for building later a still broader structure of peace. Is that not far better than being dragged piece-meal into a war when half those who might have been your friends and allies will have already been pulled down one by one? No single nation should be asked to enter into this solemn engagement unless it is assured of strong and valiant comrades banded together not only by a covenant of high ideals, but by practical military conventions. In this way we have the best chance of preventing a war, and if that fails, of surviving it unconquered.

To be precise—some of the countries who should be asked whether they will join Great Britain and France in this special duty to the League are Yugoslavia, Rumania, Hungary and Czechoslovakia. These countries can be mopped up one by one, but together they are of enormous strength. In the next place there are Bulgaria, Greece and Turkey, all states who wish to preserve their individuality and national independence, the two last of whom are already joined to us by the most cordial friendship. If this powerful group of Danubian and Balkan states were firmly united with the two great Western democracies, an immense, probably a decisive, step towards stability would be achieved.

But even that would only be a beginning. To the east of Europe lies the enormous power of Russia, a country whose form of government I detest, but which at any rate seeks no military aggression upon its neighbors, a country whose interests are peace, a country profoundly menaced by Nazi hostility, a country which lies as a great background and counterpoise at this moment to all those states of Middle Europe I have mentioned. We should certainly not go cap in hand to Soviet Russia, or count in any definite manner upon Russian action. But how improvidently foolish we should be, when dangers are so great, to put needless barriers in the way of the general association of the great Russian mass with resistance to an act of Nazi aggression.

There is, however, a third stage in the process. There is Poland; and the countries of the north, the Baltic states, the Scandinavian powers. If we had once gathered together the forces I have mentioned, we should then be in a position to offer these countries a very great measure of armed security for peace. At the present time they do not know which way to turn. But if they saw a strong, armed association, such as I have described, whose interest in peace was the same as theirs, they might easily be induced to throw in their lot with us and "make assurance double sure."

But what is this but a recreated League of Nations, devoted to its original purpose, namely, the prevention of war? If we could, therefore, get as far as this, believe me the war danger would be removed from us perhaps for our lifetime. And across the Atlantic Ocean the United States would signal her encouragement and sympathy.

I shall be told, "But this is the encirclement of Germany." I say, "No, this is the encirclement of an aggressor." Nations who are bound by the Covenant can never, however powerful they may be, menace the peace and independence of any other state. That is the essence of the conditions which bring them together. To form a war combination against a single state would be a crime. To form a combination for mutual defense against a probable aggressor is not only no crime, but the highest moral duty and virtue. We ask no security for ourselves that we are not prepared freely to extend to Germany. If Germany nourishes no aggressive designs, if Germany professes herself to be afraid of attack, let her join too; let her join the club and share fairly and equally all its privileges and safeguards.

We have made an agreement with Italy about which there are many hopes and many misgivings. No one knows, however, on which side Italy would be found to stand if Nazi Germany precipitated another great war. But Italy has great service to render to such a League as I have described. Nothing would make the Anglo-Italian agreement a reality so much as the friendly association of all these countries in maintaining the peace of Central and Southern Europe.

Now, that is a foreign policy which involves us in no commitments more entangling than those which we have already taken, and which gives us the possibility should it be successful—and one can but try—of substantial if not absolute security. There is nothing visionary or sentimental about such a policy. It is nothing more or less than common sense, and in addition it is enshrined in that great structure of international law and unity embodied in the League of Nations and the Covenant. This may be a noble dream, but it is also a practical plan, and one which I believe, if pursued with courage, comprehension and decision, would rally a peaceful Europe around a strong Britain and France. It is not even now too late to carry such a policy through to success. Then when we have gathered these forces, and by united strength removed the fear of war, then will be the time to deal with the grievances of discontented nations, to get rid of the causes of hatred and jealousy, as you will have removed the causes of fear. Then will be the time to proceed to the culmination of the whole work, namely, the broad general reduction of the hideous burden of armaments, which if it continues to grow at its present rate can only lead through bankruptcy to mutual destruction.

Before you reject this great hope with all its effort and its risk, which I in no wise conceal, consider the alternative. There is another foreign policy which you are urged to pursue. It is not to worry about all these countries of Central Europe, not to trouble yourself with preserving the Covenant of the League, to recognize that all that is foolish and vain and can never be restored, and to make a special pact of friendship with Nazi Germany. There is no reason why we should not live in a friendly manner with Germany. It is our duty to try to do so, little as we like her system of government, deeply as we are revolted by the cruel racial and religious persecution on which the flames of Nazi hatred feed themselves. Still, in making an international arrangement to preserve the peace of the world, we could no more exclude Nazi Germany than Soviet Russia. But when we are told we must make a special pact with Nazi Germany, I want to know what that pact is going to be, and at whose expense it is to be made. Undoubtedly our Government could make an agreement with Germany. All they have to do is to give her back her former colonies, and such others as she may desire; to muzzle the British press and platform by a law of censorship, and to give Herr Hitler a free hand to spread the Nazi system and dominance far and wide through Central Europe. That is the alternative foreign policy. It is one which, in my view, would be disgraceful and disastrous. In the first place it leads us straight to war. The Nazi regime, elated by this triumph, with every restraint removed, would proceed unchecked upon its path of ambition and aggression. We should be the helpless, silent, gagged, apparently consenting, spectators of the horrors which would spread through Central Europe. The Government that enforced such a policy would be swept away. The mere instinct of self-preservation would make it impossible for us to purchase a fleeting and precarious immunity at the cost of the ruin and enslavement of Europe. After an interval, long or short, we should be drawn into a war, as the United States were drawn into the Great War. But by that time we should be confronted with an antagonist, overwhelmingly powerful, and find ourselves deprived of every friend.

Have I not set out to you these issues plainly? And is there any doubt which way duty and safety point? Hitherto I have been dealing with questions about which there is confusion of thought in our country, and about which there may be a grievous division at a time when unity is vital. But now I come to an issue upon which we are all agreed, namely, the rearmament of our country for its own security, to discharge its duties, and to maintain its safety. There is a need for greater effort. There is a need for united effort. There is a need to lay aside our easy-going life, to have efficiency and a broad national plan.

A large part of our dangers and the dangers of Europe is due to the fact that we did not rearm in time. It was certainly not through lack of warning, but when we at last began it was only in a half-hearted, ramshackle, confused manner, which, though it has led to great outpourings of money, has not been attended by proportionate results. Is it not lamentable that our Air Force is not now fully equal to any Power within striking distance of these shores? Is it not grievous that the vast, flexible industry of Britain has not yet been able to produce a broad and copious flow of the latest weapons of all kinds? After all, it is nearly three years since Mr. Baldwin recognized the dangers which beset us. Late as we started we ought by now to be in a strong position. Parliament is to discuss this matter this week. There ought certainly to be a searching inquiry into the condition of the Air Force, and into the reasons why the solemn pledge given to the country by Mr. Baldwin of air parity, has been broken.

But an equal confusion and delay covers large parts of the field of munitions supply. It is greatly to be regretted that after nearly three years since the Government became alive to the dangers, and nearly five years since the danger became apparent, the equipment of our small Regular Army should be incomplete, and that the supplying of the Territorial Army with modern weapons and appliances should be only in a rudimentary stage. As for Air Raid Precautions, artillery, balloons, organization in every form, you know for yourselves—as well as the Germans know—the unhappy and discreditable conditions which prevail. This is no case for the Opposition to make party capital against the Government. Nor for the Government to try to shield incompetence and misdirection. All should set country before party. There should be a thorough and searching inquest into the mismanagement of the past and a fearless resolve to sweep away every obstacle that stands in the path of our regaining our national safety. Meanwhile everyone must do his best.

Look at the danger in which we stand. Germany has been rearming night and day for four years. For four years past they have never spent less in any year than £800,000,000 sterling on war preparation. The whole manhood of the country is harnessed to war. Even the children are organized. Every thought is turned to race assertion and the conquest of weaker, more exhausted, or less determined breeds. They are driving forward on their path. Every six weeks a new army corps is added to their active forces. Never has there been such an outpouring of munitions of war. At present we are shielded to some extent by the strength of the French army, but the German numbers are overtaking them month by month. We have still our Navy, never, happily, so supreme in European waters. But our Air Force, on which so much depends, so far from overtaking Germany, is actually falling further and further behind. If we are to place ourselves in security we must throw ourselves into the business of national defense with the vigor and concentration which Germany now displays.

It is no small or local cause we plead tonight. We must march in the good company of nations and we march under the standards of Law, of Justice and of Freedom. We must gather together round the joint strength of Britain and France and under the authority of the League all countries prepared to resist, and if possible to prevent acts of violent aggression. There is the path to safety. There are the only guarantees of Freedom. There, on the rock of the Covenant of the League of Nations alone, can we build high and enduring the temple and the towers of Peace.

THE AIR DEFENSES OF BRITAIN

The House of Commons

May 25, 1938

1938

May 12.   Lord Halifax raises before the League of Nations at Geneva the question of recognizing the Italian conquest of Abyssinia.

May 12.   The situation of the Royal Air Force debated in both Houses of Parliament. The Government replies are considered unsatisfactory and Lord Swinton, Secretary of State for Air, resigns and is succeeded by Sir Kingsley Wood.

May 13.   Visit of Herr Henlein, leader of the Sudeten Nazis, to London.

May 20–21.   Czechoslovakian forces mobilized in reply to the massing of German troops along the border.

May 25.   Mr. Hugh Dalton in the House of Commons demands an inquiry into the state of Britain's air defenses, and supports the movement for a Ministry of Supply. The Prime Minister, Mr. Chamberlain, rejects both.

THE AIR DEFENSES OF BRITAIN

I HAVE long pressed for an inquiry into the state of our air program. But the new situation which has been created by the sweeping changes in the control of the Air Ministry [1] do undoubtedly, as far as I can see, introduce a new element. I cannot feel sure that the new Minister will be helped or strengthened in his task if such an inquiry, which must needs be searching, and the results of which must certainly be disagreeable, were proceeding day by day and step by step while he is acquiring information about his new duties and his new office. Moreover, it seems to me that the case which I and others have made during the last few years, that the programs were inadequate, that they were not being fulfilled, and that the outfit of the Royal Air Force was far from satisfactory, is no longer contested by His Majesty's Government. That is a new fact, too. An inquiry would, no doubt, reveal many uncertain details, but since the broad fact of a very serious breakdown is now admitted, and there is to be a fresh start and a new surge of impulse, it seems to me that some, at least, of the arguments for an inquiry are now removed.

But this by no means implies that the position is satisfactory, or that it is improved in any way by the fact that there is a change of personnel. Someone else is going to try. We shall await with the greatest interest the statement of my right hon. Friend—not the statement he is going to make this evening, because obviously he is only going to deal with some of the issues of the Debate—but the statement that he will be in a position to make in a few weeks' time on his program and policy. I hope that he will be animated by a desire to treat the House with absolute candor, and that he will make it his rule to tell Parliament everything that he has reason to believe foreign countries already know. The credit of Gov-

[1] The resignation of Lord Swinton, and appointment of Sir Kingsley Wood.

ernment statements has been compromised by what has occurred. The House has been consistently misled about the air position. The Prime Minister himself has been misled. He was misled right up to the last moment, apparently. Look at the statement which he made in March, when he spoke about our armaments:

"The sight of this enormous, this almost terrifying, power which Britain is building up has a sobering effect, a steadying effect, on the opinion of the world." [2]

Indeed, that would be the truth, if it were supported by a solid basis of fact. But the Prime Minister himself said on the same day:

"We must take account of the aggregate and effectiveness of our resources, and in the various programs which we have put forward I can tell the House that we are satisfied that we are making the best and most effective use of these resources."

But now it appears that much greater efforts are required, and much larger programs are needed. Therefore, I say that the Prime Minister shares with the House the misfortune of being misled by statements which came, apparently, on the authority of the Air Minister.

Let me read to the House—for I think we have some grievance in this matter—a statement made by my right hon. Friend, the Minister for the Co-ordination of Defense [Sir Thomas Inskip [3]]:

"The speed of machines in production today for regular use in the Air Force would five years ago have made them serious competitors for the Schneider Cup. That fact will bring home to the Committee the extraordinary advance that has been made. These are not specimens, nor what I would call protoplanes, that are being produced, but they are machines in regular, orderly production for the regular everyday use of the Air Force.

Mr. Churchill: Are they being delivered now?

Sir T. Inskip: Yes. Some have been delivered. They are in orderly delivery, and they will be delivered in ever-increasing volume."

When does the House suppose that statement was made? Not last month, or last year. The date is July 20, 1936—twenty-two months ago. And I say that that statement certainly gave the impression to the House that all was proceeding well, that a great flow of modern machines was proceeding from the factories into the Royal Air Force. I know my right hon. Friend would be the last to mislead the House of Commons. But he

[2] March 7, 1938.
[3] Now Lord Caldecote, Lord Chief Justice.

was himself misled, because he had not the knowledge or experience, great as is his legal acumen, to enable him to conduct the necessary technical cross-examination.

I hope the new Air Minister will imitate the example of Lord Baldwin, and when he makes a mistake blurt it out in the most appalling manner, so that, at any rate, whatever we may complain about, we cannot complain that we have been misled. I have often warned the House that the air programs were falling into arrear. But I have never attacked Lord Swinton. I have never thought that he was the one to blame—certainly not the only one to blame. It is very usual for the critics of the Government— I have been a consistent critic in this matter—to discover hitherto unnoticed virtues in any Minister who is forced to resign. But perhaps I may quote—because it is directly relevant—what I said three months ago:

"It would be unfair to throw the blame on any one Minister, or upon Lord Swinton, for our deficiency. Anyone who was put in his place in July, 1935, would have made a great many mistakes, and would certainly not have been able to discharge the programs which were proclaimed within the limits assigned; but he certainly does represent—and I say this with a great feeling of sympathy for him in his task—an extremely able and wholehearted effort to do the best he possibly could to expand our air power, and the results which he has achieved would be bright if they were not darkened by the time-table, and if they were not outshone by other relative facts occurring elsewhere. Every country admires what it is doing itself, but what is not always seen is what is being done by others. I say that the hard responsibility for the failure to fulfill the promises made to us rests upon those who have governed and guided this Island for the last five years, that is to say, from the date when German rearmament in real earnest became apparent and known."

I certainly did not attempt to join in a man-hunt of Lord Swinton. I was very glad today to hear the Prime Minister's tribute to him. Certainly he deserves our sympathy. He had the confidence and friendship of the Prime Minister, he had the confidence and support of an enormous Parliamentary majority; yet he has been taken from his post at what, I think, is the worst moment in the story of air expansion. It may be that in a few months there will be a considerable flow of aircraft arriving, yet he has had to answer for his record at this particularly dark moment for him. I was reading the other day a letter from the great Duke of Marlborough, in which he said: "To remove a General in the midst of a campaign— that is the mortal stroke."

Why was he removed? Certainly not because of the inconvenience to the House of Commons.[4] The Prime Minister had given conclusive arguments against that on former occasions. When we asked for an inquiry we were told at the beginning of the Session and, later, now, "You cannot have an inquiry; that would be a court-martial on Lord Swinton." So there has been no court-martial. What has happened has been a private execution. Now there is, apparently, not even to be the usual post-mortem; or, shall I say, coroner's inquest? This is a strange episode, I must say, in Parliamentary history. I have not seen the like in my time. It almost seemed to me that occult forces were at work. Have votes of confidence no longer the virtue to sustain a Minister? Are they to be taken so much as a matter of course, a mere formality, that they no longer affect the Government? Can the earnest desire of hundreds of Members, acting in a particular way, no longer convey that sense of strength to the administration? Are the facts more powerful than the votes that are given in the Lobby? Is our business in the House of Commons to be settled outside? If so, it is a new development and I must say that I prefer the older system when Members voted with greater independence and Governments practiced a more virile candor.

But there is another reason why I am far from being reassured, and why I do not think the Prime Minister has taken the best course in the circumstances. It will be many months before my right hon. Friend knows half what Lord Swinton knows about the Air Force. The departure of this Minister is a very serious event. Was it necessary? Would it not have been a more reasonable and practical plan to leave Lord Swinton at the Air Ministry, and to free him and that Department from the whole business of supply? If, for instance, my right hon. Friend the new Secretary of State for Air had been appointed Minister of Supply, Lord Swinton could have continued to discharge the immense task—in which he has made great progress—of organizing and perfecting the Royal Air Force as a fighting service.

If that course had been adopted, a great shock to public confidence would have been avoided, and I believe we should have had more efficient service than we can possibly have for the Air Force in the next few months. Each of these Ministers, the Air Minister and the Minister of Supply, would have had an harmonious and integral task to which they could have devoted their whole energy, and the Secretary of State would

[4] It had been argued that it was a disadvantage to have a Peer as Air Minister.

not have had to be summoned from his salubrious employment[5] and forced to don the panoply of Mars, or, to put it in more homely language, we should not have been putting a round peg in a square hole.

I am very anxious to press the point of a Ministry of Supply. Let us see what is the present organization that is employed in producing armaments from British industry. It is an extraordinarily cumbrous and complex organization. First of all there is the Admiralty, with all its establishments and activities. Secondly, there is Admiral Brown's Department of the War Office. Admiral Brown is Director-General of Munitions production for the War Office, and he is a member of the Army Council. He makes for the War Office and he makes certain things for other Departments as well. Included in his sphere is the old Department of Master-General of the Ordnance, which we were told was working so splendidly a year ago, but which, when the new Secretary of State for War came along, was found to be in such a condition that it had to be transferred *en bloc* to the control of Admiral Brown. Thirdly, there is the enormous system of committees working under the Committee of Imperial Defense.

I was glad to read Lord Zetland's very full account of this in another place, and the Prime Minister has referred to some of these committees today. He mentioned particularly the Principal Supply Officers' Committee. He said it was in continuous session, which I am bound to say I heard with some surprise. I notice that there is Sir Arthur Robinson's Supply Board, which I have no doubt is in very constant function. Parallel with Sir Arthur Robinson's Supply Board, to quote the words of Lord Zetland, is a body controlled by the Board of Trade, known as the Board of Trade Supply Organization. Beneath Sir Arthur Robinson's Supply Board, we were told by the Minister for Co-ordination of Defense nearly two years ago, there were no fewer than seven main committees and no one knows how many subordinate and subsidiary committees. None of these organizations under the Committee of Imperial Defense, nor under Sir Arthur Robinson's Board, has any executive power. All these committees of the Imperial Defense Committee are deliberative and advisory. They deliberate and they advise, and the ball is flung from one to the other at weekly or fortnightly intervals.

These are not secret matters, but it is difficult to see clearly what happens. Nowhere in these committees is there power to give a series of executive orders. That is reserved, as I understand it, to the Service Departments. Consideration, yes; things considered, innumerable; done, very

[5] Sir Kingsley Wood had been Minister of Health.

few. That is why, when questions are asked on all sorts of topics, the Minister for Co-ordination of Defense is able to say, "That is being considered." "We have given our attention to this." "We are fully alive to that." "The other matter is engaging our earnest attention." "We are exploring that." No doubt it is perfectly true. I do not suppose there is any question on the subject of National Defense which is not being considered, ventilated, explored, illuminated by these innumerable committees.

I have dealt with three: the Admiralty, Admiral Brown's War Office Committee, and this cluster of committees under the Committee of Imperial Defense. Now I come to the last one, the most relevant immediately to our topic, which is the organization for ordering aircraft supplies. This again is dual. There are two quite separate aspects. In the first place there is the Director of Production of the Air Ministry, who is the opposite number of Admiral Brown at the War Office. Besides this there is this new committee which we heard so much about the other day from the Chancellor of the Duchy,[6] a committee of manufacturers, who are gathered together with my Noble Friend at their head, and they were going to put everything right in this sphere. However, owing to some oratorical fireworks, the whole of this part of the organization is to be remodeled. Moving around in this jungle, without executive power and burdened with a whole sphere of other and even more important duties, is my right hon., learned and unfortunate Friend, the Minister for Co-ordination of Defense, specially charged not merely with co-ordination, but with the preparation of the industry of the country for transition into a state of war. That is the machinery that is working at the present time.

I was surprised at my right hon. Friend. He treated the matter, when he was describing the reason against a Minister of Supply, as if everything that had happened so far was satisfactory. That apparently is his point of view. I say this machinery has failed; I say it has not delivered the goods. And this is the machinery which some people think should be replaced forthwith by an effectual Ministry of Supply under a responsible Parliamentary head and with all necessary executive powers. The Prime Minister obdurately resists this Ministry of Supply. He made difficulties today about powers, and seemed to be willing to excite a prejudice, which I do not think exists, upon the other side of the House against reasonable powers. Who has ever suggested that this Ministry should be equipped with power to prevent strikes in time of peace? I am not pre-

[6] Lord Winterton.

pared in the course of these remarks to unfold to the House the exact category of powers, but it can easily be done. There are powers that are necessary and appropriate, not to a state of war, but to an intermediate state of emergency preparation.

Why does my right hon. Friend resist this plan so obdurately? It is true that I have pressed it upon him and his predecessor for two years or more, but that is not in itself a sufficient reason. I will avail myself of the avun-·cular relationship which I hope I may still possess in respect of the Government to put it to the Prime Minister personally and even intimately. Has he ever heard of Saint Anthony the Hermit? Saint Anthony the Hermit was much condemned by the Fathers of the Church because he refused to do right when the devil told him to. My right hon. Friend should free himself from his irrational inhibition, for we are only at the beginning of our anxieties. I warn the Prime Minister of the troubles that lie ahead in this administrative sphere. He is not the only one on that bench who requires warning. Three able, industrious, loyal Ministers of the Crown have been, or are being, deeply prejudiced by being given ill-conceived and ill-assorted tasks. The Secretary of State for War, the Minister for Co-ordination of Defense and the Air Minister have all been prejudiced in their work and will be smitten in their reputation by the fact that they have been given ill-conceived and ill-assorted tasks to discharge.

The Air Minister has gone and we have another in his place, who at present has not been able fully to survey the extremely difficult ground upon which he is called to enter. When shall I be able to convince the Government that a Service Department and a Service Minister are incapable of dealing with large-scale industrial production? In time of prolonged peace, when the annual requirement of the Air Ministry or the War Office is very small, when the War Office has only to deal with Vickers, Enfield and Woolwich, when the Air Ministry can work with its small routine of selected firms, there is no difficulty. But from the moment when you require to throw yourselves for the purpose of rearmament upon the industry and labor of the nation and upon the good will of the whole mass of skilled labor and the skilled labor unions, you have created a task which requires the whole-time attention of a Minister of the Crown equipped with the full force of a great Department.

It would have been easy for the Prime Minister to have saved Lord Swinton last week. All he would have had to do was to relieve him of a task which ought not to be combined and which cannot effectively be combined with the direction of the Royal Air Force. He had only to relieve him of the task of the production of aeroplanes and aviation materials, which can be done on a gigantic scale only by civil industry. In the same way, my right hon. Friend the Minister for the Co-ordination of Defense has been throughout confronted with an unnatural task, which he has faced with his usual sturdy courage and patience, but which no man, however able, could fully discharge. I predict that there lie ahead of him, and I fear ahead of all of us, many painful realizations of the results of the discharge of this task. Nor do I except the Secretary of State for War,[7] who sails proudly and buoyantly over calmer waters than have been vouchsafed to his colleague at the Air Ministry. There is a Minister who should welcome most earnestly the creation of a Ministry of Supply.

The hon. Member who opened the Debate for the Opposition made a formidable case about the present condition of our air defenses. I cannot challenge any substantial part of the statement which he made. It should be read with profound attention by all persons who are awake to the dangers which surround our country at the present time. I consider that that alone should give the House the reason for making a decisive change in the methods of wholesale manufacture of war materials. But if ever there were to be an inquiry, certainly other aspects would come into view. I am prepared to say that the military programs are lagging equally. It is true that the Secretary of State for War has an easier method of escaping from his difficulties than the Air Minister. When deliveries of munitions and equipment fall into arrear, all he has to do is to reduce the number of divisions that he considers necessary to meet the war need. Thus, all we are able to say, as he said the other day, is that "All is proceeding according to schedule." He has the advantage, perhaps, of what we might call a double sliding-scale. The schedule is unknown, and so also are the standards towards which it is working. But these are grim times, and it is no time for the kind of rigmarole responses we had at Question Time yesterday in answer to vital questions.

We are now in the third year of openly avowed rearmament. Why is it, if all is going well, there are so many deficiencies? Why, for instance, are the Guards drilling with flags instead of machine guns? Why is it that our small Territorial Army is in a rudimentary condition? Is that all according to schedule? Why should it be, when you consider how small are our forces? Why should it be impossible to equip the Territorial Army simultaneously with the Regular Army? It would have been a

[7] Mr. Hore-Belisha.

paltry task for British industry, which is more flexible and more fertile than German industry in every sphere except munitions. We have for generations competed successfully on even terms, and even adverse terms, in the markets of the world. If Germany is able to produce in these three years equipment and armament of every kind for its Air Force and for sixty or seventy divisions of the Regular Army, how is it that we have been unable to furnish our humble, modest military forces with what is necessary? If you had given the contract to Selfridge or to the Army and Navy Stores, I believe that you would have had the stuff today.

These deficiencies of every kind, which are patent, and clearly can be seen by anyone, and are certainly known abroad, touch a more crucial point when we come to the subject which has been touched upon by all speakers today, namely, that of anti-aircraft defense. The other day the Secretary of State for War was asked about the anti-aircraft artillery. He seemed entirely contented with the position. The old 3-inch guns of the Great War, he said, had been modernized, and deliveries of the newer guns—and there is more than one type of newer gun—were proceeding "in advance of schedule." But what is the schedule? If your schedule prescribes a delivery of half a dozen, ten, a dozen, twenty, or whatever it may be, guns per month, no doubt that may easily be up to schedule and easily be in advance of it. But what is the adequacy of such a schedule to our needs? A year ago I reminded the House of the published progress of Germany in anti-aircraft artillery—thirty regiments of twelve batteries each of mobile artillery alone, aggregating something between one thousand two hundred and one thousand three hundred guns, in addition to three thousand or four thousand guns in fixed positions. They are all modern guns, not guns of 1915, but all guns made since the year 1933.

Does not that give the House an idea of the tremendous scale of these transactions? We do not need to have a gigantic army, like continental countries, but in the matter of anti-aircraft defense we are on equal terms. We are just as vulnerable, and perhaps more vulnerable. Here is the Government thinking of anti-aircraft artillery in terms of hundreds where the Germans have it today in terms of thousands. Yet we are told that "All is proceeding according to schedule. Everything is satisfactory. We are in advance of the schedule." The Prime Minister considers the organization, as it has grown up under the Committee of Imperial Defense, as the last word. He does not see how it can be improved. The Secretary of State for War, acclaiming his achievement of being in advance of schedule, almost invites us to place a chaplet of wild olives upon his brow. I assert that the Air Ministry and the War Office are absolutely incompetent to produce the great flow of weapons now required from British industry. I assert, secondly, that British industry is entirely capable of producing an overwhelming response both in respect of the air and of military material of all kinds both in quality and in quantity. But you have to organize it, and, to organize it, you must have the best brains that British industry can produce, directed by the most powerful organization that the State can supply. Without that you will not get the response.

If this is true of present peace-time rearmament, how much more is it true of the immense expansion which will be necessary on the outbreak of war. We are told that "All is ready for a Ministry of Munitions on outbreak of war." Lord Zetland tells us that all that happens is that he or some other noble personage has to press a button. I hope that it is not a button like the last gaiter button which was talked of before the war of 1870. He has only to press this button and a Ministry of Munitions will leap into being fully armed like Minerva from the head of the Minister for the Co-ordination of Defense. Do not let the House believe that, I beg of it.

You may conceivably bring together a number of functionaries of State in their varying relations. You may bring together advisory committees of business men, but what we should need if war should come would be a running concern in full activity, and from the first moment an organization which is actually shaped and molded, and an industry which is planned in every detail to take the upward leap. Otherwise, your pressing the button would result merely in producing a paper organization which would require months to undertake its job and really get its hands upon the levers, and still more months—tragic months—of agony before industry would respond to this greatly expanded scheme.

You ought now—I said this two years ago, but it is still true today—to have every factory in the country planned out, not only on paper, but with the necessary jigs, gauges and appliances handy, hung up on the spot, so that they could turn over at once in time of war to some form of war production. The exact routine change for every suitable factory should be foreseen now and elaborated, so that when you press your button you do not merely bring factories into being, but you have a living control of British industry which immediately enters into the production of munitions upon a war scale. That is only what is organized already in foreign countries, and in no country is it organized in this way so much as it is in Germany. I cannot see that there could be any objection to the view that everything ought to be prepared. It is not a very expensive job, but it is a matter of the utmost consequence.

The more you are prepared and the better you are known to be prepared, the greater is the chance of staving off war and of saving Europe from the catastrophe which menaces it. Every time we are seen to make a big new move forward there is a wave of confidence which goes through all the small countries and all the peace-loving countries of the world. Supposing it were said tomorrow that we have set up a Ministry of Supply and are making provision for turning industry over to munitions, do you not think that that would at once create a feeling of confidence and of security? As the Prime Minister said, confidence was spread through the world by the improvement of our armaments, so do not let us differ about any evidence on which we can agree.

Let me give one or two other reasons for the immediate creation of a Ministry of Supply. We are thinking at the present time in terms of production for three separate armed forces. In fact and in truth, the supply of arms for all fighting forces resolves itself into a common problem of the provision and distribution of skilled labor, raw materials, plant, machinery and technical appliances. That problem can only be dealt with comprehensively, harmoniously and economically through one central dominating control. At the present time there is inefficiency and overlapping, and there is certainly waste. Why is it that this skillful aircraft industry of Britain requires ninety thousand men, and that it produces only one-half to one-third of what is being produced by about one hundred and ten thousand men in Germany? Is that not an extraordinary fact? It is incredible that we have not been able to produce a greater supply of aeroplanes at this time. Given a plain office table, an empty field, money and labor, we should receive a flow of aeroplanes by eighteen months; yet this is the thirty-fourth month since Lord Baldwin decided that the Air Force must be tripled.

How much longer will the obvious remedies be denied? No mere change of Ministers will meet this occasion. We must have a change of system. Without a change of system you will find yourselves involved evermore in vexations and Ministers in undeserved misfortune, or in misfortune which, if it is deserved, is only because they allow these ill-assorted duties to be imposed upon them. Just consider that up to this moment we have not reached any agreement with the skilled unions, after the whole of these two years. It is only now that negotiations are beginning. If you wish to ask these skilled unions to make the sacrifices which undoubtedly are necessary, you must convince them of the emergency. Every time a Ministry of Supply is refused, the emergency is discounted and denied. At the present time the attitude of the Government is clearly that all may be carried on safely upon the existing methods, with a minimum of disturbance of the general life of the country. Surely, it is time now to proclaim the emergency. During last week-end many of us thought of those furnace fires of which the Prime Minister spoke a year or two ago, and almost felt a gust of scorching air upon our faces; and then we are told there is no emergency. Surely, this is the time when Ministers should rise to the level of events and give more effective defense protection and service to the nation which has trusted them so long.

CIVILIZATION

An Address as Chancellor to the University of Bristol

July 2, 1938

1938

May 30.   A Deputation waits upon the Prime Minister to urge the desirability of a National Register. Mr. Chamberlain declines.

May 31.   The possibility of Conscription discussed in the House of Commons.

June 8.   Nazis in Czechoslovakia present demands to the Government based upon the eight-point "Karlsbad Program."

June 14–21. The Government policy of Non-Intervention in Spain attacked in the House of Commons, following increased losses of British shipping in Spanish waters, but without success.

July 2.   The Czechoslovakian Government makes it known that several of the Sudeten-Nazi demands, presented on June 8, are unacceptable.

CIVILIZATION

THERE ARE few words which are used more loosely than the word "Civilization." What does it mean? It means a society based upon the opinion of civilians. It means that violence, the rule of warriors and despotic chiefs, the conditions of camps and warfare, of riot and tyranny, give place to parliaments where laws are made, and independent courts of justice in which over long periods those laws are maintained. That is Civilization—and in its soil grow continually freedom, comfort and culture. When Civilization reigns in any country, a wider and less harassed life is afforded to the masses of the people. The traditions of the past are cherished, and the inheritance bequeathed to us by former wise or valiant men becomes a rich estate to be enjoyed and used by all.

The central principle of Civilization is the subordination of the ruling authority to the settled customs of the people and to their will as expressed through the Constitution. In this Island we have today achieved in a high degree the blessings of Civilization. There is freedom; there is law; there is love of country; there is a great measure of good will between classes; there is a widening prosperity. There are unmeasured opportunities of correcting abuses and making further progress.

In this very week we have seen a Prime Minister at the head of a large and loyal majority bow with good grace to the customs of Parliament, and we have heard Socialist Members speaking with pride of the precedents of the early seventeenth century, and the principles of the Petition of Right.[1] In this respect for law and sense of continuity lies one of the glories of England. And more than that, there also lies in it an important part of her strength and safety. Such episodes are astonishing, but

---

[1] A reference to the Report of the Committee of Privileges which inquired into the dispute between Mr. Hore-Belisha and Mr. Duncan Sandys.

also educative, to countries where dictatorships prevail, and where no one dares to raise his hand against arbitrary power. They stir and cheer the minds of men in many lands.

We have, however, to face the problem of the turbulent, formidable world outside our shores. Why should not the same principles which have shaped the free, ordered, tolerant civilization of the British Isles and British Empire be found serviceable in the organization of this anxious world? Why should not nations link themselves together in a larger system and establish a rule of law for the benefit of all? That surely is the supreme hope by which we should be inspired and the goal towards which we should march with resolute step.

But it is vain to imagine that the mere perception or declaration of right principles, whether in one country or in many countries, will be of any value unless they are supported by those qualities of civic virtue and manly courage—aye, and by those instruments and agencies of force and science which in the last resort must be the defense of right and reason.

Civilization will not last, freedom will not survive, peace will not be kept, unless a very large majority of mankind unite together to defend them and show themselves possessed of a constabulary power before which barbaric and atavistic forces will stand in awe.

Here, then, we see the task which should command the exertions of the rising generation which fills this spacious hall, and which may bring to the life of Britain the surge of a new impulse towards the organization of world peace, and across the gulf of these eventful years prepare and bring nearer the Brotherhood of Man.

MANEUVERS IN GERMANY

Theydon Bois

August 27, 1938

1938

July 11.   Publication of the British Government's plan for the withdrawal of foreign combatants from Spain.

July 19–22. State visit of the King and Queen to Paris.

July 25.   In Spain Government troops counter-attack across the River Ebro.

August 3.   Lord Runciman arrives in Prague as "conciliator and mediator." The situation grows steadily more tense.

August 15.   German Army maneuvers of unprecedented size begin, and continue throughout the month.

August 22.   Russia informs the German Ambassador in Moscow that if Czechoslovakia is attacked she will stand by her 1935 treaty obligation to support that country.

August 26.   Herr Henlein in a proclamation to his followers orders them "to resort to self-defense, to put an end to the Marxist and irresponsible Czech elements."

MANEUVERS IN GERMANY

It is difficult for us in this ancient Forest at Theydon Bois,[1] the very name of which carries us back to Norman days—here, in the heart of peaceful, law-abiding England—to realize the ferocious passions which are rife in Europe. During this anxious month you have no doubt seen reports in the newspapers, one week good, another week bad; one week better, another week worse. But I must tell you that the whole state of Europe and of the world is moving steadily towards a climax which cannot be long delayed.

War is certainly not inevitable. But the danger to peace will not be removed until the vast German armies which have been called from their homes into the ranks have been dispersed. For a country which is itself not menaced by anyone, in no fear of anyone, to place over fifteen hundred thousand soldiers upon a war footing is a very grave step. The expense cannot be less than five or six hundred thousand pounds a day, which amounts to more than thirty millions in two months, all to be exacted from a country whose finances are already under severe strain, and whose people have long been living under what the rest of the world would call war conditions.

It seems to me, and I must tell it to you plainly, that these great forces have not been placed upon a war footing without an intention to reach a conclusion within a very limited space of time. The fabricated stories which are spread of a Marxist plot in Czechoslovakia, and the orders to the Sudeten Deutsch to arm and defend themselves, are disquieting signs, similar to those which preceded the seizure of Austria.

We are all in full agreement with the course our Government have taken in sending Lord Runciman to Prague. We hope—indeed, we

[1] In the Epping Division, Mr. Churchill's constituency.

pray—that his mission of conciliation will be successful, and certainly it looks as if the Government of Czechoslovakia were doing their utmost to put their house in order, and to meet every demand which is not designed to compass their ruin as a State. I have little doubt that Lord Runciman, if given a fair chance, would be able to bring about a friendly settlement on the spot. But it may be that outside forces, that larger and fiercer ambitions, may prevent this settlement, and then Europe and the civilized world will have to face the demands of Nazi Germany, or perhaps be confronted—and this is a possibility which you must not exclude —with some sudden violent action on the part of the German Nazi Party, carrying with it the invasion of a small country with a view to its subjugation. Such an episode would not be simply an attack upon Czechoslovakia; it would be an outrage against the civilization and freedom of the whole world. Every country would ask itself, "Whose turn will it be next?"

We have a Government which everyone knows is sincerely devoted to peace—whose whole position and policy is the maintenance of peace; who have shown they are ready to put up with affronts and injuries to which in no other period have we submitted, for the sake of peace. But it would be a mistake if any foreign Power supposed that Britain is no longer capable, if need be, of bearing her part with other nations in defending the title-deeds of mankind.

I have always wished to see Great Britain, France and Germany working together for the progress of the nations, for the reunion of the European family, and for the improvement—the vast improvement—in the conditions of the wage-earning masses which modern science has now rendered possible. Never in history have blessing and cursing been more bluntly offered to mankind, or offered on so immense a scale. It is very grievous that at this hour the fate of European peace should lie in the hands of a single man. We know that the German people do not wish for war; above all, they do not wish for war with the British Empire. Our anxieties and our hopes, therefore, center upon the extraordinary man at the summit of Germany. He has raised his country from defeat; he has brought it back again to the foremost ranks of power. It would indeed be a fatal act if he were to cast away all he has done for the German people by leading them into what would almost certainly become a world war.

My hope is, therefore, that these perils will pass. If they pass, the road will be open to many good solutions for the mutual benefit of all. The road will also be open to a large expansion in the daily life of the great masses of the people of every race. We might indeed see a movement forward which would raise the human race to new levels of security and well-being, such as have not been attained in any former age. But whatever may happen, foreign countries should know—and the Government is right to let them know—that Great Britain and the British Empire must not be deemed incapable of playing their part and doing their duty as they have done on other great occasions which have not yet been forgotten by history.

THE MUNICH AGREEMENT

The House of Commons

October 5, 1938

1938

September 1. At the suggestion of Lord Runciman, Herr Henlein takes to Herr Hitler at Berchtesgaden President Benes' plan for "cantonal self-government," together with the offer of other generous concessions.

September 8. Slight incidents in a riot stirred up by Nazis outside the prison of Maehrisch-Ostrau (Sudetenland) are seized by the German Government as an excuse for breaking off all relations with Czechoslovakia.

September 11. Lord Runciman hailed by Nazis at Petrograd as "liberator of the Sudeten Germans." Serious demonstrations, assuming the proportions of a revolt, result in 23 deaths during the 11th and 12th.

1938

September 12. Herr Hitler in an inflammatory speech at Nuremberg declares that the oppression of the Sudeten Germans must be brought to an end.

September 14. Herr Henlein issues an ultimatum, which is rejected by the Czechoslovakian Government; he flees the country.

September 15. Mr. Neville Chamberlain flies to Berchtesgaden.

September 18. At the invitation of the British Government, MM. Daladier and Bonnet come to London for a conference, at which the dismemberment of Czechoslovakia and the abandonment of pledges are agreed upon. The Czechoslovakian Government declares a "state of emergency."

September 21. The British and French Ambassadors inform President Benes that Czechoslovakia must unconditionally accept their countries' terms, or face Germany alone.

September 22. The Czechoslovakian Government, after an all-night sitting, accepts the terms. Mr. Chamberlain leaves for Godesberg.

September 24. Mr. Chamberlain returns with a Memorandum of Germany's demands, which he finds to exceed his expectation by a large margin. In the light of this Britain and France tell Czechoslovakia that, while they will bring no influence to bear on her in her decision, they will support her if she resists the additional demands. Czechoslovakia mobilizes.

September 28. The First Lord of the Admiralty, Mr. Duff Cooper, orders the mobilization of the Fleet.
In the middle of his speech in the House of Commons, Mr. Chamberlain, handed a piece of paper by Sir John Simon, announces that he has been invited to meet Herr Hitler at Munich, with M. Daladier and Signor Mussolini.

September 29. Munich Conference. Mr. Chamberlain offers further concessions on behalf of the Czechs, who are refused admittance to the conference room.

September 30. Told that Mr. Chamberlain must have an answer by noon, the Czechoslovakian Government bows to the terms dictated. General Syrovy broadcasts these to the nation at 5 p.m.

October 1. Mr. Chamberlain returns and announces at Heston Airport that he has brought "peace for our time." On arrival at Downing Street he announces that he has brought "peace with honor."

October 2. Mr. Duff Cooper, First Lord of the Admiralty, resigns. The House of Commons begins a three days' debate on the Agreement.
Poland seizes the Teschen area of Czechoslovakia.

October 5. Dr. Benes resigns.

THE MUNICH AGREEMENT

I<small>F</small> I do not begin this afternoon by paying the usual, and indeed almost invariable, tributes to the Prime Minister for his handling of this crisis, it is certainly not from any lack of personal regard. We have always, over a great many years, had very pleasant relations, and I have deeply understood from personal experiences of my own in a similar crisis the stress and strain he has had to bear; but I am sure it is much better to say exactly what we think about public affairs, and this is certainly not the time when it is worth anyone's while to court political popularity. We had a shining example of firmness of character from the late First Lord of the Admiralty two days ago. He showed that firmness of character which is utterly unmoved by currents of opinion, however swift and violent they may be. My hon. Friend the Member for South-West Hull [Mr. Law], to whose compulsive speech the House listened on Monday, was quite right in reminding us that the Prime Minister has himself throughout his conduct of these matters shown a robust indifference to cheers or boos and to the alternations of criticism or applause. If that be so, such qualities and elevation of mind should make it possible for the most severe expressions of honest opinion to be interchanged in this House without rupturing personal relations, and for all points of view to receive the fullest possible expression. Having thus fortified myself by the example of others, I will proceed to emulate them. I will, therefore, begin by saying the most unpopular and most unwelcome thing. I will begin by saying what everybody would like to ignore or forget but which must nevertheless be stated, namely, that we have sustained a total and unmitigated defeat, and that France has suffered even more than we have. The utmost my right hon. Friend the Prime Minister has been able to secure by all his immense exertions, by all the great efforts and mobilization which took place in this country, and by all the anguish and strain through which we have passed in this country—the utmost he has been able to gain for Czechoslovakia in the matters which were in dispute has been that the German dictator, instead of snatching the victuals from the table, has been content to have them served to him course by course.

The Chancellor of the Exchequer [Sir John Simon] said it was the first time Herr Hitler had been made to retract—I think that was the word—in any degree. We really must not waste time after all this long Debate upon the difference between the positions reached at Berchtesgaden, at Godesberg and at Munich. They can be very simply epitomized, if the House will permit me to vary the metaphor. One pound was demanded at the pistol's point. When it was given, £2 were demanded at the pistol's point. Finally, the dictator consented to take £1 17s. 6d. and the rest in promises of good will for the future.

Now I come to the point, which was mentioned to me just now from some quarters of the House, about the saving of peace. No one has been a more resolute and uncompromising struggler for peace than the Prime Minister. Everyone knows that. Never has there been such intense and undaunted determination to maintain and secure peace. That is quite true. Nevertheless, I am not quite clear why there was so much danger of Great Britain or France being involved in a war with Germany at this juncture if, in fact, they were ready all along to sacrifice Czechoslovakia. The terms which the Prime Minister brought back with him could easily have been agreed, I believe, through the ordinary diplomatic channels at any time during the summer. And I will say this: that I believe the Czechs, left to themselves and told they were going to get no help from the Western Powers, would have been able to make better terms than they have got after all this tremendous perturbation; they could hardly have had worse.

There never can be any absolute certainty that there will be a fight if one side is determined that it will give way completely. When one reads the Munich terms, when one sees what is happening in Czechoslovakia from hour to hour, when one is sure, I will not say of Parliamentary approval but of Parliamentary acquiescence, when the Chancellor of the Exchequer makes a speech which at any rate tries to put in a very powerful and persuasive manner the fact that, after all, it was inevitable and indeed righteous: when we saw all this—and everyone on this side of the House, including many members of the Conservative Party who are vigilant and careful guardians of the national interest, is quite clear that nothing vitally affecting us was at stake—it seems to me that one must ask, What was all the trouble and fuss about?

The resolve was taken by the British and the French Governments. Let me say that it is very important to realize that it is by no means a question which the British Government only have had to decide. I very much admire the manner in which, in the House, all references of a recriminatory nature have been repressed. But it must be realized that this resolve did not emanate particularly from one or other of the Governments but was a resolve for which both must share in common the responsibility. When this resolve was taken and the course was followed —you may say it was wise or unwise, prudent or short-sighted—once it had been decided not to make the defense of Czechoslovakia a matter of war, then there was really no reason, if the matter had been handled during the summer in the ordinary way, to call into being all this formidable apparatus of crisis. I think that point should be considered.

We are asked to vote for this Motion [1] which has been put upon the Paper, and it is certainly a Motion couched in very uncontroversial terms, as, indeed, is the Amendment moved from the Opposition side. I cannot myself express my agreement with the steps which have been taken, and as the Chancellor of the Exchequer has put his side of the case with so much ability I will attempt, if I may be permitted, to put the case from a different angle. I have always held the view that the maintenance of peace depends upon the accumulation of deterrents against the aggressor, coupled with a sincere effort to redress grievances. Herr Hitler's victory, like so many of the famous struggles that have governed the fate of the world, was won upon the narrowest of margins. After the seizure of Austria in March we faced this problem in our Debates. I ventured to appeal to the Government to go a little further than the Prime Minister went, and to give a pledge that in conjunction with France and other Powers they would guarantee the security of Czechoslovakia while the Sudeten-Deutsch question was being examined either by a League of Nations Commission or some other impartial body, and I still believe that if that course had been followed events would not have fallen into this disastrous state. I agree very much with my right hon. Friend the Member for Sparkbrook [Mr. Amery] when he said on that occasion,

---

[1] "That this House approves the policy of His Majesty's Government by which war was averted in the recent crisis and supports their efforts to secure a lasting peace."

"Do one thing or the other; either say you will disinterest yourself in the matter altogether or take the step of giving a guarantee which will have the greatest chance of securing protection for that country."

France and Great Britain together, especially if they had maintained a close contact with Russia, which certainly was not done, would have been able in those days in the summer, when they had the prestige, to influence many of the smaller states of Europe; and I believe they could have determined the attitude of Poland. Such a combination, prepared at a time when the German dictator was not deeply and irrevocably committed to his new adventure, would, I believe, have given strength to all those forces in Germany which resisted this departure, this new design. They were varying forces—those of a military character which declared that Germany was not ready to undertake a world war, and all that mass of moderate opinion and popular opinion which dreaded war, and some elements of which still have some influence upon the Government. Such action would have given strength to all that intense desire for peace which the helpless German masses share with their British and French fellow men, and which, as we have been reminded, found a passionate and rarely permitted vent in the joyous manifestations with which the Prime Minister was acclaimed in Munich.

All these forces, added to the other deterrents which combinations of Powers, great and small, ready to stand firm upon the front of law and for the ordered remedy of grievances, would have formed, might well have been effective. Between submission and immediate war there was this third alternative, which gave a hope not only of peace but of justice. It is quite true that such a policy in order to succeed demanded that Britain should declare straight out and a long time beforehand that she would, with others, join to defend Czechoslovakia against an unprovoked aggression. His Majesty's Government refused to give that guarantee when it would have saved the situation, yet in the end they gave it when it was too late, and now, for the future, they renew it when they have not the slightest power to make it good.

All is over. Silent, mournful, abandoned, broken, Czechoslovakia recedes into the darkness. She has suffered in every respect by her association with the Western democracies and with the League of Nations, of which she has always been an obedient servant. She has suffered in particular from her association with France, by whose guidance and policy she has been actuated for so long. The very measures taken by

His Majesty's Government in the Anglo-French Agreement to give her the best chance possible, namely, the 50 per cent clean cut in certain districts instead of a plebiscite, have turned to her detriment, because there is to be a plebiscite too in wide areas, and those other Powers who had claims have also come down upon the helpless victim. Those municipal elections upon whose voting the basis is taken for the 50 per cent cut were held on issues which had nothing to do with joining Germany. When I saw Herr Henlein over here he assured me that was not the desire of his people. Positive statements were made that it was only a question of home rule, of having a position of their own in the Czechoslovakian State. No one has a right to say that the plebiscite which is to be taken in areas under Saar conditions, and the clean cut of the 50 per cent areas—that those two operations together amount in the slightest degree to a verdict of self-determination. It is a fraud and a farce to invoke that name.

We in this country, as in other Liberal and democratic countries, have a perfect right to exalt the principle of self-determination, but it comes ill out of the mouths of those in totalitarian states who deny even the smallest element of toleration to every section and creed within their bounds. But, however you put it, this particular block of land, this mass of human beings to be handed over, has never expressed the desire to go into the Nazi rule. I do not believe that even now, if their opinion could be asked, they would exercise such an opinion.

What is the remaining position of Czechoslovakia? Not only are they politically mutilated, but economically and financially they are in complete confusion. Their banking, their railway arrangements, are severed and broken, their industries are curtailed, and the movement of their population is most cruel. The Sudeten miners, who are all Czechs and whose families have lived in that area for centuries, must now flee into an area where there are hardly any mines left for them to work. It is a tragedy which has occurred. There must always be the most profound regret and a sense of vexation in British hearts at the treatment and the misfortune which have overcome the Czechoslovakian Republic. They have not ended here. At any moment there may be a hitch in the program. At any moment there may be an order for Herr Goebbels to start again his propaganda of calumny and lies; at any moment an incident may be provoked, and now that the fortress line is turned, what is there to stop the will of the conqueror? Obviously, we are not in a position to give them the slightest help at the present time, except what everyone is glad to know has been done, the financial aid which the Government have promptly produced.

I venture to think that in future the Czechoslovak State cannot be maintained as an independent entity. I think you will find that in a period of time which may be measured by years, but may be measured only by months, Czechoslovakia will be engulfed in the Nazi regime. Perhaps they may join it in despair or in revenge. At any rate, that story is over and told. But we cannot consider the abandonment and ruin of Czechoslovakia in the light only of what happened only last month. It is the most grievous consequence of what we have done and of what we have left undone in the last five years—five years of futile good intentions, five years of eager search for the line of least resistance, five years of uninterrupted retreat of British power, five years of neglect of our air defenses. Those are the features which I stand here to expose and which marked an improvident stewardship for which Great Britain and France have dearly to pay. We have been reduced in those five years from a position of security so overwhelming and so unchallengeable that we never cared to think about it. We have been reduced from a position where the very word "war" was considered one which could be used only by persons qualifying for a lunatic asylum. We have been reduced from a position of safety and power—power to do good, power to be generous to a beaten foe, power to make terms with Germany, power to give her proper redress for her grievances, power to stop her arming if we chose, power to take any step in strength or mercy or justice which we thought right—reduced in five years from a position safe and unchallenged to where we stand now.

When I think of the fair hopes of a long peace which still lay before Europe at the beginning of 1933 when Herr Hitler first obtained power, and of all the opportunities of arresting the growth of the Nazi power which have been thrown away, when I think of the immense combinations and resources which have been neglected or squandered, I cannot believe that a parallel exists in the whole course of history. So far as this country is concerned, the responsibility must rest with those who have had the undisputed control of our political affairs. They neither prevented Germany from rearming, nor did they rearm ourselves in time. They quarreled with Italy without saving Ethiopia. They exploited and discredited the vast institution of the League of Nations and they neglected to make alliances and combinations which might have repaired previous errors, and thus they left us in the hour of trial without adequate national defense or effective international security.

In my holiday I thought it was a chance to study the reign of King Ethelred the Unready. The House will remember that that was a period of great misfortune, in which, from the strong position which we had gained under the descendants of King Alfred, we fell very swiftly into chaos. It was the period of Danegeld and of foreign pressure. I must say that the rugged words of the Anglo-Saxon Chronicle, written a thousand years ago, seem to me apposite, at least as apposite as those quotations from Shakespeare with which we have been regaled by the last speaker from the Opposition Bench. Here is what the Anglo-Saxon Chronicle said, and I think the words apply very much to our treatment of Germany and our relations with her. "All these calamities fell upon us because of evil counsel, because tribute was not offered to them at the right time nor yet were they resisted; but when they had done the most evil, then was peace made with them." That is the wisdom of the past, for all wisdom is not new wisdom.

I have ventured to express those views in justifying myself for not being able to support the Motion which is moved tonight, but I recognize that this great matter of Czechoslovakia, and of British and French duty there, has passed into history. New developments may come along, but we are not here to decide whether any of those steps should be taken or not. They have been taken. They have been taken by those who had a right to take them because they bore the highest executive responsibility under the Crown. Whatever we may think of it, we must regard those steps as belonging to the category of affairs which are settled beyond recall. The past is no more, and one can only draw comfort if one feels that one has done one's best to advise rightly and wisely and in good time. I, therefore, turn to the future, and to our situation as it is today. Here, again, I am sure I shall have to say something which will not be at all welcome.

We are in the presence of a disaster of the first magnitude which has befallen Great Britain and France. Do not let us blind ourselves to that. It must now be accepted that all the countries of Central and Eastern Europe will make the best terms they can with the triumphant Nazi power. The system of alliances in Central Europe upon which France has relied for her safety has been swept away, and I can see no means by which it can be reconstituted. The road down the Danube Valley to the Black Sea, the road which leads as far as Turkey, has been opened. In fact, if not in form, it seems to me that all those countries of Middle Europe, all those Danubian countries, will, one after another, be drawn into this vast system of power politics—not only power military politics but power economic politics—radiating from Berlin, and I believe this can be achieved quite smoothly and swiftly and will not necessarily entail the firing of a single shot. If you wish to survey the havoc of the foreign policy of Britain and France, look at what is happening and is recorded each day in the columns of *The Times*. Why, I read this morning about Yugoslavia—and I know something about the details of that country—

"The effects of the crisis for Yugoslavia can immediately be traced. Since the elections of 1935, which followed soon after the murder of King Alexander, the Serb and Croat Opposition to the Government of Dr. Stoyadinovitch have been conducting their entire campaign for the next elections under the slogan: 'Back to France, England, and the Little Entente; back to democracy.' The events of the past fortnight have so triumphantly vindicated Dr. Stoyadinovitch's policy. . . ."—his is a policy of close association with Germany—"that the Opposition has collapsed practically overnight; the new elections, the date of which was in doubt, are now likely to be held very soon and can result only in an overwhelming victory for Dr. Stoyadinovitch's Government." Here was a country which, three months ago, would have stood in the line with other countries to arrest what has occurred.

Again, what happened in Warsaw? The British and French Ambassadors visited the Foreign Minister, Colonel Beck, or sought to visit him, in order to ask for some mitigation in the harsh measures being pursued against Czechoslovakia about Teschen. The door was shut in their faces. The French Ambassador was not even granted an audience, and the British Ambassador was given a most curt reply by a political director. The whole matter is described in the Polish Press as a political indiscretion committed by those two powers, and we are today reading of the success of Colonel Beck's blow. I am not forgetting, I must say, that it is less than twenty years since British and French bayonets rescued Poland from the bondage of a century and a half. I think it is indeed a sorry episode in the history of that country, for whose freedom and rights so many of us have had warm and long sympathy.

Those illustrations are typical. You will see, day after day, week after week, entire alienation of those regions. Many of those countries, in fear of the rise of the Nazi power, have already got politicians, Ministers,

Governments, who were pro-German, but there was always an enormous popular movement in Poland, Rumania, Bulgaria and Yugoslavia which looked to the Western democracies and loathed the idea of having this arbitrary rule of the totalitarian system thrust upon them, and hoped that a stand would be made. All that has gone by the board. We are talking about countries which are a long way off. But what will be the position, I want to know, of France and England this year and the year afterwards? What will be the position of that Western front of which we are in full authority the guarantors? The German army at the present time is more numerous than that of France, though not nearly so matured or perfected. Next year it will grow much larger, and its maturity will be more complete. Relieved from all anxiety in the East, and having secured resources which will greatly diminish, if not entirely remove, the deterrent of a naval blockade, the rulers of Nazi Germany will have a free choice open to them as to what direction they will turn their eyes. If the Nazi dictator should choose to look westward, as he may, bitterly will France and England regret the loss of that fine army of ancient Bohemia which was estimated last week to require not fewer than 30 German divisions for its destruction.

Can we blind ourselves to the great change which has taken place in the military situation, and to the dangers we have to meet? We are in process, I believe, of adding in four years, four battalions to the British Army. No fewer than two have already been completed. Here are at least 30 divisions which must now be taken into consideration upon the French front, besides the 12 that were captured when Austria was engulfed. Many people, no doubt, honestly believe that they are only giving away the interests of Czechoslovakia, whereas I fear we shall find that we have deeply compromised, and perhaps fatally endangered, the safety and even the independence of Great Britain and France. This is not merely a question of giving up the German colonies, as I am sure we shall be asked to do. Nor is it a question only of losing influence in Europe. It goes far deeper than that. You have to consider the character of the Nazi movement and the rule which it implies. The Prime Minister desires to see cordial relations between this country and Germany. There is no difficulty at all in having cordial relations between the peoples. Our hearts go out to them. But they have no power. But never will you have friendship with the present German Government. You must have diplomatic and correct relations, but there can never be friendship between the British democracy and the Nazi power, that power which spurns Christian ethics, which cheers its onward course by barbarous paganism, which vaunts the spirit of aggression and conquest, which derives strength and perverted pleasure from persecution, and uses, as we have seen, with pitiless brutality the threat of murderous force. That power cannot ever be the trusted friend of the British democracy.

What I find unendurable is the sense of our country falling into the power, into the orbit and influence of Nazi Germany, and of our existence becoming dependent upon their good will or pleasure. It is to prevent that that I have tried my best to urge the maintenance of every bulwark of defense—first, the timely creation of an Air Force superior to anything within striking distance of our shores; secondly, the gathering together of the collective strength of many nations; and thirdly, the making of alliances and military conventions, all within the Covenant, in order to gather together forces at any rate to restrain the onward movement of this power. It has all been in vain. Every position has been successively undermined and abandoned on specious and plausible excuses.

We do not want to be led upon the high road to becoming a satellite of the German Nazi system of European domination. In a very few years, perhaps in a very few months, we shall be confronted with demands with which we shall no doubt be invited to comply. Those demands may affect the surrender of territory or the surrender of liberty. I foresee and foretell that the policy of submission will carry with it restrictions upon the freedom of speech and debate in Parliament, on public platforms, and discussions in the Press, for it will be said—indeed, I hear it said sometimes now—that we cannot allow the Nazi system of dictatorship to be criticized by ordinary, common English politicians. Then, with a Press under control, in part direct but more potently indirect, with every organ of public opinion doped and chloroformed into acquiescence, we shall be conducted along further stages of our journey.

It is a small matter to introduce into such a Debate as this, but during the week I heard something of the talk of Tadpole and Taper. They were very keen upon having a general election, a sort of, if I may say so, inverted khaki election. I wish the Prime Minister had heard the speech of my hon. and gallant friend the Member for the Abbey Division of Westminster [Sir Sidney Herbert] last night. I know that no one is more patient and regular in his attendance than the Prime Minister, and it is marvelous how he is able to sit through so much of our Debates, but it happened that by bad luck he was not here at that moment. I am sure, however, that if he had heard my hon. and gallant Friend's speech he would have felt very much annoyed that such a rumor could even have been circulated. I cannot believe that the Prime Minister, or any Prime Minister, possessed of a large working majority, would be capable of such an act of historic, constitutional indecency. I think too highly of him. Of course, if I have misjudged him on the right side, and there is a dissolution on the Munich Agreement, on Anglo-Nazi friendship, of the state of our defenses and so forth, everyone will have to fight according to his convictions, and only a prophet could forecast the ultimate result; but, whatever the result, few things could be more fatal to our remaining chances of survival as a great Power than that this country should be torn in twain upon this deadly issue of foreign policy at a moment when, whoever the Ministers may be, united effort can alone make us safe.

I have been casting about to see how measures can be taken to protect us from this advance of the Nazi power, and to secure those forms of life which are so dear to us. What is the sole method that is open? The sole method that is open is for us to regain our old island independence by acquiring that supremacy in the air which we were promised, that security in our air defenses which we were assured we had, and thus to make ourselves an island once again. That, in all this grim outlook, shines out as the overwhelming fact. An effort at rearmament the like of which has not been seen ought to be made forthwith, and all the resources of this country and all its united strength should be bent to that task. I was very glad to see that Lord Baldwin yesterday in the House of Lords said that he would mobilize industry tomorrow. But I think it would have been much better if Lord Baldwin had said that two and a half years ago, when everyone demanded a Ministry of Supply. I will venture to say to hon. Gentlemen sitting here behind the Government Bench, hon. Friends of mine, whom I thank for the patience with which they have listened to what I have to say, that they have some responsibility for all this too, because, if they had given one tithe of the cheers they have lavished upon this transaction of Czechoslovakia to the small band of Members, who were endeavoring to get timely rearmament set in motion, we should not now be in the position in which we are. Hon. Gentlemen opposite, and hon. Members on the Liberal benches, are not entitled to throw these stones. I remember for two years having to face, not only the Government's deprecation, but their stern disapproval. Lord Baldwin has now given the signal, tardy though it may be; let us at least obey it.

After all, there are no secrets now about what happened in the air and in the mobilization of our anti-aircraft defenses. These matters have been, as my hon. and gallant Friend the Member for the Abbey Division said, seen by thousands of people. They can form their own opinions of the character of the statements which have been persistently made to us by Ministers on this subject. Who pretends now that there is air parity with Germany? Who pretends now that our anti-aircraft defenses were adequately manned or armed? We know that the German General Staff are well informed upon these subjects, but the House of Commons has hitherto not taken seriously its duty of requiring to assure itself on these matters. The Home Secretary [2] said the other night that he would welcome investigation. Many things have been done which reflect the greatest credit upon the administration. But the vital matters are what we want to know about. I have asked again and again during these three years for a secret Session where these matters could be thrashed out, or for an investigation by a Select Committee of the House, or for some other method. I ask now that, when we meet again in the autumn, that should be a matter on which the Government should take the House into its confidence, because we have a right to know where we stand and what measures are being taken to secure our position.

I do not grudge our loyal, brave people, who were ready to do their duty no matter what the cost, who never flinched under the strain of last week—I do not grudge them the natural, spontaneous outburst of joy and relief when they learned that the hard ordeal would no longer be required of them at the moment; but they should know the truth. They should know that there has been gross neglect and deficiency in our defenses; they should know that we have sustained a defeat without a war, the consequences of which will travel far with us along our road; they should know that we have passed an awful milestone in our history, when the whole equilibrium of Europe has been deranged, and that the terrible words have for the time being been pronounced against the Western democracies: "Thou art weighed in the balance and found wanting." And do not suppose that this is the end. This is only the beginning of the reckoning. This is only the first sip, the first foretaste of a bitter cup which will be proffered to us year by year unless, by a supreme recovery of moral health and martial vigor, we arise again and take our stand for freedom as in the olden time.

[2] Sir Samuel Hoare.

THE DEFENSE OF FREEDOM AND PEACE

An Address to the People of the United States of America

October 16, 1938

1938

October 10. Germany completes the occupation of the ceded areas of Czechoslovakia—exceeding in many cases the agreed boundaries—while the Gestapo carries out its customary pogroms.

THE DEFENSE OF FREEDOM AND PEACE

I AVAIL myself with relief of the opportunity of speaking to the people of the United States. I do not know how long such liberties will be allowed. The stations of uncensored expression are closing down; the lights are going out; but there is still time for those to whom freedom and Parliamentary government mean something, to consult together. Let me, then, speak in truth and earnestness while time remains.

The American people have, it seems to me, formed a true judgment upon the disaster which has befallen Europe. They realize, perhaps more clearly than the French and British publics have yet done, the far-reaching consequences of the abandonment and ruin of the Czechoslovak Republic. I hold to the conviction I expressed some months ago, that if in April, May or June, Great Britain, France and Russia had jointly declared that they would act together upon Nazi Germany if Herr Hitler committed an act of unprovoked aggression against this small state, and if they had told Poland, Yugoslavia and Rumania what they meant to do in good time, and invited them to join the combination of peace-defending Powers, I hold that the German Dictator would have been confronted with such a formidable array that he would have been deterred from his purpose. This would also have been an opportunity for all the peace-loving and moderate forces in Germany, together with the chiefs of the German Army, to make a great effort to re-establish something like sane and civilized conditions in their own country. If the risks of war which were run by France and Britain at the last moment had been boldly faced in good time, and plain declarations made, and meant, how different would our prospects be today!

But all these backward speculations belong to history. It is no good using hard words among friends about the past, and reproaching one another for what cannot be recalled. It is the future, not the past, that demands our earnest and anxious thought. We must recognize that the Parliamentary democracies and liberal, peaceful forces have everywhere sustained a defeat which leaves them weaker, morally and physically, to cope with dangers which have vastly grown. But the cause of freedom has in it a recuperative power and virtue which can draw from misfortune new hope and new strength. If ever there was a time when men and women who cherish the ideals of the founders of the British and American Constitutions should take earnest counsel with one another, that time is now.

All the world wishes for peace and security. Have we gained it by the sacrifice of the Czechoslovak Republic? Here was the model democratic state of Central Europe, a country where minorities were treated better than anywhere else. It has been deserted, destroyed and devoured. It is now being digested. The question which is of interest to a lot of ordinary common people, is whether this destruction of the Czechoslovak Republic will bring upon the world a blessing or a curse.

We must all hope it will bring a blessing; that after we have averted our gaze for a while from the process of subjugation and liquidation, everyone will breathe more freely; that a load will be taken off our chests; that we shall be able to say to ourselves: "Well, that's out of the way, anyhow. Now let's get on with our regular daily life." But are these hopes well founded or are we merely making the best of what we had not the force and virtue to stop? That is the question that the English-speaking peoples in all their lands must ask themselves today. Is this the end, or is there more to come?

There is another question which arises out of this. Can peace, good will and confidence be built upon submission to wrong-doing backed by force? One may put this question in the largest form. Has any benefit or progress ever been achieved by the human race by submission to organized and calculated violence? As we look back over the long story of the nations, we must see that, on the contrary, their glory has been founded upon the spirit of resistance to tyranny and injustice, especially when these evils seemed to be backed by heavier force. Since the dawn of the Christian era a certain way of life has slowly been shaping itself among the Western peoples, and certain standards of conduct and government have come to be esteemed. After many miseries and prolonged confusion, there arose into the broad light of day the conception of the right of the individual; his right to be consulted in the government of his country; his right to invoke the law even against the State itself. Independent Courts of Justice were created to affirm and enforce this hard-won custom. Thus was assured throughout the English-speaking world, and in France by the stern lessons of the Revolution, what Kipling called, "Leave to live by no man's leave underneath the law." Now in this resides all that makes existence precious to man, and all that confers honor and health upon the state.

We are confronted with another theme. It is not a new theme; it leaps out upon us from the Dark Ages—racial persecution, religious intolerance, deprivation of free speech, the conception of the citizen as a mere soulless fraction of the state. To this has been added the cult of war. Children are to be taught in their earliest schooling the delights and profits of conquest and aggression. A whole mighty community has been drawn painfully, by severe privations, into a warlike frame. They are held in this condition, which they relish no more than we do, by a party organization, several millions strong, who derive all kinds of profits, good and bad, from the upkeep of the regime. Like the Communists, the Nazis tolerate no opinion but their own. Like the Communists, they feed on hatred. Like the Communists, they must seek, from time to time, and always at shorter intervals, a new target, a new prize, a new victim. The Dictator, in all his pride, is held in the grip of his Party machine. He can go forward; he cannot go back. He must blood his hounds and show them sport, or else, like Actaeon of old, be devoured by them. All-strong without, he is all-weak within. As Byron wrote a hundred years ago: "These Pagod things of sabre sway, with fronts of brass and feet of clay."

No one must, however, underrate the power and efficiency of a totalitarian state. Where the whole population of a great country, amiable, good-hearted, peace-loving people, are gripped by the neck and by the hair by a Communist or a Nazi tyranny—for they are the same things spelled in different ways—the rulers for the time being can exercise a power for the purposes of war and external domination before which the ordinary free Parliamentary societies are at a grievous practical disadvantage. We have to recognize this. And then, on top of all, comes this wonderful mastery of the air which our century has discovered, but of which, alas, mankind has so far shown itself unworthy. Here is this air power with its claim to torture and terrorize the women and children, the civil population of neighboring countries. This combination of medieval passion, a party caucus, the weapons of modern science, and the blackmailing power of air-bombing, is the most monstrous menace to peace, order and fertile progress that has appeared in the world since the Mongol invasions of the thirteenth century.

The culminating question to which I have been leading is whether the world as we have known it—the great and hopeful world of before the war, the world of increasing hope and enjoyment for the common man, the world of honored tradition and expanding science—should meet this menace by submission or by resistance. Let us see, then, whether the means of resistance remain to us today. We have sustained an immense disaster; the renown of France is dimmed. In spite of her brave, efficient army, her influence is profoundly diminished. No one has a right to say that Britain, for all her blundering, has broken her word—indeed, when it was too late, she was better than her word. Nevertheless, Europe lies at this moment abashed and distracted before the triumphant assertions of dictatorial power. In the Spanish Peninsula, a purely Spanish quarrel has been carried by the intervention, or shall I say the "non-intervention" (to quote the current jargon), of Dictators into the region of a world cause. But it is not only in Europe that these oppressions prevail. China is being torn to pieces by a military clique in Japan; the poor, tormented Chinese people there are making a brave and stubborn defense. The ancient empire of Ethiopia has been overrun. The Ethiopians were taught to look to the sanctity of public law, to the tribunal of many nations gathered in majestic union. But all failed; they were deceived, and now they are winning back their right to live by beginning again from the bottom a struggle on primordial lines. Even in South America, the Nazi regime begins to undermine the fabric of Brazilian society.

Far away, happily protected by the Atlantic and Pacific Oceans, you, the people of the United States, to whom I now have the chance to speak, are the spectators; and, I may add, the increasingly involved spectators of these tragedies and crimes. We are left in no doubt where American conviction and sympathies lie: but will you wait until British freedom and independence have succumbed, and then take up the cause when it is three-quarters ruined, yourselves alone? I hear that they are saying in the United States that, because England and France have failed to do their duty, therefore the American people can wash their hands of the whole business. This may be the passing mood of many people, but there is no sense in it. If things have got much worse, all the more must we try to cope with them.

For, after all, survey the remaining forces of civilization; they are overwhelming. If only they were united in a common conception of right and duty, there would be no war. On the contrary, the German people, industrious, faithful, valiant, but alas! lacking in the proper spirit of civic independence, liberated from their present nightmare would take their honored place in the vanguard of human society. Alexander the Great remarked that the people of Asia were slaves because they had not learned to pronounce the word "No." Let that not be the epitaph of the English-speaking peoples or of Parliamentary democracy, or of France, or of the many surviving Liberal states of Europe.

There, in one single word, is the resolve which the forces of freedom and progress, of tolerance and good will, should take. It is not in the power of one nation, however formidably armed, still less is it in the power of a small group of men, violent, ruthless men, who have always to cast their eyes back over their shoulders, to cramp and fetter the forward march of human destiny. The preponderant world forces are upon our side; they have but to be combined to be obeyed. We must arm. Britain must arm. America must arm. If, through an earnest desire for peace, we have placed ourselves at a disadvantage, we must make up for it by redoubled exertions, and, if necessary, by fortitude in suffering. We shall, no doubt, arm. Britain, casting away the habits of centuries, will decree national service upon her citizens. The British people will stand erect, and will face whatever may be coming.

But arms—instrumentalities, as President Wilson called them—are not sufficient by themselves. We must add to them the power of ideas. People say we ought not to allow ourselves to be drawn into a theoretical antagonism between Nazidom and democracy; but the antagonism is here now. It is this very conflict of spiritual and moral ideas which gives the free countries a great part of their strength. You see these dictators on their pedestals, surrounded by the bayonets of their soldiers and the truncheons of their police. On all sides they are guarded by masses of armed men, cannons, aeroplanes, fortifications, and the like—they boast and vaunt themselves before the world, yet in their hearts there is unspoken fear. They are afraid of words and thoughts: words spoken abroad, thoughts stirring at home—all the more powerful because forbidden—terrify them. A little mouse of thought appears in the room, and even the mightiest potentates are thrown into panic. They make frantic efforts to bar out thoughts and words; they are afraid of the workings of the human mind. Cannons, aeroplanes, they can manufacture in large quantities; but how are they to quell the natural promptings of human nature, which after all these centuries of trial and progress has inherited a whole armory of potent and indestructible knowledge?

Dictatorship—the fetish worship of one man—is a passing phase. A state of society where men may not speak their minds, where children denounce their parents to the police, where a business man or small shopkeeper ruins his competitor by telling tales about his private opinions—such a state of society cannot long endure if brought into contact with the healthy outside world. The light of civilized progress with its tolerances and co-operation, with its dignities and joys, has often in the past been blotted out. But I hold the belief that we have now at last got far enough ahead of barbarism to control it, and to avert it, if only we realize what is afoot and make up our minds in time. We shall do it in the end. But how much harder our toil for every day's delay!

Is this a call to war? Does anyone pretend that preparation for resistance to aggression is unleashing war? I declare it to be the sole guarantee of peace. We need the swift gathering of forces to confront not only military but moral aggression; the resolute and sober acceptance of their duty by the English-speaking peoples and by all the nations, great and small, who wish to walk with them. Their faithful and zealous comradeship would almost between night and morning clear the path of progress and banish from all our lives the fear which already darkens the sunlight to hundreds of millions of men.

THE CASE FOR A MINISTRY OF SUPPLY

The House of Commons: Debate on an Amendment to the Address

November 17, 1938

October 18.   The Liberal Party Executive, in a manifesto, describes the results of the Government's Foreign Policy as "an armed and precarious truce."

October 22.   Dr. Benes leaves Czechoslovakia for exile.

October 27.   Lord Stanhope appointed First Lord of the Admiralty, a post vacant since the resignation of Mr. Duff Cooper on October 2.

October 28.   Fresh outbreak of pogroms in Germany. All Polish Jews expelled from the Reich.

November 2.   Germany and Italy settle territorial differences between Czechoslovakia and Hungary—to the former's disadvantage—in the Vienna award.

November 7.   In a fit of maniac depression, H. Grynspan, 17-year-old son of a Polish Jew expelled from Germany, shoots von Rath, a member of the German Embassy staff in Paris.

November 10. German reprisals for the death of von Rath take the form of pogroms of unexampled ferocity.

November 13. Field-Marshal Goering decrees that the Jews must pay for the damage done during the persecution of them by the German mob, plus a fine of one milliard marks for the death of von Rath.

November 17. Sir Hugh Seely, Liberal, moves an Amendment to the Address, calling for a Ministry of Supply. Mr. Churchill makes the following speech in favor. But the Prime Minister is against the amendment and it is defeated.

THE CASE FOR A MINISTRY OF SUPPLY

I CONFESS that I find some difficulty in making another speech in favor of a Ministry of Supply. I have used all the arguments of urgency and I have endeavored to explain many of the processes of detail, three years ago, two years ago, and, finally, only six months ago. I have pleaded this cause in good time; I have pleaded it when it was already late; and perhaps my right hon. Friend may remember I have even adjured him not to be deterred from doing right because it was impressed on him by the devil. But neither reason nor persuasion nor coaxing has had the slightest effect against the massive obstinacy of the powers that be, the powers that have led us to where we are now. This Debate, however, differs from others we have had on the same subject. It is possible to vote tonight upon a perfectly clear issue. We are indebted to the Liberal Party for having brought the House of Commons squarely up to the fence. The House must jump that fence or swerve ignominiously away from it and, in the result, as I believe, lose a race the stakes of which not only comprise the safety of our country, but also affect great causes of world significance.

I am going to address myself particularly to hon. Friends of mine above the Gangway who sit behind the Ministers. I cannot believe that many of them do not share the anxieties which are pressing upon the thinking majority of their fellow countrymen. I appeal, therefore, to these gentlemen, but I do not appeal in suppliant terms; indeed, if at all, it is in minatory and comminatory terms. I say they have a grave responsibility for our present plight. The history of England is still to be written and unfolded. History will disentangle individual responsibility and will lay the blame on the shoulders where blame should be; but hon. Gentlemen above the Gangway—pledged, loyal, faithful supporters on all occasions of His Majesty's Government—must not imagine that they can throw their burden wholly on the Ministers of the Crown. Much power has rested with them. One healthy growl from those benches three years ago—and how different today would be the whole lay-out of our armaments production! Alas, that service was not forthcoming. We have drifted on in general good-natured acquiescence for three whole years—not for three whole years of ignorance or unawareness, but for three whole years with the facts glaring us full in the face.

We have drifted on and we have drifted down, and the question to-night is sharply, brutally even, whether we shall go on drifting or make a renewed effort to rise abreast of the level of events. I put it as bluntly as I possibly can. If only fifty Members of the Conservative Party went into the Lobby tonight to vote for this Amendment,[1] it would not affect the life of the Government, but it would make them act. It would make a forward movement of real energy. We should get our Ministry of Supply, no doubt, but, much more than that, we should get a feeling of renewed strength and a prestige outside this country which would be of real service and value. I think it right to put these points at the outset of my observations. They are not meant in any spirit but that of one who shares with hon. Gentlemen the perils of the country in which we are all involved. This is no party question. It has nothing to do with party. It is entirely an issue affecting the broad safety of the nation.

In examining the Amendment which the Liberal Party have placed upon the Paper and which has been laid before us in lucid speeches, there are three main issues which require examination. First, is the present system a sound workable system? Second, has it succeeded and is it succeeding? Third, whatever may be the difficulties in private Members' making constructive proposals, we must consider what improvements are possible. Let me take the first of these issues—is the present system succeeding? Undoubtedly much of the preliminary work has been done. Very large sums are being earned and will be earned by the contractors. [Interruption.] I regard the large sums which are earned by the contractors as a sign of progress. I am not dealing with the question of profit. Very large sums are being earned by the contractors, which will now emerge in the shape of weapons rather than of bricks and mortar, which

[1] When the division was taken the only Conservatives who followed Mr. Churchill into the Lobby were Mr. (now the Rt. Hon.) Brendan Bracken, M.P. for North Paddington, and Capt. H. Macmillan, M.P. for Stockton-on-Tees.

necessarily occupy a part of the first year of expanded munitions production. Large deliveries of all kinds of important war material are now approaching and have now begun. I do not challenge that. I rejoice in it. I certainly should not attempt to submit this case to the House by arguing on false premises.

My submission is that, broadly speaking, the original programs, when they were conceived, were less than one-third of what was then needed; that the original programs have been expanded by a series of afterthoughts which would not have occurred at the outset if a firm view had been taken of the need and scale of our rearmament; and that the deliveries of these programs, both original and supplementary, are in many cases at least twelve months lagging behind what might reasonably have been expected. Further, I submit that these evil tendencies, this lamentable lag, will continue, and that the friction, the hitches and the local and sporadic confusion will be aggravated as the scale of the business grows, unless new efforts are made to lift the whole process to a higher and more efficient basis of organization and production. That is broadly what I venture to submit to the House. The Prime Minister told us the other day, and my right hon. Friend the Minister for the Co-ordination of Defense dwelt on the point in his very patient and persuasive speech this evening, that we were engaged on a five-year plan of rearmament which had only now reached its third year. There is something in that, but it is by no means a complete and satisfactory answer. What relation has this British five-year plan to the facts of today? That is the question. Do the Government suppose that other nations are not expanding too? They say we are in the third year of our five-year plan, but the Germans are in the third year of their four-year plan.

What is the relevance of these plans to our actual needs? They are no guarantee of safety or adequacy. It is no use comparing what we have actually got at any given moment with what a plan says we ought to have. It is only useful to compare what we have got with what other people have got and with what we may need. So the only test which can be trusted is our ability from month to month to meet the dangers to which we are exposed. Everything is lagging many months behind. Consequently the entire situation for which the original plan was prepared, even assuming that it was properly measured against it, is now altogether changed. More than ever there is a need to establish without delay one supreme controlling authority over the whole field of supply and over the whole process of interweaving munitions supply with the vital trade of the nation.

I explained elaborately to the House in May the existing machinery as it was unfolded to us by the statement of the Minister, and particularly by that of Lord Zetland in another place. It is a plan, a method, a machinery of which we can only say that it is fearfully and wonderfully made.

Perhaps I may explain, in answer to a retort to me some time ago, the difference between these advisory deliberative committees and the council committees under the Ministry of Munitions which were found effective during the War—at the end of the War. The Munitions Council presided over seventy branches of munitions supplies, divided into ten or twelve groups, each of which was represented by a councilor. Consequently, it was possible to deal expeditiously with any problem of production and demand, merely by creating four or five of these chiefs of departments into a council committee. They were not advisory or deliberative personages; they were the men who actually had under them the organization and the control of those particular branches of supply, and consequently, joining together, they could in a week or even shorter produce a workable scheme for submission to the Council for the approval of the political authorities which had been at every stage prepared by the men who knew they would be answerable in their particular departments for carrying it into concrete and effective practice. It is simply darkening counsel to mix up deliberate and advisory committees, "passing the buck" from one to the other, with the grouping of executive functions in their proper sphere, with full plenary powers to carry out plans for making what is required.

I do not think there was ever any comprehensive plan on a scale appropriate to foreign programs. We have had many half-measures and many afterthoughts as different courses have emerged from successive shocks to our efforts. I have always had sympathy for my right hon. Friend, the Minister for the Co-ordination of Defense. On public grounds, at considerable personal sacrifice, he accepted nearly three years ago an office for which his high gifts and lifelong specialist training had in no way fitted him. And as the House seemed to realize at the time, although it could not shake off its inertia, the office itself was framed in a manner so curious that he really never had a chance of discharging it successfully. It was a compromise which bore in every paragraph the imprint of inter-departmental interests and rivalries.

I know how hard my right hon. Friend has tried within the limits to which he unwisely submitted himself, and I have no doubt that his tale of praiseworthy activities is a very long one and a very creditable one. He has told us tonight of some of the things he has been doing, and I have no doubt there is very much more to tell, and that he has played a very solid part in pushing this great process of production forward. But I continue to ask, Why was it that an office so irrationally conceived was devised by the Government, and why was it tolerated by the House? It could not have resulted in a smooth or abundant or rapid supply; it could not have resulted in clear definitions of our strategic needs. The mixture of these two opposite spheres and functions was sufficient to vitiate this administrative appointment from the very outset.

Such a system as I have described, with its strangely appointed, strangely shaped departmental functions, was on the face of it bound to give results which are less than satisfactory. Prima facie you would have expected a breakdown. What has been the result? I say that there has been a very great falling short of what we might have had even in the life of this Parliament, and in spite of all that has been achieved and all that is coming forward, I say that you cannot today claim that this system has succeeded. I will offer some proof of that statement. Some proof can be found in the decision referred to by my hon. and gallant Friend the Member for Wellingborough [Wing-Commander James] to substitute "adequacy" for "parity" in the air. Parity was the Government's own pledge. First-line strength was the Government's own measure. That was not invented by their critics; that was put forward by the Air Ministry, and adhered to rigorously and vehemently as long as it afforded a satisfactory line of defense. But both are now abandoned. Why are they abandoned? I say because of the lag and failure in supplies. That is the reason why this definition and this standard have both been abandoned.

Now we have "adequacy." What is adequacy? Adequacy is no standard at all. It is simply what His Majesty's Ministers at any given moment, surveying what they have got, choose to say is adequate. I shall be asked, "Have you no confidence in His Majesty's Government?" Sir, I say, "Yes and no." I have great confidence that these hon. and right hon. Friends of mine will administer faithfully and well the Constitution of this country, that they will guard its finances in a thrifty manner, that they will hunt out corruption wherever it may be found, that they will preserve the peace and order of our streets and the impartiality of our courts —and keep a general hold upon Conservative principles. [Laughter.] In all these matters I have a sincere and abiding confidence in them. But if you ask me whether I have confidence in their execution of defense programs, or even in their statements as to the degree to which those defense programs have at any moment advanced—there I must beg the House not to press me too far. [Renewed laughter.]

I am making some criticisms of a disparaging character upon some aspects of our defense, but I take this opportunity to say that in my opinion not only is the Royal Navy stronger relatively to the dangers it may have to meet than ever before, but that the Royal Air Force constitutes one of the finest and most magnificent bodies of men and scientific attainment that exist in the whole field of modern military progress. No criticism must give the idea that we have not got great and powerful air forces in this country, and nothing that I can say shall detract from that; but if an opportunity were given in secret Session I should, I think, be able to bring forward a very large number of matters of detail, and important detail, which would show that there are defects in the organization quite apart from the defects in material. But I do not intend to go into these matters about the Air Force in public, for reasons of which we have been reminded by the Minister for the Co-ordination of Defense and which readily occur to everyone here. I should very much like to see some of these matters discussed in a secret Session. I should ask to have discussions upon these matters not necessarily of an extremely secret character but without the opportunity of being overheard or having the reports read afterwards in various quarters.

I have spoken about the air, and I say that we have come to "adequacy" instead of "parity" because the system of production is ineffective. How stands the question of Anti-aircraft Defense? It is now two and a half years since I mentioned to the House that Germany had formed 30 regiments of mobile anti-aircraft artillery of 12 batteries each, aggregating 1,200 or 1,300 guns, and that they had several thousand other stationary guns for the same purpose, already manned, and I have no doubt today that there are modern anti-aircraft guns, that is, guns manufactured in the last four years in Germany, totaling not less than 7,000. What is our position? We are vulnerable, in some ways more vulnerable to air attack than any other country—once we can be reached. What is our position in anti-aircraft artillery? Here, again, I am not going unduly into detail, but the Secretary of State for War dilated, in his customary style, months ago upon the rapid production of the modern 3.7 gun, which, as everyone knows, is incomparably superior to the modernized

3-inch weapon of 20 years before. The right hon. Gentleman even went so far at one moment as to deprecate the danger of anything in the nature of a saturation of guns. But how many were available at the moment of trial? After all, it does not take three years to bring guns into being. With vigor guns can be created and deliveries begun in eighteen to twenty months. I say that the Germans, no doubt with careful previous preparations, have been making guns on an enormous scale, 6,000 or 7,000 guns every year, for four and a half years past.

How many were there available at the moment of trial here—how many which had all their appliances, without which they are useless? I am not going to answer those questions, but has the House of Commons no responsibility to satisfy itself, by methods which are open to it, and which have often been adopted in the past, upon the truth, upon the facts, in regard to this extremely important item in the defense not only of London but of our munition factories and ports throughout the country? Would any House of Commons except this one not have demanded a searching and secret inquiry into these matters? In the days of the eighteenth and nineteenth centuries Parliament would have chosen a certain number of Members whom it trusted for their discretion and would have asked them to look into the matter, and they would have reported—not the facts but whether a further effort had to be made or not. Why have we not done anything of that kind? I do not believe that any House but this would not have done it, and I do not think any Government except one which is so politically powerful as this, so beyond all political challenge, would not have conceded such a request.

Now the Secretary of State for War, I will not say incorrigible, but impenitent, tells us the new Bren gun is being produced at a maximum. What does that mean? What is the maximum? The wit of man, of a man in a fix, could not devise a more vague and misleading phrase. He also told us last week that our requirements in the matter of 3.7 guns could be met by June, perhaps even sooner. But what are the requirements? The Army List shows—and the Army List is published promptly —that our establishment of anti-aircraft units would require not more than six hundred guns all told, and of these a large part are the old 3-inch; so that one can see, within certain limits, what might be the requirements which are to be satisfactorily met by June.

Perhaps such a figure could well be realized by June, but what relation has it to our need? What relation has it to this figure which I have given of what is happening elsewhere? There is the 4.5-inch gun. We have read in the newspapers almost every day of how they are bringing out a tremendous new plan of defending the country, and how the new 4.5-inch gun is the finest thing in the world. It may well be so, but where is it? When are we to have a thousand of them? One thousand is the kind of figure in which you must think in these days. When I spoke to the Minister for the Co-ordination of Defense when we went on the deputation two and a half years ago we talked in thousands. These figures have to get into very large proportions if you are to get anything comparable in this country to what exists abroad. I am not attempting to quarrel with my right hon. Friend; on the contrary, all my remarks are couched in the most amicable sense, so far as he is concerned.

I say there is a lamentable delay attaching to this 4.5 gun. A committee of the House in a morning, with the attention which a committee can give to these matters, would discover the reason, if the House used its authority. Why does not the House use its authority? After all, if disaster comes it will not only be Ministers or Members of Parliament who will be smashed up, but it will be our long history that will come to an abrupt and melancholy end. In the anti-aircraft artillery not only was *matériel* short, but we are told of a whole host of failures to organize such *matériel* as was available at the time. The Secretary of State has confessed that there were guns lacking in predictors and dials, guns without munitions or with the wrong munitions, dumps of munitions for which there were no guns, and small items which could have been readily procured but which were lacking. Many others might be mentioned, but I am not wishing to add to this catalogue.

Take the astounding admission that modern guns available for the defense of London would have been doubled in number but for the bankruptcy of a small firm charged with an essential part. I beg the Prime Minister to face the force of that admission. He is a business man of high competence himself. Is it not shocking that such a thing should have happened? We do not want to blame the Secretary of State for War and I am not making a case against him, but if there had been a Ministry of Supply I cannot believe that the arrangements would have been so obtuse that there would not have been a follow-up department in the Ministry to see exactly what was the state of production in the different firms concerned in this very vital matter of the 3.7-inch gun.

Of course, you must have a follow-up department in any Ministry of Supply; that is to say, a little organism in the Department which, when a decision has been taken, goes two days afterwards and says: "Where is that paper? What have you done about it?" You say: "Well, I am held up by this," and they say: "We will go and find out what the matter is." In a week it reports every hitch and failure to take action, according to the label which is put on that paper as to relative priority and urgency. Such an institution, working in a Ministry of Supply, would have detected that that firm was going bankrupt, action would have been taken and you would have had double the number of guns. You ought to be thinking of these things, and they ought to be woven into your organization.

I am going to continue with the assembling of my facts to prove that the present state of affairs is not satisfactory and ought to be amended. I turn to the Army. I can speak with a little more freedom about the Army because, after all, we have the Navy, which is, I believe, in a very good condition, although no doubt capable of improvement. We have the Air Force, of which I have spoken. The Army is not a vital weapon. England will not be saved or cast away by the condition of our armies, although every effort must be made to improve them. I say that the equipment of the Regular Army is deplorable. I think it is almost unbelievable, after three years of rearming, that it should be in the present condition. I am not attacking the Secretary of State but I am stating the facts. Take the mechanized cavalry. Take the first mobile division—the only mobile division. The establishment of that division should be 700 light caterpillar vehicles and tanks. How many have we got? I should like the Secretary of State to be able to assure us that we have one-tenth or even one-twentieth in serviceable condition, with guns, gun mountings and all appurtenances. Mark you, all these regiments have been mechanized for over three years. They have been mechanized in a sense; that is to say, their horses were taken away from them. Yet their condition the other day in the crisis was such that it is no exaggeration to say that they were very largely unarmed. Take the battalions of the Guards, too. The establishment of a battalion is 52 light machine guns and 24 anti-tank rifles. How many have they got? I am not going to mention figures. I content myself by saying that they have only a small fraction of this equipment.

If these wretched conditions prevail in the leading and most famous units in the Regular Army, what do you suppose is the state of the line regiments? What do you suppose is the condition of the Territorial Force? Why, two and a half years ago, when the expansion plan was announced and the rearmament plan was begun, I said—and I was not contradicted—that the equipment of the Territorial Force with modern weapons was planned not to begin until 1940. Nothing was done to rectify that position. Recruiting for all branches of the Army has greatly improved. As the danger threatens this country, so the patriotic spirit of its young men revives. The weeks of crisis are the weeks of the best enlistment; but how scandalous, when men are coming forward, when this rich country is pouring out its money, and this vast and flexible British industry is waiting at the service of Ministers, that the Government, a National Government above all, is unable to provide them with modern weapons and fighting equipment. The whole business of supplying the British Army is a petty operation compared with the strength of the country and with its industry; yet, in the face of this lamentable failure, after three years, it is represented to us that there is no need for a change in system, that all is proceeding according to plan, and that the only possibilities are that a few readjustments may be made in the committee system on which we are proceeding.

I regard this question of the Ministry of Supply and the general issue now raised as a supreme test of the earnestness of His Majesty's Government to rearm on a scale equal to our danger. There are not wanting those of influence in this country who say, "We are already left behind and, as the task of repairing past neglect is greater than we can face, let us make the best terms we can for ourselves and accept for ourselves a position of inferiority and subordination." Those doctrines have only to be brought to the light of day to encounter the severest repudiation of the whole country. I plead this case for a Ministry of Supply in the interests, at this moment, of the Defense Ministers themselves. I address myself to them.

The Secretary of State for Air, the Secretary of State for War and the Minister for the Co-ordination of Defense have more interest in the creation of a Ministry of Supply than any other three men in this country. The Secretary of State for War is an energetic, active Minister who has made many improvements in the organization of the Army. He has improved its recruitment and given great benefits from the Treasury to the officers and men of the Regular Army. If he should be brought into discredit it will be because of the failure of supply and not because he has not been exerting himself in every direction. I do not wonder at all that he should have been tempted to break out at Cardiff the other day and to say that there can be no appreciable expansion of production under the present system. As for my right hon. Friend the Secretary of State for Air [Sir Kingsley Wood], he told us of this enormous new pro-gram he is planning; how can he possibly organize the Air Force and think out its strategic problems while, at the same time, he is responsible for running round to hundreds of firms and making sure that not one of the thousand items, each of which is indispensable, has been over-looked? I warned Lord Swinton again and again, not only publicly, and he has only now been converted. If he had had a proper Ministry of Supply in 1935 he would today be the respected head and chief of the Royal Air Force.

I say to my right hon. Friend, whom I have known for a long time, in terms of friendship, let him take warning by the fate of his predeces-sor. Let him allocate and apportion responsibilities which he cannot dis-charge himself, and which are quite unsuited to the functions and char-acter of any military department. In time of peace, when you have a very small production of munitions merely turning things over year by year for practice purposes, you can rely upon military departments in Supply, and Enfield and Woolwich will do their share for the Army; but you have reached a position in which Estimates for many hundreds of millions of pounds are being devoted and spent each year and where the whole industry of the country is being increasingly drawn in. To leave that job under the management of Service Ministers is unfair to the country, unfair to the job, and most unfair to the Ministers themselves.

Let me look at this matter from another angle, the public angle. At present the Defense Ministers are, perforce, apologists for their own failures in supply. My right hon. Friend the Air Minister has not been long enough in the office to grow a guilty conscience. They try their best, but, when failure comes, naturally they are concerned not to be in too great a hurry to have it thrust out to the public or to the House, and they are bound to minimize it as much as they can. By making the Min-isters for Air and War responsible for their own supply, and by making the harassed Minister for the Co-ordination of Defense responsible for helping them to get their supply, you get a tight combine, which cannot deliver the goods in time but which can offer any amount of concerted explanation of why they have not been delivered. If there were a Minis-try of Supply the Minister would be the poor devil who would be in the box, and the Service Departments would bring their reproaches against him. He, in his turn, would go to the Cabinet and would say: "Here, I did not get financial sanction for this. This was late. We had not had the funds for this. We had not the powers for that. There has been this difficulty with labor," or whatever might be the case. Tension, pressure and activity would be increased and stimulated by this very natural and reasonable division of functions. You would get a new energy from the very friction that would result—an energy which is vastly needed. Only the other day the Minister for the Co-ordination of Defense was arguing against a Ministry of Supply because, as he explained, there was so much importance in keeping strategic considerations and supply in harmony and in close relation. Would he not be in a far better position to procure this harmony if he presided not only over the three Defense Services but over the three Defense Services plus the shop from which they buy their goods? He would sit with his strategic functions on the top of a natural, symmetrical organization, instead of being at one moment a co-ordinator and at the next an executive producer. There would be complete harmony. Then indeed he would have a chance of success and we should have a better chance of safety.

This part of the Government's argument does not appear to be greatly hampered by undue respect for logic. The Minister for the Co-ordination of Defense declared that you cannot have a Ministry of Supply because it would divorce strategy from supply. Other Ministers say it would hamper individual production. In the same breath we are told that on the outbreak of war it would be immediately necessary and that a plan for it has been made out. In war why should you divorce strategy from supply? Supply will dictate the strategy of most of the wars that are to be fought in the future. We have been told on the highest authority that a Ministry of Supply involves dislocation of the normal business of the country, including especially the important export trade upon which we depend for our financial strength. I am sorry sometimes to hear Government speakers trying to ward off a Ministry of Supply—we know how evenly the question is balanced—by prejudicing the Labour Party and the trade unions against it. They have dilated upon the evils of compulsion. They have appealed to all those forms of particularism which, if not overridden and uplifted by a higher patriotic impulse, may well be injurious to national defense. Whoever said that a Ministry of Supply in time of peace would involve the conscription of labor? What advocate of that Ministry ever said, in the words of my right hon. Friend, that it involves a complete substitution of armaments for normal trade? The word "complete" slipped in. Who had ever suggested anything of that kind? To talk like that is putting up an Aunt Sally to knock it down again.

I will run the risk of setting forth precisely the scope of the measure which should now be introduced. That measure should have two parts. The second part would come into operation only if we were involved in a major war and the House of Commons so decided. It would, of course, take very wide and sweeping powers based upon universality of national service at a time when we should be fighting for our life. In this second part I hope and trust that there would be provision for what is called in the United States, where the study of this part of the problem has been carried very far, taking the profit out of war. We hear a lot about the conscription of wealth. I prefer the salutary principle of taking the profit out of war. If we should be involved, unhappily, in a war, let us make sure, by elaborate and carefully considered legislation beforehand, that no one is going to come out of it with private gain while others are dying for their country. All that belongs to the second part of the Bill. So far from keeping these things secret you ought to bring them out now. You want to get as much support as you can. Bring out your proposals for taking the profit out of war. The United States have published in great detail their war organization. Nothing but advantage will come.

The first part of the Bill, which we want now, would require provisions of a compulsory character to enable the Minister of Munitions Supply to control the whole of the materials of all kinds needed for national defense and to assign the priorities of their distribution not only between the different Departments of the Government but in respect of the entire trade of the country. Secondly, he should have the power to direct firms of all kinds that may be involved, to transform their production from commercial products to munitions or any such portion of their production as may be judged expedient. Thirdly, he should focus and concert, with the aid of a council of leading manufacturers, who will each preside over different spheres of the national industry, the whole process of munitions supply, and should be able to sit at the job from day to day without any other distraction.

In practice these legislative powers, which are compulsory powers, would not involve any violent overriding of customary right. The Prime Minister the other day dwelt on the invidious effect of such powers upon individual firms and said that one would be needed and another would not. But that is not the way it would work. Take, for instance, the cycle trade, which is a very complicated trade. A Minister of Supply ought to have power to say to the leaders of the cycle trade: "I require a half, or a third, or whatever it is, of your full capacity for the production of machine guns or light tanks, or whatever it may be that they are suited for. Go away and make a plan amongst yourselves. Consider carefully what is just and fair. Consider carefully the interests of the export trade, to which we attach the greatest importance, and come back in a fortnight and let us have your plan." That seems to me a perfectly reasonable way of dealing with it, and there are other great branches of industry which you could approach in a similar manner. I should like the Minister to have the legislative power to make that request; for though, no doubt, it would be proudly met by the trade, at the same time it is only right and reasonable that Parliamentary responsibility should lie behind him and that he should have the power if difficulty arose. If you are not able to get everyone in, if there are laggards who stay outside, there should be power to say: "If you are unable to make plans, I shall have to try my hand at it myself." Why is not that a perfectly reasonable and practical step? Once it was seen that the great capitalist undertakings were conforming to the national need in a generous spirit and on a great scale, I cannot believe that organized labor, as expressed through the great craft unions, would not be ready, if convinced of the justice of national policy, to make the fullest contribution in their power.

There is one further point that I must mention which arises out of the Prime Minister's speech the other day. I was very sorry to hear him make a reflection upon the preparations of 1914. I thought it was rather ungracious in him to do that. No doubt, there were mistakes, as there will always be mistakes, but nevertheless the Navy mobilized 537 ships out of 542; the ships on the sea were at their war stations before the declaration of war and we assumed command of the seas at that moment, and for 18 months 1 per cent insurance risk added to the ordinary risks of the sea was sufficient to equate all the risks of a war against the second naval Power of the world. Such a command of the sea has never been seen in the history of the country, certainly not after Trafalgar. As for the Army, within four weeks of the declaration of war six divisions fought and— it is no national vanity to claim—played a decisive part in the Battle of the Marne, and their mobilization and transportation proceeded with perfect smoothness and punctuality. It was a most remarkable feat and performance, the result of long and careful study of men like that great War Minister, Lord Haldane, and that great Staff Officer, Sir Henry Wilson. Before Christmas, 1914—let the Secretary of State turn his mind to this— there were 14 British divisions fighting in the line in France, and that with Army Estimates a half of what they are today. I hope my right hon.

Friend will not cast reflections upon the achievements of the past, even although we have all lived to see their fruits largely frittered away.

I have done, and I thank the House very much for listening to me, especially those hon. Members who do not like what I have to say. I would add this further word: This issue is not a mere administrative issue. The vote we have to give on it is in some ways a symbolic vote, going far beyond ordinary questions of administrative rearrangement. The question which we have to vote upon, in my opinion, is little less than this: Are we going to make a supreme additional effort to remain a great Power, or are we going to slide away into what seem to be easier, softer, less strenuous, less harassing courses, with all the tremendous renunciations which that decision implies? Is not this the moment when all should hear the deep, repeated strokes of the alarm bell, and when all should resolve that it shall be a call to action, and not the knell of our race and fame?

THE FRUITS OF MUNICH

Waltham Abbey

March 14, 1939

1938

November 17. Anglo-American Trade Agreement.

November 21. Czechoslovakia cedes to Germany a corridor across Czech territory, in which Germany is to build a highway connecting Vienna with Breslau.

November 23. Mr. Chamberlain and Lord Halifax visit Paris.

December 6. An agreement signed between France and Germany, forswearing the use of force in argument between the two countries—similar to that brought back by Mr. Chamberlain from Munich.

December 21. Sir John Anderson, Lord Privy Seal, introduces his scheme for air raid shelters.

January 11.   Mr. Chamberlain and Lord Halifax visit Rome, without tangible results.

January 21.   Herr Hitler dismisses Doctor Schacht and appoints Funk head of the Reichsbank.

January 22.   Germany decrees that all men over 17 not already enrolled in some similar body must receive military training in the S.A.

January 24.   Distribution to all householders of the Government's first handbook on A.R.P.; and announcement of Schedule of Reserved Occupations.

January 25.   General Franco takes Barcelona. The Catalan army collapses.

January 29.   Sir Thomas Inskip becomes Secretary of State for Dominion Affairs, and his former post of Minister for the Co-ordination of Defense is filled by Admiral of the Fleet, Lord Chatfield.

February 6.   The Prime Minister confirms M. Bonnet's statement in the French Chamber ten days before: that if either Great Britain or France were attacked the whole resources of the other would be completely at the disposal of the menaced country.

February 15.   The Chancellor of the Exchequer announces that the limit of borrowing for defense is to be raised from £400,000,000 to £800,000,000.

February 28.   Mr. Chamberlain announces that Great Britain will recognize General Franco as the government of Spain.

March 1.   The President of the Reichsbank guarantees German export trade. But the United States immediately raises her duty on German imports by 25 per cent.

March 10.   Mr. Chamberlain states that the outlook in international affairs is tranquil.

March 13.   Dr. Hacha, Dr. Benes' successor as President of Czechoslovakia, summoned to Berlin by Herr Hitler. Father Tiso declares Slovakia a separate state, which he places under German protection.

THE FRUITS OF MUNICH

COMPLAINT HAS been made in some of the outlying parts of the Constituency of my speech on the Munich Agreement. In this I pointed out that a disaster of the first magnitude had befallen France and England. Is that not so? Why do you suppose we are making all these preparations? Why do you suppose that the French military service has been lengthened, and we have promised to send nineteen divisions to the Continent? It is because in the destruction of Czechoslovakia the entire balance of Europe was changed.

The great and growing German Army is now free to turn in any direction: we do not know in what direction it will turn. The whole structure of international co-operation to protect the small country from lawless offense—all that has been broken down and cast away. I pointed out that Munich sealed the ruin of Czechoslovakia. You remember the tales we were told, how they would have a better life after they were freed from the burdens of the unwilling Sudeten Germans in their midst. Besides that, they were to have a German guarantee of their reduced frontier, and there was to be a British and French guarantee of their frontier. I held the view that these guarantees were hardly worth the paper they were written on, or the breath that uttered them. What is the position now? The Czechoslovakian Republic is being broken up before our eyes. Their gold is to be stolen by the Nazis. The Nazi system is to blot out every form of internal freedom. Their army is to be reduced to negligible proportions, or incorporated in the Nazi power. They are about to lose all symbols of an independent democratic state. Does anybody deny it?

I said that once the Czechs had given up their fortified line, a pretext could be found to take everything from them. We have seen exactly the same methods used as were used in September. Disturbances have been fomented in Slovakia which, I have no doubt, are at the instigation of the German Nazi Party. And then the German Press has set to work to vilify the Czechs, and to accuse them of violent aggression against the Germans. The next thing is to order them to reduce their army, and take into their Government whatever Ministers the Germans choose. They are being completely absorbed; and not until the Nazi shadow has been finally lifted from Europe—as lifted I am sure it will eventually be—not until then will Czechoslovakia and ancient Bohemia march once again into freedom. Why should I not have said all these things? It was the truth. It was my duty to say them. Can anybody dispute them?

I saw in one of our papers today that we were not involved in this new Czechoslovakian crisis. It seems to me quite certain that we are not going to intervene. It is too late to intervene. The Czechs have surrendered their fortress line. Its cannon are now moving to the Western Front. They are defenseless. Their railways are interrupted. They are gripped about on every side. Instead of being able to resist thirty German divisions for a considerable time, they now have no power of resistance left at all. They have to obey all orders, however cruel, that they are given. It is no use going to their aid when they are defenseless, if we would not go to their aid when they were strong. Therefore I agree entirely with those who think we should not intervene at the present time. We cannot. That is the end of it.

But to suppose that we are not involved in what is happening is a profound illusion. Although we can do nothing to stop it, we shall be sufferers on a very great scale. We shall have to make all kinds of sacrifices for our own defense that would have been unnecessary if a firm resolve had been taken at an earlier stage. We shall have to make sacrifices not only of money, but of personal service in order to make up for what we have lost. This is even more true of the French than of ourselves.

Many people at the time of the September crisis thought they were only giving away the interests of Czechoslovakia, but with every month that passes you will see that they were also giving away the interests of Britain, and the interests of peace and justice. Now I have defended this speech which has been attacked, and I say never did I make a truer statement to Parliament. Practically everything that I said has already proved true. And who are these people who go about saying that even if it were true, why state the facts? I reply, why mislead the nation? What is the use of Parliament if it is not the place where true statements can be brought before the people? What is the use of sending Members to the House of Commons who say just the popular things of the moment, and merely endeavor to give satisfaction to the Government Whips by cheering loudly every Ministerial platitude, and by walking through the Lobbies oblivious of the criticisms they hear? People talk about our Parliamentary institutions and Parliamentary democracy; but if these are to survive, it will not be because the Constituencies return tame, docile, subservient Members, and try to stamp out every form of independent judgment.

THE STRENGTH OF THE NAVY

The House of Commons: on the Navy Estimates

March 16, 1939

1939

March 15. Herr Hitler officially extends his protection to the Czech peoples and the Czechoslovakian Republic is extinguished. German troops march into Prague.

March 16. Herr Hitler, from the Hradschin, Prague, issues proclamations annexing Bohemia and Moravia.

Mr. Geoffrey Shakespeare, Parliamentary Secretary to the Admiralty, introduces the Navy Estimates.

THE STRENGTH OF THE NAVY

IT WAS a great opportunity for the Financial Secretary, both last year and this year, to have to make the general statement on behalf of the Admiralty and to present the Estimates to the House. I believe that everyone feels that he has seized this opportunity with a long arm and a firm hand, and has put it to the best possible use. I should like to associate myself with the tribute which he paid to Admiral Sir Reginald Henderson. Those of us who know that officer—and I knew him when he was gunnery lieutenant doing the gunnery trials of the ships we were building before the Great War—will realize the rare and remarkable qualities which he brought to the service of the Royal Navy. He has expended his energy, his life, his thought, his mental energy, an attribute which is rare nowadays, in the most generous manner; and if he has been stricken down by an affliction, which we all hope is only temporary, he is in exactly the same position as a brave officer who is wounded fighting for his country in action. It is well known that at the most critical period of the War this officer, then in a subordinate station, taking his career in his hands, presented facts and figures and arguments which eventually reached the highest authority—the Prime Minister—and that through that report a great change was made in our naval disposition, without which it could not be said with certainty that the submarine menace at that time would have been overcome.[1] I naturally can touch upon only very few points in the extremely important and weightily considered statement to which we have listened. The first is a very small point, but as I am dealing with the Financial Secretary to the Admiralty I would say that it has particular relevance to his office. The expense of the Navy is rising this

---

[1] By the Convoy System.

year by £23,000,000 and yet the Estimate is presented in a form which states, in a most decisive manner, a net decrease of £26,000,000. This is due, as footnotes explain, to the fact that £84,000,000 is provided by Loan or Appropriations-in-Aid in 1939 instead of £34,000,000 from that source in 1938. It would hardly be possible to make a financial statement in a more misleading, and, I must say, more silly fashion. After all, the fact that this House is providing £153,000,000 for service of the Navy in this critical year is a factor which may play an important part in maintaining stability. Why, then, state it in the worst way? I happen to know that many people, some of whom ought to know better, have been misled by the form in which these figures are presented, and by the statement that there is a net decrease of £26,000,000 in the expense of the Navy.

The same pedantic character presents itself in the case of the number of men. Here again we have the number of men—net decrease, 13,500, in Vote A. But is this really so? Is there to be a net decrease in the Navy of 13,500 this year? I should have thought that actually the Navy was increasing every year by, I suppose, 6,000 or 7,000 officers and men. That, I believe, is the fact; but, owing to some intricate convention about the form in which the bearing of personnel on Vote A during the financial year is calculated, we tell the whole world on the face of our estimate that we are reducing our man-power by 13,500. I noticed that this was made the subject of sneering abroad in countries which are inclined to say that we are unable to provide the man-power even for the highly technical services. I hope that I am right in thinking that this is only a case of clerical pedantry, of which I have no doubt the War Office are equally guilty. The same confused form of presenting the Estimates occurs also in the Army Estimates; but I still ask why, in the name of common sense, an Estimate cannot be presented to the House which states intelligibly and obviously on the face of it what are the true and salient facts of the finances of the year.

I was glad to hear the statement that even the heavy programs of new construction for which I was responsible before the War were now exceeded—220,000 tons as against 170,000 tons. I am not jealous. I am very glad that another generation is raising that effort which we made, and which proved adequate. May I point out that the increase of personnel is also most important? In 1914 Vote A reached the record total of 148,000, that is to say, it equaled the highest figure obtained by the British Navy in the height of the Napoleonic Wars. We have now 133,000 according to this Estimate as the maximum power for 1939, so there is still leeway in which to continue the increase of personnel. It must be remembered that we have not now the resources of the Mercantile Marine open to us in the same way as in 1914. The Royal Naval Reserve, owing to the shrinkage of our merchant officers and seamen, will be almost entirely needed, if not wholly, for the Merchant Service. That is a fact which makes it necessary to increase the personnel, and particularly increase the officer personnel.

I associate myself entirely with what was said by the right hon. Gentleman the Member for Hillsborough [2] that promotion from the lower deck should be opened out in the widest manner possible, and that in the manner most likely to give a real chance to those who come into the Navy by that method to rise to the highest positions of command in the naval profession. I am absolutely certain that there must be in these ships, with their enormous classes of highly trained and intricate, technical personnel, men who will make officers in large numbers to command His Majesty's ships in the future. It was in my day that we opened the gate that had been closed for many years, and it has not been kept as wide open as it ought to have been until recently. I hope that the need for expanding our personnel will make it felt that, although there are, and must be, rigid gulfs of discipline between different ranks, all may move forward and have a chance of obtaining the highest and most responsible commands.

There are several points in these Estimates which I am extremely glad to see. In the first place, we have the reinstitution of the Immediate Reserve. That is no doubt only a minor improvement. What is the Immediate Reserve? It is three or four thousand men who have served in the Fleet for 12 years, and who are coming to the Reserve to take on at a small retaining fee an extra obligation to come up in advance of a Royal Proclamation calling up the Reserves, and merely on a summons from the Admiralty. I instituted this before the War, and its convenience was proved in the early stage of the emergency. When I urged its reinstitution in 1937 I was assured that it was not necessary and would be much too expensive. Considering that it was a matter of an extra retaining fee of £5 or £6 a year to only 3,000 or 4,000 men, this seemed at the time a very absurd answer. But, of course, it was quite easy for the Admiralty and the Government, once they made up their minds, to brazen it out. All that I could say, after having made four or five attempts to persuade

[2] Mr. A. V. Alexander, now First Lord of the Admiralty.

them, was "Never force little dogs to eat mutton." Now they are eating their mutton.

The Government have been confronted with the difficulty of bringing forward the extra personnel required for minesweeping and other special services in the preliminary stages of mobilization. They would not believe the experience of the past. They brushed aside its lessons, as they have brushed aside so many lessons of the past, but now that the modern Admiralty have had a taste of it themselves there is no more argument, and this small but necessary device, which we were assured on the highest expert authority, both professional and political, was quite unnecessary, has been adopted, and I should like to congratulate the Admiralty and the Government on their decision, to which, happily, instant effect can be given.

Last year, when we looked at the program of new construction, many people were astonished to find that no destroyers were included. I said that perhaps it was due to a misprint, for nothing could be more necessary and obvious than the construction of destroyers, particularly since under the Anglo-German Naval Treaty the creation of the German U-boat fleet was authorized. We have now received the announcement that 100 per cent parity in submarine tonnage is to be constructed by Germany, and I think a very shrewd guess can be made that very much of this tonnage is already made in sections and all that is now necessary is to put these sections together. There was no part of the Parliamentary Secretary's speech more justified than the examination of the dangers which threaten the naval power of Britain at the present time. I entirely agree with him that we have the measure of the submarines. It is not merely a question of the marvelous inventions which have been perfected, but of familiarizing large portions of the Fleet to the use of these devices so that they have become a matter of ordinary routine.

I gladly add my testimony to his that it would appear that the perils which will be run by submarines in a future war are incomparably greater than the perils to which, let us not forget, the submarine succumbed in 1918. But there is this to be said in connection with destroyers. We only have this measure of the submarine, this superiority, if there is an abundance, a superabundance, of destroyers and other small craft available. Last year, for the first time, no destroyer flotilla was provided in the program, and, of course, high and technical reasons were given to show how inopportune such a provision would have been. However, this year there is not only one flotilla but two flotillas, and in addition

20 900-ton escort vessels. As to the design of these I am not particularly informed, but it would appear that these vessels are a most valuable feature. It seems a great pity that the usual flotilla was dropped last year because we should have had all the hulls built by now. I think the House is glad that the omission is being rectified, and I am glad to congratulate the Admiralty on the step that has been taken.

But there is one point upon which I cannot approve of the proposals now made. It is, I think, a serious matter which affects to a certain extent the whole of our defensive system and weakens our means of survival in the case of a major war. I am horrified to learn that the Admiralty propose to scrap the five 15-inch battleships of the Royal Sovereign class, one in 1942, one in 1943 and the rest, I suppose, in the following year. The House would hardly gather from the euphemistic phrase the Parliamentary Secretary employed—"replacement"—that these two ships are to be destroyed. That does not tell us what one would expect, that until the new ships are in commission the old ones will be kept in reserve. In other days I used to say that when the ace is out the king is the best card. These old ships can play their part, although we must be careful not to bring them into contact with new ships in the event of war.

I will outline my argument against this course in this way: Old as they are, the Royal Sovereigns have a vital and final service to render us. Under the Treaty of London, and various other agreements, we have been prevented from building any 8-inch gun cruisers for five or six years, and Germany will have at an early date in the future five 8-inch gun cruisers which will be definitely superior in speed, armor and gun power combined to any vessel in our Fleet except our battleships and our battleship-cruisers. That is a very serious matter. These German vessels in the event of war would be super-Emdens, let out upon our trade routes, and they would inflict very heavy losses. But whereas in the case of the *Emden* and her consorts, the *Karlsruhe* and *Königsberg,* we had 100 cruisers with which to envelop, pursue and destroy them, we have now a far smaller number, and it makes the problem much more serious. That is only half the story. The *Emden* was a small ship of 3,000 tons with 4-inch guns, which had only to be caught to be killed. You are going to have in the near future five super-Emdens to 10,000 tons with 8-inch guns, against which you have not only lost half the number of cruisers to bring them to book but nothing except battle-cruisers which can at once engage them and kill them in single-ship action. All this arises out of treaty entanglements which in every single respect have hampered our naval construction, made it more difficult for us to get true value for the taxpayers' money and produce the best classes of fighting vessels with the money provided.

What is the conclusion I draw from all this? It is that we shall certainly be forced in any war that may occur in the next few years to reinstitute the convoy system, not so much against the submarine as against enemy cruisers on the broad waters of the ocean. It might be a year of war before these raiding cruisers were extirpated, and meanwhile forty-five million people in this island will have to be fed and we will have to carry on our trade without which we cannot purchase the supplies we require not only for war but for keeping body and soul together. You will have to institute the convoy system on the broad waters of the ocean.

On this footing I come to the case of the five Royal Sovereigns. These are the very ships which would be the surest escorts of your ocean convoys. No raiding cruiser would dare to come within range of their 15-inch guns. Their speed is much greater than that of any convoy of merchant ships. They are the ideal vessels to bring in a three-monthly convoy of sixty, seventy or eighty vessels from Australia or the Cape, or from South America, quite safely across the oceans until they come within the regions where other escorts would be needed to deal with the submarine. The range of their enormous heavy guns would afford complete protection from a raiding cruiser, even to a very large convoy. This, at any rate in the early stages of a war, would be an enormous convenience to us. Yet these are the very ships, whose function it would cost us so many millions to provide in other ways, which are to be taken out and scrapped and destroyed although they may play a vital part in the feeding of this island.

We have heard some reasons why such a monstrous decision has been made. Under the Anglo-German Agreement no provision was made, as some of us suggested, that old ships should be counted at a lower tonnage than new ships in estimating the tonnage of German naval construction. If we keep the Royal Sovereigns, Germany would be entitled under the Treaty to build two additional battleships in the four-year period in question, and they have asked us to state in advance, as they have a right to ask, what we propose to do. We have promised to scrap or sink the first two Royal Sovereigns, and I presume that there is no hope now of rescuing the others from that imprudent decision. I put it to the House that it would be far better to let them build their two additional battleships, if they want to do so. There are two arguments for this. The first is that it will take them four years from 1942 to build the first extra battleship, and for good or ill this hideous armaments race will stand in an entirely different position in 1946. But at the mere threat of an additional German battleship arriving on the seas seven years hence we are in 1942 to destroy these important Royal Sovereigns which may be of vital service to us in the intervening years. We are to go without a real and necessary prop during a most critical period to ward off a hypothetical danger. For it may not be to Germany's interest to build the two battleships which cannot mature until the critical period is over.

And can we be sure that after we have scrapped our Royal Sovereigns Germany will not say that the situation is changed and build her battleships none the less? Such things have happened. At any rate, we should be very chary of getting rid of something of value to us on the mere possibility that thereby we may deter Germany from building something which in my view is not of very great value to her. Why should we be disturbed if Germany chooses to build an additional battleship? I would rather see her build an additional battleship than that she should build these extra squadrons of commerce raiders. I say that quite frankly.

It must be remembered that Germany, like all countries, is now at full extension in armament production, groaning and straining in that tremendous effort. Already she is spending 26 per cent of her national income on warlike preparations. All labor, skilled and unskilled, is employed to the utmost. The park railings and even iron crosses in the graveyards are being melted down for scrap. What is given to one service in these circumstances must be taken from another. This applies not only to money but especially to skilled labor and to high-quality war materials which have to be purchased across the exchange. I say frankly I would much rather see Germany build two additional battleships than that the £20,000,000 which I suppose they would cost by then should be thrown into a further expansion of the German air program. Whatever happens, whatever they do, we can keep an overwhelming lead in the line of battle. How very different is the picture in the air. There we are struggling to catch up. Why should we seek to deter Germany from consuming her substance and natural energy in a sphere where we have a sure means of keeping our supremacy, and perhaps transfer her activity into a sphere in which already, through past neglects, we are condemned to a far weaker position? Why, for the purposes of this in itself detrimental process, should we lead out to the slaughter-yards these great vessels which have a most important and probably even a vital function to discharge?

I hope this matter may be reconsidered, as the question of the Immediate Reserve was reconsidered; as the omission of a flotilla last year was reconsidered; and as the scrapping of five small cruisers in 1936, about which so much argument had to be used, was reconsidered. They were absolutely useless before it was decided not to scrap them, and now they are most valuable and important units of the Fleet. All three mistakes were made, and defended with a wealth of argument and professional authority; and they have all been repaired after a loss of valuable time. Do not let us make a fourth mistake on a far more important scale, and deprive ourselves during some most dangerous years of our history of resources which we already have in being, and of which we have need. I hope this argument may be considered. I am grieved very much to hear that commitments have already been made, but let us at any rate save the rest from that fate. It gives me a certain feeling of anxiety, when I think of the enormous demands made on the taxpayers, that vessels of this kind are simply put out of existence without any attempt to discuss the matter openly—wiped out—and then at the same time we have to come forward, as we willingly do, and provide great funds for the creation of vast new construction.

The German Navy in the next few years will not be able to form a line of battle for a general engagement. One would expect that cruisers and submarines would be sent out to attack commerce, but I think you may take it as absolutely certain that the prime object of the German Navy will be to preserve command of the Baltic, which is of supreme consequence to Germany, not only because of the supplies she can obtain from the Scandinavian countries, and the influence she can exert over them, but because the loss of naval command in the Baltic would lay the whole of the Baltic shores of Germany open to attack or possible invasions from other Baltic Powers, of which the largest and most important is, of course, the Soviet Union. Thus, you may be sure that no use will be made of the German Fleet which will compromise their loss of command of the Baltic. It was for this reason that they have been and are still quite content with a ratio of 35 per cent to the British Fleet, because that fully occupies their building resources, or all the resources they think fit to assign at present to their naval development, and because it enables them to achieve the practical and necessary object which they have in view, namely, the maintenance of command of the Baltic.

On the other hand, for Britain in time of war, the command of the Mediterranean must be the prime objective. There should be no difficulty in securing this, even if we were engaged singlehanded with any one of the Mediterranean Powers, and had at the same time to watch the debouches from the Baltic and the Elbe. Although great new British fleets which are now under construction are not yet ready, there is still an ample superiority of sea-power available to secure and hold command of the Mediterranean. The developments which have taken place, and which were described to us by the Parliamentary Secretary to the Admiralty this afternoon, in anti-submarine measures and in the anti-aircraft gunnery of our Fleet, and the structural alterations to our ships against overhead attack, are such that we may reasonably expect that our great preponderance of surface craft will make itself fully effective in future, as it has done in the past. I think it is a safe rule to treat the sailors of every country as equally brave and skillful, and I should, therefore, feel confidence in the very large British naval superiority of numbers which would exist in a war against a Mediterranean Power. This superiority would become even more ample if the British and French Fleets were acting in combination. Presumably they would be combined, as we shall never make war except as a result of unprovoked aggression upon us or upon our ally. Therefore, it seems that an overwhelming superiority will be available.

Now, there is a school of thought which favors what is called "sealing up both ends of the Mediterranean," and leaving it as a closed sea. This policy will, I hope, be rejected by the Admiralty—I hope particularly by the present First Lord of the Admiralty, who, in a matter like this, may hear the promptings of ancestral voices.[3] To gain and hold command of the Mediterranean in case of war is a high duty of the Fleet. Once that is achieved, all European land forces on the shores of North Africa will be decisively affected. Those that have command of the Mediterranean behind them can be reinforced to any extent and supplied to any extent. Those that have no such command will be like cut flowers in a vase. A hostile Power which had commitments overseas in the Mediterranean could not afford to keep its fleet in harbor; it would have to come out to make sure that communications with its forces were not intercepted or their operations interfered with by bombardment from the sea and, con-

[3] Lord Stanhope's ancestor, the first Earl (1673-1721), had commanded the army in Spain, and under the orders of the Duke of Marlborough captured Minorca in 1708.

sequently, there would be no means by which such a fleet could avoid the necessity of fighting a naval engagement, and possibly at very heavy odds.

No doubt for the first few months or weeks, while actual fighting for the command of the Mediterranean was proceeding, it would be prudent to deflect our Eastern merchant traffic round the Cape. But that in no way affects the general argument for immediate decisive operations to obtain full and unquestioned command of the inland sea. Therefore, I was very glad to hear Lord Chatfield yesterday lay down the sound doctrine that it is the duty of the Royal Navy to "seek out and destroy the enemy's fleet." That is the true note to strike. But it is not possible to be simultaneously strong everywhere. Sacrifices must be made and punishment must be taken in some theaters in order that speedy victory may be gained in the decisive theater. After the victory has been won there are ample resources which will be available to restore the position in more distant theaters. If there is anything left over which is not restored, that could be settled at the peace conference. It should not be long before we were in a position to restore the position in the more distant theaters. Therefore, I submit that the first main effort should be to secure and keep command of the Mediterranean. Lord Chatfield's statement was no doubt of general application; he did not suggest it was given a particular application; but none the less, it was most timely, because such a doctrine, vigorously applied, will influence the foreign policy of every Mediterranean Power, both in deterring possible antagonists from attacking us or our allies, and in encouraging other States bordering on the Mediterranean, who are animated by the most friendly feelings towards us, to pursue their part in confidence.

It is refreshing in times like these for us to take an afternoon off from black care and dwell upon the great and growing strength of our Navy and to feel confidence that the new inventions in the air and under the water, properly countered as they have been and are being, do not in any decisive degree deprive us of the measureless resources of sea power with all that has so often followed in their train.

THE INVASION OF ALBANIA

The House of Commons

April 13, 1939

1939

March 17.   Mr. Chamberlain, at Birmingham, denounces Germany in terms of unexpected strength.

March 20.   Alarmed by the fate of Czechoslovakia, Rumania hastens to sign a trade agreement with Germany.

March 21.   The Lithuanian Foreign Minister, invited to Berlin, surrenders Memel to Germany.

March 21–23.   Visit of M. Lebrun, President of the French Republic, to London.

March 29.   In Spain Col. Casado surrenders the remains of the Republican Government territory to General Franco.

March 31.   Great Britain guarantees Poland against aggression.

April 6.   Colonel Beck, Polish Foreign Minister, visits London.

April 7 (Good Friday). Italy invades Albania.

April 12.   The Constituent Assembly at Tirana offers the crown of Albania to King Victor Emmanuel, who graciously accepts it.

THE INVASION OF ALBANIA

I FIND myself in general agreement with the Prime Minister's statement on Government policy this afternoon, so far as it goes. I do not press my right hon. Friend to denounce the Anglo-Italian Agreement, which he made when he parted with my right hon. Friend the Member for Warwick and Leamington[1] and assumed himself the main direction of our foreign affairs. It would no doubt be very painful to the Prime Minister formally to repudiate an instrument on which he staked so much. The Agreement, of course, has been violated in every material respect by Italy, but I do not feel that anything would be gained by a denouncement with bell, book and candle at this juncture. It certainly represents a sincere, if hitherto unrequited, attempt on the part of Great Britain to dwell on terms of friendship with Italy and with the Italian people in the Mediterranean Sea. I think the Government are quite right to let this Agreement stand *De bene esse*, as the lawyers say. This is a term of art which they apply to things that do not matter very much. In spite of the bad faith with which we have been treated by the Italian Government, I am still not convinced that Italy has made up her mind, particularly the Italian nation, to be involved in a mortal struggle with Great Britain and France in the Mediterranean.

We must remember that if we had an unpleasant experience at the hands of the Italian Government, Germany had a much more grievous experience of Italian policy at the outbreak of the Great War. That wears an agreeable aspect in British recollection, but a somewhat different impression of what occurred is sustained in Germany. It may be assumed that Germany would like to make sure of Italy by getting her into a war with the Western Powers before any main strokes were delivered in the

[1] Mr. Anthony Eden.

113

central or north European theater. I am afraid we have reached a point when we are bound to look at matters in this somewhat realistic way. If it is in the Nazi interest that this should happen, it seems to me not in our interest to facilitate their task. As long as the Government have no illusions about the Agreement with the Italian Government, I shall not press them to take the step of denouncing it merely to relieve their natural feelings of indignation at the manner in which they have been treated. We can readily imagine that it must have been a great disappointment and surprise to the Prime Minister to be treated in this way by a dictator in whom he placed particular trust, and in whom he advised us to place particular trust. Everyone knows that his motives have been absolutely straightforward and sincere. We all sympathize with him, and we all sympathize with ourselves, too.

I am also in agreement with the practical steps which the Prime Minister has announced on behalf of His Majesty's Government to give a guarantee to Greece and to make even more effective arrangements with Turkey. The validity of this guarantee rests, of course, mainly upon British sea power and upon the fact that the British and French Fleets combined have a superiority in the Mediterranean which might well be considered decisive, in the absence of unknown factors which at present we cannot accurately measure.

Here I really must ask the Government to maintain a continuous state of vigilance in the Mediterranean, a state of vigilance appropriate to the tension which exists and to the strain which undoubtedly is being put upon our naval power. I cannot feel that the dispositions of the British Fleet in the recent crisis conformed to the ordinary dictates of prudence. Last Tuesday week before we separated, Lord Stanhope, the First Lord of the Admiralty, made a speech which caused alarm. It was not a very happily phrased speech perhaps, but it at any rate indicated that the most extreme conditions of vigilance were being maintained in the Home Fleet. The crews of anti-aircraft guns were not allowed even to leave their posts in order to attend an entertainment in their own ship.

What was the condition of the Mediterranean Fleet at that time? There is no secret about it. The facts have been in all the newspapers. They are known at home and abroad. The position of every ship which puts into any foreign port is known and telegraphed. I am not giving away anything that is not absolutely known, and I think it should be understood here as well as it is understood elsewhere. Moreover, the Fleet has now been concentrated, and therefore it is quite safe; but it is extremely necessary, to avoid future difficulties, to discuss what actually happened when the Albanian stroke was delivered. According to published statements in the newspapers of all countries, the Fleet was scattered from one end of the Mediterranean to the other. Of the five great capital ships one was at Gibraltar, another in the eastern Mediterranean, and the remaining three were lolling about outside various widely separated Italian ports, two of them not attended by their protective flotillas. The destroyer flotillas themselves were dispersed along the European and African shores, and a number of cruisers were crowded in Malta harbor, without the protection which is given by the powerful anti-aircraft batteries of the battleships. I do not understand at all how this situation, which has now been rectified, was allowed to arise.

After all, we are in very serious times; not a moment for merely passing the time of day. I was astounded to see what had happened, and I did not believe it until I saw it proclaimed in the newspapers. How can you reconcile the extreme extra precautions, the vigilance, taken at Portsmouth, with the simultaneous carrying out of the long published routine program of the Admiralty for the Easter period? It was published, I believe, in February, exactly where they were all to go, and it was carried out as if nothing was to happen, and at the same moment the Home Fleet is told, "No, you cannot have leave." At the very time that the Fleet was suffered to disperse in this manner it was known that the Italian Fleet was concentrated in the Straits of Otranto and that troops were being assembled and embarked on transports, which presumably were intended for some serious enterprise. It is incredible to me that, when all this intelligence had come to hand and when the First Lord of the Admiralty considered that a state of tension existed requiring the utmost precautions at home, the Mediterranean Fleet was not concentrated, and at sea. These matters touch the very life of the State, and I trust that improvidences of this character will not be repeated in the anxious months which lie before us.

I want to draw the attention of the House to the "timing" of the Italian stroke. The British habit of the week-end and the great regard which the British pay to holidays which coincide with festivals of the Church, is studied abroad. You can see it on many occasions, and that moment is the dangerous moment. I do not suggest that for this particular stroke in Albania Good Friday was selected out of any desire to insult that day, but undoubtedly it was also the first day after Parliament had dispersed and consequently no immediate question could be raised. It was also known that on that day the British Fleet, according to the program which it was carrying out in a perfectly calm and peaceful manner, would be dispersed in all quarters; and from every point of view they were able to say, "The coast is clear." I can well believe that if our Fleet had been watching these events before they happened—after all it is before events happen that you want to be ready, not afterwards—I can well believe that if our Fleet had been concentrated and cruising in the southern part of the Ionian Sea, the Albanian adventure would never have been undertaken. Instead of their gathering the transports and men and our Ambassador in Rome going to see Count Ciano and saying, "What is the meaning of all this?" we should have had the Italian Chargé d'Affaires visiting the Foreign Secretary here, and saying, "We are very much surprised to see the apparition of a great united concentration of the British Fleet in the Mediterranean waters, not far from the mouth of the Adriatic Sea." Then it might be that explanations would have been interchanged, and that some steps could have been taken with perfect safety which would have given us at any rate a chance to recover something like the initiative in foreign policy.

Here let me say a word about the British Intelligence Service. After 25 years' experience in peace and war I believe it to be the finest service of its kind in the world. I believe the right hon. Member for Carnarvon Boroughs [Mr. Lloyd George], who had supreme responsibility in those years, will corroborate me. I have always believed, and foreign countries have always believed, that it was the finest in the world. Yet we have seen both in the case of the subjugation of Bohemia and in the case of the invasion of Albania that Ministers of the Crown had apparently no inkling or at any rate no conviction of what was coming. I cannot believe that this is the fault of the British Secret Service. Several days before the stroke at Bohemia was made, Nazi intentions were known in many countries throughout Europe. The whole time-table was laid down, the whole program was known beforehand. Similarly in the case of Albania, the Italian concentration and preparations were reported repeatedly in the Press. We sneer at the Press, but they give an extremely true picture of a great deal that is going on, a very much fuller and more detailed picture than we are able to receive from Ministers of the Crown. At any rate, it was quite well known that gathering of troops and ships was taking place in the eastern ports of Italy. There was much talk that Albania was the quarry, although I quite agree that you could not tell in what form the assertion of Italian authority over Albania would be exerted, or to what extent the late King of Albania and the Albanian people would make themselves accommodating parties to what took place.

How was it that on the eve of the Bohemian outrage Ministers were indulging in what was called "sunshine talk," and predicting the dawn of a golden age? How was it that last week's holiday routine was observed at a time when, quite clearly, something of a very exceptional character, the consequences of which could not be measured, was imminent? I do not know. I know very well the patriotism and sincere desire to act in a manner of perfect rectitude which animates Ministers of the Crown, but I wonder whether there is not some hand which intervenes and filters down or withholds intelligence from Ministers. Certainly it was so in the case of the German air preparations four years ago. The facts were not allowed to reach high Ministers of the Crown until they had been so modified that they did not present an alarming impression. It seems to me that Ministers run the most tremendous risk if they allow the information collected by the Intelligence Department, and sent to them I am sure in good time, to be sifted and colored and reduced in consequence and importance, and if they ever get themselves into a mood of attaching importance only to those pieces of information which accord with their earnest and honorable desire that the peace of the world shall remain unbroken.

The great majority of the House, I believe, supports the Government in the policy which they are now adopting in building up a strong alliance of nations to resist further aggression. I welcome very much the language used on this matter by the Prime Minister this afternoon. He has an absolute right to the aid of all in the country in carrying out that course. I pointed out, the last time we discussed these matters, how great were the dangers of being caught whilst this process was incomplete. The essence of such a policy is speed and vigor. If it is not carried through with the utmost speed and vigor it would be better not to have started upon it at all. You can purchase short periods of perilous isolation. We have taken the opposite course; and this is no time for half measures. There is absolutely no halfway house.

If peace is to be preserved there seem to be two main steps which I trust are already being taken or will be taken with more decision immediately. The first, of course, is the full inclusion of Soviet Russia in our defensive peace bloc. When the right hon. Member for Caithness [Sir A. Sinclair] dwelt on the point of Russia and emphasized it, I heard a sort of commotion behind me. I heard the Noble Lady the Member for the

Sutton Division of Plymouth [Viscountess Astor] express her dislike of
any contact with Bolshevik Russia. Where was this dislike when she paid
a visit to Soviet Russia with Mr. Bernard Shaw? The Noble Lady was
treated with great consideration. But the point which the House should
notice—it is a very serious point, and I hope I shall be able to put it
without any offense—is that the time when she went to Russia and gave
all her applause and credit to Russia, was a time when the influence of
Russia was deeply detrimental to the interests of this country. I feel all
that has been said about Russia, and all that has been argued so powerfully by the Leader of the Liberal Party, but at the same time it must not
be supposed that it rests entirely with us. There are great dangers in
asking favors at a time like this. I do not at all think that we should be
well advised to ask favors from anyone. The other day I tried to show
the House the deep interest that Russia had against the further eastward
extension of the Nazi power. It is upon that deep, natural, legitimate
interest that we must rely, and I am sure we shall hear from the Government that the steps they are taking are those which will enable us to
receive the fullest possible co-operation from Russia, and that no prejudices on the part of England or France will be allowed to interfere with
the closest co-operation between the two countries, thus securing to our
harassed and anxious combinations the unmeasured, if somewhat uncertain, but enormous aid of the Russian power.

The second main step which, it seems to me, we should take, and
which I cannot but feel that the Government are taking, is the promotion
of unity in the Balkans. The four Balkan States and Turkey are an
immense combination. If they stand together, they are safe. They have
only to stand together to be safe. They will save their populations from
the horrors of another war and, by their massive stabilizing force, they
may well play a decisive part in averting a general catastrophe. If they
allow themselves to be divided, if they depart at all from the simple
principle of "the Balkans for the Balkan peoples," they will renew the
horrible experiences which tore and devastated every single one of them
in the Great War, and the Balkan Wars which preceded the Great War.
I am quite sure that His Majesty's Government are doing their utmost
to further the self-protective union of these States. The arrangements
that have been made with Greece and Turkey are, of course, only the
first step. The Prime Minister announced a new step today—the guarantee
that has been offered to Rumania. But these steps, although highly important and beneficial and sound and wise in all the circumstances into which

we have come, will not by themselves save the Balkans from another drenching dose of misery and ruin.

The arrangements which we are told have been made between Rumania and Turkey are also highly beneficial, and they are a step towards safety for both countries, but I submit that an arrangement between Rumania and Bulgaria is vital if the safety of the Balkans is to be secured. I well remember, more than a quarter of a century ago, being at the Admiralty and reading all the telegrams about the first Balkan War in 1912—the valiant effort of Bulgaria, the terrible losses that they suffered, the great courage of their troops, and then how by exorbitant demands, beyond what was reasonable, they drew upon themselves the malice of their two allies and suffered the most terrible tragedy of defeat and partition at the close of that war. You may say there were faults on both sides, but the curse of what was done then carried its consequences to every State throughout the Balkans during the Great War. It seems to me, since Rumania is receiving the support of the Western Powers and other Balkan States, there is very strong ground upon which she may be pressed to do her utmost to reach an amicable settlement with Bulgaria. That alone will knit up the entire structure of that part of the world and keep it free from the storm of war and, by keeping it free, perhaps influence the course of much larger matters outside.

Here let me say, with regard to the action of our country over the centuries, that in all the great struggles in which we have been engaged we have survived and emerged victorious not only because of the prowess of great commanders or because of famous battles gained by land and sea, but also because the true interests of Britain have coincided with those of so many other States and nations, and that we have been able to march in a great company along the high road of progress and freedom for all. This is certainly a condition which is established in the policy that we are now pursuing in the Balkan Peninsula. We and the French can say that we have no particular interests, no special claims which we wish to press. We receive no advantages which conflict with the general interest. This should strengthen the Government in their course, and such a policy which they have put forward, and which they are advancing, brings back across the Atlantic Ocean a reverberating echo increasingly encouraging in its tone. One sees a great design which, even now at the eleventh hour, if it could be perfected, would spare the world the worst of agonies. But all things are moving at the same moment. Year by year, month by month, they have all been moving forward together.

When we have reached certain positions in thought, others have reached certain positions in fact.

The danger is now very near. A great part of Europe is to a very large extent mobilized. Millions of men are being prepared for war. Everywhere the frontier defenses are manned. Everywhere it is felt that some new stroke is impending. If it should fall, can there be any doubt that we shall be involved? We are no longer where we were two or three months ago. We have committed ourselves in every direction, rightly in my opinion, having regard to all that has happened. It is not necessary to enumerate the countries to which, directly or indirectly, we have given or are giving guarantees. What we should not have dreamed of doing a year ago, when all was so much more hopeful, what we should not have dreamed of doing even a month ago, we are doing now. Surely, then, when we aspire to lead all Europe back from the verge of the abyss onto the uplands of law and peace, we must ourselves set the highest example. We must keep nothing back. How can we bear to continue to lead our comfortable, easy life here at home, unwilling even to pronounce the word "compulsion," unwilling even to take the necessary measure by which the armies that we have promised can alone be recruited and equipped? How can we continue—let me say it with particular frankness and sincerity—with less than the full force of the nation incorporated in the governing instrument? These very methods, which the Government owe it to the nation and to themselves to take, are not only indispensable to the duties that we have accepted but, by their very adoption, they may rescue our people and the people of many lands from the dark, bitter waters which are rising fast on every side.

THE KING'S DOMINIONS

A Speech made at the Canada Club in honor of the Rt. Hon. R. B. Bennett

April 20, 1939

1939

April 13.   Great Britain guarantees Greece and Rumania.

April 14.   President Roosevelt appeals to Herr Hitler and Signor Mussolini to pledge themselves to abstain from aggression for ten years.

April 20.   Mr. Chamberlain announces that he will form a Ministry of Supply and nominates Mr. Leslie Burgin Minister without Portfolio to consider the matter meanwhile.

THE KING'S DOMINIONS

THIS DINNER to Mr. Bennett is held at a timely moment. We all hope for a peaceful outcome, but everyone can see for himself that danger is afoot. It may not be long before the British Empire will have once again to marshal and reveal its latent strength. At such a time, Canada becomes a notable factor in world affairs. It is not only all over the Empire, but in all countries, that men are watching the attitude and action of the Canadian people and of their Government. Canada is a country of Party Government, such as we had in the days when Britain was rising to be a leading power. I must say I think we are very fortunate to have on both sides of Canadian politics capable and resolute statesmen who have a profound, inherent attachment to the great causes of individual freedom and public law, which are now so directly challenged. We must be thankful that time has been given to enable the causes which are at stake to become manifest to "all the men in all the lands" who wish to dwell together in friendship and freedom.

The policy pursued by "His Majesty's Government in Great Britain and Northern Ireland"—to use the jargon which the Statute of Westminster has decreed—may have been open to criticism for want of thoroughness and vigor. But no one can say that it has not been animated by patience and good faith, by a persistent desire to avoid war, and by an increasing willingness to run risks with other nations to prevent war. I have sometimes differed from the Prime Minister; but anyhow the fact remains that if, on some fateful day, Mr. Chamberlain is compelled by outrage and aggression to give the dread signal, there is no Party in Great Britain, there is no part of the British Empire, there is no free country, which would not feel able to share in the struggle—the hard struggle—without the slightest self-reproach of blood-guiltiness.

Some foreigners mock at the British Empire because there are no parchment bonds or hard steel shackles which compel its united action. But there are other forces, far more subtle and far more compulsive, to which the whole fabric spontaneously responds. These deep tides are flowing now. They sweep away in their flow differences of class and Party. They override the vast ocean spaces which separate the Dominions of the King. The electric telegraph is an old story; the wireless broadcast is a new one; but we rely on a process far more widespread and equally instantaneous. There are certain things which could happen, which it would not be necessary for us to argue about. No Constitutional issues would arise. Everyone, in the loneliest ranch, or in the most self-centered legislature, would see duty staring him in the face, and all hearts would have the same conviction. And not only the same conviction, but the same resolve to action.

It is because Mr. Bennett in his life-message to Canada and to the Empire has in a remarkable degree expressed and embodied these underlying truths, that we find this a particularly good occasion to do him honor.

One would underrate altogether the sentiment and repressed passion which unites the British Empire or Commonwealth, as many like to call it, by supposing that outworn Jingoism or grasping Imperialism play any important part. If we in this small island have gradually grown to a considerable estate, and have been able to give our wage-earners some relief from the harder forms of economic pressure, and to build up a decent, tolerant, compassionate, flexible, and infinitely varied society, it is because in all the great crises of our history the interest of Britain has marched with the progress and freedom of mankind. If in these hours of anxiety, but by no means of fear, we feel the surge of unity and of duty thrilling the pulses of the British race, it is because we are bound together by principles, themes and conceptions which make their appeal not only to the British Empire, but to the conscience and to the genius of humanity.

It is refreshing to find that in the great American Republic these same resolves to resist at all costs the new machine-made forms of tyranny and oppression, are also instinctive and strong. Canada has a great part to play in the relations of Great Britain and the United States. She spans the Atlantic Ocean with her loyalties; she clasps the American hand with her faith and good will. That long frontier from the Atlantic to the Pacific Oceans, guarded only by neighborly respect and honorable obligations, is an example to every country and a pattern for the future of the world.

Mr. Bennett, your guest this evening, in his memorable career has always known how to gather those forces which at the same moment consolidate the British Empire, and also make harmonious its growing comradeship with the Government and people of the United States. We owe him a lasting debt for his services. He has been true to the Old Flag. He has been true besides to all for which the Old Flag stands. We grieve that his health has exacted from him a period of repose. We rejoice to see him in our midst so strong and lively. This is not a time when we can spare a man like him. All will be needed, all must expend themselves. We know that there is nothing he has not done and nothing that he will not do to sustain and uplift the British Empire in days when everything that we have ever fought for will be at stake.

We must not turn from the path of duty. If the British Empire is fated to pass from life into history, we must hope it will not be by the slow processes of dispersion and decay, but in some supreme exertion for freedom, for right and for truth. Why is it that from so many lands men look towards us today? It is certainly not because we have gained advantages in a race of armaments, or have scored a point by some deeply planned diplomatic intrigue, or because we exhibit the blatancy and terrorism of ruthless power. It is because we stand on the side of the general need. In the British Empire we not only look out across the seas towards each other, but backwards to our own history, to Magna Charta, to Habeas Corpus, to the Petition of Right, to Trial by Jury, to the English Common Law and to Parliamentary Democracy. These are the milestones and monuments that mark the path along which the British race has marched to leadership and freedom. And over all this, uniting each Dominion with the other and uniting us all with our majestic past, is the golden circle of the Crown. What is within the circle? Not only the glory of an ancient unconquered people, but the hope, the sure hope, of a broadening life for hundreds of millions of men.

HITLER SPEAKS

An Address Broadcast to the People of the United States of America
April 28, 1939

1939

April 24. Sir Nevile Henderson returns to Berlin.

April 26. The Prime Minister announces the Government's intention to introduce Conscription.

April 28. Herr Hitler, addressing the Reichstag in Berlin, refuses to take President Roosevelt's message of peace seriously. He denounces the Anglo-German Naval treaty and the Non-Aggression Pact with Poland.

HITLER SPEAKS

THE CHARACTER and quality of Herr Hitler's speech shows a certain improvement on any he has made before. This improvement is no doubt largely due to the action of the President of the United States in sending his memorable message of peace and warning to the world a fortnight ago. President Roosevelt is the object of a good many jibes and taunts from the German Führer. The President's high purpose and great station will enable him to rise superior to these. The American democracy is likewise subjected to ridicule. They will get over that.

Part of the service rendered to the cause of peace by the intervention of the President is apparent. It may well be also that designs we do not know of were prevented, or at least suspended, by a message which has earned the gratitude of almost the whole world. The more prudent attitude adopted by Japan in refusing to join in an anti-democracy movement, which fact cannot have been absent from Herr Hitler's mind, is of course directly attributable to the movement of the United States Fleet to the Pacific Ocean. Any improvement in Herr Hitler's declaration is also due to the revival in Europe of a system of mutual aid against aggression, and to the active formation of a peace *bloc* of nations, great and small, which are all arming and ready to defend one another. Finally, it is due to the consolidation of France and to the rearmament of Britain.

Naturally we all welcome an improvement, even if only in the words spoken by the head of so great a State. But after all we have gone through in the last year it must be plainly said that words and declarations cannot by themselves restore trust and confidence unless and until they are made good by deeds and by conduct extending over a considerable time. While eight million Czechs are held in bondage, while the violation of the Munich Agreement remains unrepaired, not to mention other painful difficulties, a formidable barrier exists between Nazi Germany and the peaceful, law-respecting, liberty-loving civilization of the world.

The denunciation of the Anglo-German Naval Agreement need excite no regrets or alarm. The British Navy cannot be overtaken by any efforts which Nazi Germany may make. It would no doubt be better that those efforts should be diverted to building a German Fleet than that they should be concentrated upon the growth of air power, which is a menace to all, or upon land armaments by which smaller neighbors can be overrun.

Stripped of its verbiage and trimmings, Herr Hitler's speech reveals a wish to isolate Poland and to present an issue to Poland in the most plausible form, backed by a somber gesture. The denunciation of the Non-Aggression Pact with Poland, which was not to end until 1944, must be regarded as the most serious feature of the speech and as a new cause for anxiety. The Hitler method has always been to take one step at a time and, while reassuring others, to get one country shut up with him alone. For all these reasons it is of the highest consequence that there should be no slackening of the vigilance and preparation of the peace-seeking Powers of Europe and no diminution of the influence which the United States is exercising for the common good.

It is upon the continuance of these vast processes that any real escape from our dangers must depend. There are many passages in Herr Hitler's speech which would seem designed to induce Great Britain to abandon her precautions and to withdraw from the part she has pledged herself to play in Eastern Europe. Such blandishments have on several occasions been the prelude to acts of Nazi violence. They will not have any effect upon the now thoroughly awakened British public opinion. Above all, they will not in the slightest degree retard the growth of our defense forces.

It is quite natural that Herr Hitler should not like the way in which the Great War ended. He would rather it had ended in a German victory, and in the kind of peace treaties which Germany would have made, like the Treaty of Brest Litovsk, or the treaty with Rumania, or like the terms which were to be enforced upon Belgium even up to the middle of 1918. Whatever may be said against the Treaty of Versailles, it was an instrument mild in comparison with these German conceptions. In the German view, which Hitler shares, a peaceful Germany and Austria were fallen upon in 1914 by a gang of wicked designing nations, headed by Belgium and Serbia, and would have defended herself successfully if only she had not been stabbed in the back by the Jews. Against such opinions it is vain to argue.

But when Herr Hitler complains of the reparations exacted from Germany, we are surely entitled to point out that far more than was ever extracted in reparations was lent to Germany, part by Britain, but mostly by the United States of America, the bulk of which is not likely to be repaid. The reparation clauses of the Treaty of Versailles were never enforced, and so far from bleeding Germany white, the victorious Allies and Associated Powers poured enormous wealth into Germany after the War, and thus enabled her to modernize her industries and revive her economic well-being. Unhappily Germany has sought to use these benefits to forge a hideous apparatus of slaughter to hold the world to ransom or subject it to servitude.

The system of compulsory service now introduced into Britain in peacetime, or what is called peacetime, implies the sacrifice of the most deeply rooted habits of an island people. It is an act of faith and a symbol of Britain's resolve not to fail in her part of the conflict which is now opening for individual liberty and public law. The great causes which are afoot must march forward until they are vindicated and securely enthroned. But all the more is it necessary to proclaim that we in Britain and in France—and, I am sure, in the United States—ask no security for ourselves that we are not willing to share with a free, peaceful and happy Germany. If there be encirclement of Germany, it is not military or economic encirclement. It is a psychological encirclement. The masses of the peoples in all the countries around Germany are forcing their governments to be on their guard against tyranny and invasion, and to join for that purpose with other like-minded States. Nothing can now stop this process except a change of heart in the German leaders, or a change of those leaders. But there is no country in the Grand Alliance that is being formed in Europe, with the full sympathy and approval of the United States, that would tolerate for one moment the idea of attacking Germany, or of trying to impede her peaceful development and legitimate growth. On the contrary, the return of Germany to the circle and family of Europe, and to the wide, lofty uplands of a progressive, tolerant, prosperous civilization, remains the sovereign hope of the British, French and American democracies. And this is what is going to happen in the end.

THE NEW ARMY

The Corn Exchange, Cambridge

May 19, 1939

1939

May 6. The King and Queen leave for their tour of Canada.

May 10. The Prime Minister makes his first statement in the House of Commons on the secretive, and so far unsuccessful, negotiations with Russia.

May 12. The Anglo-Turkish Pact is announced.

May 18. The Military Training Bill, introduced early in the month, passes its third reading in the House of Commons.

THE NEW ARMY

I HAVE come here tonight because the University has desired an opportunity of testifying its resolve and conviction in a time of serious public need. The voice of the undergraduates of Cambridge has a right to be heard, and will certainly be marked, because so many of them are claimed by the new Conscription Act, now and in the next two years, and many more will take great pains to range themselves at their side. It is an honor to come forward at the call of King and Country, and to render the highest form of personal service to the State. It is also our duty to make sure the cause is good; and it is to this point that I shall first of all address my argument.

After many hesitations and long delays, some of which may cost us dear, Great Britain has resolved to take a leading part in forming and sustaining a league of armed and arming peoples to resist—if necessary by force—further acts of aggression by the Nazi and Fascist Powers. These totalitarian systems of government came into being from different causes. In Italy there was fear of Communism. In Germany there was the bitterness of defeat. Two remarkable men rose on these strong tides to dictatorial authority. Both, in the early stages, rendered great service to their countries. But both were carried away by the habit of despotism and lust of conquest, and both at the present time seem ready to array themselves against the progress and freedom of the modern age. They cannot pursue their course of aggression without bringing about a general war of measureless devastation. To submit to their encroachments would be to condemn a large portion of mankind to their rule; to resist them, either in peace or in war, will be dangerous, painful and hard. There is no use at this stage in concealing these blunt facts from anyone. No one should go forward in this business without realizing plainly both what the cost may be, and what are the issues at stake.

Let us therefore make it clear at the very outset that a number of nations are now being formed into a Grand Alliance which will in no circumstances attack the Dictator Powers. Nor will we hamper or obstruct their natural and lawful desires; nor will we invade their internal jurisdiction; nor will we seek to deprive them of their legitimate share in the expanding future of the world. Nor will we shed blood except in self-defense or common defense. We base our position absolutely on the Covenant of the League of Nations. This Covenant not only obliges loyal members of the League to proceed to one another's aid, according to their ability, but it also obliges them to provide sincere and effective means for the redress of injustice and well-founded grievances. If we use force to control force, we must also offer justice to relieve injustice. This is inherent in the Covenant of the League, and I would not myself invite, still less compel, any man or any woman—for all must do their part—to come forward on any basis which does not in the letter and in the spirit conform to the solemn and perpetual agreement signed by almost all the countries of the world. There is no element of imperial ambition in our policy; no taunts, no wordy provocation, no affront to mere pride, no diplomatic entanglements will tempt us to aggressive action. We stand together against violence and tyranny, and we seek nothing but to make a strong effort with the people of other countries to defend the reign of law and freedom for all.

The cause is good. What about the Government? Is it good, or is it bad, or is it just indifferent? As you know, I have not hesitated to speak and vote against the Government—although it is formed around the Party to which I belong—whenever I have thought it my duty to do so. In particular, I have urged for more than a year the formation of this Grand Alliance or "peace bloc of nations" which would have prevented the ruin of Czechoslovakia, and which may yet preserve Poland and the smaller States of Eastern Europe from a similar fate. I was a strong opponent of Munich, and I said so at the time, when the question did not seem so simple as it does now. Therefore, speaking at a meeting at which all Parties are represented, I have a right to ask for consideration from any Liberals and Socialists who may be here.

I submit to you that these matters of national defense and foreign policy ought to be considered upon a plane above Party, and apart from natural antagonisms which separate a Government and an Opposition.

They affect the life of the nation. They influence the fortunes of the world. I say to any Liberals and Socialists who are here tonight that it would not be right for them to allow any prejudices they may have against the present Government, or against its head, to prevent their giving a clear, plain vote upon an issue of national safety and of national duty. It is not within the power of any one of us to control or manage events. They may be well managed, or ill managed. It is our duty, so far as lies in each one of us, to do our best for the main purpose and the common cause. I hope therefore that I have now cleared the ground sufficiently to enable me to deal directly with this actual Conscription Bill.

I myself have not until quite lately pressed actual Conscription upon His Majesty's Government. Everyone knows that, owing to their neglect to prepare factories in good time for the output of equipment and munitions, and to their refusal until a few weeks ago to set up a Ministry of Supply, that there will be a shortage of these essentials for a good many months to come. I should therefore have been content with a Compulsory National Register, which ought to have been instituted at latest after the disaster of Munich, and with a declaration that National Service would be compulsory and general at the outbreak of a war.

But what has happened since? The whole scene has changed. The Government which allowed Czechoslovakia to be broken and disarmed was suddenly surprised and horrified that Herr Hitler should march into Prague and actually subjugate the Czech people. This damnable outrage opened the eyes of the blind, made the deaf hear, and even in some cases the dumb spoke. The Prime Minister felt himself to have been deceived and defrauded by Herr Hitler, just as he had been by Signor Mussolini, in whom he had put his trust. He and the Government which he leads and controls turned round over the week-end. They adopted—I trust whole-heartedly—the very policy which their opponents had long advocated. Although much has been lost, for which we shall have to pay dearly, nevertheless I still believe that this new policy contains within it the best hopes of peace; and if peace should unhappily be broken, the best hopes of victory and survival for the free nations of the world.

I was very much struck by some words uttered by General Weygand when, a few weeks ago, he attended the celebration of the twenty-first anniversary of the assumption by Marshal Foch of Supreme Command of the Allied Armies in April, 1918. Then, at a moment of great disaster, when it seemed that the French and British Armies might well be severed from each other by the German advance, the illustrious Marshal took command of the stricken field, and after a critical and even agonizing month, restored the fortunes of the war. General Weygand, who was head of his military family—as the French put it—said: "If Marshal Foch were here now, he would not waste time deploring what has been lost. He would say: 'Do not yield another yard.'"

The Government in their new policy have now made commitments of all kinds. They have made commitments which a year ago would certainly have saved the situation, and which still, if carried through with fidelity and resolution, may ward off the worst of the dangers. They have given a guarantee to Poland; they have given a guarantee to Rumania; they have given a guarantee to Greece; and they have made an alliance with Turkey—all with the object of building up a front in Eastern Europe against further acts of Nazi aggression. In addition to these new commitments, into which we have entered on the other side of Europe and to which our national honor is pledged, we consider ourselves bound by our direct interests to fight if Switzerland, Holland or Denmark is attacked. Above all, we have our obligation to France.

Some people talk sometimes as if it is very fine and generous of us to go to the help of France. But I can assure you that in the pass to which things have come, we stand at least as much in need of the aid of France as the French do of the aid of Britain. My feeling has been for several years past that the first hope of freedom and safety lies in a close association of the British and French democracies. These two ancient States, which stand at the head of European civilization, were for centuries rivals and foes. They are now united in the presence of a common danger. The French have the finest, though not the largest, army in existence at the present time. Great Britain has a Navy which as long as we preserve the sympathy and the good will of the United States of America is overwhelmingly strong upon the seas. I have always thought that the union of these two great forces, not for purposes of aggression or narrow selfish interest, but in an honorable cause, constitutes what I may call the sheet-anchor of human freedom and progress. I, therefore, have felt thankful when very slowly, tardily, inch by inch, month by month, these two neighboring countries have at last fused together in an open and unbreakable alliance, based upon the closest military, naval and air co-operation. And here is where I come to the main and urgent cause for the Conscription Bill.

The two Western Parliamentary States have made it clear that they do not take sides or seek to enlist others in the present quarrel of rival ideologies. There is the Nazi-Fascist ideology, and the Communist ideology. Britain and France are equally opposed to both. The Parliamentary States think that small peoples, acting within their rights, should not be trampled down by stronger ones. They think that civilization implies, in any society, the freedom to criticize the government of the day; free speech; free press; free thought; free religious observance; no racial persecution; fair treatment of minorities; and courts of law and justice which have an authority independent of the executive and untainted by Party bias. These are ideals which center around the League of Nations. These are the hopes of the world. These are the means by which an abundant prosperity would come to this generation. Are they to be dubbed a mere "ideology"? On the contrary, they represent that sober, decent, righteous middle path, which not only the majority of nations, but the vast majority in every nation, would desire to follow. They are well worth defending over all Europe as long as it is possible to defend them.

Nazi propaganda in France continues unceasing. "England," they say, "will fight to the last French soldier." Yet if Gibraltar were attacked, France would declare war on Germany, and of her Army—which comprises five million trained men—two millions would stand under fire generously because a British fortress had been attacked. True, we similarly should declare war if French territory were attacked. But one must think of the feelings of the average French soldier, marching with millions of his comrades on what might be a quarrel deliberately picked with us. The French do not easily understand that an island people who have not seen the watch fires of a hostile camp on their own soil for a thousand years have deep prejudices against militarism, and are historically attached to the voluntary system. They only know that they would have to stand for many terrible months against the German Army, and that we were not willing to put our prejudices aside, or depart from our normal system. They would not think it fair, and it would not be fair.

If such insidious propaganda drove a wedge between the two countries, our ruin would be both speedy and final. The principle of Collective Security implies an equally loyal self-sacrifice offered by all members in proportion to their strength and means. The contributions of different countries may vary in size, but they must be the same in form and equal in quality and comradeship. These considerations apply to every one of the countries now linked with us. Moreover, the success of our plan for preventing war depends not only upon rallying many nations, great and small, to resist aggression, but on obtaining from each the fullest possible service. Without that there is no safety. This is the real crux.

We have every reason to be contented with the reception which the Conscription Bill has received abroad. It could never have been intended to overawe Germany or Italy. In those countries they count their soldiers by the million; and Signor Mussolini says that he has eight million. Therefore the addition of two hundred thousand young men to our armed forces is no menace to the Dictator Powers. It is the effect upon our Allies and those countries to whom we have given guarantees that is important. This very limited measure makes it plain that should we unhappily be involved in another great war, the British contribution will not be only naval and in the air, but military. It will not only be a matter of money and munitions, but of the man-power of the British Empire, which, as it is gradually mobilized and trained, will make its weight tell with increasing force until the end is reached. All that one hears from France shows how important have been the advantages gained in French public and army opinion by this step. The hostile propaganda has received a convincing answer. Countries like Poland and Rumania, and in fact every country on the borders of Nazidom, have been cheered and fortified by the steps which His Majesty's Government have thought it right to take.

But the results at home are no less satisfactory. The Opposition Parties have felt it their duty to oppose the institution of compulsory military service in time of peace, and they had an absolute right to do this. When someone said to me the other day how shocking it was that the Labour Party, the Liberals and the trade unions were not all united upon the Bill, I could not help remarking that perhaps they were still impressed with the arguments which we ourselves were all being told and taught to use, up till a month ago.[1] We do not want to have any quarrel with the Opposition over this. It is quite natural that they should make their protest, and in view of all that has been said in the past, I do not see how they could have done less than they have done. But there is nothing undemocratic about this measure; it is the most democratic thing we have ever done in the Island. Provided that no exceptions are allowed, it will wear away differences between class and class, and it may also be the beginning of a far more broadly and evenly based society than we have ever known.

[1] Mr. Chamberlain had only a few weeks before condemned Conscription as "undemocratic."

The war that broke out in 1914 was a war in which the political leaders had to convince the people that the cause was good. They were able to do so, and the fact that the cause was recognized to be good bore down all other difficulties and carried us through to victory. But now the main impulse to resist Nazi dictatorship and aggression comes in every country with which we are associated from the mass of the people. Almost everywhere we see hesitating, cautious Governments, and resolute peoples. Here at home, the spirit of the people is far ahead of the Government, and perhaps even of Parliament also. There is still time for countries which are ruled by Dictators to place themselves in harmony with the vast majority of the human race and to join its irresistible forward movement.

We must not at this juncture do anything which encourages these Dictators to suppose that we are not ready with other like-minded countries to go to all lengths in doing our share of the common duty. I have heard that a very high functionary in Berlin said to Herr Hitler: "You will know that Britain is in earnest on the day when the British working-classes accept Conscription, and the Conservative Party agree to an alliance with Russia." If we wish for peace or, failing peace, victory, surely we ought to have both. This is a time when prejudices must be abandoned on either side, and a true comradeship established between all Parties and classes throughout our loyal, anxious land.

This Bill and its general acceptance is a great act of faith on the part of British democracy. At the beginning of the war of 1914 we soon had a million volunteers on our hands, for the bulk of whom no weapons were available. Ultimately over two million men demanded to be led to the Front. But after that the limits of voluntary recruitment were exhausted. The war continued and the armies could not be maintained. Then we had the hateful spectacle of volunteers who had been wounded twice or even thrice being sent back to the trenches, and of regular soldiers who had served two whole years in the Front Line being deprived of their right to claim expiry of their contract. This proved intolerable to the national sense of justice. Moreover, the two million households and families whose menfolk had borne the whole burden were infuriated by the fact that there were very large numbers of perfectly fit men remaining at home, filling at higher wages the jobs of those who had volunteered. It was this sense of wrong and injustice, which spread through the country in the spring and summer of 1916, that alone carried the Conscription Bill.

How different now! Today, before a shot has been fired, in cold blood we are taking this momentous step, and taking it with a very large measure of national acceptance. Nothing could more vividly mark the manner in which the wage-earning classes—without whom no armies can be formed—have realized the deadly nature of the assault which is being directed at their fundamental rights and liberties. What nearly two years of bloody war only attained with difficulty in 1916, is now practically conceded by the will of the Nation in a time of nominal peace. This is the point which should impress foreign countries, because it is the most explicit guarantee of the resolve of the British people to bear its part in what is now plainly a world cause.

THREE MONTHS OF TENSION

The City Carlton Club, London

June 28, 1939

1939

May 26. Following Lord Halifax's conversation with M. Maisky at Geneva on the 23rd, a fresh British note is dispatched to Moscow. On the 31st, however, Russia expresses herself still unconvinced of the British Government's good faith.

June 5. The Bank of England hands over to the Bank of International Settlements between five and six million pounds' worth of Czech assets, for the use and benefit of Germany.

June 7. The British Government decides to send Mr. William Strang, of the Foreign Office, to Moscow.

June 22. The King and Queen land in England from their tour of Canada and the United States.

THREE MONTHS OF TENSION

I TAKE a serious view of the position in which we find ourselves. It is similar to what happened last year, but with the important difference that this year no means of retreat are open to us. We had no treaty obligations to Czechoslovakia. We had never guaranteed their security. But now we have given an absolute guarantee to Poland that, if she is the object of unprovoked aggression, we in company with our French allies will be forced to declare war upon Germany. There is the brute fact which stares us in the face.

What, then, is happening in Germany? All preparations are apparently being made by the Nazis to force Poland to yield to the German demand, and if she does not yield, to attack her with very large forces, both from the west and from the south. Last year, when the subjugation of Czechoslovakia was being planned by Herr Hitler and his associates, we heard a lot of talk about German maneuvers, and great masses of German troops were gathered round that unhappy country. There were many signs of what was going on which were perfectly intelligible to well-informed people who wanted to know the truth. All these signs are present today, only on a larger scale than last year, and again we are told that it is only the autumn maneuvers, only sham fights, exercises for the German Army, the training of the troops. I was not deceived last year, and I warn you not to be deceived this year. The forces of aggression are actually gathering—have, indeed, already been to a large extent gathered. Many people say that nothing will happen till the harvest has been garnered, and perhaps they are right, but personally I always distrust dates which are mentioned beforehand, because they may so easily be antedated, and, after all, the harvest itself is not far off. I think we must consider July, August and September as months in which the tension of Europe

will become most severe. I feel convinced that we are entering a period
of danger, more acute and more laden with ugly facts than any which we
have ever known in the hard and disturbed period through which we
have lived.

To say this does not mean that I consider war certain. If one considers
only the German preparations, the immense massing of men and weapons,
and the tone which their government-controlled Press and Party leaders
have adopted, the only conclusion that could be drawn would be that the
worst would happen, and happen quite soon. But other factors are also
at work. All plans and preparations may be perfected, and yet the fateful
signal may not be given. Whether it will be given or not depends on the
mood, temperament and decision of a single man, who has raised himself
from an obscure position to a grisly summit from which he can perhaps
let loose upon the greater part of mankind, immeasurable catastrophe and
tribulation. If my words could reach him, as indeed they may, I would
say, "Pause, consider well before you take a plunge into the terrible unknown. Consider whether your life's work, which might now be famous
in the eyes of history, in raising Germany from prostration and defeat to
a point where all the world is waiting anxiously upon her actions—
consider whether all this may not be irretrievably cast away."

I wish I could convince Herr Hitler of the fact that the British nation
—and surely we may also say the British Empire—have reached the limit
of their patience. We have receded and acquiesced time after time in
breaches of solemn promises and treaties. This we have done out of our
desire for peace, and also no doubt because the interest of the British
Empire is peace. Herr Hitler would make a profound mistake if he persuaded himself that all these retreats were the result of cowardice and
degeneracy. When Herr Goebbels' Nazi propaganda blares and blethers
upon the ether that Britain and France have lost the capacity to make war
if it is forced upon them, we do not get angry because we know it is not
true. We know that our sufferings will be very hard and we are determined not to be guilty of bringing about a crash, the consequences of
which no man can measure. We know also that we could only throw
ourselves into such a struggle if our consciences were clear. In this free,
old, independent island we are not living in the Middle Ages. We see
great hopes for the future of all the world. We see the opportunity of
lifting, through the aid of science, all the men in all the lands to a far
higher level of well-being and culture than was ever possible before. It is
an opportunity which has never come to mankind before, and which may

not come to them again if it is cast away till generations and perhaps centuries have passed. We are determined that there shall not rest upon us the guilt and the shame of standing between the toiling masses of the world and the ever-brightening prospects which are at last within their reach. It is this sense of responsibility before the high monuments of history which has governed our policy and conduct, and no taunts or insults will move us from this determination. It would give no umbrage to Britain to dwell in the world side by side with a prosperous, happy, free, good-hearted Germany. We would welcome her arrival in the leadership, the joint leadership of the European family. Indeed, we are sure that the expanding future, on the threshold of which we stand, or might stand, will never be fully realized without active German co-operation. But if there is another act of Nazi violence, which leads to war, we shall not seek to stand aside.

We are an old nation. It is nearly a thousand years since we were conquered. We have built up our state and way of life slowly and gradually, across the centuries. Therefore we can afford to make exertions for peace which would not be easy in a race less sure of itself and of its duty. There are two supreme obligations which rest upon a British government. They are of equal importance. One is to strive to prevent war, and the other is to be ready if war should come.

As you know, I have been a persistent critic of the present Government, both in their foreign policy and in their measures for defense. My warnings and censures for the last six years are on record, and today no one is asking me to take one word back. If I support the Government today, it is not because I have changed my views. It is because the Government have in principle and even in detail adopted the policy I have urged. I only hope they have not adopted it too late to prevent war. When danger is at a distance, when there is plenty of time to make the necessary preparations, when you can bend twigs instead of having to break massive boughs—it is right, indeed it is a duty, to sound the alarm. But when danger comes very near, when it is plain that not much more can be done in the time that may be available, it is no service to dwell upon the shortcomings or neglects of those who have been responsible. The time to be frightened is when evils can be remedied; when they cannot be fully remedied they must be faced with courage. When danger is far off we may think of our weakness; when it is near we must not forget our strength.

I was glad to hear the Prime Minister say with all his knowledge of our affairs that our defenses were in such good order, and that we can face the future with calm confidence. This is no time to analyze a statement like this in detail—certainly not in public—but I believe the Prime Minister is quite right in believing that the Navy is stronger now relatively to the navies of Europe than it was at the beginning of the late War, when it was found strong enough. I believe he is quite right in saying that our Air Force has made a great advance in the last twelve months. It may not be in size as large as we were solemnly promised—namely, the equal of any air force within striking distance of our shores. That promise has not been made good. But I think it no exaggeration to state that the Royal Air Force is a massive organization of the highest quality, both in men and machines. The vast flexible power of British wealth and industry has now for several years been concentrated upon the creation of a great Air Force, the results are now coming rapidly to hand, and I trust that its strength will not be underrated in certain quarters at the present time. As to the Army, we have the men. With the approach of danger the men came forward. How splendid it has been to see conscription carried by almost universal assent, and to see all these young men coming forward, feeling that it is an honor to be called upon: grieved and crestfallen when physical disability prevented any of them from taking their places in the ranks. I was strongly encouraged by reading about the immensely improved physique of the new militia. We have heard a lot from German and Italian sources of the miserable character of the youth reared under the conditions of democracy. Now we find that they are of a far higher standard than in the Great War, and even then they were good enough. Even then we saw proud military empires ask for armistice in the open field, and some countries which are boastful today were glad to have British and French soldiers to help them defend their native soil.

What a vindication all this has been for our social services and those who have worked for them! There is no more far-seeing investment for a nation than to put milk, food and education into young children. If you add to that respect for law, knowledge of the traditions of the country and love of freedom, you have at any rate the foundations of national survival. Is it not also refreshing to find that the introduction of compulsory service has not prevented or even checked an immense flow of volunteering by those who were outside the class summoned to the Colors? The men are all right and the men are there. If only our Government had made the necessary preparations to have a great store of equip ment and munitions in good time, as they might easily have done, as they were repeatedly urged to do, we should soon have the Army in as high a state of preparedness as our Navy and our Air Force. However, the Prime Minister has at last agreed to a Ministry of Supply, and now we can only trust everything will be accomplished as fast as possible.

But let me now return, thus fortified, to the supreme issue which lies before us. What is Herr Hitler going to do? Is he going to try to blow up the world or not? The world is a very heavy thing to blow up. An extraordinary man at a pinnacle of power may create a great explosion, and yet the civilized world may remain unshaken. The enormous fragments and splinters of the explosion may clatter down upon his own head and destroy him and all who stand around him, but the world will go on. Civilization will not succumb; the working people in the free countries will not be enslaved again. If war is forced upon the world by the Nazi Party of Germany nearly three-quarters of the human race will directly or indirectly loose their weight against them; and I have no doubt that, after a struggle which will certainly be severe and may be long, democracy and civilization will beat off the assault and resume its onward march.

We are told from many quarters that the German Dictator cannot be made to believe that His Majesty's Government will fight for Danzig. What is Danzig? Danzig is not only a city. It has become a symbol. An act of violence against the Polish Republic, whether it arises from without or from within, will raise an issue of world importance. The Foreign Secretary has told us that force will be met by force, and not one voice in Britain has been raised to contradict him. An attack upon Poland at the present time would be a decisive and irrevocable event. It is of the highest importance that the Nazi Party in Germany should not mislead themselves upon the temper of the British and French democracies.

I see that Herr Goebbels and his Italian counterpart, Signor Gayda, have been jeering at us because we have not gone to war with Japan, on account of the insults to which Englishmen and New Zealanders have been subjected at Tientsin. They say that this shows we are effete, and that is what Germany and Italy are being taught today. But perhaps thinking men in these Dictator countries, if they are allowed to know the truth, will feel that we may be keeping what strength we have for someone else. I am glad that the Government have not been provoked into taking their eye off the target. These studied insults and affronts from the Japanese, a nation hitherto renowned for their good manners, might well have been a trap to lure us away from the seas, where any major trouble which may arise will be decided.

We ought not to send our Fleet to the Far East until we are sure of our position in the Mediterranean, and probably then it will not be necessary. I do not believe that Japan, deeply entangled in China—nay, bleeding at every pore in China—her strength ebbing away in a wrongful and impossible task, and with the whole weight of Russia upon her in the north of China, will wish to make war upon the British Empire until she sees how matters go in Europe. Therefore, we should approve both patience and firmness in the attitude of our Government towards the problem of the Far East.

We all hope that a full and solid alliance will be made with Russia without further delay. It would seem that the Russian claim that we should all stand together in resisting an act of aggression upon the Baltic States was just and reasonable, and I trust we shall meet it in the fullest manner. Frankly, I don't understand what we have been boggling at all these weeks. At the point to which we have come, these additional guarantees do not add much to our danger. Actually they do not add one tithe to our danger compared to what will be gained in collective security by an alliance between England, France and Russia. The main interests of the Russian State are menaced by Nazidom, and all those who feel themselves thus threatened can naturally and confidently pool their resources and share risks.

Lastly, and most weighty among the factors which may preserve the peace of the world, there is the intimate comprehension of the cause of freedom now at stake in Europe which is shown by the United States. We ask for favors from no nation. Every country must judge its own interest and duty for itself; but the understanding, the good will and the sympathy of the great republic is a very real encouragement to us in these months and weeks of increasing anxiety.

Where is it all to end? To try and buy off Nazidom, or any other sign of moral weakness, would only be to bring near the very thing we still hope may be averted. We certainly cannot go on like this. Throughout the whole country people of all classes and parties have the same feelings. Business is at a standstill. The progress of the whole world is blocked. All its resources are being devoured by armaments. No one can plan ahead. We live from crisis to crisis. There is a profound and almost universal conviction throughout the land that we shall not escape our dangers by recoiling from them. The time has come when we must confront them and surmount them. We have a Government which has proved and over-proved its fidelity to the cause of peace, and if that Government declares that national safety and national honor compel us to resist outrage and aggression, we shall all have to do our best. And it may well be that what we do will be enough to save the world, if not from war and suffering, at least from servitude and shame.

THE SUMMER ADJOURNMENT

The House of Commons

August 2, 1939

1939

July 3. The Prime Minister in the House of Commons announces that reports point to large-scale military measures in and around Danzig.

July 4. Agreement made between Germany and Italy by which the German inhabitants in Southern Tyrol are to be transported to the Reich. About 200,000 persons are affected.

July 15. Count Ciano, Italian Foreign Secretary, returns from an official visit to Spain without effecting an Italo-Spanish treaty.

July 27. The opposition in the House of Commons proposes that in view of the international situation Parliament, after rising on August 4, should meet again two weeks later for a statement. Mr. Chamberlain declines.

August 2. Mr. Chamberlain proposes that the House rise from August 4 until October 3. This is attacked from all sides of the House, but the Prime Minister is unmoved and has his way.

THE SUMMER ADJOURNMENT

I MUST say I regret the terms of the Government's Motion, and, although not altogether for the same reasons, I find myself endorsing the pleas which have been advanced from both the Opposition Parties in the House. But I still hope that the Prime Minister has not said his last word on this subject. It is in that hope that I venture to offer a few reasons for my opposition to the Motion. This House is sometimes disparaged in this country, but abroad it counts. Abroad, the House of Commons is counted, and especially in Dictator countries, as a most formidable expression of the British national will and an instrument of that will in resistance to aggression. Surely that is a fact which must be admitted. The Dictators themselves have not been slow to notice that minority opinion in this House has seemed in one way to influence the course of Government action. It is in accordance with minority opinion in this House that we have come together upon a foreign policy upon which all are now agreed, a foreign policy which the two Dictator States deeply deprecate. Therefore, I say that we count largely in their thoughts.

If you wish to check this by examination, see how oddly they have timed various strokes which have been made in the recent past for occasions when the House has risen and the Members are on their holidays. Take the latest of all, the Albanian outrage at Easter. It was nicely timed for the moment when it was known that Parliament was scattered, when the Ministers were scattered—and when the Mediterranean Fleet, unfortunately, was scattered, too. They timed it for that purpose. Then look at last year, when we parted in similar circumstances to the present. Until then there were no suspicious troop movements in Germany. It was only then that there began all these movements for the pretended peaceful purposes of a local maneuver. It may sound rather a vain thing for a Member of

Parliament to say, but it seems to me that this House is a recognized addition to the defenses of Great Britain, that we are safer when the House is sitting, and that the power and will of this House count very much, and, properly commanded, will reinforce the power of His Majesty's Government. Therefore, it seems to me that it would be regrettable if we were to go out of action just at a time when the situation is becoming most acute.

I would not press this argument so far as to suggest that if the House goes on sitting night and day there will be no crisis. That would, indeed, be exaggerating the argument, but I have the feeling that things are in a great balance, and that even minor matters of a favorable character cannot be neglected if they can be thrown in on the right side of the scale. Therefore, I should regret it very much if we were now to pass a Resolution scattering ourselves to the winds till October. This is an odd moment for the House to declare that it will go on a two months' holiday. It is only an accident that our summer holidays coincide with the danger months in Europe, when the harvests have been gathered, and when the powers of evil are at their strongest. The situation in Europe is graver than it was at this time last year. The German Government have already 2,000,000 men under arms actually incorporated in their Army. When the new class joins before the end of August more than 500,000 will be added to this number automatically. All along the Polish frontier from Danzig to Cracow there are heavy massings of troops, and every preparation is being made for a speedy advance. There are five German divisions in a high state of mobility around Breslau alone. The roads, as the Leader of the Liberal Party mentioned, towards Poland through Czechoslovakia are being raised to the highest condition. Quarries are being opened for material, by enforced Czechoslovak labor.

I have been told—I may be wrong, but I have not always been wrong—that many of the public buildings and of the schools in large parts of Czechoslovakia, Bohemia certainly, have been cleared and prepared for the accommodation of wounded. But that is not the only place. There is a definite movement of supplies and troops through Austria towards the east. The right hon. Gentleman who leads the Opposition put his finger upon another danger spot which might easily be exchanged for the one which now occupies our thoughts. There is the strained situation in the Tyrol, most significant as indicating the tenseness of the situation, where Herr Hitler has been willing to do the thing which must have caused him the greatest wrench in order to make sure of his Italian confederates.

All these are terribly formidable signs. And on our side, too, and among our Allies, are great preparations. The Fleet is largely mobilized. We congratulate the Government on the timely step they have taken, and we support them in it. As many men as can possibly be accommodated in camps are in training, and the anti-aircraft gunners are at their stations. Is this, then, the moment that we should separate and declare that we separate until the 3rd October? Who can doubt that there is going to be a supreme trial of will power, if not indeed a supreme trial of arms. At this moment in its long history, it would be disastrous, it would be pathetic, it would be shameful for the House of Commons to write itself off as an effective and potent factor in the situation, or reduce whatever strength it can offer to the firm front which the nation will make against aggression.

Then, of course, it is asked, "Do you trust the Prime Minister?" The Leaders of both Oppositions made it perfectly clear that they did not trust him, but that is not the position of some of those who are anxious that an arrangement should be reached by which Parliament will not pass entirely out of being for so long a time; that is not the position which we on this side of the House adopt. I, personally, accept what the Prime Minister says, and when he makes solemn public declarations I believe that he will do his best to carry them out. I trust his good faith in every respect, but that does not really dispose of the whole issue. It might be that his good faith was in no way in question, either about the rising of the House or other matters at all, but there might be a difference of judgment. I use the word "judgment" with some temerity, because my right hon. Friend twitted me some time ago about that notorious defect which I have in my composition. I have not looked up all his own declarations in any captious spirit, and I will not pursue that this afternoon, but it is quite clear that the judgment which the Prime Minister might form upon the facts as they unfolded would be a legitimate and natural topic upon which differences of opinion would arise between us.

Take, for instance, a very late example, this question of Danzig. The Leader of the Labour Party stated how grievous the situation was in Danzig, and my right hon. Friend said that the situation was exaggerated. That was only two days ago, but now we read in *The Times* that the official Gazette of Poland has made a statement of the facts in Danzig which goes much further than the statement put forward by the Leaders of the Labour Party which my right hon. Friend the Prime Minister thought was exaggerated. So there may be differences, quite honest differences, upon the emphasis and upon the facts; and it is in respect of these differences which arise when men are working on the same policy that an interchange of opinion in the House of Commons would be from time to time most desirable. It is a very hard thing, and I hope it will not be said, for the Government to say to the House, "Begone! Run off and play. Take your gas masks with you. Do not worry about public affairs. Leave them to the gifted and experienced Ministers"—who, after all, so far as our defenses are concerned, landed us where we were landed in September last year, and who, after all—I make all allowances for the many difficulties—have brought us in foreign policy at this moment to the point where we have guaranteed Poland and Rumania, after having lost Czechoslovakia, and not having gained Russia.

This is, indeed, a hard, an unreasonable and unnatural proposal, especially when the House is agreed upon the basis of policy, and when, if it has a difference with the Government, it is because it desires to urge them more vigorously forward and not to hinder them in the policy which they have declared. I did hope that my right hon. Friend would have taken exactly the opposite point of view, and that the roles would be reversed. I should have expected to see him come down to the House, and, at that Box, assume an air of exceptional gravity, and say that he regretted that he had to make a demand on the good will and patience of the House, and upon its public spirit; but that the circumstances were such that he could not bear the whole responsibility for months at a time without recourse to the sense of the Commons and that, therefore, he must ask the House to come back on frequent occasions during the interval. Then it would have been for the Opposition to say, "Of course it is very serious, but if the Prime Minister demands it on a policy on which we are agreed, it will be our duty to comply with his request."

How would it be if we came back in three weeks' time, just before the end of August so that we could all be in complete agreement? I should think it would be a pretty safe thing to adjourn for a fortnight or three weeks now. Surely we are not going to ask either that we should stay here night and day, or that we should never come back. That is far too narrow a dilemma. Lord Balfour used to say that this was a singularly ill-contrived world, but that it was not so ill-contrived as that. I would like to endorse the argument that it will not be so easy to recall Parliament once it has been dispersed. The reason is that events move on from day to day, and it is very difficult to say at what point a situation is being created which requires the recall of Parliament. Moreover, the recall of

Parliament in the present circumstances will denote a situation of the gravest emergency, because the Fleet is already mobilized. The recall of Parliament will mean in all probability that something has occurred which brings us right up against the supreme decision.

I should have thought that it would be a matter of foresight and prudent convenience to have had a day at the end of August up your sleeve. If the date were the 22nd or 25th August, or whatever it might be, then, if all is well, very few people need come. The Ministers need not attend. After all, we are all in the same boat. I noticed a sort of spirit on these benches to try and run this matter through on ordinary Party loyalty, but we are not going to get through these troubles on the basis of Party loyalty and calling everyone who differs unpatriotic. If that sort of atmosphere were created I am sure that it would be absolutely swept away by the country.

I am very sensitive to the atmosphere of the House, and I think that the effort ought to be to try to bring us as much together as possible, and not to imagine that people will be deterred from saying what they intend to say at any time because it causes unpopularity, or because there is a sort of organized scowl directed at them. I think it would be a very wise and prudent step from the point of view of national administration to have this date which you could put your hand on if needed and, if not, it would pass off as nothing but a needless formality. I suggest and hope that that may be weighed and considered by my right hon. Friend.

There is only one thing more that I wish to say, and it is in the nature of an appeal to my right hon. Friend. He wrote a letter in a recent election—Monmouthshire, I think—appealing for national unity. What does national unity mean? It surely means that reasonable sacrifices of Party opinions, personal opinion, and Party interest should be made by all in order to contribute to the national security. Here is an opportunity for my right hon. Friend to take a quite important step to put himself in a better relation with those forces in the country who lie outside the ranks of his numerous and faithful adherents. This is not an occasion when the House should part with reproaches and with difference of opinion. On the contrary, we ought to part as friends who are facing common problems and resolved to aid each other as far as it is possible. I hope, indeed, that my right hon. Friend will even at this moment not refuse to take into consideration the opinion of the House as a whole, including minorities in the House, and, if they want to meet again at the end of the month, endeavor to meet them upon that point. If he were to do so now, I tell him here that he would render a great service to his country, because this country cannot be guided through its present difficulties except by the Leader of the Conservative Party, and the Leader of the Conservative Party will never be chosen from any quarter except by that Party itself. It is, therefore, necessary for him to do his utmost to conciliate other opinion, now so widely estranged, and make himself the true leader of the nation as a whole.

EUROPE IN SUSPENSE

An Address Broadcast to the People of the United States of America

August 8, 1939

1939

Mid-July—August.   Under various guises Germany pours troops into the Free City of Danzig.

August 3.   Sir Thomas Inskip says: "War today is not only not inevitable but is unlikely. The Government have good reason for saying that."

August 6.   Notice is given to the Polish customs officials on the East Prussian frontier of Danzig that they cannot continue their duties. The Polish Commissioner-General in Danzig insists that they continue their duties, and the measure is suspended for the time being. Herr Foerster, Gauleiter of Danzig, goes to Berchtesgaden for instructions.

EUROPE IN SUSPENSE

HOLIDAY TIME, ladies and gentlemen! Holiday time, my friends across the Atlantic! Holiday time, when the summer calls the toilers of all countries for an all too brief spell from the offices and mills and stiff routine of daily life and breadwinning, and sends them to seek if not rest at least change in new surroundings, to return refreshed and keep the myriad wheels of civilized society on the move.

Let me look back—let me see. How did we spend our summer holidays twenty-five years ago? Why, those were the very days when the German advance guards were breaking into Belgium and trampling down its people on their march towards Paris! Those were the days when Prussian militarism was—to quote its own phrase—"hacking its way through the small, weak, neighbor country" whose neutrality and independence they had sworn not merely to respect but to defend.

But perhaps we are wrong. Perhaps our memory deceives us. Dr. Goebbels and his Propaganda Machine have their own version of what happened twenty-five years ago. To hear them talk, you would suppose that it was Belgium that invaded Germany! There they were, these peaceful Prussians, gathering in their harvests, when this wicked Belgium—set on by England and the Jews—fell upon them; and would no doubt have taken Berlin, if Corporal Adolf Hitler had not come to the rescue and turned the tables. Indeed, the tale goes further. After four years of war by land and sea, when Germany was about to win an overwhelming victory, the Jews got at them again, this time from the rear. Armed with President Wilson's Fourteen Points they stabbed, we are told, the German armies in the back, and induced them to ask for an armistice, and even persuaded them, in an unguarded moment, to sign a paper saying that it was they and not the Belgians who had been the ones to begin the War. Such is history as it is taught in topsy-turvydom.

And now it is holiday again, and where are we now? Or, as you sometimes ask in the United States—where do we go from here? There is a hush over all Europe, nay, over all the world, broken only by the dull thud of Japanese bombs falling on Chinese cities, on Chinese Universities or near British and American ships. But then, China is a long way off, so why worry? The Chinese are fighting for what the founders of the American Constitution in their stately language called: "Life, liberty and the pursuit of happiness." And they seem to be fighting very well. Many good judges think they are going to win. Anyhow, let's wish them luck! Let's give them a wave of encouragement—as your President did last week, when he gave notice about ending the commercial treaty. After all, the suffering Chinese are fighting our battle—the battle of democracy. They are defending the soil, the good earth, that has been theirs since the dawn of time against cruel and unprovoked aggression. Give them a cheer across the ocean—no one knows whose turn it may be next. If this habit of military dictatorships' breaking into other people's lands with bomb and shell and bullet, stealing the property and killing the proprietors, spreads too widely, we may none of us be able to think of summer holidays for quite a while.

But to come back to the hush I said was hanging over Europe. What kind of a hush is it? Alas! it is the hush of suspense, and in many lands it is the hush of fear. Listen! No, listen carefully; I think I hear something—yes, there it was quite clear. Don't you hear it? It is the tramp of armies crunching the gravel of the parade-grounds, splashing through rain-soaked fields, the tramp of two million German soldiers and more than a million Italians—"going on maneuvers"—yes, only on maneuvers! Of course it's only maneuvers—just like last year. After all, the Dictators must train their soldiers. They could scarcely do less in common prudence, when the Danes, the Dutch, the Swiss, the Albanians—and of course the Jews—may leap out upon them at any moment and rob them of their living-space, and make them sign another paper to say who began it. Besides, these German and Italian armies may have another work of Liberation to perform. It was only last year they liberated Austria from the horrors of self-government. It was only in March they freed the Czechoslovak Republic from the misery of independent existence. It is only two years ago that Signor Mussolini gave the ancient kingdom of Abyssinia its Magna Charta. It is only two months ago that little Albania got its writ of Habeas Corpus, and Mussolini sent in his Bill of Rights for King Zog to pay. Why, even at this moment, the mountaineers of the Tyrol, a German-speaking population who have dwelt in their beautiful valleys for a thousand years, are being *liberated,* that is to say, uprooted, from the land they love, from the soil which Andreas Hofer died to defend. No wonder the armies are tramping on when there is so much liberation to be done, and no wonder there is a hush among all the neighbors of Germany and Italy while they are wondering which one is going to be "liberated" next.

The Nazis say that they are being encircled. They have encircled themselves with a ring of neighbors who have to keep on guessing who will be struck down next. This kind of guesswork is a very tiring game. Countries, especially small countries, have long ceased to find it amusing. Can you wonder that the neighbors of Germany, both great and small, have begun to think of stopping the game, by simply saying to the Nazis on the principle of the Covenant of the League of Nations: "He who attacks any, attacks all. He who attacks the weakest will find he has attacked the strongest"? That is how we are spending our holiday over here, in poor weather, in a lot of clouds. We hope it is better with you.

One thing has struck me as very strange, and that is the resurgence of the one-man power after all these centuries of experience and progress. It is curious how the English-speaking peoples have always had this horror of one-man power. They are quite ready to follow a leader for a time, as long as he is serviceable to them; but the idea of handing themselves over, lock, stock and barrel, body and soul, to one man, and worshiping him as if he were an idol—that has always been odious to the whole theme and nature of our civilization. The architects of the American Constitution were as careful as those who shaped the British Constitution to guard against the whole life and fortunes, and all the laws and freedom of the nation, being placed in the hands of a tyrant. Checks and counter-checks in the body politic, large devolutions of State government, instruments and processes of free debate, frequent recurrence to first principles, the right of opposition to the most powerful governments, and above all ceaseless vigilance, have preserved, and will preserve, the broad characteristics of British and American institutions. But in Germany, on a mountain peak, there sits one man who in a single day can release the world from the fear which now oppresses it; or in a single day can plunge all that we have and are into a volcano of smoke and flame.

If Herr Hitler does not make war, there will be no war. No one else is going to make war. Britain and France are determined to shed no blood except in self-defense or in defense of their Allies. No one has ever dreamed of attacking Germany. If Germany desires to be reassured against attack by her neighbors, she has only to say the word and we will give her the fullest guarantees in accordance with the principles of the Covenant of the League. We have said repeatedly we ask nothing for ourselves in the way of security that we are not willing freely to share with the German people. Therefore, if war should come there can be no doubt upon whose head the blood-guiltiness will fall. Thus lies the great issue at this moment, and none can tell how it will be settled.

It is not, believe me, my American friends, from any ignoble shrinking from pain and death that the British and French peoples pray for peace. It is not because we have any doubts how a struggle between Nazi Germany and the civilized world would ultimately end that we pray tonight and every night for peace. But whether it be peace or war—peace with its broadening and brightening prosperity, now within our reach, or war with its measureless carnage and destruction—we must strive to frame some system of human relations in the future which will bring to an end this prolonged hideous uncertainty, which will let the working and creative forces of the world get on with their job, and which will no longer leave the whole life of mankind dependent upon the virtues, the caprice, or the wickedness of a single man.

WAR

The House of Commons

September 3, 1939

1939

August 10.   Herr Foerster, speaking to Anti-Poland demonstrators at Danzig, says that Poland wants to annex the whole of East Prussia, and "smash Germany in bloody war."

August 13.   Dr. Burckhardt, League of Nations Commissioner of Danzig, is invited by Herr Hitler to a conference at Berchtesgaden.

August 13.   Mr. Churchill visits the Maginot Line at the invitation of the French General Staff.

August 22. Herr von Ribbentrop goes to Moscow to sign a Non-Aggression Pact between Germany and Soviet Russia.

August 23. King Leopold broadcasts an appeal for peace.

August 24. The Russo-German Pact is signed in Moscow by Herr von Ribbentrop and M. Molotoff.

Parliament meets and passes the Emergency Powers Bill in one day.

The Pope broadcasts a "paternal message to the world" appealing for peace. President Roosevelt appeals to the King of Italy to assist in maintaining peace.

August 25. The Anglo-Polish Treaty of Mutual Assistance is signed in London. President Roosevelt sends two appeals to Herr Hitler. Herr Hitler cancels the Tannenberg celebrations.

August 27. Herr Hitler refuses M. Daladier's plea that there should be one more attempt at direct negotiation between Germany and Poland, and affirms that Danzig and the Corridor must return to the Reich.

August 28. Sir Nevile Henderson flies back to Berlin with the British Government's reply. France closes the German frontier.

August 29. Queen Wilhelmina and King Leopold offer to mediate. Germany finally occupies Slovakia.

August 30. The British Government replies in uncompromising terms to Herr Hitler's further note.

August 31. Germany broadcasts a 16-point plan for settlement with Poland. The Pope appeals for a truce.

September 1. Germany invades Poland without a declaration of War. Herr Foerster announces the return of Danzig to the Reich. Parliament votes an emergency grant of £500,000,000. The British and French Ambassadors are instructed to notify the German Government that unless German troops are immediately withdrawn from Poland, Britain and France will fulfill their treaty obligations.

September 3. Britain presents a two-hour ultimatum to Germany, expiring at 11 A.M. At 11:15 Great Britain declares war on Germany. France declares war at 5 P.M.

The War Cabinet is appointed, with Mr. Churchill as First Lord of the Admiralty. Mr. Eden returns as Secretary of State for the Dominions.

WAR

In this solemn hour it is a consolation to recall and to dwell upon our repeated efforts for peace. All have been ill-starred, but all have been faithful and sincere. This is of the highest moral value—and not only moral value, but practical value—at the present time, because the wholehearted concurrence of scores of millions of men and women, whose co-operation is indispensable and whose comradeship and brotherhood are indispensable, is the only foundation upon which the trial and tribulation of modern war can be endured and surmounted. This moral conviction alone affords that ever-fresh resilience which renews the strength and energy of people in long, doubtful and dark days. Outside, the storms of war may blow and the lands may be lashed with the fury of its gales, but in our own hearts this Sunday morning there is peace. Our hands may be active, but our consciences are at rest.

We must not underrate the gravity of the task which lies before us or the temerity of the ordeal, to which we shall not be found unequal. We must expect many disappointments, and many unpleasant surprises, but we may be sure that the task which we have freely accepted is one not beyond the compass and the strength of the British Empire and the French Republic. The Prime Minister said it was a sad day, and that is indeed true, but at the present time there is another note which may be present, and that is a feeling of thankfulness that, if these great trials were to come upon our Island, there is a generation of Britons here now ready to prove itself not unworthy of the days of yore and not unworthy of those great men, the fathers of our land, who laid the foundations of our laws and shaped the greatness of our country.

This is not a question of fighting for Danzig or fighting for Poland. We are fighting to save the whole world from the pestilence of Nazi tyranny and in defense of all that is most sacred to man. This is no war of domination or imperial aggrandizement or material gain; no war to shut any country out of its sunlight and means of progress. It is a war, viewed in its inherent quality, to establish, on impregnable rocks, the rights of the individual, and it is a war to establish and revive the stature of man. Perhaps it might seem a paradox that a war undertaken in the name of liberty and right should require, as a necessary part of its processes, the surrender for the time being of so many of the dearly valued liberties and rights. In these last few days the House of Commons has been voting dozens of Bills which hand over to the executive our most dearly valued traditional liberties. We are sure that these liberties will be in hands which will not abuse them, which will use them for no class or party interests, which will cherish and guard them, and we look forward to the day, surely and confidently we look forward to the day, when our liberties and rights will be restored to us, and when we shall be able to share them with the peoples to whom such blessings are unknown.

THE FIRST MONTH OF WAR

An Address Broadcast

October 1, 1939

1939

September 5.   The German Army cuts the Polish Corridor.

September 7.   The Polish garrison at Westerplatte, outside Danzig, surrenders after heroic resistance.

September 9.   The War Cabinet announces that its preparations will be based on the presumption of a three years' war. Canada declares war.

September 11.   It is announced that the B.E.F. has arrived in France.

September 17.   Russia invades Poland. The Polish Army collapses. The Germans issue a 12-hour ultimatum to Warsaw.

September 18.   H.M.S. *Courageous,* aircraft-carrier, is torpedoed and sunk. The German and Russian Armies meet at Brest Litovsk. The Polish Government enters Rumania.

September 21.   General von Fritsch shot on the Polish front.

September 22.   The partition of Poland announced by Germany and Russia. Warsaw still resists.

September 27.   Warsaw surrenders. Sir John Simon introduces the first War Budget.

THE FIRST MONTH OF WAR

THE BRITISH EMPIRE and the French Republic have been at war with Nazi Germany for a month tonight. We have not yet come at all to the severity of fighting which is to be expected; but three important things have happened.

First, Poland, has been again overrun by two of the great Powers which held her in bondage for 150 years, but were unable to quench the spirit of the Polish nation. The heroic defense of Warsaw shows that the soul of Poland is indestructible, and that she will rise again like a rock, which may for a spell be submerged by a tidal wave, but which remains a rock.

What is the second event of this first month? It is, of course, the assertion of the power of Russia. Russia has pursued a cold policy of self-interest. We could have wished that the Russian armies should be standing on their present line as the friends and allies of Poland instead of as invaders. But that the Russian armies should stand on this line was clearly necessary for the safety of Russia against the Nazi menace. At any rate, the line is there, and an Eastern Front has been created which Nazi Germany does not dare assail. When Herr von Ribbentrop was summoned to Moscow last week, it was to learn the fact, and to accept the fact, that the Nazi designs upon the Baltic States and upon the Ukraine must come to a dead stop.

I cannot forecast to you the action of Russia. It is a riddle wrapped in a mystery inside an enigma; but perhaps there is a key. That key is Russian national interest. It cannot be in accordance with the interest or the safety of Russia that Germany should plant itself upon the shores of the Black Sea, or that it should overrun the Balkan States and subjugate the Slavonic peoples of southeastern Europe. That would be contrary to the historic life-interests of Russia.

But in this quarter of the world—the southeast of Europe—these interests of Russia fall into the same channel as the interests of Britain and France. None of these three Powers can afford to see Rumania, Yugoslavia, Bulgaria, and above all Turkey, put under the German heel. Through the fog of confusion and uncertainty we may discern quite plainly the community of interests which exists between England, France and Russia—a community of interests to prevent the Nazis' carrying the flames of war into the Balkans and Turkey. Thus, my friends, at some risk of being proved wrong by events, I will proclaim tonight my conviction that the second great fact of the first month of the war is that Hitler, and all that Hitler stands for, have been and are being warned off the east and the southeast of Europe.

What is the third event? Here I speak as First Lord of the Admiralty, with especial caution. It would seem that the U-boat attack upon the life of the British Isles has not so far proved successful. It is true that when they sprang out upon us and we were going about our ordinary business, with two thousand ships in constant movement every day upon the seas, they managed to do some serious damage. But the Royal Navy has immediately attacked the U-boats, and is hunting them night and day—I will not say without mercy, because God forbid we should ever part company with that—but at any rate with zeal and not altogether without relish. And it looks tonight very much as if it is the U-boats who are feeling the weather, and not the Royal Navy or the world-wide commerce of Britain. A week has passed since a British ship, alone or in convoy, has been sunk or even molested by a U-boat on the high seas; and during the first month of the war we have captured by our efficient contraband control 150,000 tons more German merchandise—food, oil, minerals and other commodities—for our own benefit than we have lost by all the U-boat sinkings put together. In fact, up to date—please observe I make no promises (we must deal in performance and not in promises) —up to date we have actually got 150,000 tons of very desirable supplies into this Island more than we should have got if war had not been declared, and if no U-boat had ever cast sailormen to their fate upon the stormy seas. This seems to be a very solid, tangible fact which has emerged from the first month of the war against Nazidom.

Of course, we are told that all the U-boats have gone home just to tell their master about their exploits and their experiences. But that is not true, because every day we are attacking them upon the approaches to the British Isles. Some undoubtedly have preferred to go off and sink the unprotected neutral ships of Norway and Sweden. I hope the day will come when the Admiralty will be able to invite the ships of all nations to join the British convoys, and to insure them on their voyages at a reasonable rate. We must, of course, expect that the U-boat attack upon the sea-borne commerce of the world will be renewed presently on a greater scale. We hope, however, that by the end of October we shall have three times as many hunting-craft at work as we had at the beginning of the war; and we hope that by the measures we have taken, our means of putting down this pest will grow continually. I can assure you we are taking great care about all that.

Therefore, to sum up the results of the first month, let us say that Poland has been overrun, but will rise again; that Russia has warned Hitler off his Eastern dreams; and that U-boats may be safely left to the care and constant attention of the British Navy.

Now I wish to speak about what is happening in our own Island. When a peaceful democracy is suddenly made to fight for its life, there must be a lot of trouble and hardship in the process of turning over from peace to war. I feel very keenly for those thousands—scores of thousands of them—who wish to throw themselves into the fight at once, but for whom we cannot find full scope at the present time. All this will clear as we get into our stride. His Majesty's Government is unitedly resolved to make the maximum effort of which the British nation is capable, and to persevere, whatever may happen, until decisive victory is gained. Meanwhile, patriotic men and women, especially those who understand the high causes in human fortunes which are now at stake, must not only rise above fear; they must also rise above inconvenience and, perhaps most difficult of all, above boredom. Parliament will be kept in session, and all grievances or muddles or scandals, if such there be, can be freely ventilated or exposed there. In past times the House of Commons has proved itself an instrument of national will power capable of waging stern wars. Parliament is the shield and expression of democracy, and Ministers of the Crown base themselves upon the Parliamentary system. You have seen the power of Parliament manifested in the last week, when a Budget, gigantic in its burdens—a Budget which would have infuriated everybody a year ago—has been accepted with prompt and stolid resolve.

In other fields our work goes forward. A large army has already gone to France. British armies upon the scale of the effort of the Great War are in preparation. The British people are determined to stand in the line with the splendid Army of the French Republic, and share with them, as fast and as early as we can, whatever may be coming towards us both. It may be that great ordeals are coming to us in this Island from the air. We shall do our best to give a good account of ourselves; and we must always remember that the command of the seas will enable us to bring the immense resources of Canada and the New World into play as a decisive ultimate air factor, a factor beyond the reach of what we have to give and take over here.

Directions have been given by the Government to prepare for a war of at least three years. That does not mean that victory may not be gained in a shorter time. How soon it will be gained depends upon how long Herr Hitler and his group of wicked men, whose hands are stained with blood and soiled with corruption, can keep their grip upon the docile, unhappy German people. It was for Hitler to say when the war would begin; but it is not for him or for his successors to say when it will end. It began when he wanted it, and it will end only when we are convinced that he has had enough.

The Prime Minister has stated our war aims in terms which cannot be bettered, and which cannot be too often repeated. These are his words: "To redeem Europe from the perpetual and recurring fear of German aggression, and enable the peoples of Europe to preserve their independence and their liberties."

That is what the British and French nations are fighting for. How often have we been told that we are the effete democracies whose day is done, and who must now be replaced by various forms of virile dictatorships and totalitarian despotism? No doubt at the beginning we shall have to suffer, because of having too long wished to lead a peaceful life. Our reluctance to fight was mocked at as cowardice. Our desire to see an unarmed world was proclaimed as the proof of our decay. Now we have begun. Now we are going on. Now, with the help of God, and with the conviction that we are the defenders of civilization and freedom, we are going to persevere to the end.

After all, Great Britain and France together are eighty-five millions, even in their homelands alone. They are united in their cause; they are convinced of their duty. Nazidom, with all its tyrannical power, controls no more than that. They, too, have eighty-five millions; but of these at least sixteen millions are newly conquered Czechs, Slovakians and Austrians, who are writhing under their cruel yoke and have to be held down by main force. We have other resources. We have the oceans, and with the oceans the assurance that we can bring the vast latent power of the British and French Empires to bear upon the decisive points. We have the freely given ardent support of the twenty millions of British citizens in the self-governing Dominions of Canada, Australia, New Zealand and South Africa. We have, I believe, the heart and the moral conviction of India on our side. We believe we are entitled to the respect and good will of the world, and particularly of the United States.

Here I am in the same post as I was twenty-five years ago. Rough times lie ahead; but how different is the scene from that of October, 1914! Then the French Front, with its British Army fighting in the line, seemed to be about to break under the terrible impact of German Imperialism. Then Russia had been laid low at Tannenberg; then the whole might of the Austro-Hungarian Empire was in battle against us; then the brave, warlike Turks were about to join our enemies. Then we had to be ready night and day to fight a decisive sea battle with a formidable German fleet almost, in many respects, the equal of our own. We faced those adverse conditions then; we have nothing worse to face tonight.

In those days of 1914 also, Italy was neutral; but we did not know the reason for her neutrality. It was only later on that we learned that by a secret clause in the original Treaty of the Triple Alliance, Italy had expressly reserved to herself the right to stand aside from any war which brought her into conflict with Great Britain. Much has happened since then. Misunderstandings and disputes have arisen, but all the more do we appreciate in England the reason why this great and friendly nation of Italy, with whom we have never been at war, has not seen fit to enter the struggle.

I do not underrate what lies before us, but I must say this: I cannot doubt we have the strength to carry a good cause forward, and to break down the barriers which stand between the wage-earning masses of every land and that free and more abundant daily life which science is ready to afford. That is my conviction, and I look back upon the history of the past to find many sources of encouragement. Of all the wars that men have fought in their hard pilgrimage, none was more noble than the great Civil War in America nearly eighty years ago. Both sides fought with high conviction, and the war was long and hard. All the heroism of the South could not redeem their cause from the stain of slavery, just as all the courage and skill which the Germans always show in war will not free them from the reproach of Nazism, with its intolerance and its brutality. We may take good heart from what happened in America in those famous days of the nineteenth century. We may be sure that the world will roll forward into broader destinies. We may remember the words of old John Bright after the American Civil War was over, when he said to an audience of English working folk: "At last after the smoke of the battlefield had cleared away, the horrid shape which had cast its shadow over the whole continent had vanished and was gone for ever."

THE LOSS OF THE *ROYAL OAK*
AND THE WAR AT SEA

The House of Commons

November 8, 1939

1939

September 30.   A new Polish Government, with M. Raczkiewicz as President and General Sikorski as Prime Minister, takes the oath at Paris.

October 2.   Reports begin to arrive of a German raider in the South Atlantic, later identified as the *Graf Spee*.

October 6.   Herr Hitler in a speech to the Reichstag makes in vague terms his "last peace offer" to the Allies.
Russia inquires of Finland whether she would be prepared to send a special envoy to Moscow to discuss differences.

October 9.   The American ship *City of Flint* seized by the pocket battleship *Deutschland*.

October 10.   Finland sends Dr. Paasikivi to Moscow, and makes preparations to resist if necessary.

October 14.   H.M.S. *Royal Oak* sunk at Scapa Flow, with considerable loss of life.

October 19.   A Treaty of Mutual Assistance between Britain, France and Turkey is signed at Ankara.

October 23.   Finnish delegates return to Moscow for a second conference.

October 27.   The United States repeals its arms embargo. King Leopold reiterates his intention of remaining neutral.

November 3.   In a conference at the Kremlin Russia officially demands territorial concessions from Finland.

November 4.   President Roosevelt signs the American Neutrality Bill.
The *City of Flint* reaches a Norwegian port, and is released.

November 7.   Queen Wilhelmina and King Leopold issue another appeal for peace.

THE LOSS OF THE *ROYAL OAK*
AND THE WAR AT SEA

IT IS NOW established that the *Royal Oak* was sunk in the early hours of 14th October by a German U-boat which penetrated the defenses of the land-locked anchorage of Scapa Flow. These defenses were of two kinds. First, the physical obstructions by nets, booms and blockships; and secondly, by small patrolling craft upon the approaches to the various entrances or Sounds, which are seven in number.

Neither the physical obstructions nor the patrolling craft were in that state of strength and efficiency required to make the anchorage absolutely proof, as it should have been, against the attack of a U-boat on the surface or half-submerged at high water. Measures had been taken, and were being taken, to improve the physical obstructions, and the last blockship required reached Scapa Flow only on the day after the disaster occurred. All the more was it necessary, while these defenses were incomplete, that the patrolling craft should have been particularly numerous. But from a variety of causes connected with the movements of the Fleet, which was not at that time using the anchorage, these patrolling craft were reduced below what was required. I am unable to enter into details, because a full explanation—and no explanation is worth giving unless it is full—would reveal to the enemy matters which would throw a light upon our methods of defense. This light would illuminate for them not only the past but the future. It would not be right to discuss in public, in time of war, these intimate matters of naval defense, and I ask the House with confidence to support the Admiralty in their decision. I must content myself by saying that the long and famed immunity which Scapa Flow, with its currents and defenses, had gained in the last war, had led to a too easy valuation of the dangers which were present. An undue degree of risk was accepted, both at the Admiralty and in the Fleet. At the same time I must point out that many risks are being accepted inevitably by the Fleets and by the Admiralty as part of the regular routine of keeping the seas, and these risks which were unadvisedly run at Scapa Flow seemed to highly competent and responsible persons to be no greater than many others.

No more striking measure of the strong sense of security against U-boats which dominated all minds at Scapa Flow can be found than in the fact that, after one torpedo from the first volley had actually struck the *Royal Oak,* none of the vigilant and experienced officers conceived that it could be a torpedo. The danger from the air was the one first apprehended, and large numbers of the crew took up their air-raid stations under the armor, and were thereby doomed, while at the same time the captain and admiral were examining the alternative possibilities of an internal explosion. It was in these conditions that the second volley of torpedoes was discharged. Thus the forfeit has been claimed, and we mourn the loss of eight hundred gallant officers and men, and of a ship which, although very old, was of undoubted military value.

The inquiries which have been completed have brought all the knowable facts to our attention. The Admiralty, upon whom the broad responsibility rests, are resolved to learn this bitter lesson, namely, that in this new war, with its many novel complications, nothing must be taken for granted; and that every joint in our harness must be tested and strengthened so far as our resources and ingenuity allow. Having most carefully considered the issues involved in this particular case, I propose to take such steps within the Service as are proper and necessary, but I do not intend to embark upon a judicial inquiry with a view to assigning blame to individuals. Such a course would impose an additional burden upon those who, afloat and ashore, are engaged in an intense and deadly and, as many may well think, not wholly unsuccessful struggle. It is on this struggle that all our thought and strength must be concentrated.

During this opening phase of the war the Royal Navy has suffered a greater loss of life than all the other forces, French and British, on sea, on land and in the air combined. Every loss inflicted on us by the enemy has been at once announced. In addition, since the outbreak of war one of our submarines, His Majesty's ship *Oxley,* has been destroyed by an accidental explosion in circumstances which made its publication inadvisable at the time. So far the *Royal Oak, Courageous* and *Oxley* are the only losses we have had of His Majesty's ships of war, but they are, of course, serious losses. The war at sea has, in fact, been the only war which has been proceeding on a full scale, but the House will not suppose that these losses are the only events which have been taking place at sea. What I told the House under much reserve six weeks ago, I can now repeat with more assurance, namely, that we are gaining a definite mastery over the U-boat attack. In the second four weeks of war the British tonnage lost by enemy action—72,000 tons—was less than half the amount lost during the first four weeks; and against the loss we may set 52,000 tons captured from the enemy, 27,000 tons purchased from foreigners, and 57,000 tons of new-built ships, leaving in these four weeks a net gain of 64,000 tons. During the first eight weeks of war our net loss of tonnage has been less than one-third of 1 per cent. This, of course, takes no account of the important chartering operations from neutrals which are in progress. It is interesting to note that one of the most valuable of recent prizes was captured from the enemy by the *Ark Royal,* which the German wireless has sunk so many times. When I recall the absurd claims which they are accustomed to shout around the world, I cannot resist saying we should be quite content to engage the entire German Navy, using only the vessels which at one time or another they have declared they have destroyed.

A not less favorable balance is presented when we turn from the tonnage of ships to that of cargo. More than 10,000,000 tons of cargo were brought into this country in British and neutral ships in the first eight weeks of the war; less than a quarter of a million tons have been lost. But over 400,000 tons of cargo consigned to Germany have been captured, and, even taking into account 50,000 tons of exports which were lost, there remains a balance of over 100,000 tons in our favor.

But here again I must make a qualification. The institution of the convoy system, which is proving so good a protection, imposes a delay upon the movement of shipping which is in fact a reduction of its carrying capacity. These delays will be greatly diminished as the system comes into full use and habit, and the first two months while all is being organized afford no true measure of the degree of restriction which convoys impose. Moreover, in these two months we have been withdrawing several hundreds of our largest merchant vessels in order to give them their defensive armaments, and this is still going on. I hope, therefore, for still better results in the future and for an increasing diminution up to a certain point of the inevitable delays which follow from convoy, from zigzagging and from traversing the oceans by wide and unexpected routes. When we contemplate the difficulty of carrying on in full activity our vast processes of commerce, and the need of being prepared at a hundred points and on a thousand occasions in the teeth of the kind of severe attack to which we are being subjected, I feel that credit is due to the many thousands of persons who, in every quarter of the globe, are contributing to the achievement, and especially to the central machinery and direction which is in fact holding the seas free, as they have never been at any time in any war in which we have been engaged.

Now I turn to the offensive against the U-boats. It is very difficult to give assured figures, because many a marauder who is sunk in deep water leaves no trace behind. There must be a doubt and dispute about every case in which we have not a survivor, or a corpse, or a wreck to show. But I think it would be a fairly sound conservative estimate that the losses of U-boats lie between two and four in every week, according to the activity which prevails. Of course, when many are out there are more losses to commerce and more U-boats are killed. On the other side, however, there is a factor which has to be considered. I have not hitherto mentioned to the House the German building. We must assume that perhaps two new U-boats are added every week to the hostile strength, and in 10 weeks of war this would be 20. At any rate, our expectation is that we must face a hundred U-boats available in January, less whatever sinkings have occurred in the interval, which is a matter that cannot now be predicted. It will be seen, therefore, that, although we are making headway, a long and unrelenting struggle lies before us. For this our preparations are moving forward on the largest scale. Three times as many hunting craft are now at work as at the outbreak of the war, and very large reinforcements of vessels, specially adapted to this task, will flow increasingly from the spring of 1940 onwards. Therefore, it would seem that, judged upon the material basis alone, we may face the future with confidence.

But, as I have reminded the House earlier in the Session, it is not only the material basis which will decide this struggle. Training the crews and especially providing the skilled officers will be the hardest part of the enemy's task. Moreover, a conflict from which, perhaps, one in four of each excursion never returns, and the others with grievous experiences, is one which must have in it many deterrent factors. We are exposed to a form of attack justly considered abominable, but we are making successful headway against it. I must warn the House that continual losses must be expected. No immunity can be guaranteed at any time. There will not be in this war any period when the seas will be completely safe; but neither will there be, I believe, any period when the full necessary traffic of the Allies cannot be carried on. We shall suffer and we shall suffer continuously; but by perseverance, and by taking measures on the largest scale, I feel no doubt that in the end we shall break their hearts.

In addition to the U-boat menace we have to face the attack of the surface raider. It is certain that one and possibly two of the so-called pocket battleships has been out upon the Atlantic trade routes during the last six weeks. My hon. Friend the Member for Plaistow [Mr. Thorne] asked me the other day whether any attempt was being made to pursue them. I hope that my hon. Friend will not be shocked if I say that the answer is in the affirmative. But what is remarkable is that although these powerful vessels have been lying athwart the stream of convoys and the individual vessels crossing the Atlantic they have not been able, or have not dared, so far—and I speak under the greatest reserve—to make any captures worth considering. Only two ships aggregating 10,000 tons have been sunk so far by surface action, compared with 212,000 by the U-boats. Of course, in the vast ocean it is only when a victim is struck down that any trace of the attacker is revealed. When we remember how seriously the outbreak of these surface raiders was viewed before the war began, it is a matter of some reassurance that they have been at large for a considerable time without any appreciable damage or inconvenience to our trade. On the other hand, let me again strike the note of warning, because the element of risk is never absent from us any more than it is from the raiding enemy. But up to the present not only has the U-boat campaign been controlled, but also the attack by surface raiders both by warships or by armed merchantmen has not developed in any serious way.

At this point I must speak of the remarkable contribution of the French Navy, which has not for many generations been so powerful or so efficient. Under the long care of Admiral Darlan and M. Campinchi, the Minister of Marine, a magnificent fighting and seafaring force has been developed. Not only have we been assisted in every way agreed upon before the war, but besides a whole set of burdens have been lifted off our shoulders by the loyal and ever-increasingly vigorous co-operation of the French Fleet. It seems to me a wonderful thing that when France is making so great an effort upon land she should at the same time offer to the Allied cause so powerful a reinforcement by sea.

The House must not underrate the extreme exertions that are required from our sailors and our officers, both in the Royal Navy and in the Merchant Service, in carrying forward almost uninterruptedly the whole world-wide business of British and Allied commerce. Happily the reinforcements which are coming to the Fleets and to the flotillas will give an easement which is greatly needed, both by men and machinery. We must indeed pay our tribute both to the composure and coolness with which risks are taken and warded off in the great ships, and to the hitherto unexhausted energy of the flotilla service. At the Admiralty we are now in a position to consider some mitigation of these severe conditions; and without indulging in any over-confident opinion, I feel after the ninth week of the war that, so far as the sea is concerned—and the sea has often proved decisive in the end—we may cherish good hopes that all will be well.

TEN WEEKS OF WAR

An Address Broadcast

November 12, 1939

1939

November 8.   Reported attempt on the life of Herr Hitler in the Bürger-
brau cellar at Munich.

November 10.   Finland and Russia reach a deadlock.

TEN WEEKS OF WAR

I THOUGHT it would be a good thing for me to tell you now how well the war has turned for the Allies during the first ten weeks. It is quite plain that the power of the British Empire and the French Republic to restore and revive the life of the Polish, Czech and Slovak peoples, as well as to do a few other things which I will mention later, has been growing every day. Peaceful Parliamentary countries, which aim at freedom for the individual and abundance for the mass, start with a heavy handicap against a dictatorship whose sole theme has been war, the preparation for war, and the grinding up of everything and everybody into its military machine. In our Island particularly we are very easy-going in time of peace. We should like to share the blessings of peace with every nation; and to go on enjoying them ourselves. It is only after many vain attempts to remain at peace that we have been at last forced to go to war. We tried again and again to prevent this war, and for the sake of peace we put up with a lot of things happening which ought not to have happened. But now we are at war, and we are going to make war, and persevere in making war, until the other side have had enough of it. We are going to persevere as far as we can to the best of our ability; which is not small and is always growing.

You know I have not always agreed with Mr. Chamberlain; though we have always been personal friends. But he is a man of very tough fiber, and I can tell you that he is going to fight as obstinately for victory as he did for peace. You may take it absolutely for certain that either all that Britain and France stand for in the modern world will go down, or that Hitler, the Nazi regime and the recurring German or Prussian menace to Europe will be broken and destroyed. That is the way the matter lies and everybody had better make up his mind to that solid, somber fact.

Nowadays we are assailed by a chorus of horrid threats. The Nazi Government exudes through every neutral State inside information of the frightful vengeance they are going to wreak upon us, and they also bawl it around the world by their leather-lunged propaganda machine. If words could kill, we should be dead already. But we are not disturbed by these blood-curdling threats. Indeed, we take them as a sign of weakness in our foes. We do not make threats in time of war. If at any time we should have some ideas of an offensive character, we should not talk about them; we should try to see how they worked out in action.

We do not at all underrate the power and malignity of our enemies. We are prepared to endure tribulation. But we made up our minds about all this ten weeks ago, and everything that has happened since has made us feel that we were right then and are still right now. No one in the British Islands supposed this was going to be a short or easy war. Nothing has ever impressed me so much as the calm, steady, business-like resolution with which the masses of our wage-earning folk and ordinary people in our great cities faced what they imagined would be a fearful storm about to fall on them and their families at the very first moment. They all prepared themselves to have the worst happen to them at once, and they braced themselves for the ordeal. They did not see what else there was to do.

We have been agreeably surprised that ten weeks have been allotted to us to get into fighting trim. We are in a very different position from what we were ten weeks ago. We are far stronger than we were ten weeks ago; we are far better prepared to endure the worst malice of Hitler and his Huns than we were at the beginning of September. Our Navy is stronger. Our anti-U-boat forces are three times as numerous. Our Air Force is much stronger. Our Army is growing in numbers and improving in training every day. Our Air Raid Precautions are very different from what they were at the outbreak of war. The attack of the U-boats has been controlled and they have paid a heavy toll. Nearly all the German ocean-going ships are in hiding and rusting in neutral harbors, while our world-wide trade steadily proceeds in 4,000 vessels, of which 2,500 are constantly at sea.

The superior quality of our Air Force has been proved both in pilots and machines over the enemy. Our aircraft shot down fifteen German oversea raiders, without losing one machine in the combats. Now the

mists and storms of winter wrap our Island and make continuous bombing attack of military objectives far more difficult. We have a marked
advantage in the higher range of science applied to war, and this is
improving with every week that passes.

I do not doubt myself that time is on our side. I go so far as to say
that if we come through the winter without any large or important event
occurring we shall in fact have gained the first campaign of the war:
and we shall be able to set about our task in the spring far stronger,
better organized and better armed than ever before. Let us therefore bear
discomfort and many minor—and even perhaps needless—vexations with
comprehending patience, because we are all the time moving forward
towards greater war strength, and because Germany is all the time, under
the grip of our economic warfare, falling back in oil and other essential
war supplies.

It may be, of course, that at any time violent and dire events will open.
If so, we shall confront them with resolution. If not, we shall profit to
the full by the time at our disposal. But Field-Marshal Goering—who is
one of the few Germans who has been having a pretty good time for the
last few years—says that we have been spared so far because Nazi Germany is so humane. They cannot bear to do anything to hurt anybody.
All they ask for is the right to live and to be let alone to conquer and kill
the weak. Their humanity forbids them to apply severities to the strong.
It may be true: but when we remember the bestial atrocities they have
committed in Poland, we do not feel we wish to ask for any favors to be
shown us. We shall do our duty as long as we have life and strength.

A long succession of important events has moved in our favor since
the beginning of the war. Italy, which we had feared would be drawn
from her historic partnership with Britain and France in the Mediterranean—a partnership which will become increasingly fruitful—has
adopted a wise policy of peace. No quarrel has developed between us
and Japan. These two great Powers, which had joined Nazi Germany
in the Anti-Comintern Pact, find it difficult to accommodate themselves
to the change of front towards Bolshevism which Herr Hitler and his
bad adviser, Herr von Ribbentrop—that prodigious contortionist—have
perpetrated. No one can underrate the importance of the Treaty of
Alliance between Britain and France with Turkey. The Russian Soviet
Government, embodied in the formidable figure of Stalin, has barred off
once and for ever all Nazi dreams of an advance in the east. The left
paw of the Bear bars Germany from the Black Sea; the right paw

disputes with her the control of the Baltic. Whatever history may record about these events, the fact which we have to reckon with is perfectly plain. Nazi Germany is barred off from the east, and has to conquer the British Empire and the French Republic or perish in the attempt.

So now these boastful and bullying Nazis are looking with hungry eyes for some small countries in the west which they can trample down and loot, as they have trampled down and looted Austria, Czechoslovakia and Poland. Now they turn their fierce, but also rather circumspect, glare upon the ancient, civilized and unoffending Dutch and Belgian nations. They have not chosen to molest the British Fleet, which has awaited their attack in the Firth of Forth during the last week; they recoil from the steel front of the French Army along the Maginot Line; but their docile conscripts are being crowded in vast numbers upon the frontiers of Holland and Belgium. To both these States the Nazis have given the most recent and solemn guarantees; no wonder anxiety is great. No one believes one word Herr Hitler and the Nazi Party say, and therefore we must regard that situation as grave.

I shall not attempt to prophesy whether the frenzy of a cornered maniac will drive Herr Hitler into the worst of all his crimes; but this I will say without a doubt: that the fate of Holland and Belgium, like that of Poland, Czechoslovakia and Austria, will be decided by the victory of the British Empire and the French Republic. If we are conquered, all will be enslaved, and the United States will be left single-handed to guard the rights of man. If we are not destroyed, all these countries will be rescued and restored to life and freedom.

It is indeed a solemn moment when I speak to you on this tenth Sunday after the outbreak of war. But it is also a moment sustained by resolve and hope. I am in the singular position of having lived through the early months of the last German war upon Europe in the same position, in charge of the British Admiralty, as I am now. I am therefore very careful not to say anything of an over-confident or unduly sanguine nature. I am sure we have very rough weather ahead; but I have this feeling: that the Germany which assaults us all today is a far less strongly built and solidly founded organism than that which the Allies and the United States forced to beg for armistice twenty-one years ago. I have the sensation and also the conviction that that evil man over there and his cluster of confederates are not sure of themselves, as we are sure of ourselves; that they are harassed in their guilty souls by the thought and by the fear of an ever-approaching retribution for their crimes, and for the orgy of destruction in which they have plunged us all. As they look out tonight from their blatant, panoplied, clattering Nazi Germany, they cannot find one single friendly eye in the whole circumference of the globe. Not one! Russia returns them a flinty stare; Italy averts her gaze; Japan is puzzled and thinks herself betrayed. Turkey and the whole of Islam have ranged themselves instinctively but decisively on the side of progress. The hundreds of millions of people in India and in China, whatever their other feelings, would regard with undisguised dread a Nazi triumph, well knowing what their fate would soon be. The great English-speaking Republic across the Atlantic Ocean makes no secret of its sympathies or of its self-questionings, and translates these sentiments into actions of a character which anyone may judge for himself. The whole world is against Hitler and Hitlerism. Men of every race and clime feel that this monstrous apparition stands between them and the forward move which is their due, and for which the age is ripe. Even in Germany itself there are millions who stand aloof from the seething mass of criminality and corruption constituted by the Nazi Party machine. Let them take courage amid perplexities and perils, for it may well be that the final extinction of a baleful domination will pave the way to a broader solidarity of all the men in all the lands than we could ever have planned if we had not marched together through the fire.

TRAFFIC AT SEA

The House of Commons

December 6, 1939

November 13. German raiders drop bombs on the Shetlands—the first to fall on British soil.

November 17. In the South African elections General Smuts is returned with a large majority in favor of fighting by Britain's side.

November 21. Great Britain announces that as a reprisal for Germany's breaches of Sea Law she will seize all German exports.

November 26. The *Rawalpindi*, British armed merchant cruiser, is sunk in the North Atlantic by the pocket battleship *Deutschland*.

November 28. Russia denounces her Pact of Non-Aggression with Finland.

November 30. Russia invades Finland.

TRAFFIC AT SEA

THE MAIN attack of the enemy has so far been concentrated upon the Royal Navy and the sea-borne commerce upon which the British Islands and British Empire depend. We have always, as I reminded the House the other day, considerably more than 2,000 ships at sea, and between 100 and 150 ships move every day in and out of our harbors in the United Kingdom alone. This immense traffic has to be maintained in the teeth of a constant U-boat attack, which never hesitates to break the conventions of civilized warfare to which Germany has so recently subscribed. We have also been frequently attacked from the air. Mining on a large scale has been practiced against us; and latterly magnetic mines have been dropped from aeroplanes or laid by submarines on the approaches to our harbors, with the intention of destroying British, and still more, apparently, neutral commerce. These mines have been laid contrary to the accepted rules of sea warfare and of specific German engagements in regard to them. Besides this, two of the so-called "pocket" battleships, and certainly one other cruiser, have been loose for many weeks in the North and South Atlantic, or near Madagascar in the Indian Ocean.

The Admiralty task has been to bring in our immense world-wide traffic in spite of this opposition. Besides this, we have to cleanse the seas of all German commerce, and to arrest every German vessel and every scrap of cargo in which Germany is interested. Broadly speaking, as I shall presently show, these considerable duties have, up to the present, been successfully discharged. The destruction of the U-boats is proceeding normally, and in accordance with the estimate I gave to the House of between two and four a week, that is to say, at a rate superior to what we believe to be the German power of replacing U-boats and of replacing the competently trained U-boat captains and crews. When I see statements, as I have done lately, that the Germans during 1940 will have as many as 400 U-boats in commission, and that they are producing these vessels by what is called "the chain-belt system," I wonder if they are producing the U-boat captains and crews by a similar method. If so, it seems likely that our rate of destruction might well undergo a similar expansion.

Enterprise and daring have been shown by U-boat commanders, who seek to emulate the exploit of Scapa Flow by penetrating into our defended harbors, and several graves of U-boats lie upon their approaches. The rate of destructions varies, of course, with the number of U-boats which are actively hunting. This fluctuates from time to time, and we have noticed three periods of maximum activity, interspersed with periods of minimum activity, when, presumably, the bulk of the raiders return home for rest and refreshment. In the last week they have been active, and we are inclined to think that five certainly have met their fate, either from our flotillas or from the ardent, skillful and invaluable co-operation of the Royal Air Force and particularly of the Coastal Command. These figures are, of course, independent of any results achieved by the French Navy.

Nevertheless, this struggle proceeds upon a margin which, though adequate, is not extravagant; and when we consider the possibility, as we always must, of some unexpected development of numbers by the enemy, it is a comfort to feel that very great reinforcements to our hunting craft in home waters, which have already been tripled since the beginning of the war, will come into service during 1940. I must again repeat the warning which I gave to the House in September: that a steady flow of losses must be expected, that occasional disasters will occur, and that any failure upon our part to act up to the level of circumstances would immediately be attended by grave dangers. It is, however, my sure belief that we are getting the better of this menace to our life. We are buffeted by the waves, but the ocean tides flow steady and strong in our favor.

In the course of this war the U-boats have tended to turn from using the gun to using the torpedo, and from summoning ships on the surface to sinking them at sight without warning or provision for the crews. This carries them into a form of warfare at once more ruthless and at the same time far less effective. The underwater attack by torpedo can only be delivered at a quarter of the speed that it is possible for a U-boat to move on the surface, and the chances of their intercepting ships or convoys are, therefore, greatly reduced. In addition to our armed merchant cruisers we have armed already more than a thousand merchant ships for self-defensive purposes, and this process is continuing with all possible speed. It will not be long before we shall have two thousand vessels so armed. These merchant ships, in accordance with the oldest rights of the sea, fire back when they are attacked. The merchant captains and seamen show a resolute disposition to defend themselves, and many duels are fought in which the U-boat, fearing to be damaged, and thus to be unable to dive, gives up the attack and is beaten off. The efficacy of the Asdic method of detection is increasingly proved, and as our margin in hunting craft increases, as it has done and will do rapidly, the ordeal to which the U-boat is subjected will become ever more severe.

The convoy system is now in full operation. Very few ships have been attacked in convoy; less than one in 750 has been sunk. Nevertheless, we must remember that convoy involves a certain definite loss of carrying power, since the ships have to wait during the assembly of the convoy, and the convoy must travel at the speed of the slowest ship. This loss is being steadily reduced by the institution of slow and fast convoys, and by other appropriate measures; but a certain delay must always remain, a certain diminution, that is to say, in the actual fertility of our convoys.

In consequence of our defense and the defense of our merchant ships, the U-boats have found it easier to attack neutral shipping than to attack the vessels of Britain and France. They prefer increasingly to attack the ships of countries with whom they are at peace, rather than those of the countries with whom they are at war. The figures are remarkable. The losses of British merchant ships in October were half what they were in September, and in November they were only two-thirds of what they were in October. There has been a strong and steady diminution of loss among all ships obeying Admiralty directions or joining our convoys. Quite the contrary has been the case with the neutrals. They lost half as much again in the second month as they did in the first, and double as much in the third month of the war as they did in the second. It is indeed, as the Prime Minister said the other day, a strange war—it is a strange kind of warfare for the German Navy to engage in, when, driven off the shipping of their declared enemy, they console themselves by running amok among the shipping of neutral nations. This fact ought to encourage neutrals to charter their ships to Great Britain for the duration of the war, when they can be sure of making larger profits than they have ever made in peace, and have a complete guarantee against loss. The Ministry of Shipping have already arranged the charter of several millions of tonnage, and it seems probable that this healthy process will continue, to mutual and even to general advantage.

In the last few weeks the German U-boats, having largely abandoned the gun for the torpedo, have descended from the torpedo to the mine. This is about the lowest form of warfare that can be imagined. It is the warfare of the I.R.A., leaving the bomb in the parcels office at the railway station. The magnetic mine, deposited secretly by the U-boat under the cloak of darkness in the approaches to our harbors, or dropped by parachutes from aircraft, may perhaps be Herr Hitler's much-vaunted secret weapon. It is certainly a characteristic weapon, and one that will no doubt be for ever associated with his name. More than half our losses in the last month have been due to the magnetic mine, but two-thirds of the total losses from the use of this mine have fallen not upon belligerents but upon neutrals. In fact, in the third month of the war, neutral losses by mine have been twice as great as British losses, and neutral losses of all kinds have been one-third greater than belligerent losses. These losses have fallen upon Swedish, Norwegian, Danish, Belgian, Finnish, Yugoslav, Dutch, Greek, Italian and Japanese vessels, who have had to pay a heavy toll for remaining in friendly relations with Germany. So far as the sea war is concerned, German friendship has proved far more poisonous than German enmity.

The magnetic mine is neither new nor mysterious. As the Prime Minister announced in his broadcast, its secrets are known to us. Indeed, the preparation of counter-measures was already far advanced before the first magnetic mine was laid in British waters. I do not wish, however, in any way to underrate the magnitude or intensity of the effort which will be required and is now forthcoming to cope with this latest manifestation of Nazi culture. Many variants are being developed and applied, and as an interim measure, before the full scientific treatment can be given to this procedure, we have found it necessary to call upon a large number of trawlers to assist in the dredging of our harbors. The service of minesweeping is one of peculiar danger and one calculated to try the strongest nerves because of the silence and constant uncertainty of destruction in which those who engage in it must dwell. The fact of this serious danger was sufficient to bring forward an overwhelming response from the fishermen, the trawler crews, when called upon to come to their country's assistance. Offices when they opened on the Saturday night at some of the fishing ports were thronged and had to be kept open all night and on the Sunday, and in a very short time a full complement was made up of these fisher folk, eager to serve their country in a manner which they felt would be really effective.

The recklessness of this latest attack upon neutrals, and the breach of international agreements which it involves, have led us to place a retaliatory embargo upon the export of all goods of German ownership or origin. This measure was taken in the late war, when it worked with surprising smoothness and efficiency. German oversea exporting power was rapidly destroyed, and with it perished all power of building up new credits abroad. No serious inconvenience need be caused to neutrals. They have only to avoid carrying tainted goods in their ships, and they can easily obtain a certificate from the British Consular officers in neutral countries, which will enable them to proceed upon their outward voyages without interference or delay from us. It is satisfactory to learn that goods for export are already piling up on the German quays and in their warehouses to such an extent that, we are told, they hamper the handling of incoming merchandise. This latter congestion will, however, be relieved as our blockade tightens through the growing strength of our patrolling and blockading squadrons.

A strident effort has been made by German propaganda to persuade the world that we have laid these magnetic mines ourselves in the fairways of our own harbors, in order, apparently, to starve ourselves out. When this inanity expired amid general derision, the alternative claim was made that the sinking of the neutrals by mine was another triumph of German science and seamanship, and should convince all nations that the German mastery of the seas was complete. This claim may be tested by a general survey of the results of the first three months of war. We began the war with 21 million tons of merchant shipping. This figure, of course, includes ships on the Great Lakes of North America, and a number of very small coastal vessels. Out of this total we have lost during the three months in which we have been subject to severe and concentrated attack by all kinds of methods, fair and foul, by U-boat, by mine, by surface raider, and by the hazards of the sea, about 340,000 tons. Against this we have gained by transfer from foreign flags, independent of the large chartering operations to which I have referred, by prizes taken from the enemy, and by the new vessels we are building on a very large scale, about 280,000 tons, leaving a net loss of about 60,000 tons.

We should have to go back to the Hundred Years' War in order to provide sufficient time and scope for inroads of this degree to make any serious impression upon the scale of our Mercantile Marine. For every

1,000 tons of British shipping sunk, 110,000 tons have entered or left the ports of this threatened Island, which we are told upon the enemy's authority is beleaguered and beset on all sides, in the first three months of war. In the month of November, nearly a quarter of a million tons of our shipping entered or cleared from our harbors for every 1,000 tons lost, a proportion of 250 to one. If the House feels that these facts are reassuring and worthy of acknowledgment, their debt is due to the officers and men of the Royal Navy and of the Merchant Service, and also, in increasing measure, to their comrades of the Royal Air Force, as well as to our Allies, the French, about whom I spoke on the last occasion, and to the small though highly efficient Polish flotillas which have lent us their aid.

The losses which have fallen upon the protecting warships of the Royal Navy are necessarily heavier in proportion than those which affect the Mercantile Marine. His Majesty's warships run greater risks as, unlike merchant ships, they have to seek the enemy wherever he may be. The Navy has never been so many days at sea each month as in this war, and it has been plying in the most dangerous waters. The price for sea control must be paid. It is often heavy. We have made a rule to publish all losses of British warships by enemy action, at the earliest moment after it has been possible to inform the relatives of the survivors. There has been no exception to this rule. We do not publish damage to His Majesty's ships unless this becomes widely known, or is certainly known to the enemy. These ships can be repaired very often within a few weeks, and there is not the slightest reason why we should be at pains to inform the enemy of matters which he cannot find out for himself, but greatly desires to know. We have lost, in these three months of war, two great ships, the *Courageous* and the *Royal Oak,* two destroyers, and the submarine which was blown up by accident—in all, about 50,000 tons. We have at present building, much of it in an advanced stage, nearly 1,000,000 tons of warships of all classes. We have also lost one of our fifty armed merchant cruisers, the *Rawalpindi,* whose glorious fight against overwhelming odds deserves the respect and honor of the House and of the nation.

However, our losses in warships during the first three months of war of 1914 were more than double those we have now suffered. Of course war is full of ugly and unpleasant surprises. No one must indulge in easy habits of mind, or relax for one moment the vigilant attention to the fortunes of the State, and that fearless desire to measure the rea facts and understand them and master them, which are incumbent upon all citizens, and still more upon their Parliamentary representatives. If I have given this afternoon facts and figures of reassurance, it is only because the House and the nation can alike be trusted to use these good tidings only as a stimulus and fortification to the much greater efforts which will be certainly required from us as this fierce and obstinate conflict rises to its full height. We have the means, and we have the opportunity, of marshaling the whole vast strength of the British Empire, and of the Mother Country, and directing these steadfastly and unswervingly to the fulfillment of our purpose and the vindication of our cause; and for each and for all, as for the Royal Navy, the watchword should be, "Carry on, and dread nought."

THE BATTLE OF THE PLATE

An Address Broadcast

December 18, 1939

1939

December 12.   Russia rejects the League of Nations' offer of mediation in the Finnish War.

December 13.   The German pocket battleship *Graf Spee* engaged in the South Atlantic by H.M.S. *Exeter*, *Ajax* and *Achilles*, and driven into the River Plate.

December 15.   The *Graf Spee* refuels and begins repairs.

               The Finns wreck and abandon the nickel mines at Salmijärvi.

December 17.   The *Graf Spee* is scuttled outside Montevideo.

THE BATTLE OF THE PLATE

THE NEWS which has come from Montevideo has been received with thankfulness in our island, and with unconcealed satisfaction throughout the greater part of the world. The pocket battleship *Graf Spee,* which has for many weeks been preying upon the trade of the South Atlantic, has met her doom, and throughout a vast expanse of water peaceful shipping of all nations may, for a spell at least, enjoy the freedom of the seas.

The end of the raider came in the form most serviceable to those who have taken up arms in accordance with the Covenant of the League, and to all adherents of the cause of law and freedom in every land. The German pocket battleship, in spite of her far heavier metal and commanding range, was driven to take refuge in a neutral harbor by the three British cruisers whose names are on every lip. Once in harbor she had the choice of submitting in the ordinary manner to internment, which would have been unfortunate for her, or of coming out to fight and going down in battle, like the *Rawalpindi,* which would have been honorable to her. She discovered a third alternative. She came out, not to fight, but to sink herself in the fairway of a neutral State from whom she had received such shelter and succor as international law prescribes. At that time the pocket battleship *Graf Spee* knew that the British heavy ships *Renown* and *Ark Royal* were still a thousand miles away, oiling at Rio. All that awaited her outside the harbor were the two six-inch gun cruisers, the *Ajax* and *Achilles,* who had chased her in, and the eight-inch gun cruiser *Cumberland,* which had arrived to take the place of the damaged *Exeter.*

Our own losses have not been slight. There is no harm now in stating that the *Ajax,* in which was Commodore Harwood, now by His Majesty's pleasure Rear-Admiral Sir Henry Harwood, K.C.B., had two out of her four turrets knocked out; while the *Exeter* bore up against forty to fifty hits, many of them from shells three times the weight of those she could fire back, that three of her eight-inch guns were smashed, and that she sustained nearly a hundred casualties, by far the greater part killed. Nevertheless, the *Exeter* remained outside the harbor of Montevideo ready, although crippled, to take part in a fresh action, and she only departed to care for her wounded and her injuries when she was relieved by the timely arrival of the *Cumberland*.

Here at home in the North Sea, our British submarines have had the best week I can remember in this or the last war. British submarines suffer from the serious disadvantage that they have very few targets to attack. They are not allowed, by the custom of the sea and by the conventions to which we have subscribed, to sink merchant ships without warning, or without being able to provide for the safety of the merchant crews. British submarines do not wage war on neutral vessels. They do not attack humble fishing boats. They have to work for the most part among the minefields within the strongly defended waters of the Heligoland Bight. It is only when a German warship is sighted that they are able to use their power and skill. The German warships hardly ever venture out of port, and then only for furtive dashes. Consequently, the exploits of His Majesty's submarine *Salmon* last week are remarkable and praiseworthy in the highest degree.

First, she blew to pieces, by a volley of torpedoes, one of the largest German U-boats, which was going out upon a raiding foray. Secondly, she rightly abstained from torpedoing the *Bremen* when that enormous ship was at her mercy. Her third encounter was the most important. On Thursday last she observed through her periscope the German Fleet proceeding to sea on one of its rare excursions. She fired six torpedoes at the cruiser squadron which was accompanying the German battlecruisers, and she hit one 6,000-ton cruiser with one torpedo, and a second cruiser of equal size with two. These cruisers may have been able to limp home, though that is by no means certain in the case of one of them, and when they have reached home they will be out of action for many a long month. Meanwhile, the entire German Fleet abandoned whatever enterprise they had in view and returned in haste and dudgeon to the harbors they had so recently quitted. Now today, His Majesty's submarine *Ursula* reports that on the fourteenth she sank a 6,000-ton cruiser of the *Koeln* class, although it was surrounded by no fewer than six German destroyers. Thus, a considerable proportion of the total German cruiser strength had been sunk or put out of action in a single week, and that the same week in which, on almost the other side of the globe, the pocket battleship *Graf Spee* met her inglorious end.

The Nazi Navy and Air Force are venting their wrath for these heavy blows by redoubling their efforts to sink the fishing-smacks and drown the fishermen in the North Sea; and all yesterday and today their Air Force has been trying to bomb individual unarmed merchant ships, including an Italian ship, which were moving up and down the east coast of Britain. I am glad to tell you, however, that the heat of their fury has far exceeded the accuracy of their aim. Out of twenty-four ships attacked by bombs yesterday and today, only six small boats engaged in fishing and one small coasting vessel have been sunk, and the bulk of the others, including the Italian, have not even been hit.

Now that several successes have been achieved by the Royal Navy, I take the opportunity of drawing the attention of the public to the fact that the present satisfactory position in the naval war is due to the care and conduct of operations by the First Sea Lord, Admiral of the Fleet Sir Dudley Pound, and also to the Naval Staff at the Admiralty, of whom Rear-Admiral Phillips is the Deputy Chief. Although from time to time a success is recorded, it must not be forgotten that risks are being run all over the world in the protection of trade and for the control of the seas, and that preparations have to be made in many quarters, most of which are never needed, and consequently never see the light of day. The Commander-in-Chief of the Main Fleet, Admiral Sir Charles Forbes, has from the beginning of the war maintained the strong guard required in the Atlantic and the North Sea, keeping his ships almost constantly at sea under continued menace of U-boats, aircraft and mines. The Main Fleet has been more days at sea since this war began than has ever been required in any equal period of modern naval war. These responsibilities could not have been discharged if the professional skill of the Admiral had not been sustained by unwearied vigilance and a buoyancy of spirit in the face of many dangers.

But after all, no leadership or expert naval direction could be successful unless it were supported by the whole body of officers and men of the Navy. It is upon these faithful, trusty servants in the great ships and cruisers that the burden falls directly day after day. In particular, the flotillas of destroyers, of submarines watching the throat of the Elbe, of anti-submarine craft, of mine-sweepers multiplying on all our coasts—all these have undergone, and are undergoing, a toil and strain which only those who are informed in detail, can understand. Many vexatious tasks lie before the Royal Navy and before its comrades in the Merchant Navy, and, as I always warn you, rough and violent times lie ahead, but everything that has happened since the beginning of this war should give the nation confidence that in the end the difficulties will be surmounted, the problems solved, and duty done.

A HOUSE OF MANY MANSIONS

An Address Broadcast

January 20, 1940

1939

December 19. The 32,000-ton German liner *Columbus* scuttled.
    Captain Hans Langsdorff, commander of the *Graf Spee,* shoots himself.

December 21. The Finns counter-attack on the narrow "waist-line" front.

December 27. Disastrous earthquake in Anatolia.

1940

January 5. Mr. Hore-Belisha is succeeded in the office of Secretary of State for War by Mr. Oliver Stanley. Sir Andrew Duncan becomes President of the Board of Trade, and Sir John Reith Minister of Information.

January 6-11. At Suomussalmi the Finns annihilate the Russian 44th Division.

A HOUSE OF MANY MANSIONS

EVERYONE wonders what is happening about the war. For several months past the Nazis have been uttering ferocious threats of what they are going to do to the Western Democracies—to the British and French Empires— when once they set about them. But so far it is the small neutral States that are bearing the brunt of German malice and cruelty. Neutral ships are sunk without law or mercy—not only by the blind and wanton mine, but by the coldly considered, deliberately aimed, torpedo. The Dutch, the Belgians, the Danes, the Swedes, and, above all, the Norwegians, have their ships destroyed whenever they can be caught upon the high seas. It is only in the British and French convoys that safety is to be found. There, in those convoys, it is five-hundred-to-one against being sunk. There, controlling forces are at work which are steadily keeping the seas open, steadily keeping the traffic going, and establishing order and free-dom of movement amid the waves of anarchy and sea-murder.

We, the aggrieved and belligerent Powers who are waging war against Germany, have no need to ask for respite. Every week our commerce grows; every month our organization is improved and reinforced. We feel ourselves more confident day by day of our ability to police the seas and oceans and to keep open and active the salt-water highways by which we live, and along which we shall draw the means of victory. It seems pretty certain that half the U-boats with which Germany began the war have been sunk, and that their new building has fallen far behind what we expected. Our faithful Asdic detector smells them out in the depths of the sea and, with the potent aid of the Royal Air Force, do not doubt that we shall break their strength and break their pur-pose.

The magnetic mine, and all the other mines with which the narrow waters, the approaches to this Island, are strewn, do not present us with any problem which we deem insoluble. It must be remembered that in the last war we suffered very grievous losses from mines, and that at the climax more than six hundred British vessels were engaged solely upon the task of mine-sweeping. We must remember that. We must always be expecting some bad thing from Germany, but I will venture to say that it is with growing confidence that we await the further developments or variants of their attack.

Here we are, after nearly five months of all they can do against us on the sea, with the first U-boat campaign for the first time being utterly broken, with the mining menace in good control, with our shipping virtually undiminished, and with all the oceans of the world free from surface raiders. It is true that the *Deutschland* escaped the clutches of our cruisers by the skin of her teeth, but the *Spee* still sticks up in the harbor of Montevideo as a grisly monument and as a measure of the fate in store for any Nazi warship which dabbles in piracy on the broad waters. As you know, I have always—after some long and hard experience—spoken with the utmost restraint and caution about the war at sea, and I am quite sure that there are many losses and misfortunes which lie ahead of us there; but in all humility and self-questioning I feel able to declare that at the Admiralty, as, I have no doubt, at the French Ministry of Marine, things are not going so badly after all. Indeed, they have never gone so well in any naval war. We look forward as the months go by to establishing such a degree of safe sailings as will enable the commerce of all the nations whose ships accept our guidance, not only to live but to thrive. This part—this sea affair—at least, of the Nazi attack upon freedom is not going to bar the path of justice or of retribution.

Very different is the lot of the unfortunate neutrals. Whether on sea or on land, they are the victims upon whom Hitler's hate and spite descend. Look at the group of small but ancient and historic States which lie in the North; or look again at that other group of anxious peoples in the Balkans or in the Danube basin behind whom stands the resolute Turk. Every one of them is wondering which will be the next victim on whom the criminal adventurers of Berlin will cast their rending stroke. A German major makes a forced landing in Belgium with plans for the invasion of that country whose neutrality Germany has so recently promised to respect. In Rumania there is deep fear lest by some deal between Moscow and Berlin they may become the next object of aggression. German intrigues are seeking to undermine the newly strengthened solidarity of the southern Slavs. The hardy Swiss arm and man their mountain passes. The Dutch—whose services to European freedom will be remembered long after the smear of Hitler has been wiped from the human path—stand along their dykes, as they did against the tyrants of bygone days. All Scandinavia dwells brooding under Nazi and Bolshevik threats.

Only Finland—superb, nay, sublime—in the jaws of peril—Finland shows what free men can do. The service rendered by Finland to mankind is magnificent. They have exposed, for all the world to see, the military incapacity of the Red Army and of the Red Air Force. Many illusions about Soviet Russia have been dispelled in these few fierce weeks of fighting in the Arctic Circle. Everyone can see how Communism rots the soul of a nation; how it makes it abject and hungry in peace, and proves it base and abominable in war. We cannot tell what the fate of Finland may be, but no more mournful spectacle could be presented to what is left to civilized mankind than that this splendid Northern race should be at last worn down and reduced to servitude worse than death by the dull brutish force of overwhelming numbers. If the light of freedom which still burns so brightly in the frozen North should be finally quenched, it might well herald a return to the Dark Ages, when every vestige of human progress during two thousand years would be engulfed.

But what would happen if all these neutral nations I have mentioned—and some others I have not mentioned—were with one spontaneous impulse to do their duty in accordance with the Covenant of the League, and were to stand together with the British and French Empires against aggression and wrong? At present their plight is lamentable; and it will become much worse. They bow humbly and in fear to German threats of violence, comforting themselves meanwhile with the thought that the Allies will win, that Britain and France will strictly observe all the laws and conventions, and that breaches of these laws are only to be expected from the German side. Each one hopes that if he feeds the crocodile enough, the crocodile will eat him last. All of them hope that the storm will pass before their turn comes to be devoured. But I fear—I fear greatly—the storm will not pass. It will rage and it will roar, ever more loudly, ever more widely. It will spread to the South; it will spread to the North. There is no chance of a speedy end except through united action; and if at any time Britain and France, wearying of the struggle, were to make a shameful peace, nothing would remain for the smaller States of Europe, with their shipping and their possessions, but to be divided between the opposite, though similar, barbarisms of Nazidom and Bolshevism.

The one thing that will be most helpful in determining the action of neutrals is their increasing sense of the power and resolution of the Western Allies. These small States are alarmed by the fact that the German armies are more numerous, and that their Air Force is still more numerous, and also that both are nearer to them than the forces of Great Britain and France. Certainly it is true that we are facing numerical odds; but that is no new thing in our history. Very few wars have been won by mere numbers alone. Quality, will power, geographical advantages, natural and financial resources, the command of the sea, and, above all, a cause which rouses the spontaneous surgings of the human spirit in millions of hearts—these have proved to be the decisive factors in the human story. If it were otherwise, how would the race of men have risen above the apes; how otherwise would they have conquered and extirpated dragons and monsters; how would they have ever evolved the moral theme; how would they have marched forward across the centuries to broad conceptions of compassion, of freedom, and of right? How would they ever have discerned those beacon lights which summon and guide us across the rough dark waters, and presently will guide us across the flaming lines of battle towards better days which lie beyond?

Numbers do not daunt us. But judged even by the test of numbers we have no reason to doubt that once the latent, and now rapidly growing, power of the British nation and Empire are brought, as they must be, and as they will be, fully into line with the magnificent efforts of the French Republic, then, even in mass and in weight, we shall not be found wanting. When we look behind the brazen fronts of Nazidom—as we have various means of doing—we see many remarkable signs of psychological and physical disintegration. We see the shortages of raw materials which already begin to hamper both the quality and the volume of their war industry. We feel the hesitancy of divided counsels, and the pursuing doubts which assail and undermine those who count on force and force alone.

In the bitter and increasingly exacting conflict which lies before us we are resolved to keep nothing back, and not to be outstripped by any in service to the common cause. Let the great cities of Warsaw, of Prague, of Vienna banish despair even in the midst of their agony. Their liberation is sure. The day will come when the joybells will ring again throughout Europe, and when victorious nations, masters not only of their foes but of themselves, will plan and build in justice, in tradition, and in freedom a house of many mansions where there will be room for all.

A TIME TO DARE AND ENDURE

The Free Trade Hall, Manchester

January 27, 1940

1940

January 20-26.   Russian assault north of Lake Ladoga, which eventually fails.

January 23.   The Chancellor of the Exchequer announces improvements in the Old Age Pensions system, introducing pensions for women at 60.

A TIME TO DARE AND ENDURE

WE HAVE been five months at war against the world's greatest military power and the world's greatest air power. When the war began in September most of us expected that very soon our cities would be torn and charred by explosion and fire, and few would have dared to plan for the end of January a splendid gathering such as I see before me here this afternoon. I know of nothing more remarkable in our long history than the willingness to encounter the unknown, and to face and endure whatever might be coming to us, which was shown in September by the whole mass of the people of this Island in the discharge of what they felt sure was their duty. There never was a war which seemed so likely to carry its terrors at once into every home, and there never was a war into which the whole people entered with the same united conviction that, God helping, they could do no other.

This was no war planned and entered upon by a Government, or a class, or a Party. On the contrary, the Government labored for peace to the very end; and during those last days the only fear in Britain was lest, weighted down by their awful responsibilities, they should fail to rise up to the height of the occasion. They did not fail, and the Prime Minister led us forward in one great body into a struggle against aggression and oppression, against wrong-doing, faithlessness and cruelty, from which there can be no turning back. We cannot tell what the course of that struggle will be, into what regions it will carry us, how long it will last, or who will fall by the way. But we are sure that in the end right will win, that freedom will not be trampled down, that a truer progress will open, and a broader justice will reign. And we are determined to play our part worthily, faithfully, and to the end.

So far the war in the west has fallen almost solely upon the Royal

Navy, and upon those parts of the Royal Air Force who give the Navy invaluable help. But I think you will agree that up to date the Navy has not failed the nation. Continual losses there have been, and continual losses there will be. When you remember that we have hundreds of war-ships always running risks upon the sea in order to protect thousands of British and neutral merchant ships spread about the vast ocean spaces of the globe, or crowding into our Island gateways, you will realize that we shall have to pay an unrelenting toll for the mastery of the seas. Many hundreds of Naval homes in our dockyard cities have been darkened by irreparable loss. I am sure the sympathy and affection of the British people goes out to our sailormen—Royal Navy, Merchant Marine, trawlers, mine-sweepers, fisherfolk, and all who love them and depend upon them as they toil day by day and night by night upon the dangerous stormy waters, doing their duty with unrivaled skill and with cheerful, unquestioning courage, that we may eat our daily bread each day, and that our cause may prosper.

Let no one therefore be disheartened when he reads of daily losses, or listens to them reiterated by the B.B.C. Let all remember that now, at the end of five months of vehement naval war, it is five hundred to one against any ship which obeys Admiralty instructions and joins a British convoy being sunk, and that out of nearly seven thousand five hundred ships convoyed, only fifteen have been lost; that our convoy system is becoming more refined and rapid as the weeks go by; that the volume of our imports and exports, inevitably checked by change from peace to war, is now steadily increasing; that the ships we have captured and the ships we have built have almost made good the losses we have suffered; and that very important reinforcements are approaching both our Navy and our merchant shipping to meet new dangers and new assaults which may very easily come upon us in the future.

We are embarking upon a widespread system of rationing. That is not because there is danger of famine or because the Navy has not done its part in keeping open the oceans, the seas and the harbors. We are ration-ing ourselves because we wish to save every ton of imports, to increase our output of munitions, and to maintain and extend our export trade, thus gaining the foreign credits wherewith to buy more munitions and more materials of war, in order that the whole life-energy of the British nation and of the British Empire, and of our Allies, may be directed to the last ounce, to the last inch, to the task we have in hand. This is no time for ease and comfort. It is the time to dare and endure. That is why we are rationing ourselves, even while our resources are expanding. That is why we mean to regulate every ton that is carried across the sea and make sure that it is carried solely for the purpose of victory.

But now on this question of food let me turn from the sea to the land, and from those who plow the main to those who plow, or should plow, the manor. In our national effort there is need for all kinds of activity, and there is room, or room must be found, for all—men and women, old and young—to serve in one way or another. We must plow up the land. We must organize agriculture, upon at least the 1918 scale. We must grow more food and accommodate ourselves as much as possible to eat the kind of food we can grow. The cost of living must, so far as possible, be kept down by abundance of simple food and necessaries. In this way we may lighten the task of the Navy, increase its mobility, and free its striking forces for offensive action.

I have no doubt that from time to time you ask yourselves the question: Why is it that we have not yet been attacked from the air? Why is it that those severe ordeals for which we had braced ourselves on the outbreak of war have not been imposed upon us during these long five months? It is a question I am always turning over in my mind, and, like so many questions in this war, it is difficult to answer. Is it that they are saving up for some orgy of frightfulness which will soon come upon us, or is it because so far they have not dared? Is it because they dread the superior quality of our fighter aircraft? Is it because they have feared the massive counterstroke which they would immediately receive from our powerful bombing force? No one can say for certain. But one thing is sure: it is not from any false sense of delicacy that they have so far refrained from subjecting us to this new and odious form of attack. Nor is it out of lovingkindness.

We know from what they did in Poland that there is no brutality or bestial massacre of civilians by air bombing which they would not readily commit if they thought it were for their advantage. But here is a chapter of war which they have not chosen to open upon us, because they cannot tell what may be written in its final pages. But then the question arises, Ought we to have begun? Ought we, instead of demonstrating the power of our Air Force by dropping leaflets all over Germany, to have dropped bombs? But there I am quite clear that our policy has been right.

In this peaceful country, governed by public opinion, democracy and Parliament, we were not as thoroughly prepared at the outbreak as this Dictator State whose whole thought was bent upon the preparation for war. Everyone knows how far better organized we are now, and how much stronger our defenses of all kinds are, than at the beginning of the war. We have striven hard to make the most of the time of preparation that has been gained, and there is no doubt that an enormous advance has been made both in the protection of the civil population and in the punishment which would be inflicted upon the raiders. Not only have our air defenses and shelters been substantially improved, but our armies at home and abroad, which are now very large, are steadily maturing in training and in quality; and the whole preparation of our munition industries under the spell of war has rolled forward with gathering momentum. Therefore I feel I was right in saying in one of my earliest broadcasts that if we reached the spring without any interruption of our sea-borne trade, and without anything happening on land or in the air, we should, in fact, have gained the opening campaign of the war.

We cannot, however, place in the field immediately the great armies which we need, and which we are determined to form, and for which millions of eager men stand ready. We have to increase very largely our manufacture of munitions and equipment of all kinds. The immense plants and factories needed can only gradually come into full production. We are of course much further ahead than we were at this time in the last war, and, guided by the experiences of that war, we ought to make far more rapid progress. But we have to make a huge expansion of our labor force, and especially of those capable of performing skilled or semi-skilled operations. Here we must specially count for aid and guidance upon our Labour colleagues and trade union leaders. I can speak with some knowledge about this, having presided over the former Ministry of Munitions in its culminating phase. Millions of new workers will be needed, and more than a million women must come boldly forward into our war industry—into the shell plants and munitions works, and into the aircraft factories.

If trade unionists, from patriotic or international motives, lay aside for the duration of the war any of the special craft usages which they have so carefully built up, they need have no fear that these will not be fully restored to them after the war is won. Nearly a million women were employed in the last war in 1918 under the Ministry of Munitions. They did all kinds of things that no one had ever expected them to do before, and they did them very well. But after the war was over they all went back home, and were no obstacles to the resumption of normal conditions of British life and labor. Without this expansion of labor, and without allowing the women of Britain to enter the struggle, as they desire to do, we should fail utterly to bear our fair share of the burden which France and Britain have jointly assumed, and which we must now carry forward together to the end, or perish miserably in slavery and ruin.

During this time of war great powers are entrusted to the executive government. Nevertheless, we exercise them under the constant supervision of Parliament, and with a wide measure of free debate. We have a stern and resolute House of Commons, which is not likely at all to flag or weaken in the conflict upon which it entered unanimously, and I do not doubt it is a House of Commons which will not hesitate, if emergency requires it, to approve and to enforce all measures necessary for the safety of the State. During the last two hundred and fifty years the British Parliament has fought several great and long European wars with unwearied zeal and tenacity, and carried them all to a successful conclusion. In this war they are fighting not only for themselves, but for Parliamentary institutions wherever they have been set up all over the globe.

In our country public men are proud to be the servants of the people. They would be ashamed to be their masters. Ministers of the Crown feel themselves strengthened by having at their side the House of Commons and the House of Lords sitting with great regularity, and acting as a continual stimulus to their activities. Of course, it is quite true that there is often severe criticism of the Government in both Houses. We do not resent the well-meant criticism of any man who wishes to win the war. We do not shrink from fair criticism, and that is the most dangerous of all. On the contrary, we take it earnestly to heart and seek to profit by it. Criticism in the body politic is like pain in the human body. It is not pleasant, but where would the body be without it? No health or sensibility would be possible without continued correctives and warnings of pain.

It is in this fear of criticism that the Nazi and Bolshevik dictatorships run their greatest risk. They silence all criticism by the concentration camp, the rubber truncheon, or the firing party. Thus the men at the top must very often only be fed with the facts which are palatable to them. Scandals, corruption and shortcomings are not exposed, because there are no independent voices. Instead of being exposed, they continue to fester behind the pompous frontage of the State. The men at the top may be very fierce and powerful, but their ears are deaf, their fingers are numb; they cannot feel their feet as they move forward in the fog and darkness of the immeasurable and the unknown. One of the things that this war is going to prove is whether in modern times the full strength of nations can be realized for war under totalitarian systems working through an Ogpu or a Gestapo. Certainly what we have seen of the Russian effort when opposed to the heroic Finns should give the British and French democracies and Parliaments additional confidence in their own struggle with the Nazi despotism.

Herr Hitler boasts that he has ninety millions under his rod, but nearly twenty of these millions have to be forcibly held down by the others. We and the French have eighty-five millions in our homelands, and twenty millions more in the British Dominions whose armies are hastening to the battle front; and besides this there are vast populations of men of other races who owe allegiance to the Crown or the French Republic spread about the surface of the globe whose sure instinct leads them to regard Nazism as a deadly menace to their future progress. All these inexhaustible resources will steadily and surely, through the command of the seas, be brought to bear upon the evil things whose wickedness has cast its shadow upon mankind and seeks to bar its forward march.

Let us look for a moment at what Nazi Germany inflicts upon the peoples she has subjugated to her rule. The German invaders pursue with every method of cultural, social and economic oppression their intention of destroying the Czech nation. Students are shot by scores and tormented in concentration camps by thousands. All the Czech universities have closed—amongst them the Charles University of Prague which, founded in 1348, was the first university in Central Europe; the clinics in Central Europe, the laboratories, the libraries of the Czech universities have been pillaged or destroyed. The works of their national writers have been removed from the public libraries. More than two thousand periodicals and newspapers have been suppressed. Prominent writers, artists and professors have been herded into the concentration camps. The public administration and judicature have been reduced to chaos. The Czech lands have been plundered, and every scrap of food and useful portable article carried off into Germany by organized brigandage or common theft. The property of the Churches is maladministered and engrossed by German commissars. A hundred thousand Czech workmen have been led off into slavery to be toiled to death in Germany. Eight millions of Czechs—a nation famous and recognizable as a distinct community for many centuries past in Europe—writhe in agony under the German and Nazi tyranny.

But everything that is happening to the Czechs pales in comparison with the atrocities which as I speak here this afternoon are being perpetrated upon the Poles. In German-occupied Poland the most hideous form of terrorism prevails. In this there are two distinct phases. In the first the Germans tried to cow the population by shooting individuals picked at random from the towns. At one place where they had decided to shoot thirty-five people they collected thirty-four, and then, finding themselves one short, went into a chemist's shop and seized the first person they saw to make up the tally. But later on they became more discriminating— they made careful search for the natural leaders of Polish life: the nobles, the landowners, the priests, as well as prominent workmen and peasants. It is estimated that upwards of fifteen thousand intellectual leaders have been shot. These horrible mass executions are a frequent occurrence. At one place three hundred were lined up against the wall; at another a group of drunken German officers are said to have shot seventy hostages in prison; at another a hundred and thirty-six Polish students, some of whom were only twelve or thirteen years old, were butchered. Torture has been used. Press gangs seize men and women in the streets and drive them off in droves to forced labor in Germany. Famine stalks not only amid the ruins of Warsaw, but far and wide throughout that ancient country which a few months ago was the home of a people of over thirty-five millions, with a history extending back far beyond anything that Germany can boast.

"The horror and inexcusable excesses committed on a helpless and home-less people," declared the Papal broadcasts from the Vatican on the 22nd of this month, "have been established by the unimpeachable testimony of eye-witnesses. The crowning iniquity"—says the Vatican broadcast—"lies in the cynical suppression of all but the merest suggestion of religious worship in the lives of one of the most pious and devotional of the peoples of Europe." From these shameful records we may judge what our own fate would be if we fell into their clutches. But from them also we may draw the force and inspiration to carry us forward upon our journey and not to pause or rest till liberation is achieved and justice done.

Come then: let us to the task, to the battle, to the toil—each to our part, each to our station. Fill the armies, rule the air, pour out the munitions, strangle the U-boats, sweep the mines, plow the land, build the ships, guard the streets, succor the wounded, uplift the downcast, and honor the brave. Let us go forward together in all parts of the Empire, in all parts of the Island. There is not a week, nor a day, nor an hour to lose.

THE NAVY IS HERE

A Speech delivered at the Luncheon given by the City of London to the Officers and Men of the Exeter *and* Ajax, *at the Guildhall*

February 23, 1940

January 29.	A German bomber machine-guns the East Dudgeon lightship, killing all the crew but one.
January 31.	H.M.S. *Ajax* arrives at Plymouth.
February 12.	The first contingents of the Australian and New Zealand Expeditionary Forces arrive at Suez.
February 14.	The British Government issues a general license for any British subjects who wish to volunteer to fight for Finland.
February 15.	H.M.S. *Exeter* arrives at Plymouth, and is welcomed home by the First Lord of the Admiralty.
February 16.	Sweden refuses Finland's appeal for the passage of foreign troops through Swedish territory.
February 17.	H.M.S. *Cossack* attacks the German naval auxiliary *Altmark* in Josling Fjord and sets free 299 British prisoners—seamen from the ships sunk by the *Graf Spee*.
February 19.	It is announced that north of Lake Ladoga the Finns have destroyed the Russian 18th Division.
February 23.	H.M.S. *Achilles* arrives home at Auckland, New Zealand.

THE NAVY IS HERE

My COLLEAGUES of the Board of Admiralty and of the War Cabinet are grateful to you for inviting us here today to share the hospitality which the City of London has extended to the victors of the River Plate. It is an occasion at once joyous, memorable and unique. It is the highest compliment your ancient Corporation could give to the officers and men of the *Exeter* and *Ajax* and through them to the whole of our Navy, upon whom, under Providence, our lives and State depend from hour to hour.

I do not suppose that the bonds which unite the British Navy to the British nation—and they have taken a long time to form—or those which join the Navy and the Mercantile Marine were ever so strong as they are today. The brunt of the war so far has fallen upon the sailormen, and their comrades in the Coastal Air Force, and we have already lost nearly 3,000 lives in a hard, unrelenting struggle which goes on night and day and is going on now without a moment's respite. The brilliant sea fight which Admiral Harwood conceived, and which those who are here executed, takes its place in our naval annals, and I might add that in a dark, cold winter it warmed the cockles of the British heart. But it is not only in those few glittering, deadly hours of action, which rivet all eyes, that the strain falls upon the Navy. Far more does it fall in the weeks and months of ceaseless trial and vigilance on cold, dark, stormy seas from whose waves at any moment death and destruction may leap with sullen roar. There is the task which these men were discharging and which their comrades are discharging. There was the task from which, in a sense, the fierce action was almost a relief.

Here let me say a word for the naval members of the Board of Admiralty and especially for the First Sea Lord, Sir Dudley Pound, and his Deputy-Chief of Naval Staff (the newly promoted Vice-Admiral

Phillips) for the skillful combination for which they have been responsible. You must remember that for one stroke that goes home, for one clutch that grips the raider, there are many that miss their mark on the broad oceans; for every success there are many disappointments. You must never forget that the dangers that are seen are only a small part of those that are warded off by care and foresight, and therefore pass unnoticed. The Admiralty and the Fleet are learning together the special conditions of this hard and novel war; and, although mistakes and accidents will certainly occur, and sorrow will fall from time to time upon us, we hope that from Whitehall the sense of resolution and design at the center will impart itself to all afloat, and will lighten the burden of their task and concert the vigor of their action. It is not, for instance, a mere coincidence that has brought the *Achilles* out of the vast Pacific Ocean to the shores of far-off New Zealand, in order to receive in the Antipodes the same warm-hearted welcome as her sisters the *Ajax* and the *Exeter* are receiving now in dear old London.

The spirit of all our forces serving on salt water has never been more strong and high than now. The warrior heroes of the past may look down, as Nelson's monument looks down upon us now, without any feeling that the island race has lost its daring or that the examples they set in bygone centuries have faded as the generations have succeeded one another. It was not for nothing that Admiral Harwood, as he instantly at full speed attacked an enemy which might have sunk any one of his ships by a single successful salvo from its far heavier guns, flew Nelson's immortal signal, of which neither the new occasion, nor the conduct of all ranks and ratings, nor the final result were found unworthy.

To the glorious tale of the action off the Plate there has recently been added an epilogue—the rescue last week by the *Cossack* and her flotilla, under the nose of the enemy and amid the tangles of one-sided neutrality, of the British captives taken from the sunken German raider. Their rescue at the very moment when these unhappy men were about to be delivered over to German bondage proves that the long arm of British sea power can be stretched out, not only for foes but also for faithful friends. And to Nelson's signal of 135 years ago, "England expects that every man will do his duty," there may now be added last week's not less proud reply: "The Navy is here!"

THE NAVY ESTIMATES

The House of Commons: introducing the Supplementary Estimate

February 27, 1940

1940

February 25. Mr. Sumner Welles, President Roosevelt's special envoy, arrives in Rome.

February 26. The Finns lose the important island fortress of Koivisto, protecting the right flank of the Mannerheim Line.

THE NAVY ESTIMATES

I come before the House on behalf of the Navy to ask for a few men, some ships, and a little money, to enable them to carry on their work which has become important to us all at the present time. In making this request I am emboldened by the remarkable consideration with which naval affairs have been treated during this war by all Parties in the House. It seems to me that since I last presented Navy Estimates in wartime— 25 years ago, almost to a day—there has grown up a very much wider comprehension of the conditions under which the Navy and the Admiralty do their duty; of their difficulties, and of the certainty that mistakes will be made both at Whitehall and on salt water; and that, however hard we try, a painful drain of losses will be sustained. I am grateful to the House—not only to my hon. Friends on this side, but to the right hon. Member who speaks for the Opposition and to the Leader of the Liberal Party, for this spirit of tolerance, of understanding, and even indulgence with which we have been and are being treated; and I can assure the House that it will only make us more zealous in the discharge of our task, in order to give satisfaction and win approval by producing good results. The earnestness and vigor with which Parliament is supporting the Crown in waging this very grievous war, and the unstinted money contribution which the House of Commons has made for that purpose impose the highest obligation upon the armed Forces, and upon the Parliamentary Ministers entrusted with their superintendence and direction.

I regret that it is not expedient to lay precise facts and figures of the proposed strength and cost of the Navy in the coming year before the House, as we should naturally desire to do. In the first place, it is physically impossible to make exact estimates for contingencies which are constantly changing; and, in the second place, there is no need to tell the enemy more than is good for him about what we are doing. We therefore ask the House to show us a special mark of confidence by allowing us to present only token votes. But this must not in the slightest degree relax or baffle the vigilance of Parliament in preventing waste and exposing errors, should such be detected.

The Parliamentary Committees which the House desired, and which the Chancellor of the Exchequer instituted, are now at work in all three Services. I have given particular directions at the Admiralty that all officials and officers required shall attend before them and assist them in their work. Many have already been examined, but they can be recalled at any time, and there are many others who have not yet been seen; and all these have full liberty to disclose all matters bearing on the subject except those which, being of a specially secret nature, the Committee themselves would not desire to know. Should any difficulty arise, I hold myself entirely at the disposal of the Committee examining Admiralty expenditure. I hope they will not confine themselves to taking evidence in London, but will go to the naval ports and establishments and see things on the spot for themselves.

Of course, there is bound to be both extravagance and waste in time of war. In our country, accustomed to strict Parliamentary supervision, this waste arises very rarely from fraud or corruption. It arises sometimes from inefficiency, and is capable of correction. It arises most of all, I think, from excessive zeal in preparing against dangers which often change, and sometimes fade as soon as they are faced; and still more from the well-intentioned desire of every branch and section to reach 100 per cent standard of safety—which, of course, is never attainable in war. An officer, in any station, serves his country best by asking for no more than he needs for his task. It is not patriotic to ask for the moon—and you do not get it, either. The Navy has borne, and is bearing, the main weight of the war up to the present, and many vexatious and dangerous forms of attack are directed upon us; but if at any time in the future it becomes apparent that we have got the upper hand in an even more marked and decisive form than at present, I shall be the first to propose a review of our resources and requirements—and we have quite a lot—in order to aid the national war-effort in other directions. That time has not yet come. We must clearly expect that attacks will be delivered upon the sea-power by which we live, on which all depends, on a far greater scale than anything we have so far beaten back and beaten down. We have been making, from the outset of war, immense additional preparations to meet these reinforced attacks, whether they come from U-boats, or from the mine-laying of various kinds, or from the air.

I have undertaken, at the request of the Cabinet, to try to make a large increase in the rate of merchant shipbuilding in order to replace inevitable losses. Obviously we have to balance one form of building against the other, and that is best done by making the Admiralty responsible for both. I hope to get, not only leading employers, but also leading trade unionists, into the new department, so that both sides will be represented, will have a place in the honor of success, and will, I trust, pull together as they have never pulled before.

The U-boat has been steadily driven from using the gun, with all its great advantages of speed, upon the surface into the more ruthless but less effective warfare by the torpedo; and it has been largely driven from using the torpedo to the laying of mines, magnetic and others, in the approaches to our harbors. The ordinary moored mines were familiar to us in the last war, and we had at one time upwards of 600 vessels engaged solely on the task of sweeping them up and keeping the channels clear. The use of the magnetic mine produces an additional complication. There is nothing particularly new or novel about it, although mechanically it is very nicely made. I feel entitled to say that we see our way to mastering this magnetic mine and other variants of the same idea. How this has been achieved is a detective story written in a language of its own. Magnetism is a fairly exact science, and its complications and refinements can all be explored and measured. To be modest, we do not feel at all outdone in science in this country by the Nazis. There are, of course, two stages in the process of dealing with the magnetic mine. The first is finding out what to do, and the second is applying this knowledge to practical conditions upon a very large scale. We are now far advanced upon the second stage, and although we must expect, perhaps in the immediate future, further much heavier attacks upon us by this method, we believe we shall find ourselves equipped to deal with them. To cope with the mining attack, we have had to call upon the fishing fleets and upon the fishermen. Although this year we shall have about a quarter of a million sailors at our disposal, we had at the end of November to call for many thousand volunteers for mine-sweeping duties. There was a most willing response, but the engagement was for only three months. It is now clear that it must be greatly prolonged. The service is, of course, not only dangerous but arduous in a very high degree. However, our volunteers from the fishing fleets seem to have taken a liking to it, probably because everybody knows how very necessary it is to the country and that the job has to be done by men bred to the sea. In many seaports over 75 per cent of those who volunteered for three months in November now wish to continue for the duration, and the Admiralty are going to meet their wish.

Thousands of guns of all sorts and sizes are being issued to our merchant and fishing fleets. The Nazis have retorted by saying that this entitles them to break all the conventions which they had already broken many times over. They may, of course, apply their methods on a larger scale, but they have not for some time been able to descend to any new levels of cruelty and disgrace. I suppose the House realizes that Herr Hitler and his Nazis have quite definitely exceeded the worst villainies which Imperial Germany committed in the late war. This brings me to a point that I should like to put to the House. One of the most extraordinary things that I have ever known in my experience is the way in which German illegalities, atrocities, and brutalities are coming to be accepted as if they were part of the ordinary day-to-day conditions of war. Why, Sir, the neutral Press makes more fuss when I make a speech telling them what is their duty than they have done when hundreds of their ships have been sunk and many thousands of their sailors have been drowned or murdered—for that is the right word—on the open sea. Apparently, according to the present doctrine of neutral States, strongly endorsed by the German Government, Germany is to gain one set of advantages by breaking all the rules and committing foul outrages upon the seas, and then go on and gain another set of advantages through insisting, whenever it suits her, upon the strictest interpretation of the International Code she has torn to pieces. It is not at all odd that His Majesty's Government are getting rather tired of it. I am getting rather tired of it myself. For my part, I say without hesitation that in the interpretation of the rules and conventions affecting neutrals humanity rather than legal pedantry must be our guide; and, judging by the *Altmark* episode, which gave so much pleasure last week, this seems to be the opinion, not only of the British nation, but of the civilized world.

Let us look at the foundations upon which our sea power rests. Some people think that great battleships are no use at all, that they are only anxieties at sea and a useless burden in port. Everyone sees this war being fought from day to day by the small craft, and they see that the little ships have always to go ahead to protect the big ones, so they ask, "Why have the big ones at all?" But this is a very superficial view. If we had not got at the present time an unquestioned superiority in battleships, the German heavy cruisers would come out into the Atlantic Ocean, and, without fear of being brought to account, would be able to obstruct, if not to arrest, the whole of the enormous trade without which we could not live. They might make temporary bases in distant quarters of the globe, they might establish themselves in positions where we should have no means whatever with which to attack them, and in this way they would soon bring about our mortal ruin. Happily, we have far greater strength in capital ships than the enemy; and if at any time they break out, as they may do, we are always ready to meet them with much larger forces and bring them to battle and destroy them, as we did in the isolated case of the *Graf Spee,* although, of course, this would have to be on a much larger scale. Without a superior battle fleet we could not exercise any command of the sea, nor even keep ourselves alive in food.

During the last war we had to keep always ready 30 or 40 battleships, with all their attendant squadrons and flotillas, at short notice, in order to fight a main battle with the enemy at any time. But now this preoccupation is greatly diminished. The enemy have only two really big ships, and they cannot attempt to form a line of battle. We, on the other hand, have at least three, if not four, possible lines of battle, not one of which the enemy could face in a fought-out engagement. Therefore we are able to dispose our ships much more widely about the oceans, and at the same time to keep ample force at hand and always at sea ready to engage his principal vessels should they present themselves; and it is upon this fact that the whole of our sea control depends.

However, it must be remembered that at this moment there are no modern battleships in action. Many are building in various countries, but none is in commission. Through the various treaties into which we entered, and upon which I have sometimes expressed my opinion in former times, all our capital ships are old. Some have been rebuilt, but all except three were approved by me when I was last at the Admiralty more than a quarter of a century ago. In fact, we are fighting this war with the battleships of the last war. This does not affect surface fighting, because our new ships will come along as soon as theirs, and in much greater numbers. In a short time the Fleet will be reinforced by five modern battleships of the *King George V* class, against which the enemy, in a similar time, can only bring two. Therefore, we shall not be at any disadvantage so far as surface fighting is concerned.

But the fact that we are using old ships at this present time adds to our anxiety, because the attack from under-water or from the air has become far more formidable since they were built; for the torpedoes, mines and air bombs of 1940 are now applied to the structures of a bygone generation. Where one torpedo with a 500 lbs. head was fired in 1915, six may be fired in a volley with much heavier heads in 1940. The air bombs descending almost vertically are also a menace which ought not to be underrated, and which did not exist when most of our battleships were built. But the new ships which we are building, which we have accelerated, and which will be ready in time, are capable of standing up to the air bomb, and are far better adapted to under-water explosions than anything we have today. I do not wish, however, to raise any undue apprehensions about the strength of our existing ships. When the *Barham* was hit by a torpedo, although an old ship, she stood up well to the heavy blow and was able to proceed under her own steam. She will soon be repaired and ready for sea. Again, when in the early part of December the *Nelson,* the Home Fleet flagship, a more modern ship but still 15 years old, was damaged by a magnetic mine, she was able to return to harbor under her own steam. She too will soon be rejoining the Fleet. This secret, of which many thousands of people were necessarily aware, was very well kept and has only just leaked out into Germany after it has ceased to have any importance. Apart from the *Royal Oak* and the *Courageous,* no other large ship has been damaged or sunk since the outbreak of the war.

Where then, Sir, do we stand at the end of the first six months of war? We have lost 63,000 tons of warships, or about half the losses of the first six months of the last war. We have lost on the balance of loss and gain less than 200,000 tons of merchant shipping, taking new building and prizes on the one side, out of a total of 21,000,000 of all types or 17½ million in ocean-going shipping, flying the British flag. This figure of less than 200,000 tons in six months may be compared with 450,000 tons net loss in the single deadly month of April, 1917. We have captured more cargoes in tonnage destined for the enemy than we have lost ourselves. During the first two months of war there was inevitable dislocation. But each month there has been a steady improvement in spite of the deterioration of the weather, and in January the Navy carried safely into British harbors, in the teeth of the U-boats, of the mines, and of the winter gales and fog, considerably more than four-fifths of the peacetime average taken over the whole, summer and winter alike, of the three preceding years.

Our imports, measured in tons—and it is with tonnage that the Navy is concerned—were equal in December and January to our imports coming in in those months of the last peace-time year of 1938. But now, with spring and summer at hand, there is to be expected a considerable normal seasonal increase in the volume of traffic by sea, and apart from any new development of enemy action, a matter which can never be overlooked in any provisions for the future, there is no reason why we should not improve upon these figures. When we consider the great number of British ships which have been withdrawn for Naval Service, or for the transport of our armies across the Channel or across the globe, there is nothing in these results which—to put it mildly—should cause despondency or alarm, or which justifies the idea that we cannot carry on our national life, and the war upon which the national life is centered, with increasing vigor. Any reductions and austerities in home consumption, which we have found, or may find, it necessary to impose upon ourselves, are not due to any failure of the Navy to keep the seas open, but to the need of making prudent preparations against the unknown, and of raising our war effort to the highest pitch.

In 1915, speaking from this Box, I was able to say that our command of the seas was more thorough than ever before in our history, and—although I was not allowed to preside over it—it so continued for more than eighteen months. I will not make any prophecies about the future, which is doubly veiled by the obscurities and uncertainties of war. But personally I shall not be content, nor do I think the House should be content, if we do not reach and maintain a control of the seas equal to the highest standards of the last war and enable the Navy once again to play a decisive part in the general victory of the Allies.

A STERNER WAR

An Address Broadcast

March 30, 1940

1940

March 2.	Mr. Sumner Welles has an interview with Herr Hitler in Berlin.
March 7.	The 85,000-ton *Queen Elizabeth* docks in New York after a secret maiden voyage from the Clyde.
March 11.	Mr. Sumner Welles arrives in London.
March 13.	Peace agreement between Finland and Russia announced.
March 18.	Herr Hitler and Signor Mussolini meet on the Brenner Pass.
March 20.	In France M. Daladier's Government resigns; M. Paul Reynaud is asked by the President to form a Cabinet.
March 27.	In the Canadian General Elections Mr. Mackenzie King's Liberal Government is returned with a greatly increased majority.

A STERNER WAR

IT SEEMS rather hard when spring is caressing the land, and when, after the rigors of winter, our fields and woodlands are reviving, that all our thoughts must be turned and bent upon sterner war. When I spoke to you six months ago, I said that if we reached the spring without any great event occurring, we should in fact have gained an important success. I still feel that this additional period of preparation has been an invaluable help to the Allies. Peaceful Parliamentary nations have more difficulty in transforming themselves into vast war-making organisms than Dictator States who glorify war and feed their youth on dreams of conquest. The British Empire and the French Republic are now joined together in indissoluble union so that their full purposes may be accomplished, and immense progress has been made in almost every direction—in strengthening our forces, in improving our defenses, and adapting our whole economy and way of life to the service of the common cause.

Up to the present, time has been on our side; but time is a changeable ally. He may be with you in one period and against you in another, and then if you come through that other, he may return again more faithful than before. It seems to me, taking a general view, that an intensification of the struggle is to be expected, and we are certainly by no means inclined to shrink from it. We must not boast, or speak in terms of vain conceit and overconfidence. We have never underrated the terrible nature of what we undertook when, after striving so long for peace, we set ourselves to the task of dealing with the Nazi and German menace and of dealing with it in such a fashion as would clear the path of human progress and enable all countries, great and small, old and new, to breathe freely for a long time to come. We do not minimize our task. But we can now measure it in its enormous magnitude more exactly than we could before we came into contact with our adversary on the sea and in the air.

People often ask me, Will the war be long or short? It might have been a very short war—perhaps indeed there might have been no war—if all the neutral States who share our convictions upon fundamental matters, and who openly or secretly sympathize with us, had stood together at one signal and in one line. We did not count on this, we did not expect it, and therefore we are not disappointed or dismayed. We trust in God and in our own arm uplifted in a cause which we devoutly feel carries with it the larger hopes and harmonies of mankind. But the fact that many of the smaller States of Europe are terrorized by Nazi violence and brutality into supplying Germany with the materials of modern war— this fact may condemn the whole world to a prolonged ordeal with grievous unmeasured consequences in many lands. Therefore I cannot assure you that the war will be short, and still less that it will be easy.

It is, I think, our duty to try so far as our strength lies not only to win the war, but to curtail as far as possible its devouring course. Some few weeks ago I spoke about the action of the neutral States who have the misfortune to be Germany's neighbors. We have the greatest sympathy for these forlorn countries, and we understand their dangers and their point of view; but it would not be right, or in the general interest, that their weakness should feed the aggressor's strength and fill to overflowing the cup of human woe. There can be no justice if in a mortal struggle the aggressor tramples down every sentiment of humanity, and those who resist him remain entangled in the tatters of violated legal conventions. Hardly a day passes without fresh outrages of a barbarous character being inflicted upon the shipping and sailors of all European countries. Their ships are sunk by mine or by torpedo, or by bombs from the air, and their crews are murdered or left to perish, unless we are able to rescue them. Swedes, Norwegians, Danes, and even Italians, and many more I could mention, have been the victims of Hitler's murderous rage. In his frenzy, this wicked man and the criminal regime which he has conceived and erected increasingly turn their malice upon the weak, upon the lonely, and above all upon the unarmed vessels of countries with which Germany is still supposed to be in friendly relations.

Such a form of warfare has never been practiced since the effectual suppression of piracy on the high seas. And this is the monstrous power which even the very neutrals who have suffered and are suffering most are forced to supply with the means of future aggression. This is the power before whom, even while they writhe in anger, they are forced to bow, and whose victory would mean their own enslavement. Why, only yesterday, while the sailors from a British submarine were carrying ashore on stretchers eight emaciated Dutchmen whom they had rescued from six days' exposure in an open boat, Dutch aviators in Holland, in the name of strict and impartial neutrality, were shooting down a British aircraft which had lost its way. I do not reproach the Dutch, our valiant allies of bygone centuries; my heart goes out to them in their peril and distress, dwelling as they do in the cage with the tiger. But when we are asked to take as a matter of course interpretations of neutrality which give all the advantages to the aggressor and inflict all the disadvantages upon the defenders of freedom, I recall a saying of the late Lord Balfour: "This is a singularly ill-contrived world, but not so ill-contrived as that."

All these outrages upon the sea, which are so clearly visible, pale before the villainous deeds which are wrought upon the helpless Czechs and Austrians, and they sink almost into insignificance before the hideous agony of Poland. What a frightful fate has overtaken Poland! Here was a community of nearly thirty-five millions of people, with all the organization of a modern government, and all the traditions of an ancient State, which in a few weeks was dashed out of civilized existence to become an incoherent multitude of tortured and starving men, women and children, ground beneath the heel of two rival forms of withering and blasting tyranny. The other day in a well-known British harbor I inspected the crew of a Polish destroyer. I have rarely seen a finer body of men. I was stirred by their discipline and bearing. Yet how tragic was their plight! Their ship was afloat, but their country had foundered. But as I looked around upon all the great ships of war which lay at their anchors, and at all the preparations which were being made on every side to carry this war forward at all costs as long as may be necessary, I comforted myself with the thought that when these Polish sailors have finished their work with the British Navy, we will take particular care that they once more have a home to go to. Although the fate of Poland stares them in the face, there are thoughtless dilettanti or purblind worldlings who sometimes ask us: "What is it that Britain and France are fighting for?" To this I answer: "If we left off fighting you would soon find out."

We shall follow this war wherever it leads us; but we have no wish to broaden the area of conflict. At the outbreak, seven months ago, we did not know that Italy would not be our enemy. We were not sure that Japan would not be our enemy. Many people, on the other hand, had hoped that Russia would re-enter the comity of nations and help to shield working folk all over the world from Nazi aggression. But none of these things, bad or good, has happened. We have no quarrel with the Italian or Japanese peoples. We have tried, and we shall try, our best to live on good terms with them.

All's quiet upon the Western Front; and today, this Saturday, so far, nothing has happened on the sea or in the air. But more than a million German soldiers, including all their active divisions and armored divisions, are drawn up ready to attack, at a few hours' notice, all along the frontiers of Luxembourg, of Belgium and of Holland. At any moment these neutral countries may be subjected to an avalanche of steel and fire; and the decision rests in the hands of a haunted, morbid being, who, to their eternal shame, the German peoples in their bewilderment have worshiped as a god. That is the situation of Europe tonight. And can anyone wonder that we are determined to bring such a hideous state of alarm and menace to an end, and to bring it to an end as soon as may be, and to bring it to an end once and for all? Few there are tonight who, looking back on these last seven months, would doubt that the British and French peoples were right to draw the sword of justice and of retribution. Fewer still there are who would wish to sheathe it till its somber, righteous work is done.

NORWAY

The House of Commons

April 11, 1940

1940

April 8.   While German transports are already on their way to Scandinavia, Britain mines Norwegian waters.

April 9.   Germany invades Norway and Denmark. The latter does not resist.

April 10.   First battle of Narvik between British and German destroyers.

NORWAY

I AM sure I shall receive the indulgence of the House if by any chance there should be some minor error in fact or detail in the statement I am going to make, or if it has not received that thorough and prolonged preparation which I have always endeavored to give to any observations I have had to offer to the House. We are working under very sharp pressure in these times, and I have been most anxious to give the House the fullest possible information agreeable with the public interest; that being the strongly expressed direction and desire which I have received from the Prime Minister and my colleagues in the Cabinet.

The strange and unnatural calm of the last few weeks was violently broken on Monday morning by the German invasion of Norway and Denmark. This crime had, of course, been long and elaborately prepared, and it was actually set in motion in the last week of March. For several months past we have received information of large numbers of German merchant ships being fitted as transports and of numerous small vessels being assembled in various Baltic ports and, also, in the mouths of the River Elbe. But no one could tell when or against what peaceful country they would be used. Holland, Denmark, Norway and Sweden were, as it seemed, all equally liable to a sudden, brutal, capricious and, in any case, unprovoked attack. Which would be selected as the first victims or when the blow would be struck remained, inevitably, a matter of pure speculation.

The Nazi German Government is accustomed to spreading through its channels a continuous flow of threats and rumors. These are put forth by all their agents in neutral countries, by the "hangers-on" of their legations and by their sympathizers and backers, wherever they may be found. All these countries have been threatened, and as the German Government are not restrained by law or scruple, and as they have an obvious preference for striking at the weak rather than the strong, all the small countries on their borders were, and still are, in a high state of alarm. Even those neutrals who have done the most to placate Germany, and have been the greatest aid to her, could not feel any sense of security that they would not be attacked without any reason or without any warning, swiftly overrun, reduced to bondage and pillaged of all their property, especially all eatables. Fear was, therefore, general in all these unfortunate countries, and none of them could tell, and none of us could tell, which one of them would be the next to be devoured.

In the small hours of Monday morning we learned that Norway and Denmark had drawn the unlucky numbers in this sinister lottery. Denmark, of course, had special reason for apprehension, not only because she was the nearest and the weakest of Germany's neighbors, but because she had a recent treaty with Germany guaranteeing her from all molestation and because she was engaged in active commerce both with Germany and Great Britain, the continuance of which in time of war had been foreseen by Germany, and was guaranteed by special trade arrangements between the German and Danish Governments. This, obviously, placed her in a position of peculiar danger.

The extraordinary configuration of the Norwegian western coast provides a kind of corridor, or covered way, as everyone knows, through which neutral trade and German ships of all kinds, warships and others, could be moved to and fro through the Allied blockade, within the territorial waters of Norway and Sweden, until they were under the effective protection of the German Air Force in North Germany. They could go to and fro along this route without molestation. The existence of this geographical and legal covered way has been the greatest disadvantage which we have suffered and the greatest advantage which Germany has possessed in her efforts to frustrate the British and Allied blockade. Warships moved up and down it as they thought it convenient. U-boats used it as they thought fit. Stray German liners and merchant ships, trying to get back to Germany from outer seas, followed this route, which is over 800 miles long, and can be entered or quitted at any convenient point. There has been no greater impediment to the blockade of Germany than this Norwegian corridor. It was so in the last war, and it has been so in this war. Therefore, the British Navy has been forced to watch an endless procession of German and neutral ships carrying contraband of all kinds to Germany, which at any moment they could have stopped, but which they were forbidden to touch by those very same conventions of inter-national law which Germany, in this war, as in the last, has treated with the utmost contempt.

During the last war, when we were associated with the United States, the Allies felt themselves so deeply injured by this covered way, then being used specially for U-boats setting out on their marauding expedi-tions, that the British, French and United States Governments together induced the Norwegians to lay a minefield in their territorial waters, across the covered way, in order to prevent the abuse by U-boats of this channel. It was only natural that the Admiralty, since this war began, should have brought this precedent—although it is not exactly on all fours, and there are some differences—this modern and highly respectable precedent, to the notice of His Majesty's Government and should have urged that we should be allowed to lay a minefield of our own in Norwegian terri-torial waters in order to compel this traffic which was passing in and out to Germany to come out into the open sea and take a chance of being brought into the contraband control, or being captured as enemy prize by our blockading squadrons and flotillas. It was only natural and it was only right that His Majesty's Government should have been long reluctant to incur the reproach of even a technical violation of international law. After all, we are seeking to establish the reign of international law, and anyone can see the dilemma upon which those who have to consider these matters are liable to be impaled in such a situation as that. It is in-tolerable that the good cause should suffer by respecting the conventions which those who champion the bad cause have profited by tearing to pieces. But gradually, as this cruel, deadly war has deepened and darkened, the feeling grew that it was placing an undue burden upon the Allies to allow this traffic to continue and that it was intolerable to watch, week after week, the ships passing down this corridor carrying the iron ore to make the shells which will strike down the young men of France and Britain in the campaign of 1941.

It was, therefore, decided at last—and the scruples caused us injury at the same time as they did us honor—to interrupt this traffic and make it come out into the open sea. Every precaution was taken to avoid the slightest danger to neutral ships or any loss of life, even to enemy merchant ships, by the minefields which were laid and declared on Monday last at dawn, and British patrolling craft were actually stationed around them in order to warn all ships off these dangerous areas. The German Gov-ernment have sought to make out that their invasion of Norway and of

Denmark was a consequence of our action in closing the Norwegian corridor. It can, however, undoubtedly be proved that not only had their preparations been made nearly a month before, but that their actual movements of troops and ships had begun before the British and French minefields were laid. No doubt they suspected they were going to be laid. It must indeed have appeared incomprehensible to them that they had not been laid long before. They therefore decided in the last week of March to use the Norwegian corridor to send empty ore ships northward, filled with military stores and German soldiers, concealed below decks, in order at the given moment to seize the various ports on the Norwegian seaboard which they considered to have military value.

I here must say a word about Norway. We have the most profound sympathy with the Norwegian people. We have understood the terrible dilemma in which they have been placed. Their sentiments, like those of every other small country, were with the Allies. They writhed in helpless anger while scores of their ships were wantonly sunk and many hundreds of their sailors cruelly drowned. They realize fully that their future independence and freedom are bound up with the victory of the Allies. But the feeling of powerlessness in the ruthless grip of Nazi wrath made them hope against hope until the last moment that at least their soil and their cities would not be polluted by the trampling of German marching columns or their liberties and their livelihood stolen away by foreign tyrants. But this hope has been in vain. Another violent outrage has been perpetrated by Nazi Germany against a small and friendly Power, and the Norwegian Government and people are today in arms to defend their hearths and homes. We shall aid them to the best of our ability, we shall conduct the war in common with them, and we shall make peace only when their rights and freedom are restored. In their very large, wild, mountainous country—freedom, it is said, dwells in the mountains—in their very large country, sparsely populated, but rugged and full of positions where free men can shelter and can fight, they should be able to maintain vigorous and prolonged resistance, costing enormous labor to those who wish to subjugate them to tyranny.

But what an example this Norwegian episode is to other neutral countries! What an example it is of the danger of supposing that friendly relations with Germany, or friendly assurances from Germany, or treaties of any kind, or friendly offices rendered to Germany, or advantages given to Germany—what a danger to suppose that any of these are the slightest protection against a murderous onslaught the moment it is thought by

Germany that any advantage can be gained by such action! If the Norwegian Government had not been so very strict and severe in enforcing their neutrality against us and in leaving their corridor open to German operations and machinations, and if they had entered into confidential relations with us, it would have been very easy to give them more timely and more opportune support than is now possible. It is not the slightest use blaming the Allies for not being able to give substantial help and protection to neutral countries if they are held at arm's length by the neutral countries until those countries are actually attacked on a scientifically prepared plan by Germany. And I trust that the fact that the strict observance of neutrality by Norway has been a contributory cause of the sufferings to which she is now exposed and in the limits of aid which we can give her will be meditated upon by other countries who may tomorrow, or a week hence, or a month hence find themselves the victims of an equally elaborately worked-out staff plan for their destruction and enslavement.

I now address myself to the question which I believe has been asked in some quarters, What is the Navy doing? As I told the House in the Debate upon the Navy Estimates, we were deprived during all the long winter months of the great strategic advantages of Scapa Flow, but during all that time we labored with might and main to make that base a safe and sure home for the Fleet. About five weeks ago the Home Fleet returned to Scapa Flow and has been resting there or operating from there ever since. We have been exposed to continual air-raid alarms and numerous air raids, but we have now very powerful anti-aircraft batteries in action, together with various other methods of defense, and very good arrangements have been made with the Royal Air Force and with our home squadrons of the Fleet Air Arm, so that an adequate number of squadrons are disposed within striking distance.

In all, there have been five raids on Scapa Flow—many alarms, but five raids. My right hon. Friend the Leader of the Opposition, who paid a visit to that spot, was, I gather, by accident so unfortunate as just to miss one of those exhilarating experiences. In the first raid a cruiser was hit aft, which necessitated several weeks of repair but no more than that. Otherwise, up to the time I am speaking, there has been no vessel hit or damaged in Scapa Flow, no objective of the slightest military importance has been hit on shore, and very few people have been hurt. The enemy has shown himself increasingly gun-shy in his attacks on Scapa, and this is hardly to be wondered at, since the batteries, especially when reinforced by the powerful batteries of the Fleet, can deliver what is probably far the heaviest concentration of anti-aircraft fire in the world. It is a tremendous fire, and in the latest raid, which took place last night at dusk, 60 aircraft attacked in successive waves without doing the slightest damage, although they themselves suffered the loss of at least six aircraft, the credit for which is divided between—I might almost say disputed between—the batteries and the very excellently combined and skillfully used air squadrons. We are ready to fight this matter out at Scapa Flow. It is of the utmost importance to the Fleet to make themselves comfortable there, and the repeated attacks give a practice to the batteries against high-speed aircraft which no towed target which we have been able to devise can possibly supply. It is most necessary to have further encounters between the batteries and enemy aircraft and between the Fleet and enemy aircraft if our gunnery is to develop its full efficiency, and, of course, we must always be prepared when we run risks for occasional losses.

The Fleet was, therefore, in instant readiness at Scapa Flow when, on Sunday night, news was received from the air reconnaissance—our air reconnaissance ranges over the whole of the North Sea—that German battle cruisers, with a number of other cruisers and vessels and destroyers, were out at sea and moving very swiftly northwards. The Commander-in-Chief immediately put to sea to find them and bring them to action. At the same time, independently of this, a strong British naval force was approaching Narvik in order to lay a minefield off the Norwegian coast for the purposes which I described to the House a few moments ago. The minefield was laid according to plan at daylight on Monday morning. The task of the minelayers accomplished, they withdrew to the westward in order to avoid the risk of any collision with Norwegian war vessels maintaining their neutrality, which they had been specially enjoined to respect and take every precaution against infringing.

One of the destroyers of this northern force which went to lay mines lost a man overboard on Sunday afternoon and stayed behind some time to pick him up. This destroyer, the *Glowworm,* was proceeding northwards to rejoin its force when, at 8 o'clock on Monday morning, she saw first one and then two enemy destroyers, which she engaged. She then reported an unknown enemy ship before her to the northward. These incidents came to us one by one at few-minute intervals as they occurred, but the last message ended abruptly, and we can only conclude that the *Glowworm* has been sunk by the greatly superior forces of the enemy which she had to encounter. The *Glowworm's* light has been quenched, but there is no reason why a large proportion of her crew should not have been saved if the ordinary humanity of fighting men, which is a different thing from the humanity of some Governments, has been practiced by the enemy. This chance encounter showed that major elements of the enemy Navy were at sea and that considerable events were in train.

Since then fighting has been continuous night and day, without stopping, and is going on now—a widely dispersed, but none the less a general, action between large numbers of German ships and aircraft and such forces as we are able to bring into action. A great deal has been reported in the newspapers, a great deal of what has taken place and even more than has taken place, because, of course, we have not reoccupied the ports on the Norwegian coast. These are rumors which come from neutral sources and are naturally given currency. During Monday morning it looked as though the enemy forces which had sunk the *Glowworm,* and which contained German battle-cruisers and other enemy ships, would be caught between our forces in the north and the main Home Fleet, both of which were superior. However, they got away, and here I must make a digression about the conditions of sea war.

You may look at the map and see flags stuck in at different points and consider that the result will be certain, but when you get out on the sea, with its vast distances, its storms and mists, and with night coming on and all the uncertainties which exist, you cannot possibly expect that the kind of conditions which would be appropriate to consider in respect of the movements of armies have any application to the chance and haphazard conditions of collisions by ships of war at sea. On Tuesday the Fleet was cruising to the southward about the level of Bergen, when, during the afternoon, it was attacked continuously by German aircraft. The usual tales were put out by the German wireless of several battleships and cruisers being sunk or seriously damaged. I know that some of my friends were concerned at these blatant exaggerations. Actually, two cruisers were slightly damaged by splinters, but this did not at all interfere with their work, and they are still with the Fleet at their stations. One very heavy bomb hit the flagship, the *Rodney,* but her very strong deck armor resisted the impact, and she was not affected in any way by the explosions except that three officers and seven men were injured. As far as the structure of our ships of war is concerned, this incident must be regarded as satisfactory. The cruiser *Aurora,* which had joined the Fleet, was subjected to five successive bombing attacks, all of which were pressed home with courage and all of which failed; but a destroyer, the *Gurkha,* which was accompanying her and to some extent escorting her, was hard hit and listed heavily and sank after four and a half hours, during which the crew, or almost all of the crew, were rescued. The same afternoon the destroyer *Zulu* sank a German U-boat off the Orkneys.

Meanwhile, far to the north off Narvik, on this Tuesday morning at daybreak, the *Renown,* one of our battle-cruisers, perceived the *Scharnhorst* and a 10,000-ton *Hipper*-class cruiser, which had evidently come up with the force the day before, in the distance dimly. Amid snowstorms, a tempestuous day, sea running high, gales blowing furiously, our battle-cruiser opened fire at 18,000 yards. After three minutes the enemy replied, but almost immediately turned away. After nine minutes the *Renown* observed hits on the forward structure of the German battle-cruiser, and thereafter her whole armament stopped firing. Later her after-turret began firing under local control. The speed the enemy battle-cruiser maintained was very great, and the *Renown* had to push to 24 knots through very heavy seas breaking over her forward turrets and guns. After a further two minutes of firing, a vertical column of smoke from what they call a possible second hit was observed on the *Scharnhorst,* which then turned away and directly retired at a high speed without further firing. During this period a shell had passed through our vessel about the water line without bursting. We had something like that in the case of the *Exeter,* and it seems to show that Nazi workmanship is not all of a piece. A second shell went through the foremast, carrying away the main aerial. There were no casualties on board the *Renown.* The destroyers which were with her were unable to keep up in the heavy seas at the speed at which she was going.

The 10,000-ton *Hipper* cruiser now drew across the battleship *Scharnhorst.* The two ships of this class, the *Scharnhorst* and *Gneisenau,* are of 25,000 tons and most formidable vessels. The *Hipper* threw a smoke-screen across her to cover her retreat. The *Renown* opened fire on the *Hipper,* which turned away. Both ships now retired at high speed, the *Hipper* swinging to fire a broadside from time to time, and also dodging. Firing was intermittent, as all the time snowstorms were sweeping across and closing the view, and the sea was running very high, but in the end we much regret to say that they succeeded in leaving us. Firing finally ceased at 29,000 yards, when they became quite invisible. Someone will say, "If you had all this news on Tuesday morning, why have you been saving it up for the House of Commons?" All I can say is that I have been most anxious to obtain this information, because the *Renown* signals broke off when they became interesting, and we never heard another word from her until a few hours ago upon that subject. Although she made various signals, she did not think it necessary to tell us what had happened. I must emphasize this, that when sailors are fighting they busy themselves so much upon that, and take so much interest in that, that they quite forget for a long time to tell us what they are doing, which sometimes causes some embarrassment to the Admiralty and even more to the Minister of Information.

I am still on Tuesday. On Tuesday night we gave orders to our destroyers to blockade the West Fjord, that great stretch of water fifty or sixty miles long leading up to Narvik. Our orders to those destroyers were to attack the enemy who had got in there and especially to destroy the store ships in which they had smuggled their soldiers up the Norwegian corridor, and on which they must depend for working up the efficiency of their defenses. There were six destroyers and a U-boat reported, and, moreover, it was to be expected that they had landed a certain number of guns in the twenty-four hours they had been there. The Germans are very quick in landing and making themselves fortified; they are very nimble about these things. From what we heard at the Admiralty late on Tuesday night, we thought the operation so hazardous that at 1 o'clock in the morning we told the captain of the destroyer flotilla that he must be the sole judge of whether to attack or not, and we would support him, whatever he did and whatever happened. In these circumstances, Captain Warburton-Lee entered with five destroyers and attacked the enemy destroyers, and such guns as they could have landed in the interval. In the beginning all that they reported to us was what they had lost—nothing more—and I let it go out, because I do not think we ought to have a kind of mealy-mouthed attitude towards these matters. We have embarked on this war, and we must take our blows. Therefore, I put the report out, although there was nothing to relieve it, as it were. We are not children to be kept in the dark, and we can take what is coming to us as well as any other country.

As soon as the further report was received at about 1 o'clock, I prepared it for the Prime Minister, who immediately gave it to the House of Commons and to the country, through the Press, at the same time. The moment we get any news, be it bad or good, once we can rely on it, we shall present it to Parliament, the broadcast and the Press. I am all for propaganda and publicity, but the best propaganda is results, and I must

say that I think these are coming to hand in no unsatisfactory manner.
The result of this hard, fierce fight in the Narvik Fjord—half the com-
batant vessels were knocked out on each side—is worthy of any of the
records which are preserved with such respect in the long history of the
Navy. What was gained was the destruction of these store ships, as well
as the crippling of the force, and on the way back the two destroyers,
who were escorting their wounded comrade out of the Fjord, unpursued
by the enemy, who had received an equal battering, got the *Rauenfels,*
full of reserve ammunition with which, I suppose, it was intended to turn
Narvik into a kind of Sebastopol or Gibraltar. This ship was blown up,
and we must regard that as simplifying the task which obviously might
be among those which lie ahead of us.

Now I come to Wednesday. On that day a very determined attack was
made by two waves of 12 planes each of the Royal Air Force on two
German cruisers sheltering in the Bergen Fjord and covering German
troops that had been landed there. One of these light cruisers was hit, and
we have not seen anything of her since. She may be at the bottom or hiding in some fjord, but subsequent reconnaissance has not revealed her
presence. At dusk on Wednesday, the Fleet Air Arm came onto the scene
for the first time in this war. They have been very anxious to come into
action with their Skuas, which are perhaps not the latest pattern of aircraft. They have a long range, and they flew from the Orkneys and
attacked the remaining German cruiser at Bergen, which was moored
alongside. Sixteen of them attacked in successions of threes, all making
low bombing dives and casting their 500-pound bombs at the lowest
point. They secured three hits, and out of the 16, 15 returned. Then a little
later, when a reconnaissance aircraft was sent over, no cruiser was seen
where this one had been lying—only a streak of oil about a mile long
smearing the surface of the harbor. It looks as if a result has been obtained.

Today, Thursday, at daybreak, torpedo-carrying aircraft of the Fleet
Air Arm, 18 in number, have attacked enemy shipping in the harbor
of Trondheim. We had hoped to get a *Hipper*-class cruiser which was
reported certainly to be there. She had, however, vanished in the night,
and all we got was a destroyer, which was hit by a torpedo. This form of
attack by torpedo from the air is very old. I saw it when I was First Lord
before the last war and was deeply interested in it. It was used once at
the Dardanelles. It carries with it great hopes and possibilities which
have never been fully developed, but we must have more practice and

experience in the use of this unaccustomed weapon. This we hope to obtain as the fighting proceeds during the summer.

In my task of answering the question, "What is the Navy doing?" I am getting too near the range of current and pending operations to be able to make any further report to the House, but I hope I have to some extent answered the question which has been asked, and shown that the Navy has not been idle or negligent, and that it is actively proceeding on the tasks confided to it by Parliament. I shall look forward to making a further statement to Parliament a little later on. I will, however, venture to make a few general observations and attempt to survey the results up to date. When we speak of the command of the seas, that does not mean that the Royal Navy and its French ally command every part of the seas at the same moment or at every moment. It only means that we can make our will prevail ultimately in any part of the seas which may be selected for operations, and thus indirectly we can make our will prevail in every part of the seas. That is what command of the seas means. Anything more foolish than to suppose that the life and strength of the Royal Navy—which, allow me to remind the House, is engaged in bringing in through the U-boats the immense traffics of this country—anything, I say, more foolish than to suppose that the life and strength of the Royal Navy should have been expended in ceaselessly patrolling up and down the Norwegian and Danish coasts, a target for the U-boats, wearing out their crews and machinery on the chance that Hitler would launch a blow like this—anything more foolish than that nobody can imagine. I say with great respect that a man who makes such a suggestion is hardly qualified to offer advice to the nation in these serious times.

In my view, which is shared by my skilled advisers, Herr Hitler has committed a grave strategic error in spreading the war so far to the north and in forcing the Scandinavian people, or peoples, out of their attitude of neutrality. We have suffered from nothing in our blockade policy so much as the denial of the Norwegian coast, and that cursed corridor is now closed forever. Hitler has effected his German lodgments of various strengths at many points of the Norwegian coasts, and he has felled with a single hammer blow the inoffensive Kingdom of Denmark, but we shall take all we want of this Norwegian coast now, with an enormous increase in the facility and in the efficiency of our blockade. We are also at this moment occupying the Faroe Islands, which belong to Denmark and which are a strategic point of high importance, and whose people showed every disposition to receive us with warm regard. We shall shield the Faroe Islands from all the severities of war and establish ourselves there conveniently by sea and air until the moment comes when they will be handed back to the Crown and people of a Denmark liberated from the foul thraldom in which they have been plunged by the German aggression. The question of Iceland needs further consideration, because Iceland is, as it were, a Dominion of the Danish Kingdom. What I can say about Iceland at the moment is that no German will be allowed to set foot there with impunity.

In the upshot, it is the considered view of the Admiralty that we have greatly gained by what has occurred in Scandinavia and in northern waters in a strategic and military sense. For myself, I consider that Hitler's action in invading Scandinavia is as great a strategic and political error as that which was committed by Napoleon in 1807, when he invaded Spain. Hitler has violated the independence and soil of virile peoples dwelling in very large and expansive countries capable of maintaining, with British and French aid, prolonged resistance to his soldiers and his Gestapo. He has almost doubled the efficiency of the Allied blockade. He has made a whole series of commitments upon the Norwegian coast for which he will now have to fight, if necessary, during the whole summer, against Powers possessing vastly superior naval forces and able to transport them to the scenes of action more easily than he can. I cannot see any counter-advantage which he has gained except the satisfaction of another exercise of the brutal lust of unbridled power. I cannot see any satisfaction which he has gained which is any adequate offset to these substantial and enduring facts. Grieved as we all are at the suffering and misery which are now extended to wider areas, I must declare to the House that I feel that we are greatly advantaged by what has occurred, provided we act with unceasing and increasing vigor to turn to the utmost profit the strategic blunder into which our mortal enemy has been provoked.

I have two things more to say before I sit down. The first is a very serious thought. Everyone must recognize the extraordinary precision and the reckless gambling which have flung the whole German Fleet out upon the savage seas of war as if it were a mere counter, to be cast away for a particular operation. We and the French are far stronger than the German Navy. We have enough to maintain control of the Mediterranean, and, at the same time, we can carry on all our operations in the North Sea. But out of the very much smaller forces of the German Navy, most grievous losses have been already sustained. Four German cruisers—that is to say, nearly half their total pre-war strength and much more than their existing strength in cruisers—have been sunk, and a number of German destroyers together with several more U-boats have been destroyed, all since Sunday.

Up to the time I speak, those losses have been sustained by the German Navy. After all, a navy is an integral organization, with its battleships, cruisers and its destroyers, and that navy must be regarded as deeply mutilated in respect of this extraordinarily important and indeed indispensable cruiser element. Our submarines, which, I can assure the House, were by no means asleep, have taken heavy toll from the German transports and store ships now crossing into Scandinavia. We have given them the fullest liberty of action in all cases where humanity does not impose restraints. All German ships in the Skagerrak and the Kattegat will be sunk,[1] and by night all ships will be sunk, as opportunity serves. We are not going to allow the enemy to supply their armies across these waters with impunity. They have already ordered all merchant vessels out of this area, and in this respect our advice coincides with theirs. We hope to take unceasing toll. Up to the present nearly a dozen ships, some of large tonnage, have been sunk or captured, either in the Skagerrak and the Kattegat, or in other parts of the North Sea, or in attempting to bring supplies to the forces which were landed at Narvik. The Norwegian batteries have had their successes, and I must consider the German Fleet crippled in important respects.

But, Mr. Speaker—and this is the gravity of the thought which I venture to submit to the House—the very recklessness with which Hitler and his advisers have cast the interests of the German Navy upon the wild waters to meet all that moves thereon—this very recklessness makes me feel that these audacious, costly operations may be only the prelude to far larger events which impend on land. We have probably arrived now at the first main clinch of the war. But we certainly find no reason in the fact of what has just happened, and still less in our own hearts, to deter us from entering upon any further trials that may lie before us. While we will not prophesy or boast about battles still to be fought, we feel ourselves ready to encounter the utmost malice of the enemy and to devote all our life strength to achieve the victory in what is a world cause.

One word more. There never was a time when the Navy was treated more kindly by the British nation or by the House or when it was regarded with more admiration, nay, I will say affection. It is worthy of

[1] I.e., Liable to be sunk.

your confidence. But showing confidence in the Navy does not only mean applauding it in good days when some glittering success may be proclaimed. It means that those, and they are legion, who repose their faith in our sailormen and their leaders will not falter or become distressed if, for three or four days at a time, silence and darkness and dubious news lie over the sea or come from the sea, and that each one who has that confidence and faith will make it his duty to sustain those who are of lesser faith. Each of them will have his part in the great drama of human progress, now so vividly unfolded before us.

THE WITHDRAWAL FROM NORWAY

The House of Commons

May 8, 1940

April 13. Second naval action at Narvik; H.M.S. *Warspite* and escorting destroyers sink seven German destroyers.

April 14. Britain mines the whole Baltic coast of Germany.

April 15. The presence of a British Expeditionary Force in Norway is announced.

April 23. Sir John Simon introduces his second war budget.

May 2. The British Military forces south of Trondheim withdraw and embark at Andalsnes.

May 3. Further British forces withdraw at Namsos. The Norwegian Commander-in-Chief leaves with them.

May 8. Following a vigorous attack by Mr. Herbert Morrison, the Prime Minister states that the challenge will be treated as a vote of confidence. The debate is wound up by Mr. Churchill in the following speech. But the Government majority falls to 81.

THE WITHDRAWAL FROM NORWAY

I would like to say a few things about the subject of the Norwegian campaign and also about the general war. In this war we are frequently asked, "Why do you not take the initiative, why do you repeatedly wait and wonder where the enemy is going to strike you next?" Obviously, he has many choices open. We always seem to be waiting, and when we are struck, then we take some action. "Why," it is asked, "is the next blow not going to be struck by Britain?" The reason for this serious disadvantage of our not having the initiative is one which cannot speedily be removed, and it is our failure in the last five years to maintain or regain air parity in numbers with Germany. That is an old story, and it is a long story—a very long story, let me remind the House—because for the first two years, when I, with some friends, was pressing this upon the House, it was not only the Government who objected, but both the Opposition Parties. In the last two years or so, they came round, and gave great and valuable aid, but the fact remains that we failed to achieve the air parity which was considered to be vital to our security. The fact of our numerical deficiency in the air, in spite of our superiority in quality, both in men and material—which is, I believe, established—has condemned us, and will condemn us for some time to come, to a great deal of difficulty and suffering and danger, which we must endure with firmness, until more favorable conditions can be established, as assuredly they will be established.

The right hon. Gentleman [Mr. A. V. Alexander] asked me a number of questions about the Skagerrak and why we had not cut the communications there. Our present naval preponderance, it is said, ought to make it feasible for us to dominate the Skagerrak with our surface ships and thus cut the communications with Oslo from the first moment and continuously. But the immense enemy air strength which can be brought to bear upon our patrolling craft had made this method far too costly to be adopted. It could only be enforced by maintaining a standing surface patrol—and a patrol, mark you, not of detroyers—because it is close to the enemy air bases and it is also close to their cruisers and their battle-cruisers, of which they still retain two. Consequently, very important forces would have to be employed, in order to maintain a steady surface patrol, and the losses which would be inflicted upon that patrol from the air would, undoubtedly, very soon constitute a naval disaster. We have to face a fact like that.

Then, it is said, "Instead of maintaining a regular patrol, you might have had a raid." Here again, air strength, in this period when the nights are already shortening, impedes the approaching forces, and either the transports are removed from the area and sent back to their ports, or adequate forces are provided by the enemy to deal with the approaching raid. I am sorry, indeed, that things should be so, but it would be very foolish in these days, when we are repeatedly asked, in almost every speech, to face facts, if they were ignored. We therefore adopted the submarine blockade as the only method at our disposal, and in doing this, I followed the opinion of our naval authorities, who are responsible for handling the fleets not only from the Admiralty but on the ships at sea.

Here let me say a word about responsible opinion. There is a great deal of difference between being responsible for giving an order, on which the loss of several valuable ships might swiftly follow, and merely expressing an opinion, however well-informed, however sincere, however courageous, without such responsibility. I have to be guided in the advice which I offer to the Cabinet by responsible naval expert opinion, just as the right hon. Gentleman would be guided by it if he were occupying the place which he once occupied with a very considerable measure of naval esteem. Therefore we limited our operations in the Skagerrak to the submarines. In order to make this work as effective as possible, the usual restrictions which we have imposed on the actions of our submarines were relaxed. As I told the House, all German ships by day and all ships by night were to be sunk as opportunity served. This statement was most falsely and grotesquely twisted and travestied into a sort of promise that all German ships would be sunk. I have seen an echo coming from the United States. No one could ever have given so absurd a promise as that. I said the toll would be heavy, and heavy indeed it has been. There has been a ghastly success; seven thousand or eight thousand men have been drowned, and thousands of corpses have been washed up on the rocks at the entrance of Oslo. At the foot of the lighthouse the most frightful scenes have been witnessed. But what does the loss of seven thousand or eight thousand men matter to a totalitarian State? What do they matter to a Government such as that which we are fighting? They are not announced, no criticism is allowed, no murmur is allowed and no news. If there is a cry or a whimper, it is promptly dealt with by a brutal blow. Therefore that heavy loss does not operate in the moral or psychological sphere at all at the present time.

Well, then, the question was asked by a very influential person, not a Member of the House, Mr. Bevin—who is a friend of mine, working hard for the public cause, and a man who has much help to give and who asked in a public speech— "Why, when we went into Narvik on the first occasion, did you not send a big ship in with the destroyers and Captain Warburton-Lee?" I think that he should have his answer, and I will give it. The reason was that the only ship available was a battle-cruiser, and we only have three battle-cruisers, and we felt that it would be a very great damage to the balance of the Fleet if we lost a battle-cruiser. We thought it very likely that a ship going in might be lost. We later sent the *Warspite* there; but it did not look so easy the day before it was done as the day after. The craven and inept authorities of the Admiralty who took that risk were very much relieved to find that there were no controlled minefields laid, no special traps of one kind or another in the fjord, no destroyer lurking in some angle where it could fire its bouquet of torpedoes at the *Warspite*. We were very glad to know that a submarine which followed up was effectively sunk by an aircraft of the *Warspite* herself. All these are very different things when looked at beforehand than they are when looked at after. But what would have been said if it had been sunk? Who was the madman who sent one of our most valuable ships into narrow, congested waters like these where it could easily fall a prey to the many dangers surrounding it? It is easy when you have no responsibility. If you dare, and forfeit is exacted, it is murder of our sailors; if you are prudent, you are craven, cowardly, inept and timid.

Then we were asked why we did not go into Bergen, Trondheim and other ports in the first few hours. My right hon. Friend the Member for Sparkbrook [Mr. Amery] said we had been rather led astray or decoyed away by the two German heavy battle-cruisers which came out to sea, and that they were a fake and a lure. They may have been a fake and a lure, but they were certainly a reality. If we had tried to send transports carrying troops across waters where they, although unlocated, were known to be lurking, they might have cut the whole squadron of transports to rags. It would have been a very tragic incident, and we were happily spared from it. The only object of going into these fjords, unless you had troops to land and fight the Germans who had just arrived, would have been to destroy such enemy cruisers and destroyers as were there. These were largely destroyed from the air by the Fleet Air Arm. As for the two that were lurking in Trondheim harbor, one was a destroyer and one a small torpedo boat, and they were overlooked by the air. It would not have been justifiable to undertake to force Trondheim Fjord merely for the purpose of cleaning up that very small item.

I now come to the much more important question of Trondheim. There is no dispute that it was our duty to do our best to help the Norwegians and that the capture and defense of Trondheim was the best way to do it. My eye has always been fixed on Narvik; there, it seemed to me, was a port which might lead to some decisive achievement in the war. But when the German outrage occurred, there is no dispute that we were bound to go to the aid of the Norwegians and that Trondheim was the place. A plan was prepared by the joint staffs for two diversionary landings at Namsos and Andalsnes and for a direct landing in Trondheim Fjord of a force superior to that of the enemy which had seized that port. This was undoubtedly a hazardous operation. The forts at the entrance presented no serious difficulty, and the guns were not of a very formidable character; but the fact that a very large number of valuable ships would have to be continuously exposed for many hours to close bombing meant that grievous losses might be sustained. And although perhaps only one in two or three hundred bombs hit—we have had scores of ships under hours and hours of bombing—yet every now and again there is a hit, and the injury is disproportionate altogether to the power and value of the aircraft which inflicts it. Nevertheless, the Navy were perfectly ready to carry the troops in, and no one doubted their ability to do so.

Why, then, was this plan, which was timed for 25th April, abandoned? It was abandoned because, on the 17th, the two diversionary landings had made good progress, and it seemed much easier to capture Trondheim by this method than to incur the heavy cost of direct attack. I must make it perfectly clear that the Admiralty never withdrew their offer or considered the operation impracticable in the naval aspect. Grave doubts were, however, entertained by the Military as to the possibility of making an opposed landing under heavy hostile air superiority, apart from the existence of machine guns, and in these circumstances the Chiefs of Staff, and not only the Chiefs of Staff but their Deputies or Vice-Chiefs, as they are now called, without the slightest difference of opinion, so far as I am aware, advised that it would be less costly and surer to convert the diversionary landings into the main attack. No one has the slightest right to suggest that the Navy withdrew from this undertaking or that the politicians overruled the Admirals. I take the fullest responsibility—and so do the Prime Minister and the other Ministers concerned —for having accepted the unanimous view of our expert advisers. I thought they were right at the time and on the information we then had, and I have seen no reason to alter my view by what I have learned since.

However, the situation rapidly became worse. In the first place, the German thrust north of Oslo developed enormous strength. The Norwegians were unable to hold the mountain passes, and they did not destroy the roads and railways. By the 25th or 26th the possibility of the arrival in the region south of Trondheim of very large German forces, thoroughly equipped and maintained, had to be foreseen. At the same time the intense and continuous bombing of the bases at Namsos and Andalsnes prevented the landing at these small fishing ports of any large reinforcements, even of the artillery and of the many supplies for the infantry we had already landed. It was therefore necessary either to withdraw the troops, or leave them to be destroyed by overwhelming force. The decision to withdraw was undoubtedly sound, and the extrication and the re-embarkation of those 12,000 men—for that is all there were, less than a division—was accomplished with very great skill and, I may also add, with very good luck.

Now, that is the story of what happened, and why. As I have said, all the responsible Naval and Military and Air authorities, together with the Ministers principally concerned, and the War Cabinet, were at every stage united; and I expect that if any dozen Members of this House had been brought into this matter day by day they would equally have been united. But that does not, of course, end the question. Even if we assume that that view is right, and that we could have been masters of Trondheim— or its ruins, for such it would have speedily become—by 25th April, the question immediately arose: Could we have brought to bear a sufficient army south of Trondheim to hold the invader or drive him off? It is true that we should have had one good aerodrome together with proper quays for landing larger forces, and artillery, and that we might by this time, perhaps, have been building up a front on a line south of Trondheim, between the sea and the Swedish border; but even if we had, at the present time, got 25,000 or 30,000 Allied troops into action on this front, which, in view of the enemy's air superiority, is highly questionable, such a force would not have been able to arrive in time or been equipped with the necessary artillery in time, or been able to get anything like equal air support in time. I do not believe that it would have been able to withstand the immense weight of the attack which was being delivered by the Germans from their magnificent base at Oslo and up the two lines of railway and road from Oslo to the north. There can be no doubt whatever that the German base at Oslo and the German communications northward were incomparably superior to anything that we could have obtained at Trondheim, and at the various small ancillary landing places which we used. It would have been a very unsatisfactory struggle, at a great disadvantage and at disproportionate cost to the Allies. There are already over 120,000 German troops operating in South and Central Norway; and, although we could have thrown in continual reinforcements, I cannot believe that there was the slightest chance of ultimate success, and it would have been a struggle between an army based on Trondheim and a German army based on Oslo. That aspect of the matter had to be considered by the military experts as to whether the Germans could reinforce more quickly than we could. There was no means by which their air superiority could have been overcome. We should therefore have been committed to a forlorn operation on an ever-increasing scale.

Therefore, whatever view we may take of the chances of the attack on Trondheim, the decision to abandon it, although it was taken for different reasons from those I have just mentioned, was not only reasonable at the time, but has, I believe, saved us in the upshot from a most disastrous entanglement. It often happens in war that an operation which is successful on a small scale becomes vicious if it is multiplied by three, four, or five times. We must be careful not to exhaust our Air Force in view of the much graver dangers which might come upon us at any time, and also not to throw such a strain on our flotillas and anti-aircraft cruisers as might hamper the general mobility of the Fleet. There are other waters of which we have to think besides the Norwegian waters, and I can think of nothing more likely to bring new adversaries down upon us in other waters than the spectacle of our being too largely absorbed under the most unfavorable conditions in a protracted struggle around Trondheim. Of course, if Sweden had come to the rescue of

Norway, if her troops had entered, as they could easily have done, and if her air bases had been at the disposal of the Royal Air Force, very different positions might have been established. There has, unhappily, never been any chance of that. The Swedish Government, like many other people, have confined themselves to adverse criticism of His Majesty's Government. We are now fighting hard for Northern Norway, and in particular for Narvik, and I will not attempt to predict how the struggle will go, nor will I give any information about it all. I will content myself with saying that the conditions in that area are much more equal so far as ability to reinforce it is concerned—much more equal and much more favorable than those which would have developed in Central Norway.

I must say a word about my hon. and gallant Friend the Admiral,[1] to whom we listened with so much pleasure yesterday, when he made the best speech I have heard him make. I sympathize intensely with his desire to lead a valiant attack and to repeat in Scandinavian waters the immortal glories of the Zeebrugge Mole, but I am sorry that this natural impulse should have led him to cast aspersions upon his old shipmates and his old staff officers, Sir Dudley Pound and Vice-Admiral Phillips, and to speak in disparaging terms of them. I did not know them before I went to the Admiralty. I went there, as the House knows, on the day that war broke out. Eight months of war have led me to feel a very strong and solid confidence in them and also in the Commander-in-Chief of the Home Fleet, Sir Charles Forbes—confidence in their capacity and massive good sense and in their knowledge, which is kept constantly up-to-date by contacts with modern conditions—and I believe the Fleet itself has confidence in them. Therefore, when my hon. and gallant Friend came to me with his plan for forcing an entrance into Trondheim, I could only tell him that there was already a plan very similar to his, though I thought his was to some extent to be preferred; but that we had abandoned the plan.

I have dealt, as far as I can in the time open to me, with the details of this Trondheim story, but I must say that I cannot recede at all from the statement I made, which has been much criticized, that this invasion of Norway by Hitler has been a cardinal political and strategic error. In the brown hours, when baffling news comes, and disappointing news, I always turn for refreshment to the reports of the German wireless. I love to read the lies they tell of all the British ships they have sunk so

[1] Sir Roger Keyes.

many times over, and to survey the fools' paradise in which they find it necessary to keep their deluded serfs and robots. The Germans have claimed to have sunk or damaged 11 battleships; actually, two have been slightly damaged—neither of them withdrawn for a day from the service. They have claimed three aircraft carriers heavily damaged; the facts are that one was slightly injured by a near miss, and that it is still going on in the service. They have declared that they have sunk or damaged 28 cruisers; actually, one anti-aircraft cruiser has sustained damage. As to destroyers, and so forth—I could go on, but I will not. The only point on which they have not exaggerated is the sinking of trawlers. We have, unhappily, lost 11 trawlers in the Government service at one time or another; and that explains all these "battleships" in the German accounts.

My right hon. Friend the Member for Carnarvon [Mr. Lloyd George] said we must not mention calculations of profit and loss, but I do not agree. Calculations of profit and loss are our life. We win by these calculations of the ships we sink. It seems to me that, although Hitler's sudden overrunning of the vast regions of Norway has had astonishing and unwelcome effects, nevertheless, the advantages rest substantially with us. I will give some of the facts which are worth mentioning. Hitler has certainly lost ten lives for one—not that he cares for that, I agree. He has condemned a large part of the Scandinavian Peninsula and Denmark to enter the Nazi empire of Hungryland. He has committed an act of self-blockade. We see no reason why our control over the commerce of the seas should not become even more effective now that the Norwegian corridor exists no longer, and now that unhappy Denmark, when her reserves have been devoured, will no longer be the purveyor of bacon and butter and the channel of trade and communications with the outer world.

Although Hitler has treacherously received a large part of Norway it is perhaps forgotten that, like our own people, the Norwegians live largely by the sea. The French and the British Mercantile Marine can now rely upon the invaluable support and co-operation of the Norwegian merchant fleet, the fourth largest in the world, and on the services of seamen whose skill and daring are well known. Also we have taken into our service a very large amount of Danish shipping which will be of the greatest assistance. These are notable facts when we remember that the British and French losses through enemy action since the war are barely eight hundred thousand tons, and the captures and the building have already made good three-quarters of that loss.

PRIME MINISTER

The House of Commons

May 13, 1940

1940

May 10.   Germany invades Holland and Belgium. The British Army answers the appeal of King Leopold and moves north into Belgium.

Mr. Neville Chamberlain resigns the office of Prime Minister and the King invites Mr. Churchill to form a new Administration.

May 13.   The Dutch Royal Family arrives in London.

PRIME MINISTER

On Friday evening last I received His Majesty's Commission to form a new Administration. It was the evident wish and will of Parliament and the nation that this should be conceived on the broadest possible basis and that it should include all Parties, both those who supported the late Government and also the Parties of the Opposition. I have completed the most important part of this task. A War Cabinet has been formed of five Members, representing, with the Opposition Liberals, the unity of the nation. The three Party Leaders have agreed to serve, either in the War Cabinet or in high executive office. The three Fighting Services have been filled. It was necessary that this should be done in one single day, on account of the extreme urgency and rigor of events. A number of other key positions were filled yesterday, and I am submitting a further list to His Majesty tonight. I hope to complete the appointment of the principal Ministers during tomorrow. The appointment of the other Ministers usually takes a little longer, but I trust that, when Parliament meets again, this part of my task will be completed, and that the Administration will be complete in all respects.

I considered it in the public interest to suggest that the House should be summoned to meet today. Mr. Speaker agreed, and took the necessary steps, in accordance with the powers conferred upon him by the Resolution of the House. At the end of the proceedings today, the Adjournment of the House will be proposed until Tuesday, 21st May, with, of course, provision for earlier meeting if need be. The business to be considered during that week will be notified to Members at the earliest opportunity.

I now invite the House, by the Resolution which stands in my name, to record its approval of the steps taken and to declare its confidence in the new Government.

To form an Administration of this scale and complexity is a serious undertaking in itself, but it must be remembered that we are in the preliminary stage of one of the greatest battles in history, that we are in action at many points in Norway and in Holland, that we have to be prepared in the Mediterranean, that the air battle is continuous, and that many preparations have to be made here at home. In this crisis I hope I may be pardoned if I do not address the House at any length today. I hope that any of my friends and colleagues, or former colleagues, who are affected by the political reconstruction, will make all allowance for any lack of ceremony with which it has been necessary to act. I would say to the House, as I said to those who have joined this Government: "I have nothing to offer but blood, toil, tears, and sweat."

We have before us an ordeal of the most grievous kind. We have before us many, many long months of struggle and of suffering. You ask, What is our policy? I will say: "It is to wage war, by sea, land and air, with all our might and with all the strength that God can give us: to wage war against a monstrous tyranny, never surpassed in the dark, lamentable catalogue of human crime. That is our policy." You ask, What is our aim? I can answer in one word: Victory—victory at all costs, victory in spite of all terror, victory however long and hard the road may be; for without victory there is no survival. Let that be realized; no survival for the British Empire; no survival for all that the British Empire has stood for; no survival for the urge and impulse of the ages, that mankind will move forward towards its goal. But I take up my task with buoyancy and hope. I feel sure that our cause will not be suffered to fail among men. At this time I feel entitled to claim the aid of all, and I say, "Come then, let us go forward together with our united strength."

"BE YE MEN OF VALOR"

An Address Broadcast

May 19, 1940

May 14.   The Dutch Commander-in-Chief orders the Dutch Army to cease
fire. In Belgium the battle of the Meuse begins. The Secretary of
State for War, Mr. Anthony Eden, announces the formation of the
Home Guard.

May 15.   Queen Wilhelmina broadcasts a message that, though the Dutch
Army has been beaten in the field, Holland will continue the
struggle.
The Germans cross the Meuse between Meziéres and Namur.
Their attack turns west, driving behind the French defenses.

May 17.   The Germans enter Brussels.

May 19.   General Weygand succeeds General Gamelin as French Commander-in-Chief. The Germans take St. Quentin.

"BE YE MEN OF VALOR"

I SPEAK to you for the first time as Prime Minister in a solemn hour for the life of our country, of our Empire, of our Allies, and, above all, of the cause of Freedom. A tremendous battle is raging in France and Flanders. The Germans, by a remarkable combination of air bombing and heavily armored tanks, have broken through the French defenses north of the Maginot Line, and strong columns of their armored vehicles are ravaging the open country, which for the first day or two was without defenders. They have penetrated deeply and spread alarm and confusion in their track. Behind them there are now appearing infantry in lorries, and behind them, again, the large masses are moving forward. The re-groupment of the French armies to make head against, and also to strike at, this intruding wedge has been proceeding for several days, largely assisted by the magnificent efforts of the Royal Air Force.

We must not allow ourselves to be intimidated by the presence of these armored vehicles in unexpected places behind our lines. If they are behind our Front, the French are also at many points fighting actively behind theirs. Both sides are therefore in an extremely dangerous position. And if the French Army, and our own Army, are well handled, as I believe they will be; if the French retain that genius for recovery and counter-attack for which they have so long been famous; and if the British Army shows the dogged endurance and solid fighting power of which there have been so many examples in the past—then a sudden transformation of the scene might spring into being.

It would be foolish, however, to disguise the gravity of the hour. It would be still more foolish to lose heart and courage or to suppose that well-trained, well-equipped armies numbering three or four millions of men can be overcome in the space of a few weeks, or even months, by a scoop, or raid of mechanized vehicles, however formidable. We may look with confidence to the stabilization of the Front in France, and to the general engagement of the masses, which will enable the qualities of the French and British soldiers to be matched squarely against those of their adversaries. For myself, I have invincible confidence in the French Army and its leaders. Only a very small part of that splendid Army has yet been heavily engaged; and only a very small part of France has yet been invaded. There is good evidence to show that practically the whole of the specialized and mechanized forces of the enemy have been already thrown into the battle; and we know that very heavy losses have been inflicted upon them. No officer or man, no brigade or division, which grapples at close quarters with the enemy, wherever encountered, can fail to make a worthy contribution to the general result. The Armies must cast away the idea of resisting behind concrete lines or natural obstacles, and must realize that mastery can only be regained by furious and unrelenting assault. And this spirit must not only animate the High Command, but must inspire every fighting man.

In the air—often at serious odds, often at odds hitherto thought overwhelming—we have been clawing down three or four to one of our enemies; and the relative balance of the British and German Air Forces is now considerably more favorable to us than at the beginning of the battle. In cutting down the German bombers, we are fighting our own battle as well as that of France. My confidence in our ability to fight it out to the finish with the German Air Force has been strengthened by the fierce encounters which have taken place and are taking place. At the same time, our heavy bombers are striking nightly at the tap-root of German mechanized power, and have already inflicted serious damage upon the oil refineries on which the Nazi effort to dominate the world directly depends.

We must expect that as soon as stability is reached on the Western Front, the bulk of that hideous apparatus of aggression which gashed Holland into ruin and slavery in a few days will be turned upon us. I am sure I speak for all when I say we are ready to face it; to endure it; and to retaliate against it—to any extent that the unwritten laws of war permit. There will be many men and many women in this Island who, when the ordeal comes upon them, as come it will, will feel comfort, and even a pride, that they are sharing the perils of our lads at the Front—soldiers, sailors and airmen, God bless them—and are drawing away from them a part at least of the onslaught they have to bear. Is not this the appointed time for all to make the utmost exertions in their power? If the battle is to be won, we must provide our men with ever-increasing quantities of the weapons and ammunition they need. We must have, and have quickly, more aeroplanes, more tanks, more shells, more guns. There is imperious need for these vital munitions. They increase our strength against the powerfully armed enemy. They replace the wastage of the obstinate struggle; and the knowledge that wastage will speedily be replaced enables us to draw more readily upon our reserves and throw them in now that everything counts so much.

Our task is not only to win the battle—but to win the war. After this battle in France abates its force, there will come the battle for our Island —for all that Britain is, and all that Britain means. That will be the struggle. In that supreme emergency we shall not hesitate to take every step, even the most drastic, to call forth from our people the last ounce and the last inch of effort of which they are capable. The interests of property, the hours of labor, are nothing compared with the struggle for life and honor, for right and freedom, to which we have vowed ourselves.

I have received from the Chiefs of the French Republic, and in particular from its indomitable Prime Minister, M. Reynaud, the most sacred pledges that whatever happens they will fight to the end, be it bitter or be it glorious. Nay, if we fight to the end, it can only be glorious.

Having received His Majesty's commission, I have formed an Administration of men and women of every Party and of almost every point of view. We have differed and quarreled in the past; but now one bond unites us all—to wage war until victory is won, and never to surrender ourselves to servitude and shame, whatever the cost and the agony may be. This is one of the most awe-striking periods in the long history of France and Britain. It is also beyond doubt the most sublime. Side by side, unaided except by their kith and kin in the great Dominions and by the wide Empires which rest beneath their shield—side by side, the British and French peoples have advanced to rescue not only Europe but mankind from the foulest and most soul-destroying tyranny which has ever darkened and stained the pages of history. Behind them—behind us —behind the Armies and Fleets of Britain and France—gather a group of shattered States and bludgeoned races: the Czechs, the Poles, the Norwegians, the Danes, the Dutch, the Belgians—upon all of whom the long night of barbarism will descend, unbroken even by a star of hope, unless we conquer, as conquer we must; as conquer we shall.

Today is Trinity Sunday. Centuries ago words were written to be a call and a spur to the faithful servants of Truth and Justice: "Arm yourselves, and be ye men of valor, and be in readiness for the conflict; for it is better for us to perish in battle than to look upon the outrage of our nation and our altar. As the Will of God is in Heaven, even so let it be."

THE CAPITULATION OF KING LEOPOLD

The House of Commons

May 28, 1940

May 21.   The Germans reach Abbeville.

May 22.   The Belgian Army holds on the Scheldt. The Germans advance northwards from Abbeville along the Channel coast. The British Government passes in one day a new Emergency Powers Act, giving them complete power over persons and property for the prosecution of the war.

May 23.   The Germans reach Boulogne. Sir Samuel Hoare appointed Ambassador to Spain.

May 24.   The Germans reach Calais; they begin the siege of the ancient citadel.

May 27.   The Belgian Army, on the left of the British, severely handled.

May 28.   King Leopold surrenders. The Belgian Government repudiates the capitulation and remains with the Allies.

THE CAPITULATION OF KING LEOPOLD

THE HOUSE will be aware that the King of the Belgians yesterday sent a plenipotentiary to the German Command asking for a suspension of arms on the Belgian front. The British and French Governments instructed their generals immediately to dissociate themselves from this procedure and to persevere in the operations in which they are now engaged. However, the German Command has agreed to the Belgian proposals, and the Belgian Army ceased to resist the enemy's will at four o'clock this morning.

I have no intention of suggesting to the House that we should attempt at this moment to pass judgment upon the action of the King of the Belgians in his capacity as Commander-in-Chief of the Belgian Army. This Army has fought very bravely and has both suffered and inflicted heavy losses. The Belgian Government has dissociated itself from the action of the King and, declaring itself to be the only legal Government of Belgium, has formally announced its resolve to continue the war at the side of the Allies, who have come to the aid of Belgium at her urgent appeal. Whatever our feelings may be upon the facts so far as they are known to us, we must remember that the sense of brotherhood between the many peoples who have fallen into the power of the aggressor and those who still confront him will play its part in better days than those through which we are passing.

The situation of the British and French Armies, now engaged in a most severe battle and beset on three sides and from the air, is evidently extremely grave. The surrender of the Belgian Army in this manner adds appreciably to their grievous peril. But the troops are in good heart, and are fighting with the utmost discipline and tenacity; and I shall, of course, abstain from giving any particulars of what, with the powerful assistance of the Royal Navy and the Royal Air Force, they are doing or hope to do. I expect to make a statement to the House on the general position when the result of the intense struggle now going on can be known and measured. This will not, perhaps, be until the beginning of next week.

Meanwhile, the House should prepare itself for hard and heavy tidings. I have only to add that nothing which may happen in this battle can in any way relieve us of our duty to defend the world cause to which we have vowed ourselves; nor should it destroy our confidence in our power to make our way, as on former occasions in our history, through disaster and through grief to the ultimate defeat of our enemies.

DUNKIRK

The House of Commons

June 4, 1940

1940

May 29.   The defense of Dunkirk and the evacuation of the B.E.F. begin.

May 30.   The vanguard of the French Army commanded by General Prioux, cut off in Flanders, fights its way through to Dunkirk.

June 1.   Lord Gort, under instructions from the Government, returns to England. Mr. Eden announces that four-fifths of the Army has already been evacuated from Dunkirk.

June 3.   A thousand bombs dropped on Paris by German aircraft.

June 3-4.   The last Allied troops leave Dunkirk.

DUNKIRK

From the moment that the French defenses at Sedan and on the Meuse were broken at the end of the second week of May, only a rapid retreat to Amiens and the south could have saved the British and French Armies who had entered Belgium at the appeal of the Belgian King; but this strategic fact was not immediately realized. The French High Command hoped they would be able to close the gap, and the Armies of the north were under their orders. Moreover, a retirement of this kind would have involved almost certainly the destruction of the fine Belgian Army of over 20 divisions and the abandonment of the whole of Belgium. Therefore, when the force and scope of the German penetration were realized and when a new French Generalissimo, General Weygand, assumed command in place of General Gamelin, an effort was made by the French and British Armies in Belgium to keep on holding the right hand of the Belgians and to give their own right hand to a newly created French Army which was to have advanced across the Somme in great strength to grasp it.

However, the German eruption swept like a sharp scythe around the right and rear of the Armies of the north. Eight or nine armored divisions, each of about four hundred armored vehicles of different kinds, but carefully assorted to be complementary and divisible into small self-contained units, cut off all communications between us and the main French Armies. It severed our own communications for food and ammunition, which ran first to Amiens and afterwards through Abbeville, and it shore its way up the coast to Boulogne and Calais, and almost to Dunkirk. Behind this armored and mechanized onslaught came a number of German divisions in lorries, and behind them again there plodded comparatively slowly the dull brute mass of the ordinary German Army and German people, always so ready to be led to the trampling down in other lands of liberties and comforts which they have never known in their own.

I have said this armored scythe-stroke almost reached Dunkirk—almost but not quite. Boulogne and Calais were the scenes of desperate fighting. The Guards defended Boulogne for a while and were then withdrawn by orders from this country. The Rifle Brigade, the 60th Rifles, and the Queen Victoria's Rifles, with a battalion of British tanks and 1,000 Frenchmen, in all about four thousand strong, defended Calais to the last. The British Brigadier was given an hour to surrender. He spurned the offer, and four days of intense street fighting passed before silence reigned over Calais, which marked the end of a memorable resistance. Only 30 unwounded survivors were brought off by the Navy, and we do not know the fate of their comrades. Their sacrifice, however, was not in vain. At least two armored divisions, which otherwise would have been turned against the British Expeditionary Force, had to be sent to overcome them. They have added another page to the glories of the light divisions, and the time gained enabled the Graveline water lines to be flooded and to be held by the French troops.

Thus it was that the port of Dunkirk was kept open. When it was found impossible for the Armies of the north to reopen their communications to Amiens with the main French Armies, only one choice remained. It seemed, indeed, forlorn. The Belgian, British and French Armies were almost surrounded. Their sole line of retreat was to a single port and to its neighboring beaches. They were pressed on every side by heavy attacks and far outnumbered in the air.

When, a week ago today, I asked the House to fix this afternoon as the occasion for a statement, I feared it would be my hard lot to announce the greatest military disaster in our long history. I thought—and some good judges agreed with me—that perhaps 20,000 or 30,000 men might be re-embarked. But it certainly seemed that the whole of the French First Army and the whole of the British Expeditionary Force north of the Amiens-Abbeville gap would be broken up in the open field or else would have to capitulate for lack of food and ammunition. These were the hard and heavy tidings for which I called upon the House and the nation to prepare themselves a week ago. The whole root and core and brain of the British Army, on which and around which we were to build, and are to build, the great British Armies in the later years of the war, seemed about to perish upon the field or to be led into an ignominious and starving captivity.

'That was the prospect a week ago. But another blow which might well have proved final was yet to fall upon us. The King of the Belgians had called upon us to come to his aid. Had not this Ruler and his Government severed themselves from the Allies, who rescued their country from extinction in the late war, and had they not sought refuge in what has proved to be a fatal neutrality, the French and British Armies might well at the outset have saved not only Belgium but perhaps even Poland. Yet at the last moment, when Belgium was already invaded, King Leopold called upon us to come to his aid, and even at the last moment we came. He and his brave, efficient Army, nearly half a million strong, guarded our left flank and thus kept open our only line of retreat to the sea. Suddenly, without prior consultation, with the least possible notice, without the advice of his Ministers and upon his own personal act, he sent a plenipotentiary to the German Command, surrendered his Army, and exposed our whole flank and means of retreat.

I asked the House a week ago to suspend its judgment because the facts were not clear, but I do not feel that any reason now exists why we should not form our own opinions upon this pitiful episode. The surrender of the Belgian Army compelled the British at the shortest notice to cover a flank to the sea more than 30 miles in length. Otherwise all would have been cut off, and all would have shared the fate to which King Leopold had condemned the finest Army his country had ever formed. So in doing this and in exposing this flank, as anyone who followed the operations on the map will see, contact was lost between the British and two out of the three corps forming the First French Army, who were still farther from the coast than we were, and it seemed impossible that any large number of Allied troops could reach the coast.

The enemy attacked on all sides with great strength and fierceness, and their main power, the power of their far more numerous Air Force, was thrown into the battle or else concentrated upon Dunkirk and the beaches. Pressing in upon the narrow exit, both from the east and from the west, the enemy began to fire with cannon upon the beaches by which alone the shipping could approach or depart. They sowed magnetic mines in the channels and seas; they sent repeated waves of hostile aircraft, sometimes more than a hundred strong in one formation, to cast their bombs upon the single pier that remained, and upon the sand dunes upon which the troops had their eyes for shelter. Their U-boats, one of which was sunk, and their motor launches took their toll of the vast traffic which now began. For four or five days an intense struggle reigned. All their armored divisions—or what was left of them—together with great masses of infantry and artillery, hurled themselves in vain upon the ever-narrowing, ever-contracting appendix within which the British and French Armies fought.

Meanwhile, the Royal Navy, with the willing help of countless merchant seamen, strained every nerve to embark the British and Allied troops; 220 light warships and 650 other vessels were engaged. They had to operate upon the difficult coast, often in adverse weather, under an almost ceaseless hail of bombs and an increasing concentration of artillery fire. Nor were the seas, as I have said, themselves free from mines and torpedoes. It was in conditions such as these that our men carried on, with little or no rest, for days and nights on end, making trip after trip across the dangerous waters, bringing with them always men whom they had rescued. The numbers they have brought back are the measure of their devotion and their courage. The hospital ships, which brought off many thousands of British and French wounded, being so plainly marked were a special target for Nazi bombs; but the men and women on board them never faltered in their duty.

Meanwhile, the Royal Air Force, which had already been intervening in the battle, so far as its range would allow, from home bases, now used part of its main metropolitan fighter strength, and struck at the German bombers and at the fighters which in large numbers protected them. This struggle was protracted and fierce. Suddenly the scene has cleared, the crash and thunder has for the moment—but only for the moment—died away. A miracle of deliverance, achieved by valor, by perseverance, by perfect discipline, by faultless service, by resource, by skill, by unconquerable fidelity, is manifest to us all. The enemy was hurled back by the retreating British and French troops. He was so roughly handled that he did not hurry their departure seriously. The Royal Air Force engaged the main strength of the German Air Force, and inflicted upon them losses of at least four to one; and the Navy, using nearly 1,000 ships of all kinds, carried over 335,000 men, French and British, out of the jaws of death and shame, to their native land and to the tasks which lie immediately ahead. We must be very careful not to assign to this deliverance the attributes of a victory. Wars are not won by evacuations.

But there was a victory inside this deliverance, which should be noted. It was gained by the Air Force. Many of our soldiers coming back have not seen the Air Force at work; they saw only the bombers which escaped its protective attack. They underrate its achievements. I have heard much talk of this; that is why I go out of my way to say this. I will tell you about it.

This was a great trial of strength between the British and German Air Forces. Can you conceive a greater objective for the Germans in the air than to make evacuation from these beaches impossible, and to sink all these ships which were displayed, almost to the extent of thousands? Could there have been an objective of greater military importance and significance for the whole purpose of the war than this? They tried hard, and they were beaten back; they were frustrated in their task. We got the Army away; and they have paid fourfold for any losses which they have inflicted. Very large formations of German aeroplanes—and we know that they are a very brave race—have turned on several occasions from the attack of one-quarter of their number of the Royal Air Force, and have dispersed in different directions. Twelve aeroplanes have been hunted by two. One aeroplane was driven into the water and cast away by the mere charge of a British aeroplane, which had no more ammunition. All of our types—the Hurricane, the Spitfire and the new Defiant—and all our pilots have been vindicated as superior to what they have at present to face.

When we consider how much greater would be our advantage in defending the air above this Island against an overseas attack, I must say that I find in these facts a sure basis upon which practical and reassuring thoughts may rest. I will pay my tribute to these young airmen. The great French Army was very largely, for the time being, cast back and disturbed by the onrush of a few thousands of armored vehicles. May it not also be that the cause of civilization itself will be defended by the skill and devotion of a few thousand airmen? There never has been, I suppose, in all the world, in all the history of war, such an opportunity for youth. The Knights of the Round Table, the Crusaders, all fall back into the past—not only distant but prosaic; these young men, going forth every morn to guard their native land and all that we stand for, holding in their hands these instruments of colossal and shattering power, of whom it may be said that

"Every morn brought forth a noble chance
And every chance brought forth a noble knight,"

deserve our gratitude, as do all of the brave men who, in so many ways and on so many occasions, are ready, and continue ready, to give life and all for their native land.

I return to the Army. In the long series of very fierce battles, now on this front, now on that, fighting on three fronts at once, battles fought by two or three divisions against an equal or somewhat larger number of the enemy, and fought fiercely on some of the old grounds that so many of us knew so well—in these battles our losses in men have exceeded 30,000 killed, wounded and missing. I take occasion to express the sympathy of the House to all who have suffered bereavement or who are still anxious. The President of the Board of Trade[1] is not here today. His son has been killed, and many in the House have felt the pangs of affliction in the sharpest form. But I will say this about the missing: We have had a large number of wounded come home safely to this country, but I would say about the missing that there may be very many reported missing who will come back home, some day, in one way or another. In the confusion of this fight it is inevitable that many have been left in positions where honor required no further resistance from them.

Against this loss of over 30,000 men, we can set a far heavier loss certainly inflicted upon the enemy. But our losses in material are enormous. We have perhaps lost one-third of the men we lost in the opening days of the battle of 21st March, 1918, but we have lost nearly as many guns— nearly one thousand—and all our transport, all the armored vehicles that were with the Army in the north. This loss will impose a further delay on the expansion of our military strength. That expansion had not been proceeding as fast as we had hoped. The best of all we had to give had gone to the British Expeditionary Force, and although they had not the numbers of tanks and some articles of equipment which were desirable, they were a very well and finely equipped Army. They had the first-fruits of all that our industry had to give, and that is gone. And now here is this further delay. How long it will be, how long it will last, depends upon the exertions which we make in this Island. An effort the like of which has never been seen in our records is now being made. Work is proceeding everywhere, night and day, Sundays and week days. Capital and Labor have cast aside their interests, rights, and customs and put them into the common stock. Already the flow of munitions has leaped forward. There is no reason why we should not in a few months over-

[1] Sir Andrew Duncan, now Minister of Supply.

take the sudden and serious loss that has come upon us, without retarding the development of our general program.

Nevertheless, our thankfulness at the escape of our Army and so many men, whose loved ones have passed through an agonizing week, must not blind us to the fact that what has happened in France and Belgium is a colossal military disaster. The French Army has been weakened, the Belgian Army has been lost, a large part of those fortified lines upon which so much faith had been reposed is gone, many valuable mining districts and factories have passed into the enemy's possession, the whole of the Channel ports are in his hands, with all the tragic consequences that follow from that, and we must expect another blow to be struck almost immediately at us or at France. We are told that Herr Hitler has a plan for invading the British Isles. This has often been thought of before. When Napoleon lay at Boulogne for a year with his flat-bottomed boats and his Grand Army, he was told by someone, "There are bitter weeds in England." There are certainly a great many more of them since the British Expeditionary Force returned.

The whole question of home defense against invasion is, of course, powerfully affected by the fact that we have for the time being in this Island incomparably more powerful military forces than we have ever had at any moment in this war or the last. But this will not continue. We shall not be content with a defensive war. We have our duty to our Ally. We have to reconstitute and build up the British Expeditionary Force once again, under its gallant Commander-in-Chief, Lord Gort. All this is in train; but in the interval we must put our defenses in this Island into such a high state of organization that the fewest possible numbers will be required to give effective security and that the largest possible potential of offensive effort may be realized. On this we are now engaged. It will be very convenient, if it be the desire of the House, to enter upon this subject in a secret Session. Not that the Government would necessarily be able to reveal in very great detail military secrets, but we like to have our discussions free, without the restraint imposed by the fact that they will be read the next day by the enemy; and the Government would benefit by views freely expressed in all parts of the House by Members with their knowledge of so many different parts of the country. I understand that some request is to be made upon this subject, which will be readily acceded to by His Majesty's Government.

We have found it necessary to take measures of increasing stringency, not only against enemy aliens and suspicious characters of other nationalities, but also against British subjects who may become a danger or a nuisance should the war be transported to the United Kingdom. I know there are a great many people affected by the orders which we have made who are the passionate enemies of Nazi Germany. I am very sorry for them, but we cannot, at the present time and under the present stress, draw all the distinctions which we should like to do. If parachute landings were attempted and fierce fighting attendant upon them followed, these unfortunate people would be far better out of the way, for their own sakes as well as for ours. There is, however, another class, for which I feel not the slightest sympathy. Parliament has given us the powers to put down Fifth Column activities with a strong hand, and we shall use those powers, subject to the supervision and correction of the House, without the slightest hesitation until we are satisfied, and more than satisfied, that this malignancy in our midst has been effectively stamped out.

Turning once again, and this time more generally, to the question of invasion, I would observe that there has never been a period in all these long centuries of which we boast when an absolute guarantee against invasion, still less against serious raids, could have been given to our people. In the days of Napoleon the same wind which would have carried his transports across the Channel might have driven away the blockading fleet. There was always the chance, and it is that chance which has excited and befooled the imaginations of many Continental tyrants. Many are the tales that are told. We are assured that novel methods will be adopted, and when we see the originality of malice, the ingenuity of aggression, which our enemy displays, we may certainly prepare ourselves for every kind of novel stratagem and every kind of brutal and treacherous maneuver. I think that no idea is so outlandish that it should not be considered and viewed with a searching, but at the same time, I hope, with a steady eye. We must never forget the solid assurances of sea power and those which belong to air power if it can be locally exercised.

I have, myself, full confidence that if all do their duty, if nothing is neglected, and if the best arrangements are made, as they are being made, we shall prove ourselves once again able to defend our Island home, to ride out the storm of war, and to outlive the menace of tyranny, if necessary for years, if necessary alone. At any rate, that is what we are going to try to do. That is the resolve of His Majesty's Government—every man of them. That is the will of Parliament and the nation. The British Empire and the French Republic, linked together in their cause and in their need, will defend to the death their native soil, aiding each other like good comrades to the utmost of their strength. Even though large tracts of Europe and many old and famous States have fallen or may fall into the grip of the Gestapo and all the odious apparatus of Nazi rule, we shall not flag or fail. We shall go on to the end, we shall fight in France, we shall fight on the seas and oceans, we shall fight with growing confidence and growing strength in the air, we shall defend our Island, whatever the cost may be, we shall fight on the beaches, we shall fight on the landing grounds, we shall fight in the fields and in the streets, we shall fight in the hills; we shall never surrender, and even if, which I do not for a moment believe, this Island or a large part of it were subjugated and starving, then our Empire beyond the seas, armed and guarded by the British Fleet, would carry on the struggle, until, in God's good time, the New World, with all its power and might, steps forth to the rescue and the liberation of the old.

A MESSAGE TO THE PEOPLE

Broadcast June 17, 1940

June 5. The Germans attack on the Somme and Aisne.

June 6. M. Daladier dropped from the French Cabinet.

June 10. Italy declares war on France and Britain.

June 11. First R.A.F. raids on Libya. Fighting in Somaliland.

June 12. Rouen and Rheims fall.

June 13. The British Government promises the utmost help in their power to France and renew their pledge to continue the struggle.

June 14. The Germans occupy Paris, and make rapid progress through Champagne.

June 16. M. Reynaud resigns and Marshal Pétain forms a new Government. German troops near Dijon.

June 17. Marshal Pétain sues for peace.

A MESSAGE TO THE PEOPLE

THE NEWS from France is very bad and I grieve for the gallant French people who have fallen into this terrible misfortune. Nothing will alter our feelings towards them or our faith that the genius of France will rise again. What has happened in France makes no difference to our actions and purpose. We have become the sole champions now in arms to defend the world cause. We shall do our best to be worthy of this high honor. We shall defend our Island home, and with the British Empire we shall fight on unconquerable until the curse of Hitler is lifted from the brows of mankind. We are sure that in the end all will come right.

THEIR FINEST HOUR

*A Speech delivered first to the House of Commons
and then Broadcast, June 18, 1940*

1940

June 18. German forces reach the Swiss frontier. Herr Hitler and Signor Mussolini meet at Munich to agree on terms for France. German forces reach Cherbourg, and cross the Loire at several points.

THEIR FINEST HOUR

I spoke the other day of the colossal military disaster which occurred when the French High Command failed to withdraw the northern Armies from Belgium at the moment when they knew that the French front was decisively broken at Sedan and on the Meuse. This delay entailed the loss of fifteen or sixteen French divisions and threw out of action for the critical period the whole of the British Expeditionary Force. Our Army and 120,000 French troops were indeed rescued by the British Navy from Dunkirk but only with the loss of their cannon, vehicles and modern equipment. This loss inevitably took some weeks to repair, and in the first two of those weeks the battle in France has been lost. When we consider the heroic resistance made by the French Army against heavy odds in this battle, the enormous losses inflicted upon the enemy and the evident exhaustion of the enemy, it may well be thought that these 25 divisions of the best-trained and best-equipped troops might have turned the scale. However, General Weygand had to fight without them. Only three British divisions or their equivalent were able to stand in the line with their French comrades. They have suffered severely, but they have fought well. We sent every man we could to France as fast as we could re-equip and transport their formations.

I am not reciting these facts for the purpose of recrimination. That I judge to be utterly futile and even harmful. We cannot afford it. I recite them in order to explain why it was we did not have, as we could have had, between twelve and fourteen British divisions fighting in the line in this great battle instead of only three. Now I put all this aside. I put it on the shelf, from which the historians, when they have time, will select their documents to tell their stories. We have to think of the future and not of the past. This also applies in a small way to our own affairs at home. There are many who would hold an inquest in the House of Commons on the conduct of the Governments—and of Parliaments, for they are in it, too—during the years which led up to this catastrophe. They seek to indict those who were responsible for the guidance of our affairs. This also would be a foolish and pernicious process. There are too many in it. Let each man search his conscience and search his speeches. I frequently search mine.

Of this I am quite sure, that if we open a quarrel between the past and the present, we shall find that we have lost the future. Therefore, I cannot accept the drawing of any distinctions between Members of the present Government. It was formed at a moment of crisis in order to unite all the Parties and all sections of opinion. It has received the almost unanimous support of both Houses of Parliament. Its Members are going to stand together, and, subject to the authority of the House of Commons, we are going to govern the country and fight the war. It is absolutely necessary at a time like this that every Minister who tries each day to do his duty shall be respected; and their subordinates must know that their chiefs are not threatened men, men who are here today and gone tomorrow, but that their directions must be punctually and faithfully obeyed. Without this concentrated power we cannot face what lies before us. I should not think it would be very advantageous for the House to prolong this Debate this afternoon under conditions of public stress. Many facts are not clear that will be clear in a short time. We are to have a secret Session on Thursday, and I should think that would be a better opportunity for the many earnest expressions of opinion which Members will desire to make and for the House to discuss vital matters without having everything read the next morning by our dangerous foes.

The disastrous military events which have happened during the past fortnight have not come to me with any sense of surprise. Indeed, I indicated a fortnight ago as clearly as I could to the House that the worst possibilities were open; and I made it perfectly clear then that whatever happened in France would make no difference to the resolve of Britain and the British Empire to fight on, "if necessary for years, if necessary alone." During the last few days we have successfully brought off the great majority of the troops we had on the line of communication in France; and seven-eighths of the troops we have sent to France since the beginning of the war—that is to say, about 350,000 out of 400,000 men—are safely back in this country. Others are still fighting with the French, and fighting with considerable success in their local encounters against the enemy. We have also brought back a great mass of stores, rifles and munitions of all kinds which had been accumulated in France during the last nine months.

We have, therefore, in this Island today a very large and powerful military force. This force comprises all our best-trained and our finest troops, including scores of thousands of those who have already measured their quality against the Germans and found themselves at no disadvantage. We have under arms at the present time in this Island over a million and a quarter men. Behind these we have the Local Defense Volunteers, numbering half a million, only a portion of whom, however, are yet armed with rifles or other firearms. We have incorporated into our Defense Forces every man for whom we have a weapon. We expect very large additions to our weapons in the near future, and in preparation for this we intend forthwith to call up, drill and train further large numbers. Those who are not called up, or else are employed upon the vast business of munitions production in all its branches—and their ramifications are innumerable—will serve their country best by remaining at their ordinary work until they receive their summons. We have also over here Dominions armies. The Canadians had actually landed in France, but have now been safely withdrawn, much disappointed, but in perfect order, with all their artillery and equipment. And these very high-class forces from the Dominions will now take part in the defense of the Mother Country.

Lest the account which I have given of these large forces should raise the question: Why did they not take part in the great battle in France? I must make it clear that, apart from the divisions training and organizing at home, only 12 divisions were equipped to fight upon a scale which justified their being sent abroad. And this was fully up to the number which the French had been led to expect would be available in France at the ninth month of the war. The rest of our forces at home have a fighting value for home defense which will, of course, steadily increase every week that passes. Thus, the invasion of Great Britain would at this time require the transportation across the sea of hostile armies on a very large scale, and after they had been so transported they would have to be continually maintained with all the masses of munitions and supplies which are required for continuous battle—as continuous battle it will surely be.

Here is where we come to the Navy—and after all, we have a Navy. Some people seem to forget that we have a Navy. We must remind them. For the last thirty years I have been concerned in discussions about the possibilities of oversea invasion, and I took the responsibility on behalf of the Admiralty, at the beginning of the last war, of allowing all regular troops to be sent out of the country. That was a very serious step to take, because our Territorials had only just been called up and were quite untrained. Therefore, this Island was for several months practically denuded of fighting troops. The Admiralty had confidence at that time in their ability to prevent a mass invasion even though at that time the Germans had a magnificent battle fleet in the proportion of 10 to 16, even though they were capable of fighting a general engagement every day and any day, whereas now they have only a couple of heavy ships worth speaking of—the *Scharnhorst* and the *Gneisenau*. We are also told that the Italian Navy is to come out and gain sea superiority in these waters. If they seriously intend it, I shall only say that we shall be delighted to offer Signor Mussolini a free and safeguarded passage through the Straits of Gibraltar in order that he may play the part to which he aspires. There is a general curiosity in the British Fleet to find out whether the Italians are up to the level they were at in the last war or whether they have fallen off at all.

Therefore, it seems to me that as far as sea-borne invasion on a great scale is concerned, we are far more capable of meeting it today than we were at many periods in the last war and during the early months of this war, before our other troops were trained, and while the B.E.F. had proceeded abroad. Now, the Navy have never pretended to be able to prevent raids by bodies of 5,000 or 10,000 men flung suddenly across and thrown ashore at several points on the coast some dark night or foggy morning. The efficacy of sea power, especially under modern conditions, depends upon the invading force being of large size. It has to be of large size, in view of our military strength, to be of any use. If it is of large size, then the Navy have something they can find and meet and, as it were, bite on. Now, we must remember that even five divisions, however lightly equipped, would require 200 to 250 ships, and with modern air reconnaissance and photography it would not be easy to collect such an armada, marshal it, and conduct it across the sea without any powerful naval forces to escort it; and there would be very great possibilities, to put it mildly, that this armada would be intercepted long before it reached the coast, and all the men drowned in the sea or, at the worst, blown to pieces with their equipment while they were trying to land. We also have a great system of minefields, recently strongly reinforced, through which we alone know the channels. If the enemy tries to sweep passages through these minefields, it will be the task of the Navy to destroy the mine-sweepers and any other forces employed to protect them. There should be no difficulty in this, owing to our great superiority at sea.

Those are the regular, well-tested, well-proved arguments on which we have relied during many years in peace and war. But the question is whether there are any new methods by which those solid assurances can be circumvented. Odd as it may seem, some attention has been given to this by the Admiralty, whose prime duty and responsibility it is to destroy any large sea-borne expedition before it reaches, or at the moment when it reaches, these shores. It would not be a good thing for me to go into details of this. It might suggest ideas to other people which they have not thought of, and they would not be likely to give us any of their ideas in exchange. All I will say is that untiring vigilance and mind-searching must be devoted to the subject, because the enemy is crafty and cunning and full of novel treacheries and stratagems. The House may be assured that the utmost ingenuity is being displayed and imagination is being evoked from large numbers of competent officers, well-trained in tactics and thoroughly up to date, to measure and counterwork novel possibilities. Untiring vigilance and untiring searching of the mind is being, and must be, devoted to the subject, because, remember, the enemy is crafty and there is no dirty trick he will not do.

Some people will ask why, then, was it that the British Navy was not able to prevent the movement of a large army from Germany into Norway across the Skagerrak? But the conditions in the Channel and in the North Sea are in no way like those which prevail in the Skagerrak. In the Skagerrak, because of the distance, we could give no air support to our surface ships, and consequently, lying as we did close to the enemy's main air power, we were compelled to use only our submarines. We could not enforce the decisive blockade or interruption which is possible from surface vessels. Our submarines took a heavy toll but could not, by themselves, prevent the invasion of Norway. In the Channel and in the North Sea, on the other hand, our superior naval surface forces, aided by our submarines, will operate with close and effective air assistance.

This brings me, naturally, to the great question of invasion from the air, and of the impending struggle between the British and German Air Forces. It seems quite clear that no invasion on a scale beyond the capacity of our land forces to crush speedily is likely to take place from the air until our Air Force has been definitely overpowered. In the meantime, there may be raids by parachute troops and attempted descents of air-borne soldiers. We should be able to give those gentry a warm reception, both in the air and on the ground, if they reach it in any condition to continue the dispute. But the great question is: Can we break Hitler's air weapon? Now, of course, it is a very great pity that we have not got an Air Force at least equal to that of the most powerful enemy within striking distance of these shores. But we have a very powerful Air Force which has proved itself far superior in quality, both in men and in many types of machine, to what we have met so far in the numerous and fierce air battles which have been fought with the Germans. In France, where we were at a considerable disadvantage and lost many machines on the ground when they were standing round the aerodromes, we were accustomed to inflict in the air losses of as much as two to two-and-a-half to one. In the fighting over Dunkirk, which was a sort of no-man's-land, we undoubtedly beat the German Air Force, and gained the mastery of the local air, inflicting here a loss of three or four to one day after day. Anyone who looks at the photographs which were published a week or so ago of the re-embarkation, showing the masses of troops assembled on the beach and forming an ideal target for hours at a time, must realize that this re-embarkation would not have been possible unless the enemy had resigned all hope of recovering air superiority at that time and at that place.

In the defense of this Island the advantages to the defenders will be much greater than they were in the fighting around Dunkirk. We hope to improve on the rate of three or four to one which was realized at Dunkirk; and in addition all our injured machines and their crews which get down safely—and, surprisingly, a very great many injured machines and men do get down safely in modern air fighting—all of these will fall, in an attack upon these Islands, on friendly soil and live to fight another day; whereas all the injured enemy machines and their complements will be total losses as far as the war is concerned.

During the great battle in France, we gave very powerful and continuous aid to the French Army, both by fighters and bombers; but in spite of every kind of pressure we never would allow the entire metropolitan fighter strength of the Air Force to be consumed. This decision was painful, but it was also right, because the fortunes of the battle in France could not have been decisively affected even if we had thrown in our entire fighter force. That battle was lost by the unfortunate strategical opening, by the extraordinary and unforeseen power of the armored columns, and by the great preponderance of the German Army in numbers. Our fighter Air Force might easily have been exhausted as a mere accident in that great struggle, and then we should have found ourselves at the present time in a very serious plight. But as it is, I am happy to inform the House that our fighter strength is stronger at the present time relatively to the Germans, who have suffered terrible losses, than it has ever been; and consequently we believe ourselves possessed of the capacity to continue the war in the air under better conditions than we have ever experienced before. I look forward confidently to the exploits of our fighter pilots—these splendid men, this brilliant youth—who will have the glory of saving their native land, their island home, and all they love, from the most deadly of all attacks.

There remains, of course, the danger of bombing attacks, which will certainly be made very soon upon us by the bomber forces of the enemy. It is true that the German bomber force is superior in numbers to ours; but we have a very large bomber force also, which we shall use to strike at military targets in Germany without intermission. I do not at all underrate the severity of the ordeal which lies before us; but I believe our countrymen will show themselves capable of standing up to it, like the brave men of Barcelona, and will be able to stand up to it, and carry on in spite of it, at least as well as any other people in the world. Much will depend upon this; every man and every woman will have the chance to show the finest qualities of their race, and render the highest service to their cause. For all of us, at this time, whatever our sphere, our station, our occupation or our duties, it will be a help to remember the famous lines:

> "He nothing common did or mean,
> Upon that memorable scene."

I have thought it right upon this occasion to give the House and the country some indication of the solid, practical grounds upon which we base our inflexible resolve to continue the war. There are a good many people who say, "Never mind. Win or lose, sink or swim, better die than submit to tyranny—and such a tyranny." And I do not dissociate myself from them. But I can assure them that our professional advisers of the three Services unitedly advise that we should carry on the war, and that there are good and reasonable hopes of final victory. We have fully informed and consulted all the self-governing Dominions, these great communities far beyond the oceans who have been built up on our laws and on our civilization, and who are absolutely free to choose their course, but are absolutely devoted to the ancient Motherland, and who feel themselves inspired by the same emotions which lead me to stake our all upon duty and honor. We have fully consulted them, and I have received from their Prime Ministers, Mr. Mackenzie King of Canada, Mr. Menzies of Australia, Mr. Fraser of New Zealand, and General Smuts of South Africa—that wonderful man, with his immense profound mind, and his eye watching from a distance the whole panorama of European affairs—I have received from all these eminent men, who all have Governments behind them elected on wide franchises, who are all there because they represent the will of their people, messages couched in the most moving terms in which they endorse our decision to fight on, and declare themselves ready to share our fortunes and to persevere to the end. That is what we are going to do.

We may now ask ourselves: In what way has our position worsened since the beginning of the war? It has worsened by the fact that the Germans have conquered a large part of the coast line of Western Europe, and many small countries have been overrun by them. This aggravates the possibilities of air attack and adds to our naval preoccupations. It in no way diminishes, but on the contrary definitely increases, the power of our long-distance blockade. Similarly, the entrance of Italy into the war increases the power of our long-distance blockade. We have stopped the worst leak by that. We do not know whether military resistance will come to an end in France or not, but should it do so, then of course the Germans will be able to concentrate their forces, both military and industrial, upon us. But for the reasons I have given to the House these will not be found so easy to apply. If invasion has become more imminent, as no doubt it has, we, being relieved from the task of maintaining a large army in France, have far larger and more efficient forces to meet it.

If Hitler can bring under his despotic control the industries of the countries he has conquered, this will add greatly to his already vast armament output. On the other hand, this will not happen immediately, and we are now assured of immense, continuous and increasing support in supplies and munitions of all kinds from the United States; and especially of aeroplanes and pilots from the Dominions and across the oceans, coming from regions which are beyond the reach of enemy bombers.

I do not see how any of these factors can operate to our detriment on balance before the winter comes; and the winter will impose a strain upon the Nazi regime, with almost all Europe writhing and starving under its cruel heel, which, for all their ruthlessness, will run them very hard. We must not forget that from the moment when we declared war on the 3rd September it was always possible for Germany to turn all her Air Force upon this country, together with any other devices of invasion she might conceive, and that France could have done little or nothing to prevent her doing so. We have, therefore, lived under this danger, in principle and in a slightly modified form, during all these months. In the meanwhile, however, we have enormously improved our methods of defense, and we have learned what we had no right to assume at the beginning, namely, that the individual aircraft and the individual British pilot have a sure and definite superiority. Therefore, in casting up this dread balance-sheet and contemplating our dangers with a disillusioned eye, I see great reason for intense vigilance and exertion, but none whatever for panic or despair.

During the first four years of the last war the Allies experienced nothing but disaster and disappointment. That was our constant fear: one blow after another, terrible losses, frightful dangers. Everything miscarried. And yet at the end of those four years the morale of the Allies was higher than that of the Germans, who had moved from one aggressive triumph to another, and who stood everywhere triumphant invaders of the lands into which they had broken. During that war we repeatedly asked ourselves the question: How are we going to win? and no one was able ever to answer it with much precision, until at the end, quite suddenly, quite unexpectedly, our terrible foe collapsed before us, and we were so glutted with victory that in our folly we threw it away.

We do not yet know what will happen in France or whether the French resistance will be prolonged, both in France and in the French Empire overseas. The French Government will be throwing away great opportunities and casting adrift their future if they do not continue the war in accordance with their Treaty obligations, from which we have not felt able to release them. The House will have read the historic declaration in which, at the desire of many Frenchmen—and of our own hearts—we have proclaimed our willingness at the darkest hour in French history to conclude a union of common citizenship in this struggle. However matters may go in France or with the French Government, or other French Governments, we in this Island and in the British Empire will never lose our sense of comradeship with the French people. If we are now called upon to endure what they have been suffering, we shall emulate their courage, and if final victory rewards our toils they shall share the gains, aye, and freedom shall be restored to all. We abate nothing of our just demands; not one jot or tittle do we recede. Czechs, Poles, Norwegians, Dutch, Belgians have joined their causes to our own. All these shall be restored.

What General Weygand called the Battle of France is over. I expect that the Battle of Britain is about to begin. Upon this battle depends the survival of Christian civilization. Upon it depends our own British life, and the long continuity of our institutions and our Empire. The whole fury and might of the enemy must very soon be turned on us. Hitler knows that he will have to break us in this Island or lose the war. If we can stand up to him, all Europe may be free and the life of the world may move forward into broad, sunlit uplands. But if we fail, then the whole world, including the United States, including all that we have known and cared for, will sink into the abyss of a new Dark Age made more sinister, and perhaps more protracted, by the lights of perverted science. Let us therefore brace ourselves to our duties, and so bear ourselves that, if the British Empire and its Commonwealth last for a thousand years, men will still say, "This was their finest hour."

THE FALL OF FRANCE

The House of Commons

June 25, 1940

1940

June 21. Hitler receives French plenipotentiaries in Marshal Foch's railway carriage in the Forest of Compiègne. He dictates his armistice terms. The Polish Cabinet lands in England.

June 22. Herr Hitler's armistice terms are accepted by Marshal Pétain's plenipotentiaries. General de Gaulle in London raises the standard of Free France.

June 24. Armistice between France and Italy signed. Herr Hitler proclaims, "The war in the West is ended."

June 25. Hostilities in France cease at 12:35 A.M.

THE FALL OF FRANCE

THE HOUSE will feel profound sorrow at the fate of the great French nation and people, to whom we have been joined so long in war and peace, and whom we have regarded as trustees with ourselves for the progress of a liberal culture and tolerant civilization in Europe. There is no use or advantage in wasting strength and time upon hard words and reproaches. We hope that life and power will be given to us to rescue France from the ruin and bondage into which she has been cast by the might and fury of the enemy—and by other causes. We hope, however, that the French Empire, stretching all over the world, and still protected by sea power, will continue the struggle at the side of its Allies. We hope that it may become the seat of a government which will strive steadfastly for victory, and will organize armies of liberation.

These are matters which Frenchmen alone can decide. We find it difficult to believe that the interests of France and the spirit of France will find no other expression than in the melancholy decisions which have been taken by the Government at Bordeaux. We shall certainly aid, to the best of our ability and resources, any movement or any action by Frenchmen outside the power of the enemy, to work for the defeat of Nazi German barbarism and for the freedom and restoration of France. What our relations will be with the Bordeaux Government I cannot tell. They have delivered themselves over to the enemy, and lie wholly in his power. He may do much by blandishments or by severities, by propaganda, and by the choosing of pro-German Ministers to make our relations difficult. We do not know whether we shall be allowed to have any British representative in the restricted region called "unoccupied France," because that is entirely surrounded by and under the control of the enemy; but, relying upon the true genius of the French people, and their judgment upon what has happened, when they are allowed to know the facts, we shall endeavor to keep such contacts as are possible through the bars of their prison. Meanwhile we must look to our own salvation and effectual defense, upon which not only British but French, European, and world-wide fortunes depend.

The safety of Great Britain and the British Empire is powerfully, though not decisively, affected by what happens to the French Fleet. When it became clear that the defeat and subjugation of France was imminent and that her fine Army, on which so many hopes were set, was reeling under the German flail, M. Reynaud, the courageous Prime Minister, asked me to come to Tours, which I did on 13th June, accompanied by the Foreign Secretary and the Minister for Aircraft Production, Lord Beaverbrook. I see that some accounts have been given of these conversations by the Bordeaux Government which do not at all correspond with the facts. We have, of course, a record kept by one of the Cabinet secretaries who came with us, and I do not propose to go into this now at any length. M. Reynaud, after dwelling on the conditions at the Front and the state of the French Army, with which I was well acquainted, asked me whether Great Britain would release France from her obligations not to negotiate for an armistice or peace without the consent of her British Ally. Although I knew how great French sufferings were, and that we had not so far endured equal trials or made an equal contribution in the field, I felt bound to say that I could not give consent. I said that there would be no use in adding mutual reproaches to the other miseries we might have to bear, but that I could not give consent. We agreed that a further appeal should be made by M. Reynaud to the United States and that if the reply was not sufficient to enable M. Reynaud to go on fighting —and he, after all, was the fighting spirit—then we should meet again and take a decision in the light of the new factors.

On the 16th I received a message from M. Reynaud, who had then moved to Bordeaux, to say that the American response was not satisfactory, and requesting the formal release of France from her obligations under the Anglo-French Agreement. The Cabinet was immediately convened, and we sent a message, of which I do not give the exact text, but I give the general substance—*Separate negotiations, whether for armistice or peace, depend upon an agreement made by Britain with the French Republic and not with any particular French administration or statesman. They therefore involve the honor of France. However, in view of all they have suffered, and of the forces evidently working upon them, and pro-*

vided that the French Fleet is dispatched to British ports and remains there while the negotiations are conducted, His Majesty's Government will give their consent to the French Government's asking what terms of armistice would be open to them.—It was also made clear that His Majesty's Government were resolved to continue the war, altogether apart from French aid, and dissociated themselves from such inquiries about an armistice.

The same evening, the 16th, when I was preparing, at M. Reynaud's invitation, to go to see him, and I was in fact in the train, I received news that he had been overthrown and that a new Government under Marshal Pétain had been formed, which Government had been formed for the prime purpose of seeking an armistice with Germany. In these circumstances, we naturally did everything in our power to secure proper arrangements for the disposition of the French Fleet. We reminded the new Government that the condition indispensable to their release had not been complied with, the condition being that it should be sent to a British port. There was plenty of time to do it, and it would have made no difference to the negotiations: the terms could hardly have been more severe than they were. In order to reinforce the earnestness with which we held our views, we sent the First Sea Lord and the First Lord [1] as well as Lord Lloyd [2] to establish what contacts were possible with the new Ministers. Everything was, of course, fusing into collapse at that time, but many solemn assurances were given that the Fleet would never be allowed to fall into German hands. It was, therefore, "with grief and amazement," to quote the words of the Government statement which we issued on Sunday, that I read Article 8 of the Armistice terms.

This Article, to which the French Government have subscribed, says that the French Fleet, excepting that part left free for the safeguarding of French interests in the Colonial Empire, shall be collected in ports to be specified and there demobilized and disarmed under German or Italian control. From this text it is clear that the French war vessels under this Armistice pass into German and Italian control while fully armed. We note, of course, in the same Article the solemn declaration of the German Government that they have no intention of using them for their own purposes during the war. What is the value of that? Ask half a dozen countries what is the value of such solemn assurance. Furthermore, the

---

[1] Admiral Sir Dudley Pound, First Sea Lord; Mr. A. V. Alexander, First Lord of the Admiralty.

[2] Secretary of State for the Colonies.

same Article 8 of the Armistice excepts from the operation of such assurances and solemn declarations those units necessary for coast surveillance and mine-sweeping. Under this provision it would be possible for the German Government to reserve, ostensibly for coast surveillance, any existing units of the French Fleet. Finally, the Armistice can at any time be voided on any pretext of non-observance, and the terms of Armistice explicitly provide for further German claims when any peace between Germany and France comes to be signed. Such, in a very brief epitome, are the salient points in this lamentable and also memorable episode, of which no doubt a much fuller account will be given by history. The House would naturally not expect me to say anything about the future. The situation at the present time is so uncertain and obscure that it would be contrary to the public interest for me to attempt to pronounce or speculate upon it, but I may well have more to say should the House permit me to make a further statement next week. In the meantime, I hope that the House will continue to extend their full confidence to His Majesty's Government and will believe that neither patience nor resolution will be lacking in the measures they may think it right to take for the safety of the Empire.

THE TRAGEDY OF THE FRENCH FLEET

The House of Commons

July 4, 1940

June 26. M. Corbin, French Ambassador in London, resigns.

June 27. Russia in an ultimatum to Rumania demands the return of Bessarabia and Bukovina.

June 29. Rumania accepts Russia's terms and Russian forces begin to occupy the ceded territory.

June 29. Marshal Balbo crashes in Libya and is killed.

July 1. Rumania, subjected to Axis pressure, renounces the Anglo-French guarantee of her integrity. Russia completes her occupation of the ceded portions of Rumania two and a half days ahead of schedule.

July 3. Great Britain assumes control over those portions of the French Fleet lying in British waters, and, after an ultimatum is rejected by their commander, disables the French ships of war at Oran.

THE TRAGEDY OF THE FRENCH FLEET

It is with sincere sorrow that I must now announce to the House the measures which we have felt bound to take in order to prevent the French Fleet from falling into German hands. When two nations are fighting together under long and solemn alliance against a common foe, one of them may be stricken down and overwhelmed, and may be forced to ask its ally to release it from its obligations. But the least that could be expected was that the French Government, in abandoning the conflict and leaving its whole weight to fall upon Great Britain and the British Empire, would have been careful not to inflict needless injury upon their faithful comrade, in whose final victory the sole chance of French freedom lay, and lies.

As the House will remember, we offered to give full release to the French from their treaty obligations, although these were designed for precisely the case which arose, on one condition, namely, that the French Fleet should be sailed for British harbors before the separate armistice negotiations with the enemy were completed. This was not done, but on the contrary, in spite of every kind of private and personal promise and assurance given by Admiral Darlan to the First Lord and to his Naval colleague, the First Sea Lord of the British Admiralty, an armistice was signed which was bound to place the French Fleet as effectively in the power of Germany and its Italian following as that portion of the French Fleet was placed in our power when many of them, being unable to reach African ports, came into the harbors of Portsmouth and Plymouth about ten days ago. Thus I must place on record that what might have been a mortal injury was done to us by the Bordeaux Government with full knowledge of the consequences and of our dangers, and after rejecting all our appeals at the moment when they were abandoning the Alliance, and breaking the engagements which fortified it.

There was another example of this callous and perhaps even malevolent treatment which we received, not indeed from the French nation, who have never been and apparently never are to be consulted upon these transactions, but from the Bordeaux Government. This is the instance: There were over 400 German air pilots who were prisoners in France, many of them, perhaps most of them, shot down by the Royal Air Force. I obtained from M. Reynaud a personal promise that these pilots should be sent for safekeeping to England, and orders were given by him to that effect; but when M. Reynaud fell, these pilots were delivered over to Germany, in order, no doubt, to win favor for the Bordeaux Government with their German masters, and to win it without regard to the injury done to us. The German Air Force already feels acutely the shortage of high-grade pilots, and it seemed to me particularly odious, if I may use the word, that these 400 skilled men should be handed over with the sure knowledge that they would be used to bomb this country, and thus force our airmen to shoot them down for the second time over. Such wrongful deeds I am sure will not be condoned by history, and I firmly believe that a generation of Frenchmen will arise who will clear their national honor from all countenance of them.

I said last week that we must now look with particular attention to our own salvation. I have never in my experience seen discussed in a Cabinet so grim and somber a question as what we were to do about the French Fleet. It shows how strong were the reasons for the course which we thought it our duty to take, that every Member of the Cabinet had the same conviction about what should be done and there was not the slightest hesitation or divergence among them, and that the three Service Ministers, as well as men like the Minister of Information[1] and the Secretary of State for the Colonies, particularly noted for their long friendship with France, when they were consulted were equally convinced that no other decision than that which we took was possible. We took that decision, and it was a decision to which, with aching hearts but with clear vision, we unitedly came. Accordingly, early yesterday morning, 3rd July, after all preparations had been made, we took the greater part of the French Fleet under our control, or else called upon them, with adequate force, to comply with our requirements. Two battleships, two light cruisers, some submarines, including a very large one, the *Surcouf,* eight destroyers and approximately 200 smaller but extremely useful mine-sweeping and anti-submarine craft which lay for the most part at Portsmouth

[1] Mr. Duff Cooper.

and Plymouth, though there were some at Sheerness, were boarded by superior forces, after brief notice had been given wherever possible to their captains.

This operation was successfully carried out without resistance or bloodshed except in one instance. A scuffle arose through a misunderstanding in the submarine *Surcouf,* in which one British leading seaman was killed and two British officers and one rating wounded, and one French officer killed and one wounded. For the rest, the French sailors in the main cheerfully accepted the end of a period of uncertainty. A considerable number, 800 to 900, have expressed an ardent desire to continue the war, and some have asked for British nationality. This we are ready to grant without prejudice to the other Frenchmen, numbered by thousands, who prefer to fight on with us as Frenchmen. All the rest of those crews will be immediately repatriated to French ports, if the French Government are able to make arrangements for their reception by permission of their German rulers. We are also repatriating all French troops who were in this country, excepting those who, of their own free will, have volunteered to follow General de Gaulle in the French Forces of Liberation, of whom he is chief. Several French submarines have also joined us independently, and we have accepted their services.

Now I turn to the Mediterranean. At Alexandria, where a strong British battle fleet is lying, there are, besides a French battleship, four French cruisers, three of them modern 8-inch gun vessels, and a number of smaller ships. These have been informed that they cannot be permitted to leave harbor and thus fall within the power of the German conquerors of France. Negotiations and discussions, with the details of which I need not trouble the House, have necessarily been taking place, and measures have now been taken to ensure that those ships, which are commanded by a very gallant Admiral, shall be sunk or otherwise made to comply with our wishes. The anguish which this process has, naturally, caused to the British and French naval officers concerned may be readily imagined, when I tell the House that only this morning, in the air raid upon Alexandria by Italian aircraft, some of the French ships fired heavily and effectively with us against the common enemy. We shall, of course, offer the fullest facilities to all French officers and men at Alexandria who wish to continue the war, and will provide for them and maintain them during the conflict. We have also promised to repatriate all the rest, and every care in our power will be taken, if they allow it, for their safety and their comfort. So much for Alexandria.

But the most serious part of the story remains. Two of the finest vessels of the French Fleet, the *Dunkerque* and the *Strasbourg,* modern battle-cruisers much superior to *Scharnhorst* and *Gneisenau*—and built for the purpose of being superior to them—lay with two battleships, several light cruisers, and a number of destroyers and submarines and other vessels at Oran and at its adjacent military port of Mers-El-Kebir on the northern African shore of Morocco. Yesterday morning, a carefully chosen British officer, Captain Holland, late Naval Attaché in Paris, was sent on in a destroyer and waited upon the French Admiral Gensoul. After being refused an interview, he presented the following document, which I will read to the House. The first two paragraphs of the document deal with the general question of the Armistice, which I have already explained in my own words. The fourth paragraph begins as follows—this is the operative paragraph:

"It is impossible for us, your comrades up to now, to allow your fine ships to fall into the power of the German or Italian enemy. We are determined to fight on to the end, and if we win, as we think we shall, we shall never forget that France was our Ally, that our interests are the same as hers, and that our common enemy is Germany. Should we conquer, we solemnly declare that we shall restore the greatness and territory of France. For this purpose, we must make sure that the best ships of the French Navy are not used against us by the common foe. In these circumstances, His Majesty's Government have instructed me [that is, the British Admiral] to demand that the French Fleet now at Mers-El-Kebir and Oran shall act in accordance with one of the following alternatives:

"(*a*) Sail with us and continue to fight for victory against the Germans and Italians.

"(*b*) Sail with reduced crews under our control to a British port. The reduced crews will be repatriated at the earliest moment.

"If either of these courses is adopted by you, we will restore your ships to France at the conclusion of the war or pay full compensation, if they are damaged meanwhile.

"(*c*) Alternatively, if you feel bound to stipulate that your ships should not be used against the Germans or Italians unless these break the Armistice, then sail them with us, with reduced crews, to some French port in the West Indies—Martinique, for instance—where they can be demilitarized to our satisfaction or be perhaps entrusted to the United States and remain safe until the end of the war, the crews being repatriated.

"If you refuse these fair offers, I must, with profound regret, require you to sink your ships within six hours.

"Finally, failing the above, I have the orders of His Majesty's Government to use whatever force may be necessary to prevent your ships from falling into German or Italian hands."

We had hoped that one or other of the alternatives which we presented would have been accepted, without the necessity of using the terrible force of a British battle squadron. Such a squadron arrived before Oran two hours after Captain Holland and his destroyer. This battle squadron was commanded by Vice-Admiral Somerville, an officer who distinguished himself lately in the bringing off of over 100,000 Frenchmen during the evacuation from Dunkirk. Admiral Somerville was further provided, besides his battleships, with a cruiser force and strong flotillas. All day the parleys continued, and we hoped until the afternoon that our terms would be accepted without bloodshed. However, no doubt in obedience to the orders dictated by the Germans from Wiesbaden, where the Franco-German Armistice Commission is in session, Admiral Gensoul refused to comply and announced his intention of fighting. Admiral Somerville was, therefore, ordered to complete his mission before darkness fell, and at 5:53 P.M. he opened fire upon this powerful French Fleet, which was also protected by its shore batteries. At 6 P.M. he reported that he was heavily engaged. The action lasted for some ten minutes and was followed by heavy attacks from our naval aircraft, carried in the *Ark Royal*. At 7:20 P.M. Admiral Somerville forwarded a further report, which stated that a battle-cruiser of the *Strasbourg* class was damaged and ashore; that a battleship of the *Bretagne* class had been sunk, that another of the same class had been heavily damaged, and that two French destroyers and a seaplane carrier, *Commandant Teste,* were also sunk or burned.

While this melancholy action was being fought, either the battle-cruiser *Strasbourg* or the *Dunkerque,* one or the other, managed to slip out of harbor in a gallant effort to reach Toulon or a North African port and place herself under German control, in accordance with the Armistice terms of the Bordeaux Government—though all this her crew and captain may not have realized. She was pursued by aircraft of the Fleet Air Arm and hit by at least one torpedo. She may have been joined by other French vessels from Algiers, which were well placed to do so and to reach Toulon before we would overtake them. She will, at any rate, be out of action for many months to come.

I need hardly say that the French ships were fought, albeit in this unnatural cause, with the characteristic courage of the French Navy, and every allowance must be made for Admiral Gensoul and his officers, who felt themselves obliged to obey the orders they received from their Government and could not look behind that Government to see the German dictation. I fear the loss of life among the French and in the harbor must have been very heavy, as we were compelled to use a severe measure of force and several immense explosions were heard. None of the British ships taking part in the action was in any way affected in gun-power or mobility by the heavy fire directed upon them. I have not yet received any reports of our casualties, but Admiral Somerville's Fleet is, in all military respects, intact and ready for further action. The Italian Navy, for whose reception we had also made arrangements and which is, of course, considerably stronger numerically than the Fleet we used at Oran, kept prudently out of the way. However, we trust that their turn will come during the operations which we shall pursue to secure the effectual command of the Mediterranean.

A large proportion of the French Fleet has, therefore, passed into our hands or has been put out of action or otherwise withheld from Germany by yesterday's events. The House will not expect me to say anything about other French ships which are at large except that it is our inflexible resolve to do everything that is possible in order to prevent them falling into the German grip. I leave the judgment of our action, with confidence, to Parliament. I leave it to the nation, and I leave it to the United States. I leave it to the world and history.

Now I turn to the immediate future. We must, of course, expect to be attacked, or even invaded, if that proves to be possible—it has not been proved yet—in our own Island before very long. We are making every preparation in our power to repel the assaults of the enemy, whether they be directed upon Great Britain, or upon Ireland, which all Irishmen, without distinction of creed or party, should realize is in imminent danger. These again are matters upon which we have clear views. These preparations are constantly occupying our toil from morn till night, and far into the night. But, although we have clear views, it would not, I think, be profitable for us to discuss them in public, or even, so far as the Government are concerned, except under very considerable reserve in a private Session. I call upon all subjects of His Majesty, and upon our Allies, and well-wishers—and they are not a few—all over the world, on both sides of the Atlantic, to give us their utmost aid. In the fullest harmony with our Dominions, we are moving through a period of extreme danger and of splendid hope, when every virtue of our race will be tested, and all that we have and are will be freely staked. This is no time for doubt or weakness. It is the supreme hour to which we have been called.

I will venture to read to the House a message which I have caused to be sent to all who are serving in positions of importance under the Crown, and if the House should view it with sympathy, I should be very glad to send a copy of it to every Member for his own use—not that such exhortations are needed. This is the message:

"On what may be the eve of an attempted invasion or battle for our native land, the Prime Minister desires to impress upon all persons holding responsible positions in the Government, in the fighting Services, or in the Civil Departments, their duty to maintain a spirit of alert and confident energy. While every precaution must be taken that time and means afford, there are no grounds for supposing that more German troops can be landed in this country, either from the air or across the sea, than can be destroyed or captured by the strong forces at present under arms. The Royal Air Force is in excellent order and at the highest strength it has yet attained. The German Navy was never so weak, nor the British Army at home so strong as now. The Prime Minister expects all His Majesty's servants in high places to set an example of steadiness and resolution. They should check and rebuke expressions of loose and ill-digested opinion in their circle, or by their subordinates. They should not hesitate to report, or if necessary remove, any officers or officials who are found to be consciously exercising a disturbing or depressing influence, and whose talk is calculated to spread alarm and despondency. Thus alone will they be worthy of the fighting men, who, in the air, on the sea, and on land, have already met the enemy without any sense of being outmatched in martial qualities."

In conclusion, I feel that we are entitled to the confidence of the House and that we shall not fail in our duty, however painful. The action we have already taken should be, in itself, sufficient to dispose once and for all of the lies and rumors which have been so industriously spread by German propaganda and through Fifth Column activities that we have the slightest intention of entering into negotiations in any form and through any channel with the German and Italian Governments. We shall, on the contrary, prosecute the war with the utmost vigor by all the means that are open to us until the righteous purposes for which we entered upon it have been fulfilled.

THE WAR OF THE UNKNOWN WARRIORS

An Address Broadcast

July 14, 1940

July 5.   The Pétain Government breaks off diplomatic relations with Britain.

July 8.   The Navy disables the new French battleship *Richelieu* at Dakar.

July 11.   Germany seizes all French gold and securities.

July 12.   Britain agrees to close the Burma road to armaments traffic for three months.

THE WAR OF THE UNKNOWN WARRIORS

During the last fortnight the British Navy, in addition to blockading what is left of the German Fleet and chasing the Italian Fleet, has had imposed upon it the sad duty of putting effectually out of action for the duration of the war the capital ships of the French Navy. These, under the Armistice terms, signed in the railway coach at Compiègne, would have been placed within the power of Nazi Germany. The transference of these ships to Hitler would have endangered the security of both Great Britain and the United States. We therefore had no choice but to act as we did, and to act forthwith. Our painful task is now complete. Although the unfinished battleship, the *Jean Bart,* still rests in a Moroccan harbor and there are a number of French warships at Toulon and in various French ports all over the world, these are not in a condition or of a character to derange our preponderance of naval power. As long, therefore, as they make no attempt to return to ports controlled by Germany or Italy, we shall not molest them in any way. That melancholy phase in our relations with France has, so far as we are concerned, come to an end.

Let us think rather of the future. Today is the fourteenth of July, the national festival of France. A year ago in Paris I watched the stately parade down the Champs Elysées of the French Army and the French Empire. Who can foresee what the course of other years will bring? Faith is given to us to help and comfort us when we stand in awe before the unfurling scroll of human destiny. And I proclaim my faith that some of us will live to see a fourteenth of July when a liberated France will once again rejoice in her greatness and in her glory, and once again stand forward as the champion of the freedom and the rights of man. When the day dawns, as dawn it will, the soul of France will turn with comprehension and with kindness to those Frenchmen and Frenchwomen, wherever they may be, who in the darkest hour did not despair of the Republic.

In the meantime, we shall not waste our breath nor cumber our thought with reproaches. When you have a friend and comrade at whose side you have faced tremendous struggles, and your friend is smitten down by a stunning blow, it may be necessary to make sure that the weapon that has fallen from his hands shall not be added to the resources of your common enemy. But you need not bear malice because of your friend's cries of delirium and gestures of agony. You must not add to his pain; you must work for his recovery. The association of interest between Britain and France remains. The cause remains. Duty inescapable remains. So long as our pathway to victory is not impeded, we are ready to discharge such offices of good will toward the French Government as may be possible, and to foster the trade and help the administration of those parts of the great French Empire which are now cut off from captive France, but which maintain their freedom. Subject to the iron demands of the war which we are waging against Hitler and all his works, we shall try so to conduct ourselves that every true French heart will beat and glow at the way we carry on the struggle; and that not only France, but all the oppressed countries in Europe may feel that each British victory is a step towards the liberation of the Continent from the foulest thralldom into which it has ever been cast.

All goes to show that the war will be long and hard. No one can tell where it will spread. One thing is certain: the peoples of Europe will not be ruled for long by the Nazi Gestapo, nor will the world yield itself to Hitler's gospel of hatred, appetite and domination.

And now it has come to us to stand alone in the breach, and face the worst that the tyrant's might and enmity can do. Bearing ourselves humbly before God, but conscious that we serve an unfolding purpose, we are ready to defend our native land against the invasion by which it is threatened. We are fighting *by* ourselves alone; but we are not fighting *for* ourselves alone. Here in this strong City of Refuge which enshrines the title-deeds of human progress and is of deep consequence to Christian civilization; here, girt about by the seas and oceans where the Navy reigns; shielded from above by the prowess and devotion of our airmen— we await undismayed the impending assault. Perhaps it will come tonight. Perhaps it will come next week. Perhaps it will never come. We must show ourselves equally capable of meeting a sudden violent shock or

—what is perhaps a harder test—a prolonged vigil. But be the ordeal sharp or long, or both, we shall seek no terms, we shall tolerate no parley; we may show mercy—we shall ask for none.

I can easily understand how sympathetic onlookers across the Atlantic, or anxious friends in the yet-unravished countries of Europe, who cannot measure our resources or our resolve, may have feared for our survival when they saw so many States and kingdoms torn to pieces in a few weeks or even days by the monstrous force of the Nazi war machine. But Hitler has not yet been withstood by a great nation with a will power the equal of his own. Many of these countries have been poisoned by intrigue before they were struck down by violence. They have been rotted from within before they were smitten from without. How else can you explain what has happened to France?—to the French Army, to the French people, to the leaders of the French people?

But here, in our Island, we are in good health and in good heart. We have seen how Hitler prepared in scientific detail the plans for destroying the neighbor countries of Germany. He had his plans for Poland and his plans for Norway. He had his plans for Denmark. He had his plans all worked out for the doom of the peaceful, trustful Dutch; and, of course, for the Belgians. We have seen how the French were undermined and overthrown. We may therefore be sure that there *is* a plan—perhaps built up over years—for destroying Great Britain, which after all has the honor to be his main and foremost enemy. All I can say is that any plan for invading Britain which Hitler made two months ago must have had to be entirely recast in order to meet our new position. Two months ago —nay, one month ago—our first and main effort was to keep our best Army in France. All our regular troops, all our output of munitions, and a very large part of our Air Force, had to be sent to France and maintained in action there. But now we have it all at home. Never before in the last war—or in this—have we had in this Island an Army comparable in quality, equipment or numbers to that which stands here on guard tonight. We have a million and a half men in the British Army under arms tonight, and every week of June and July has seen their organization, their defenses and their striking power advance by leaps and bounds. No praise is too high for the officers and men—aye, and civilians—who have made this immense transformation in so short a time. Behind these soldiers of the regular Army, as a means of destruction for parachutists, air-borne invaders, and any traitors that may be found in our midst (but I do not believe there are many—woe betide them, they will get short shrift)—behind the regular Army we have more than a million of the Local Defense Volunteers, or, as they are much better called, the "Home Guard." These officers and men, a large proportion of whom have been through the last war, have the strongest desire to attack and come to close quarters with the enemy wherever he may appear. Should the invader come to Britain, there will be no placid lying down of the people in submission before him, as we have seen, alas, in other countries. We shall defend every village, every town, and every city. The vast mass of London itself, fought street by street, could easily devour an entire hostile army; and we would rather see London laid in ruins and ashes than that it should be tamely and abjectly enslaved. I am bound to state these facts, because it is necessary to inform our people of our intentions, and thus to reassure them.

This has been a great week for the Royal Air Force, and for the Fighter Command. They have shot down more than five to one of the German aircraft which have tried to molest our convoys in the Channel or have ventured to cross the British coast line. These are, of course, only the preliminary encounters to the great air battles which lie ahead. But I know of no reason why we should be discontented with the results so far achieved; although, of course, we hope to improve upon them as the fighting becomes more widespread and comes more inland. Around all lies the power of the Royal Navy. With over a thousand armed ships under the White Ensign, patrolling the seas, the Navy, which is capable of transferring its force very readily to the protection of any part of the British Empire which may be threatened, is capable also of keeping open communication with the New World, from whom, as the struggle deepens, increasing aid will come. Is it not remarkable that after ten months of unlimited U-boat and air attack upon our commerce, our food reserves are higher than they have ever been, and we have a substantially larger tonnage under our own flag, apart from great numbers of foreign ships in our control, than we had at the beginning of the war?

Why do I dwell on all this? Not, surely, to induce any slackening of effort or vigilance. On the contrary. These must be redoubled, and we must prepare not only for the summer, but for the winter; not only for 1941, but for 1942; when the war will, I trust, take a different form from the defensive, in which it has hitherto been bound. I dwell on these elements in our strength, on these resources which we have mobilized and control—I dwell on them because it is right to show that the good cause *can* command the means of survival; and that while we toil through the dark valley we can see the sunlight on the uplands beyond.

I stand at the head of a Government representing all Parties in the State—all creeds, all classes, every recognizable section of opinion. We are ranged beneath the Crown of our ancient monarchy. We are supported by a free Parliament and a free Press; but there is one bond which unites us all and sustains us in the public regard—namely (as is increasingly becoming known), that we are prepared to proceed to all extremities, to endure them and to enforce them; *that* is our bond of union in His Majesty's Government tonight. Thus only, in times like these, can nations preserve their freedom; and thus only can they uphold the cause entrusted to their care.

But all depends now upon the whole life-strength of the British race in every part of the world and of all our associated peoples and of all our well-wishers in every land, doing their utmost night and day, giving all, daring all, enduring all—to the utmost—to the end. This is no war of chieftains or of princes, of dynasties or national ambition; it is a war of peoples and of causes. There are vast numbers, not only in this Island but in every land, who will render faithful service in this war, but whose names will never be known, whose deeds will never be recorded. This is a War of the Unknown Warriors; but let all strive without failing in faith or in duty, and the dark curse of Hitler will be lifted from our age.

THE WAR SITUATION I

The House of Commons

August 20, 1940

1940

August 2.   Lord Beaverbrook, Minister of Aircraft Production, joins the War Cabinet.

August 4.   The Prime Minister warns the nation that the danger of invasion is still great.

August 12, 14, 16.   Determined air attacks against this country are repulsed by the R.A.F., the enemy losing 217 aeroplanes in these three days.

THE WAR SITUATION I

ALMOST A year has passed since the war began, and it is natural for us, think, to pause on our journey at this milestone and survey the dark, vide field. It is also useful to compare the first year of this second war gainst German aggression with its forerunner a quarter of a century ago. Although this war is in fact only a continuation of the last, very great differences in its character are apparent. In the last war millions of men ought by hurling enormous masses of steel at one another. "Men and hells" was the cry, and prodigious slaughter was the consequence. In his war nothing of this kind has yet appeared. It is a conflict of strategy, f organization, of technical apparatus, of science, mechanics and morale. he British casualties in the first 12 months of the Great War amounted) 365,000. In this war, I am thankful to say, British killed, wounded, risoners and missing, including civilians, do not exceed 92,000, and of ese a large proportion are alive as prisoners of war. Looking more idely around, one may say that throughout all Europe, for one man illed or wounded in the first year perhaps five were killed or wounded 1 1914-15.

The slaughter is only a small fraction, but the consequences to the elligerents have been even more deadly. We have seen great countries ith powerful armies dashed out of coherent existence in a few weeks. We ave seen the French Republic and the renowned French Army beaten to complete and total submission with less than the casualties which ey suffered in any one of half a dozen of the battles of 1914-18. The tire body—it might almost seem at times the soul—of France has suc-mbed to physical effects incomparably less terrible than those which ere sustained with fortitude and undaunted will power 25 years ago. lthough up to the present the loss of life has been mercifully diminished,

the decisions reached in the course of the struggle are even more profoun
upon the fate of nations than anything that has ever happened since bar
baric times. Moves are made upon the scientific and strategic boards
advantages are gained by mechanical means, as a result of which score
of millions of men become incapable of further resistance, or judg
themselves incapable of further resistance, and a fearful game of ches
proceeds from check to mate by which the unhappy players seem to b
inexorably bound.

There is another more obvious difference from 1914. The whole of th
warring nations are engaged, not only soldiers, but the entire population
men, women and children. The fronts are everywhere. The trenches ar
dug in the towns and streets. Every village is fortified. Every road i
barred. The front line runs through the factories. The workmen ar
soldiers with different weapons but the same courage. These are grea
and distinctive changes from what many of us saw in the struggle o
a quarter of a century ago. There seems to be every reason to believ
that this new kind of war is well suited to the genius and the resource
of the British nation and the British Empire; and that, once we get prop
erly equipped and properly started, a war of this kind will be mor
favorable to us than the somber mass slaughters of the Somme and Pass
chendaele. If it is a case of the whole nation fighting and suffering to
gether, that ought to suit us, because we are the most united of all th
nations, because we entered the war upon the national will and with ou
eyes open, and because we have been nurtured in freedom and individua
responsibility and are the products, not of totalitarian uniformity, bu
of tolerance and variety. If all these qualities are turned, as they are bein
turned, to the arts of war, we may be able to show the enemy quite a lo
of things that they have not thought of yet. Since the Germans drove th
Jews out and lowered their technical standards, our science is definitel
ahead of theirs. Our geographical position, the command of the sea, an
the friendship of the United States enable us to draw resources from th
whole world and to manufacture weapons of war of every kind, bu
especially of the superfine kinds, on a scale hitherto practiced only b
Nazi Germany.

Hitler is now sprawled over Europe. Our offensive springs are bein
slowly compressed, and we must resolutely and methodically prepar
ourselves for the campaigns of 1941 and 1942. Two or three years ar
not a long time, even in our short, precarious lives. They are nothing i
the history of the nation, and when we are doing the finest thing in th

world, and have the honor to be the sole champion of the liberties of all Europe, we must not grudge these years or weary as we toil and struggle through them. It does not follow that our energies in future years will be exclusively confined to defending ourselves and our possessions. Many opportunities may lie open to amphibious power, and we must be ready to take advantage of them. One of the ways to bring this war to a speedy end is to convince the enemy, not by words, but by deeds, that we have both the will and the means, not only to go on indefinitely, but to strike heavy and unexpected blows. The road to victory may not be so long as we expect. But we have no right to count upon this. Be it long or short, rough or smooth, we mean to reach our journey's end.

It is our intention to maintain and enforce a strict blockade, not only of Germany, but of Italy, France, and all the other countries that have fallen into the German power. I read in the papers that Herr Hitler has also proclaimed a strict blockade of the British Islands. No one can complain of that. I remember the Kaiser doing it in the last war. What indeed would be a matter of general complaint would be if we were to prolong the agony of all Europe by allowing food to come in to nourish the Nazis and aid their war effort, or to allow food to go in to the subjugated peoples, which certainly would be pillaged off them by their Nazi conquerors.

There have been many proposals, founded on the highest motives, that food should be allowed to pass the blockade for the relief of these populations. I regret that we must refuse these requests. The Nazis declare that they have created a new unified economy in Europe. They have repeatedly stated that they possess ample reserves of food and that they can feed their captive peoples. In a German broadcast of 27th June it was said that while Mr. Hoover's plan for relieving France, Belgium and Holland deserved commendation, the German forces had already taken the necessary steps. We know that in Norway when the German troops went in, there were food supplies to last for a year. We know that Poland, though not a rich country, usually produces sufficient food for her people. Moreover, the other countries which Herr Hitler has invaded all held considerable stocks when the Germans entered and are themselves, in many cases, very substantial food producers. If all this food is not available now, it can only be because it has been removed to feed the people of Germany and to give them increased rations—for a change—during the last few months. At this season of the year and for some months to come, there is the least chance of scarcity as the harvest has just been gathered in. The only agencies which can create famine in any part of Europe, now and during the coming winter, will be German exactions or German failure to distribute the supplies which they command.

There is another aspect. Many of the most valuable foods are essential to the manufacture of vital war material. Fats are used to make explosives. Potatoes make the alcohol for motor spirit. The plastic materials now so largely used in the construction of aircraft are made of milk. If the Germans use these commodities to help them to bomb our women and children, rather than to feed the populations who produce them, we may be sure that imported foods would go the same way, directly or indirectly, or be employed to relieve the enemy of the responsibilities he has so wantonly assumed. Let Hitler bear his responsibilities to the full, and let the peoples of Europe who groan beneath his yoke aid in every way the coming of the day when that yoke will be broken. Meanwhile, we can and we will arrange in advance for the speedy entry of food into any part of the enslaved area, when this part has been wholly cleared of German forces, and has genuinely regained its freedom. We shall do our best to encourage the building up of reserves of food all over the world, so that there will always be held up before the eyes of the peoples of Europe, including—I say deliberately—the German and Austrian peoples, the certainty that the shattering of the Nazi power will bring to them all immediate food, freedom and peace.

Rather more than a quarter of a year has passed since the new Government came into power in this country. What a cataract of disaster has poured out upon us since then! The trustful Dutch overwhelmed; their beloved and respected Sovereign driven into exile; the peaceful city of Rotterdam the scene of a massacre as hideous and brutal as anything in the Thirty Years' War; Belgium invaded and beaten down; our own fine Expeditionary Force, which King Leopold called to his rescue, cut off and almost captured, escaping as it seemed only by a miracle and with the loss of all its equipment; our Ally, France, out; Italy in against us; all France in the power of the enemy, all its arsenals and vast masses of military material converted or convertible to the enemy's use; a puppet Government set up at Vichy which may at any moment be forced to become our foe; the whole western seaboard of Europe from the North Cape to the Spanish frontier in German hands; all the ports, all the airfields on this immense front employed against us as potential springboards of invasion. Moreover, the German air power, numerically so far outstripping ours, has been brought so close to our Island that what we used to dread greatly has come to pass and the hostile bombers not only reach our shores in a few minutes and from many directions, but can be escorted by their fighting aircraft. Why, Sir, if we had been confronted at the beginning of May with such a prospect, it would have seemed incredible that at the end of a period of horror and disaster, or at this point in a period of horror and disaster, we should stand erect, sure of ourselves, masters of our fate and with the conviction of final victory burning unquenchable in our hearts. Few would have believed we could survive; none would have believed that we should today not only feel stronger but should actually be stronger than we have ever been before.

Let us see what has happened on the other side of the scales. The British nation and the British Empire, finding themselves alone, stood undismayed against disaster. No one flinched or wavered; nay, some who formerly thought of peace, now think only of war. Our people are united and resolved, as they have never been before. Death and ruin have become small things compared with the shame of defeat or failure in duty. We cannot tell what lies ahead. It may be that even greater ordeals lie before us. We shall face whatever is coming to us. We are sure of ourselves and of our cause, and that is the supreme fact which has emerged in these months of trial.

Meanwhile, we have not only fortified our hearts but our Island. We have rearmed and rebuilt our armies in a degree which would have been deemed impossible a few months ago. We have ferried across the Atlantic, in the month of July, thanks to our friends over there, an immense mass of munitions of all kinds: cannon, rifles, machine guns, cartridges and shell, all safely landed without the loss of a gun or a round. The output of our own factories, working as they have never worked before, has poured forth to the troops. The whole British Army is at home. More than 2,000,000 determined men have rifles and bayonets in their hands tonight, and three-quarters of them are in regular military formations. We have never had armies like this in our Island in time of war. The whole Island bristles against invaders, from the sea or from the air. As I explained to the House in the middle of June, the stronger our Army at home, the larger must the invading expedition be, and the larger the invading expedition, the less difficult will be the task of the Navy in detecting its assembly and in intercepting and destroying it in passage; and the greater also would be the difficulty of feeding and supplying the invaders if ever they landed, in the teeth of continuous naval and air attack on their communications. All this is classical and venerable doctrine. As in

Nelson's day, the maxim holds, "Our first line of defense is the enemy's ports." Now air reconnaissance and photography have brought to an old principle a new and potent aid.

Our Navy is far stronger than it was at the beginning of the war. The great flow of new construction set on foot at the outbreak is now beginning to come in. We hope our friends across the ocean will send us a timely reinforcement to bridge the gap between the peace flotillas of 1939 and the war flotillas of 1941. There is no difficulty in sending such aid. The seas and oceans are open. The U-boats are contained. The magnetic mine is, up to the present time, effectively mastered. The merchant tonnage under the British flag, after a year of unlimited U-boat war, after eight months of intensive mining attack, is larger than when we began. We have, in addition, under our control at least 4,000,000 tons of shipping from the captive countries which has taken refuge here or in the harbors of the Empire. Our stocks of food of all kinds are far more abundant than in the days of peace, and a large and growing program of food production is on foot.

Why do I say all this? Not, assuredly, to boast; not, assuredly, to give the slightest countenance to complacency. The dangers we face are still enormous, but so are our advantages and resources. I recount them because the people have a right to know that there are solid grounds for the confidence which we feel, and that we have good reason to believe ourselves capable, as I said in a very dark hour two months ago, of continuing the war "if necessary alone, if necessary for years." I say it also because the fact that the British Empire stands invincible, and that Nazidom is still being resisted, will kindle again the spark of hope in the breasts of hundreds of millions of down-trodden or despairing men and women throughout Europe, and far beyond its bounds, and that from these sparks there will presently come cleansing and devouring flame.

The great air battle which has been in progress over this Island for the last few weeks has recently attained a high intensity. It is too soon to attempt to assign limits either to its scale or to its duration. We must certainly expect that greater efforts will be made by the enemy than any he has so far put forth. Hostile air fields are still being developed in France and the Low Countries, and the movement of squadrons and material for attacking us is still proceeding. It is quite plain that Herr Hitler could not admit defeat in his air attack on Great Britain without sustaining most serious injury. If after all his boastings and blood-curdling threats and lurid accounts trumpeted round the world of the damage he has inflicted, of the vast numbers of our Air Force he has shot down, so he says, with so little loss to himself; if after tales of the panic-stricken British crushed in their holes cursing the plutocratic Parliament which has led them to such a plight—if after all this his whole air onslaught were forced after a while tamely to peter out, the Führer's reputation for veracity of statement might be seriously impugned. We may be sure, therefore, that he will continue as long as he has the strength to do so, and as long as any preoccupations he may have in respect of the Russian Air Force allow him to do so.

On the other hand, the conditions and course of the fighting have so far been favorable to us. I told the House two months ago that, whereas in France our fighter aircraft were wont to inflict a loss of two or three to one upon the Germans, and in the fighting at Dunkirk, which was a kind of no-man's-land, a loss of about three or four to one, we expected that in an attack on this Island we should achieve a larger ratio. This has certainly come true. It must also be remembered that all the enemy machines and pilots which are shot down over our Island, or over the seas which surround it, are either destroyed or captured; whereas a considerable proportion of our machines, and also of our pilots, are saved, and soon again in many cases come into action.

A vast and admirable system of salvage, directed by the Ministry of Aircraft Production, ensures the speediest return to the fighting line of damaged machines, and the most provident and speedy use of all the spare parts and material. At the same time the splendid—nay, astounding—increase in the output and repair of British aircraft and engines which Lord Beaverbrook has achieved by a genius of organization and drive, which looks like magic, has given us overflowing reserves of every type of aircraft, and an ever-mounting stream of production both in quantity and quality. The enemy is, of course, far more numerous than we are. But our new production already, as I am advised, largely exceeds his, and the American production is only just beginning to flow in. It is a fact, as I see from my daily returns, that our bomber and fighter strength now, after all this fighting, are larger than they have ever been. We believe that we shall be able to continue the air struggle indefinitely and as long as the enemy pleases, and the longer it continues the more rapid will be our approach, first towards that parity, and then into that superiority, in the air upon which in a large measure the decision of the war depends.

The gratitude of every home in our Island, in our Empire, and indeed throughout the world, except in the abodes of the guilty, goes out to the British airmen who, undaunted by odds, unwearied in their constant challenge and mortal danger, are turning the tide of the World War by their prowess and by their devotion. Never in the field of human conflict was so much owed by so many to so few. All hearts go out to the fighter pilots, whose brilliant actions we see with our own eyes day after day; but we must never forget that all the time, night after night, month after month, our bomber squadrons travel far into Germany, find their targets in the darkness by the highest navigational skill, aim their attacks, often under the heaviest fire, often with serious loss, with deliberate careful discrimination, and inflict shattering blows upon the whole of the technical and war-making structure of the Nazi power. On no part of the Royal Air Force does the weight of the war fall more heavily than on the daylight bombers, who will play an invaluable part in the case of invasion and whose unflinching zeal it has been necessary in the meanwhile on numerous occasions to restrain.

We are able to verify the results of bombing military targets in Germany, not only by reports which reach us through many sources, but also, of course, by photography. I have no hesitation in saying that this process of bombing the military industries and communications of Germany and the air bases and storage depots from which we are attacked, which process will continue upon an ever-increasing scale until the end of the war, and may in another year attain dimensions hitherto undreamed of, affords one at least of the most certain, if not the shortest, of all the roads to victory. Even if the Nazi legions stood triumphant on the Black Sea, or indeed upon the Caspian, even if Hitler was at the gates of India, it would profit him nothing if at the same time the entire economic and scientific apparatus of German war power lay shattered and pulverized at home.

The fact that the invasion of this Island upon a large scale has become a far more difficult operation with every week that has passed since we saved our Army at Dunkirk, and our very great preponderance of sea power enable us to turn our eyes and to turn our strength increasingly towards the Mediterranean and against that other enemy who, without the slightest provocation, coldly and deliberately, for greed and gain, stabbed France in the back in the moment of her agony, and is now marching against us in Africa. The defection of France has, of course, been deeply damaging to our position in what is called, somewhat oddly, the Middle East. In the defense of Somaliland, for instance, we had counted upon strong French forces attacking the Italians from Jibuti.

We had counted also upon the use of the French naval and air bases in the Mediterranean, and particularly upon the North African shore. We had counted upon the French Fleet. Even though metropolitan France was temporarily overrun, there was no reason why the French Navy, substantial parts of the French Army, the French Air Force and the French Empire overseas should not have continued the struggle at our side.

Shielded by overwhelming sea power, possessed of invaluable strategic bases and of ample funds, France might have remained one of the great combatants in the struggle. By so doing, France would have preserved the continuity of her life, and the French Empire might have advanced with the British Empire to the rescue of the independence and integrity of the French Motherland. In our own case, if we had been put in the terrible position of France, a contingency now happily impossible, although, of course, it would have been the duty of all war leaders to fight on here to the end, it would also have been their duty, as I indicated in my speech of 4th June, to provide as far as possible for the Naval security of Canada and our Dominions and to make sure they had the means to carry on the struggle from beyond the oceans. Most of the other countries that have been overrun by Germany for the time being have persevered valiantly and faithfully. The Czechs, the Poles, the Norwegians, the Dutch, the Belgians are still in the field, sword in hand, recognized by Great Britain and the United States as the sole representative authorities and lawful Governments of their respective States.

That France alone should lie prostrate at this moment is the crime, not of a great and noble nation, but of what are called "the men of Vichy." We have profound sympathy with the French people. Our old comradeship with France is not dead. In General de Gaulle and his gallant band, that comradeship takes an effective form. These free Frenchmen have been condemned to death by Vichy, but the day will come, as surely as the sun will rise tomorrow, when their names will be held in honor, and their names will be graven in stone in the streets and villages of a France restored in a liberated Europe to its full freedom and its ancient fame. But this conviction which I feel of the future cannot affect the immediate problems which confront us in the Mediterranean and in Africa. It had been decided some time before the beginning of the war not to defend the Protectorate of Somaliland. That policy was changed in the early months of the war. When the French gave in, and when our small forces there, a few battalions, a few guns, were attacked by all the

Italian troops, nearly two divisions, which had formerly faced the French at Jibuti, it was right to withdraw our detachments, virtually intact, for action elsewhere. Far larger operations no doubt impend in the Middle East theater, and I shall certainly not attempt to discuss or prophesy about their probable course. We have large armies and many means of reinforcing them. We have the complete sea command of the eastern Mediterranean. We intend to do our best to give a good account of ourselves, and to discharge faithfully and resolutely all our obligations and duties in that quarter of the world. More than that I do not think the House would wish me to say at the present time.

A good many people have written to me to ask me to make on this occasion a fuller statement of our war aims, and of the kind of peace we wish to make after the war, than is contained in the very considerable declaration which was made early in the autumn. Since then we have made common cause with Norway, Holland and Belgium. We have recognized the Czech Government of Dr. Benes, and we have told General de Gaulle that our success will carry with it the restoration of France. I do not think it would be wise at this moment, while the battle rages and the war is still perhaps only in its earlier stage, to embark upon elaborate speculations about the future shape which should be given to Europe or the new securities which must be arranged to spare mankind the miseries of a third World War. The ground is not new, it has been frequently traversed and explored, and many ideas are held about it in common by all good men, and all free men. But before we can undertake the task of rebuilding we have not only to be convinced ourselves, but we have to convince all other countries that the Nazi tyranny is going to be finally broken. The right to guide the course of world history is the noblest prize of victory. We are still toiling up the hill; we have not yet reached the crest-line of it; we cannot survey the landscape or even imagine what its condition will be when that longed-for morning comes. The task which lies before us immediately is at once more practical, more simple and more stern. I hope—indeed, I pray—that we shall not be found unworthy of our victory if after toil and tribulation it is granted to us. For the rest, we have to gain the victory. That is our task.

There is, however, one direction in which we can see a little more clearly ahead. We have to think not only for ourselves but for the lasting security of the cause and principles for which we are fighting and of the long future of the British Commonwealth of Nations. Some months ago we came to the conclusion that the interests of the United States and of the British Empire both required that the United States should have facilities for the naval and air defense of the Western Hemisphere against the attack of a Nazi power which might have acquired temporary but lengthy control of a large part of Western Europe and its formidable resources. We had therefore decided spontaneously, and without being asked or offered any inducement, to inform the Government of the United States that we would be glad to place such defense facilities at their disposal by leasing suitable sites in our Transatlantic possessions for their greater security against the unmeasured dangers of the future. The principle of association of interests for common purposes between Great Britain and the United States had developed even before the war. Various agreements had been reached about certain small islands in the Pacific Ocean which had become important as air fueling points. In all this line of thought we found ourselves in very close harmony with the Government of Canada.

Presently we learned that anxiety was also felt in the United States about the air and naval defense of their Atlantic seaboard, and President Roosevelt has recently made it clear that he would like to discuss with us, and with the Dominion of Canada and with Newfoundland, the development of American naval and air facilities in Newfoundland and in the West Indies. There is, of course, no question of any transference of sovereignty—that has never been suggested—or of any action being taken without the consent or against the wishes of the various Colonies concerned; but for our part, His Majesty's Government are entirely willing to accord defense facilities to the United States on a 99 years' leasehold basis, and we feel sure that our interests no less than theirs, and the interests of the Colonies themselves and of Canada and Newfoundland, will be served thereby. These are important steps. Undoubtedly this process means that these two great organizations of the English-speaking democracies, the British Empire and the United States, will have to be somewhat mixed up together in some of their affairs for mutual and general advantage. For my own part, looking out upon the future, I do not view the process with any misgivings. I could not stop it if I wished; no one can stop it. Like the Mississippi, it just keeps rolling along. Let it roll. Let it roll on full flood, inexorable, irresistible, benignant, to broader lands and better days.

THE WAR SITUATION II

The House of Commons

September 5, 1940

August 29.   French Equatorial Africa and the French Cameroons declare for General de Gaulle.

August 31.   Rumania, yielding to German and Italian pressure, cedes almost two-thirds of Transylvania to Hungary.

September 2.   A determined attack by 650 enemy aircraft is beaten back.

September 3.   The United States transfer fifty of their older destroyers to the Royal Navy. Britain agrees to lease to U.S.A. for 99 years without charge naval and air bases in the North and South Atlantic.

THE WAR SITUATION II

THE MEMORABLE transactions between Great Britain and the United States, which were foreshadowed when I last addressed the House, have now been completed. As far as I can make out, they have been completed to the general satisfaction of the British and American peoples and to the encouragement of our friends all over the world. It would be a mistake to try to read into the official notes which have passed more than the documents bear on their face. The exchanges which have taken place are simply measures of mutual assistance rendered to one another by two friendly nations, in a spirit of confidence, sympathy and good will. These measures are linked together in a formal agreement. They must be accepted exactly as they stand. Only very ignorant persons would suggest that the transfer of American destroyers to the British flag constitutes the slightest violation of international law or affects in the smallest degree the non-belligerency of the United States.

I have no doubt that Herr Hitler will not like this transference of destroyers, and I have no doubt that he will pay the United States out, if ever he gets the chance. That is why I am very glad that the army, air and naval frontiers of the United States have been advanced along a wide arc into the Atlantic Ocean, and that this will enable them to take danger by the throat while it is still hundreds of miles away from their homeland. The Admiralty tell us also that they are very glad to have these 50 destroyers, and that they will come in most conveniently to bridge the gap which, as I have previously explained to the House, inevitably intervenes before our considerable war-time program of new construction comes into service.

I suppose the House realizes that we shall be a good deal stronger next year on the sea than we are now, although that is quite strong enough for the immediate work in hand. There will be no delay in bringing the American destroyers into active service; in fact, British crews are already meeting them at the various ports where they are being delivered. You might call it the long arm of coincidence. I really do not think that there is any more to be said about the whole business at the present time. This is not the appropriate occasion for rhetoric. Perhaps I may, however, very respectfully, offer this counsel to the House: When you have got a thing where you want it, it is a good thing to leave it where it is.

The House has no doubt observed—to change the subject—that Rumania has undergone severe territorial mutilation. Personally, I have always thought that the southern part of Dobrudja ought to be restored to Bulgaria, and I have never been happy about the way in which Hungary was treated after the last war. We have not at any time adopted, since this war broke out, the line that nothing could be changed in the territorial structure of various countries. On the other hand, we do not propose to recognize any territorial changes which take place during the war, unless they take place with the free consent and good will of the parties concerned. No one can say how far Herr Hitler's empire will extend before this war is over, but I have no doubt that it will pass away as swiftly as, and perhaps more swiftly than, did Napoleon's empire, although, of course, without any of its glitter or its glory.

The general air battle, of which I spoke the last time we met together, continues. In July, there was a good deal of air activity, but August has been a real fighting month. Neither side has put out its full strength, but the Germans have made a very substantial and important effort to gain the mastery, and they have certainly put forth a larger proportion of their total air strength than we have found it necessary, up to the present, to employ against them. Their attempt to dominate the Royal Air Force and our anti-aircraft defenses, by daylight attacks, has proved very costly for them. The broad figures of three to one in machines and six to one in pilots and crews, of which we are sure, do not by any means represent the total injuries inflicted upon the enemy. We must be prepared for heavier fighting in this month of September. The need of the enemy to obtain a decision is very great, and if he has the numbers with which we have hitherto credited him, he should be able to magnify and multiply his attacks during September.

Firm confidence is felt by all the responsible officers of the Royal Air Force in our ability to withstand this largely increased scale of attack, and we have no doubt that the whole nation, taking its example from our airmen, have been proud to share their dangers and will stand up to the position grim and gay. Now is the chance of the men and women in the factories to show their mettle, and for all of us to try to be worthy of our boys in the air and not make their task longer or harder by the slightest flinching. That, I know, is the temper of the nation, and even if the average attack is doubled or trebled—which last is most unlikely—and however long it continues, we believe that we can stand it and that we shall emerge from it actually and relatively stronger in the air than we were before.

Our Air Force today is more numerous and better equipped than it was at the outbreak of the war, or even in July, and, to the best of our belief, we are far nearer to the total of the German numerical strength, as we estimate it, than we expected to be at this period in the war. I asked that the German claims of British aircraft destroyed during July and August should be added up. I was curious to see the total to which they would amount. I found them to make the surprising total of 1,921 British aircraft destroyed. That total is rather like the figures we heard about of losses among our Fleet, many ships of which have been sunk several times over. The actual figure of British losses, which we have published daily for these last two months, is 558. Our loss in pilots is, of course, happily very much less. I do not know whether Herr Hitler believes the truth of his own published figures. I hope he does. One is always content to see an enemy plunged in error and self-deception. How very differently this air attack which is now beginning has turned out from what we imagined it would be before this war! More than 150,000 beds have stood open and, thank God, empty in our war hospitals for a whole year. When the British people make up their minds to go to war they expect to receive terrible injuries. That is why we tried to remain at peace as long as possible. So far as the air attack is concerned, up to the present we have found it far less severe than what we prepared ourselves to endure and what we are still ready, if necessary, to endure. One thousand and seventy-five civilians were killed during August in Britain, and a slightly greater number seriously injured. Our sympathy goes out to the wounded and to those who are bereaved, but no one can pretend that out of 45,000,000 people these are losses which, even if multiplied as they may be two or three times, would be serious compared to the majestic world issues which are at stake. Apart from minor or readily reparable injuries, about eight hundred houses have been destroyed or damaged beyond repair. I am not talking of what can be put right very quickly or what is worth while to put right, but eight hundred houses were actually damaged beyond repair out of a total in this Island of 13,000,000 houses.

This, of course, is very different from the estimate of damage which was given to the War Committee which considered and decided against the possibility of an insurance scheme against air-raid damage to property. It would, in my judgment, be worth while for a further examination of such a scheme, particularly as it would affect the small man, and to make this examination in the light of facts which we now know and also of future possibilities about which we are in a far better position to form an opinion than we were before the war began. I have therefore asked my right hon. Friend the Chancellor of the Exchequer to consider the best way of making such a review in the light of the facts as they are today. It is very painful to me to see, as I have seen in my journeys about the country, a small British house or business smashed by the enemy's fire, and to see that without feeling assured that we are doing our best to spread the burden so that we all stand in together. Damage by enemy action stands on a different footing from any other kind of loss or damage, because the nation undertakes the task of defending the lives and property of its subjects and taxpayers against assaults from outside. Unless public opinion and the judgment of the House were prepared to separate damage resulting from the fire of the enemy from all those other forms of war loss, and unless the House was prepared to draw the distinction very sharply between war damage by bomb and shell and the other forms of loss which are incurred, we could not attempt to deal with this matter; otherwise we should be opening up a field to which there would be no bounds. If, however, we were able to embark upon such a project as would give complete insurance, at any rate up to a certain minimum figure, for everyone against war damage by shell or bomb, I think it would be a very solid mark of the confidence which after some experience we are justified in feeling about the way in which we are going to come through this war.

In the meanwhile, my right hon. Friend the Chancellor of the Exchequer, who has to give so many halfpence and take so many kicks, and upon whose wisdom and practical good sense those who have been his colleagues have learned to rely—and I can assure the House that it is no mere flattery in order to get the money out of him—has agreed to the following arrangements, in addition to the satisfactory provisions which have already been made in respect of the personal injuries and immediate needs of those smitten. At present in cases where the income of the claimant's household does not exceed £400 a year and his resources are limited, payments are made to cover damage to essential household furniture up to a maximum of £50, and similar payments are made in respect of personal clothing up to £30, subject to income limits of £400 where there are dependents and £250 where there are no dependents. It is now proposed to abolish these upper limits of £50 and £30 respectively, so that payments for damage to the furniture or clothing of persons of limited means will now be made up to 100 per cent of the damage, whatever that amount may be. Hitherto there has been no provision to enable workmen to replace tools which are their personal property and the use of which is vital to their employment. It is proposed to remedy this hardship by making provision for payments for these purposes, subject to the same income limits which apply in the case of the clothing advances. Similar payments will be made to professional people within the same limits of income. Finally, there is the case of the small retailer who is not insured under the Board of Trade Commodities Insurance Scheme. Here payments up to £50 will be made within the same income limits as for clothing and tools, in order to enable those retailers to replace stocks essential to the continuance of trade. I may say that in all these three cases appropriate mitigating measures will be taken in the border-line cases lying just above the income limits.

Then there is the case of the coast towns which have been declared to be evacuation areas for the purpose of the Defense (Evacuated Areas) Regulations. Upon this a number of Members, as was their duty, have made representations to the Government. The Ministry of Health will be prepared, upon an application from the authorities of these areas, to make advances out of Exchequer funds to enable the authorities to meet liabilities for which collectable rate revenue will not suffice. These advances will be free of interest. The term "advances" in this case is understood to mean that the Government retain the right to call for repayment, but the question how far this right will be exercised will be considered after the war in the light of the financial circumstances then prevailing, both in the areas interested and in the country generally. These advances must be conditional upon the examination of the estimates of expenditure and of revenue, and for this purpose my right hon. Friend the Minister of Health will arrange for officers of the Ministry of Health to visit the towns concerned and to confer with the mayors and principal officials—

very plucky fellows, some of them; one is proud to meet them. Such conferences will afford an opportunity for advising and assisting the local authorities upon the best means of securing reasonable economy consistent with the maintenance of essential services, and they will also advise them about the collection of revenue. These local authorities will not in the present circumstances be required to increase their existing rate of poundage as a condition of financial assistance. It is recognized that the shortage of rate income will involve a deficit in the sums collected by rates levied for meeting county council precepts. It is understood that some of the local authorities are, in fact, proposing to limit their payments in respect of county precepts to that proportion of the total rate which represents the county rate which they have been able to collect. The Government propose to recognize and validate these arrangements, and if in any case an unreasonable burden was thereby thrown upon the county's resources, the Government would not refuse to consider the possibility of extending to the county council some measure of assistance.

I think the House will see that we have been endeavoring to meet the cases both of individuals and of local authorities as they are affected by the conditions into which we have moved. We must expect for some time to come to have to live our lives and to carry on our work under these strange conditions, but they are conditions to which the fortitude and adaptiveness of the British people will not, we feel, be found unequal. If, as was suggested in a recent oration, there is to be a contest of nerve, will power and endurance in which the whole British and German peoples are to engage, be it sharp or be it long, we shall not shrink from it. We believe that the spirit and temperament bred under institutions of freedom will prove more enduring and resilient than anything that can be got out of the most efficiently enforced mechanical discipline.

In the light of what we have learned so far with regard to the arrangements for air-raid warnings, we have come to the conclusion that the arrangements for air-raid warnings and what is to be done when they are given, which appears to be another question, require very considerable changes. There is really no good sense in having these prolonged banshee howlings from sirens two or three times a day over wide areas, simply because hostile aircraft are flying to or from some target which no one can possibly know or even guess. All our precaution regulations have hitherto been based on this siren call, and I must say that one must admire the ingenuity of those who devised it as a means of spreading alarm. Indeed, most people now see how very wise Ulysses was when he stopped the ears of his sailors from all siren songs and had himself tied up firmly to the mast of duty.

Now that we are settling down to the job, we must have different arrangements from those devised before the war. It is right that everyone should know now that the red warning is more in the nature of a general alert than a warning of the imminence of danger to any particular locality. In many cases it is physically impossible to give the alarm before the attack. Constant alarms come to be something in the nature of no alarm. Yet while they give no protection to very great numbers of people, who take no notice of them, they undoubtedly exercise a disturbing effect upon necessary war work. All our regulations, and much preaching, have taught people that they should take a whole series of steps, mostly of a downward character, when they hear the siren sound, and it is no use having official regulations which point one way and enjoin immediate respect for the alarm when exhortations are given, unofficially or officially, to disregard them and go on working. In our own case today, it was felt that the red warning should be taken merely as an alert, but that if special circumstances indicated the proximity of danger, then the conditions of alarm should supervene. That is exactly what we did on receiving information that there was danger of a particular kind in the vicinity; and when that special condition departed we immediately resumed our work under the conditions of alert until the "All Clear," which has now sounded, restored us to normal. Something like this unrehearsed experiment may well give us guidance in our future treatment of the problem. All our regulations require to be shaped to the new basis which is being established by actual contact with events.

The responsibility to give clear guidance to the public in time of war is imposed upon His Majesty's Government. In order to preserve the confidence shown them by the House and by the public, the Government must act with conviction. I have, therefore, asked the various Departments concerned to review the whole position as a matter of urgency. In these matters one must expect to proceed by trial and error, and one must also try to carry public opinion along. What we want, on the one hand, is the greatest measure of real warning that is compatible with what all our people are resolved upon, namely, the active maintenance of war production. I will not make any specific announcement today, because we are in negotiation with very important bodies concerned, employers and employed, throughout the country. We want to move in these matters with sureness, precision and clarity, and no uncertainty or doubt;

and I would like to have the opportunity of a little further consultation with the different bodies that are now in touch with the Government. This is a matter, of course, which affects scores of millions of people. Therefore, I will not attempt to make any specific announcement today, but such an announcement must be made within the next week, at the latest. I think I have given the House a pretty clear indication of what is in our thoughts, and of the direction in which we are thinking of moving at the present time.

There is another point which I should like to mention, and that is this business of lighting the streets, the centers of the cities of our country. Winter is coming along, and I hope we are not going through all that gloomy business that we went through last year. I have, therefore, asked a committee of persons deeply versed in this matter, responsible people in the Departments, to meet together, and to see in what way we can make more light and cheer in the winter months, and at the same time subserve the purposes of alert and alarm. Such a course is not at all impossible, and I hope to come forward with some proposals, necessarily of a highly detailed character.

I do not mean to trespass at any length upon the time of the House this afternoon, because our affairs are evidently very largely in the region of action. No one must suppose that the danger of invasion has passed. My right hon. Friend the Secretary of State for War—to whom I would have gladly paid some compliments if he had not already forestalled me, in a very charming manner, and probably robbed any compliments of some of their intrinsic value—is absolutely right in enjoining the strictest vigilance upon the great and growing armies which are now entrusted in this country to the command of Sir Alan Brooke. I do not agree with those who assume that after the 15th September—or whatever is Herr Hitler's latest date—we shall be free from the menace of deadly attack from overseas; because winter, with its storms, its fogs, its darkness, may alter the conditions, but some of the changes cut both ways. There must not be for one moment any relaxation of effort or of wise precaution, both of which are needed to save our lives and to save our cause. I shall not, however, be giving away any military secrets if I say that we are very much better off than we were a few months ago, and that if the problem of invading Great Britain was a difficult one in June, it has become a far more difficult and a far larger problem in September.

Indeed, while all this preparation for home defense has been going forward on a gigantic scale, we have not hesitated to send a continuous stream of convoys with reinforcements to the Middle East. In particular, a few days ago we found it possible almost to double the effective strength of our Fleet in the eastern Mediterranean by sending some of our most powerful modern vessels to reinforce the flag of Sir Andrew Cunningham, the Admiral in the eastern Mediterranean. This movement, while plainly visible to the Italians, was not molested by them. Some of our great ships touched at Malta on the way, and carried a few things that were needed by those valiant islanders and their garrison, who, under a remarkably resolute Governor, General Dobbie, are maintaining themselves with the utmost constancy. We must expect heavy fighting in the Middle East before very long. We have every intention of maintaining our positions there with our utmost strength, and of increasing our sea power, and the control which follows from sea power, throughout the Mediterranean, not only in the eastern basin but in the western basin. In this way, both at home and abroad, we shall persevere along our course, however the winds may blow.

EVERY MAN TO HIS POST

An Address Broadcast

September 11, 1940

1940

September 6. King Carol of Rumania abdicates.

September 7. Air battle over London in which 65 raiders are brought down. Raiders return in force after dark and begin the determined and indiscriminate night bombing of London and its suburbs that is to go on for months.

EVERY MAN TO HIS POST

WHEN I said in the House of Commons the other day that I thought it improbable that the enemy's air attack in September could be more than three times as great as it was in August, I was not, of course, referring to barbarous attacks upon the civil population, but to the great air battle which is being fought out between our fighters and the German Air Force.

You will understand that whenever the weather is favorable, waves of German bombers, protected by fighters, often three or four hundred at a time, surge over this Island, especially the promontory of Kent, in the hope of attacking military and other objectives by daylight. However, they are met by our fighter squadrons and nearly always broken up; and their losses average three to one in machines and six to one in pilots.

This effort of the Germans to secure daylight mastery of the air over England is, of course, the crux of the whole war. So far it has failed conspicuously. It has cost them very dear, and we have felt stronger, and actually are relatively a good deal stronger, than when the hard fighting began in July. There is no doubt that Herr Hitler is using up his fighter force at a very high rate, and that if he goes on for many more weeks he will wear down and ruin this vital part of his Air Force. That will give us a very great advantage.

On the other hand, for him to try to invade this country without having secured mastery in the air would be a very hazardous undertaking. Nevertheless, all his preparations for invasion on a great scale are steadily going forward. Several hundreds of self-propelled barges are moving down the coasts of Europe, from the German and Dutch harbors to the ports of northern France; from Dunkirk to Brest; and beyond Brest to the French harbors in the Bay of Biscay.

Besides this, convoys of merchant ships in tens of dozens are being moved through the Straits of Dover into the Channel, dodging along from port to port under the protection of the new batteries which the Germans have built on the French shore. There are now considerable gatherings of shipping in the German, Dutch, Belgian and French harbors—all the way from Hamburg to Brest. Finally, there are some preparations made of ships to carry an invading force from the Norwegian harbors.

Behind these clusters of ships or barges, there stand very large numbers of German troops, awaiting the order to go on board and set out on their very dangerous and uncertain voyage across the seas. We cannot tell when they will try to come; we cannot be sure that in fact they will try at all; but no one should blind himself to the fact that a heavy, full-scale invasion of this Island is being prepared with all the usual German thoroughness and method, and that it may be launched now—upon England, upon Scotland, or upon Ireland, or upon all three.

If this invasion is going to be tried at all, it does not seem that it can be long delayed. The weather may break at any time. Besides this, it is difficult for the enemy to keep these gatherings of ships waiting about indefinitely, while they are bombed every night by our bombers, and very often shelled by our warships which are waiting for them outside.

Therefore, we must regard the next week or so as a very important period in our history. It ranks with the days when the Spanish Armada was approaching the Channel, and Drake was finishing his game of bowls; or when Nelson stood between us and Napoleon's Grand Army at Boulogne. We have read all about this in the history books; but what is happening now is on a far greater scale and of far more consequence to the life and future of the world and its civilization than these brave old days of the past.

Every man and woman will therefore prepare himself to do his duty, whatever it may be, with special pride and care. Our fleets and flotillas are very powerful and numerous; our Air Force is at the highest strength it has ever reached, and it is conscious of its proved superiority, not indeed in numbers, but in men and machines. Our shores are well fortified and strongly manned, and behind them, ready to attack the invaders, we have a far larger and better equipped mobile Army than we have ever had before.

Besides this, we have more than a million and a half men of the Home Guard, who are just as much soldiers of the Regular Army as the

Grenadier Guards, and who are determined to fight for every inch of the ground in every village and in every street.

It is with devout but sure confidence that I say: Let God defend the Right.

These cruel, wanton, indiscriminate bombings of London are, of course, a part of Hitler's invasion plans. He hopes, by killing large numbers of civilians, and women and children, that he will terrorize and cow the people of this mighty imperial city, and make them a burden and an anxiety to the Government and thus distract our attention unduly from the ferocious onslaught he is preparing. Little does he know the spirit of the British nation, or the tough fiber of the Londoners, whose forebears played a leading part in the establishment of Parliamentary institutions and who have been bred to value freedom far above their lives. This wicked man, the repository and embodiment of many forms of soul-destroying hatred, this monstrous product of former wrongs and shame, has now resolved to try to break our famous Island race by a process of indiscriminate slaughter and destruction. What he has done is to kindle a fire in British hearts, here and all over the world, which will glow long after all traces of the conflagration he has caused in London have been removed. He has lighted a fire which will burn with a steady and consuming flame until the last vestiges of Nazi tyranny have been burnt out of Europe, and until the Old World—and the New—can join hands to rebuild the temples of man's freedom and man's honor, upon foundations which will not soon or easily be overthrown.

This is a time for everyone to stand together, and hold firm, as they are doing. I express my admiration for the exemplary manner in which all the Air Raid Precautions services of London are being discharged, especially the Fire Brigade, whose work has been so heavy and also dangerous. All the world that is still free marvels at the composure and fortitude with which the citizens of London are facing and surmounting the great ordeal to which they are subjected, the end of which or the severity of which cannot yet be foreseen.

It is a message of good cheer to our fighting Forces on the seas, in the air, and in our waiting Armies in all their posts and stations, that we send them from this capital city. They know that they have behind them a people who will not flinch or weary of the struggle—hard and protracted though it will be; but that we shall rather draw from the heart of suffering itself the means of inspiration and survival, and of a victory won not only for ourselves but for all—a victory won not only for our own time, but for the long and better days that are to come.

THE WAR SITUATION III

The House of Commons

September 17, 1940

September 15. The German Air Force makes its most determined attack on Britain. It is repulsed by the R.A.F., who destroy 185 aircraft and at least 450 airmen.

THE WAR SITUATION III

I DO not feel it necessary to make any lengthy statement to the House today upon the general war position. Practically all the facts not of a secret nature have already been made public. The advance of the Italian Army from Libya is in progress. The two British platoons which have been holding Sollum have been withdrawn. Sharp fighting is taking place upon the desert flank between the armored vehicles of both sides. The enemy is still some distance from our position of resistance. We must see what happens. The deployment of the German barges and ships in preparation for the invasion of Great Britain and Ireland continues steadily, and we must expect that he will make an attempt at what he judges to be the best opportunity. All our preparations must therefore be maintained in a state of vigilance.

The process of waiting, keyed up to concert pitch day after day, is apt after a while to lose its charm of novelty. There is no doubt that it imposes a heavy strain upon all concerned, but we must not underrate the damage inflicted upon the enemy, who also has to wait, by the very heavy and prolonged nightly bombings upon his concentrations of ships and upon all the focal points of his assembly of troops. Undoubtedly serious injury has been done to his ships and barges, and meanwhile our own strength, I am able to assure the House, develops steadily by land, by sea, and above all in the air. Sunday's action was the most brilliant and fruitful of any fought upon a large scale up to that date by the fighters of the Royal Air Force. The figures have already been made public. To the best of my belief—and I have made searching inquiries and taken several cross checks—these figures are not in any way exaggerated. Neither side has yet employed more than a portion of its forces, but there are good reasons for believing at the present time that very grievous inroads are being made upon the enemy's superiority of numbers, and we may await the decision of this prolonged air battle with sober but increasing confidence.

The German attacks upon the civil population have been concentrated mainly upon London, in the hopes of terrorizing its citizens into submission or throwing them into confusion, and, of course, in the silly idea that they will put pressure upon the Government to make peace. The deliberate and repeated attacks upon Buckingham Palace and upon the persons of our beloved King and Queen are also intended, apart from their general barbarity, to have an unsettling effect upon public opinion. They have, of course, the opposite effect. They unite the King and Queen to their people by new and sacred bonds of common danger, and they steel the hearts of all to the stern and unrelenting prosecution of the war against so foul a foe.

I gave the House when I last addressed them the casualty figures up to the end of August and without prejudice to our habit of publishing the figures monthly, I may now mention that during the first half of September about 2,000 civilians—men, women and children—have been killed, and about 8,000 wounded by air bombardment. Four-fifths of these casualties have occurred in London. Many hospitals and churches and public monuments have been damaged, but the injury to our warmaking capacity has been surprisingly small. We are only now beginning to get the increased flow of production from the great programs which were started on the outbreak of the war, and it is very agreeable to see that the increases are maintained over so wide a field in spite of the enemy's fire. To show how indiscriminate and wanton is the enemy's attack, one has only to compare the figures of civilian casualties in the first fortnight of this month with the military casualties. There were, as I have said, 10,000 civilian casualties from air attack, but only some 250 of these occurred in all the Fighting Forces.

The Air Raid Precautions organization in all its branches has proved its efficiency, and the greatest discipline and devotion have been shown by all. The fire brigades are, of course, conspicuous, but in paying tribute to them there must be no disparagement to all the other forms of service which have been faithfully and punctiliously discharged. Of course, the task of preserving the health and well-being of this enormous community in the Thames Valley, exceeding 8,000,000 souls, living under artificial conditions of civilization, and supplying them with food and all other necessities, and making provision for those whose homes have been destroyed or who have had to be evacuated—all this and much else have, as the House will realize, cast a strain upon the machinery of government which calls for ceaseless exertion by all authorities concerned. I am glad to say that this heavy and intricate task is being efficiently and successfully discharged, and our whole system of life and labor is being rapidly adapted to conditions hitherto unknown to modern society. Constant adjustments have to be made and defects remedied in the light of experience. As I said last time, a great deal of our progress must be by trial and error. We have to feel our way and do our best to meet each defect as it reveals itself.

I had hoped, as I said when I last spoke during the week that has passed, to promulgate some new rules about air-raid warnings, but the intensification of the air attack has made it difficult to draw precise conclusions, and, in spite of my desire to make good my undertakings to the House, I feel that it is wiser for the moment to allow the process of local adaptation to run its course. Broadly speaking, our plan must be to use the siren, which, it may be noted, has been cut in two, as an alert and not as an alarm, and to have a system of highly trained what I may call Jim Crows, or lookout men, who will give the alarm when immediate danger is expected at any point. Upon this basis everyone must endeavor to carry on his work and see that output and the public services do not suffer or suffer only the minimum interruption. No doubt, we shall work up to a much higher standard than we have at present attained in many respects, but I feel it better to proceed empirically than, at this moment, to try to make precise conditions; because, after all, we must expect that very much more intense examples of air fighting will be experienced in future than we have yet seen.

There are some matters connected with our arrangements under air attack which I should prefer to discuss in private. I must remind the House that every word spoken in public Session can be telegraphed all over the world; and that there is no reason why we should keep the enemy informed of the details of our arrangements, and thus enable him to inflict the maximum injury upon us. We do not receive any similar information from him about his way of life; although, I am sure, our military staffs would be very much convenienced thereby. There are several things that I wish to say to the House, and I dare say there are many things that hon. Members would like to say to the Government. Therefore, I propose that we should now move into secret Session, and I declare to you, Mr. Speaker, that, casting my eyes around, I spy strangers.

THE WAR SITUATION IV

The House of Commons

October 8, 1940

September 23. General de Gaulle arrives off Dakar with a Free French force accompanied by a British naval squadron. Resistance is offered by the representatives of the Vichy Government, and de Gaulle refrains from decisive action and withdraws.

September 27. Japan joins the Axis by signing a military and economic pact with Germany and Italy.

THE WAR SITUATION IV

A MONTH has passed since Herr Hitler turned his rage and malice onto the civil population of our great cities and particularly of London. He declared in his speech of 4th September that he would raze our cities to the ground, and since then he has been trying to carry out his fell purpose. Naturally, the first question we should ask is to what extent the full strength of the German bombing force has been deployed. I will give the House the best opinion I have been able to form on what is necessarily to some extent a matter of speculation. After their very severe mauling on 15th August, the German short-range dive bombers, of which there are several hundred, have been kept carefully out of the air fighting. This may be, of course, because they are being held in reserve so that they may play their part in a general plan of invasion or reappear in some other theater of war. We have, therefore, had to deal with the long-range German bombers alone.

It would seem that, taking day and night together, nearly 400 of these machines have, on the average, visited our shores every 24 hours. We are doubtful whether this rate of sustained attack could be greatly exceeded; no doubt a concentrated effort could be made for a few days at a time, but this would not sensibly affect the monthly average. Certainly there has been a considerable tailing off in the last ten days, and all through the month that has passed since the heavy raids began on 7th September, we have had a steady decline in casualties and damage to so-called vulnerable points. We know, of course, exactly what we are doing in reply, and the size of our own bombing force; and from the many sources which are open to us we believe that the German heavy bomber pilots are being worked at least as hard as, and maybe a great deal harder than, our own. The strain upon them is, therefore, very considerable.

The bulk of them do not seem capable of anything beyond blind bombing. I always hesitate to say anything of an optimistic nature, because our people do not mind being told the worst. They resent anything in the nature of soothing statements which are not borne out by later events, and, after all, war is full of unpleasant surprises.

On the whole, however, we may, I think, under all reserve, reach provisionally the conclusion that the German average effort against this country absorbs a very considerable part of their potential strength. I should not like to say that we have the measure of their power, but we feel more confident about it than we have ever done before.

Let us now proceed to examine the effect of this ruthless and indiscriminate attack upon the easiest of all targets, namely, the great built-up areas of this land. The Germans have recently volunteered some statements of a boastful nature about the weight of explosives which they have discharged upon us during the whole war, and also on some particular occasions. These statements are not necessarily untrue, and they do not appear unreasonable to us. We were told on 23rd September that 22,000 tons of explosives had been discharged upon Great Britain since the beginning of the war. No doubt this included the mines on the coast. We were told also, on last Thursday week, that 251 tons were thrown upon London in a single night, that is to say, only a few tons less than the total dropped on the whole country throughout the last war. Now, we know exactly what our casualties have been. On that particular Thursday night 180 persons were killed in London as a result of 251 tons of bombs. That is to say, it took one ton of bombs to kill three-quarters of a person. We know, of course, exactly the ratio of loss in the last war, because all the facts were ascertained after it was over. In that war the small bombs of early patterns which were used killed ten persons for every ton discharged in the built-up areas. Therefore, the deadliness of the attack in this war appears to be only one-thirteenth of that of 1914-18. Let us say "less than one-tenth," so as to be on the safe side. That is, the mortality is less than one-tenth of the mortality attaching to the German bombing attacks in the last war. This is a very remarkable fact, deserving of profound consideration. I adduce it, because it is the foundation of some further statements, which I propose to make later on.

What is the explanation? There can only be one, namely, the vastly improved methods of shelter which have been adopted. In the last war there were hardly any air-raid shelters, and very few basements had been strengthened. Now we have this ever-growing system of shelters, among which the Anderson shelter justly deserves its fame, and the mortality has been reduced to one-thirteenth, or, say, at least one-tenth. This appears, as I say, not only to be remarkable, but also reassuring. It has altered, of course, the whole of the estimates we had made of the severity of the attacks to which we should be exposed. Whereas, when we entered the war at the call of duty and honor, we expected to sustain losses which might amount to 3,000 killed in a single night and 12,000 wounded, night after night, and made hospital arrangements on the basis of a quarter of a million casualties merely as a first provision—whereas that is what we did at the beginning of the war, we have actually had since it began, up to last Saturday, as a result of air bombing, about 8,500 killed and 13,000 wounded. This shows that things do not always turn out as badly as one expects. Also, it shows that one should never hesitate, as a nation or as an individual, to face dangers because they appear to the imagination to be so formidable. Since the heavy raiding began on 7th September, the figures of killed and seriously wounded have declined steadily week by week, from over 6,000 in the first week to just under 5,000 in the second, and from about 4,000 in the third week to under 3,000 in the last of the four weeks.

The destruction of property has, however, been very considerable. Most painful is the number of small houses inhabited by working folk which have been destroyed, but the loss has also fallen heavily upon the West End, and all classes have suffered evenly, as they would desire to do. I do not propose to give exact figures of the houses which have been destroyed or seriously damaged. That is our affair. We will rebuild them, more to our credit than some of them were before. London, Liverpool, Manchester, Birmingham may have much more to suffer, but they will rise from their ruins, more healthy and, I hope, more beautiful. We must not exaggerate the material damage which has been done. The papers are full of pictures of demolished houses, but naturally they do not fill their restricted space with the numbers that are left standing. If you go, I am told, to the top of Primrose Hill or any of the other eminences of London and look round, you would not know that any harm had been done to our city.

Statisticians may amuse themselves by calculating that after making allowance for the working of the law of diminishing returns, through the same house being struck twice or three times over, it would take ten years at the present rate for half the houses of London to be demolished. After that, of course, progress would be much slower. Quite a lot of things are going to happen to Herr Hitler and the Nazi regime before ten years are up, and even Signor Mussolini has some experiences ahead of him which he had not foreseen at the time when he thought it safe and profitable to stab the stricken and prostrate French Republic in the back. Neither by material damage nor by slaughter will the people of the British Empire be turned from their solemn and inexorable purpose. It is the practice and in some cases the duty of many of my colleagues and many Members of the House to visit the scenes of destruction as promptly as possible, and I go myself from time to time. In all my life, I have never been treated with so much kindness as by the people who have suffered most. One would think one had brought some great benefit to them, instead of the blood and tears, the toil and sweat which is all I have ever promised. On every side, there is the cry, "We can take it," but with it there is also the cry, "Give it 'em back."

The question of reprisals is being discussed in some quarters as if it were a moral issue. What are reprisals? What we are doing now is to batter continuously, with forces which steadily increase in power, each one of those points in Germany which we believe will do the Germans most injury and will most speedily lessen their power to strike at us. Is that a reprisal? It seems to me very like one. At any rate, it is all we have time for now. We should be foolish to shift off those military targets which the skill of our navigators enables us to find with a very great measure of success, to any other targets at the present stage. Although the bombing force that we are able as yet to employ is, as I have told the House on several occasions, much less numerous than that of which the enemy disposes, I believe it to be true that we have done a great deal more harm to the war-making capacity of Germany than they have done to us. Do not let us get into a sterile controversy as to what are and what are not reprisals. Our object must be to inflict the maximum harm on the enemy's war-making capacity. That is the only object that we shall pursue.

It must not be thought that the mists and storms which enshroud our Island in the winter months will by themselves prevent the German bombers from the crude, indiscriminate bombing by night of our built-up areas into which they have relapsed. No one must look forward to any relief merely from the winter weather. We have, however, been thinking about the subject for some time, and it may be that new methods will be devised to make the wholesale bombing of the civilian population by night and in fog more exciting to the enemy than it is at present. The

House will not expect me to indicate or foreshadow any of these methods. It would be much better for us to allow our visitors to find them out for themselves in due course by practical experience. I think that is much the best way to handle that particular matter.

Meanwhile, upon the basis that this will continue and that our methods will also be improving, we have to organize our lives and the life of our cities on the basis of dwelling under fire and of having always this additional—not a very serious—chance of death, added to the ordinary precarious character of human existence. This great sphere of domestic organization becomes the counterpart of our military war effort. The utmost drive and capacity of which we are capable as a Government and as a people will be thrown into this task. Nothing but the needs of the Fighting Services can stand in the way. We must try to have shelters with sleeping bunks for everyone in the areas which are liable to constant attack, and this must be achieved in the shortest possible time. As soon as it is accomplished, and in proportion as it is accomplished, people will have to go to their proper places, and above all, we must prevent large gatherings of people in any shelters which only give illusory protection against a direct hit. People must be taught not to despise the small shelter. Dispersal is the sovereign remedy against heavy casualties. In my right hon. Friend the new Minister of Home Security,[1] we have a man of warm sympathy, of resource and energy, who is well known to Londoners and has their confidence, and who will equally look after the other cities which are assailed. But do not let it be thought that the work of his predecessor, now Lord President of the Council,[2] has not been of a very high order. There is no better war horse in the Government. I am ashamed of the attacks which are made upon him in ignorant and spiteful quarters. Every one of his colleagues knows that he is a tower of strength and good sense, fearless and unflinching in storm and action. With my many burdens, I rely greatly upon him to take a part of the civil and domestic load from off my shoulders, setting me free for the more direct waging of the war. Large schemes are already on foot for providing food and hot drinks for those who sleep in shelters, and also for entertainment during the winter evenings. Far-reaching measures are being taken to safeguard the health of the people under these novel and primordial conditions. Widespread organization and relief to those whose homes are smitten is already in being and is expanding and im-

[1] Mr. Herbert Morrison.
[2] Sir John Anderson.

proving every day. All these matters will be unfolded at length, some in public, some in private Session, by the Ministers responsible for the various branches of action.

There is one scheme, however, upon which I must say a word today. The diminution of the damage done by blind bombing from what we had expected before the war, in the figures that I gave the House in the opening passage of my speech, enable us to take an enormous step forward in spreading the risk over the property of all classes, rich and poor. The Chancellor of the Exchequer, as I indicated a month ago, is preparing, and in fact has virtually completed the preparation of, a Bill for nation-wide compulsory insurance against damage to property from the enemy's fire. Immediate needs of food and shelter are already provided for; so is loss of life and limb as far as it is possible for human beings to be compensated for such calamities; but why should we have the whole value of the buildings of the country simultaneously and universally discounted and discredited by the shadow of a sporadic sky vulture? Such a course would be financially improvident and also fiscally inane. An appropriate charge levied on the capital value of buildings and structures of all kinds will provide a fund from which, supplemented if need be by a State subvention, everyone can be made sure that compensation for his house and home and place of business will be paid to him in one form or another at the end of the war, if not sooner, and that, where necessity arises in the intervening period, means of carrying on will not be withheld. We also propose to provide insurance against the risk of war damage for all forms of movable property, such as industrial plant, machinery, household effects and other personal possessions which are not at present protected by insurance. This will also be retroactive.

As I see it, we must so arrange that, when any district is smitten by bombs which are flung about at utter random, strong, mobile forces will descend on the scene in power and mercy to conquer the flames, as they have done, to rescue sufferers, provide them with food and shelter, to whisk them away to places of rest and refuge, and to place in their hands leaflets which anyone can understand to reassure them that they have not lost all, because all will share their material loss, and in sharing it, sweep it away. These schemes and measures, pursued on the greatest scale and with fierce energy, will require the concentrated attention of the House in the weeks that lie before us. We have to make a job of this business of living and working under fire, and I have not the slightest doubt that when we have settled down to it, we shall establish conditions which will be a credit to our Island society and to the whole British family, and will enable us to maintain the production of those weapons in good time upon which our whole safety and future depend. Thus we shall be able to prove to all our friends and sympathizers in every land, bond or free, that Hitler's act of mass terror against the British nation has failed as conspicuously as his magnetic mine and other attempts to strangle our sea-borne trade.

Meanwhile, what has happened to the invasion which we have been promised every month and almost every week since the beginning of July? Do not let us be lured into supposing that the danger is past. On the contrary, unwearying vigilance and the swift and steady strengthening of our Forces by land, sea and air which is in progress must be at all costs maintained. Now that we are in October, however, the weather becomes very uncertain, and there are not many lucid intervals of two or three days together in which river barges can cross the narrow seas and land upon our beaches. Still, those intervals may occur. Fogs may aid the foe. Our armies, which are growing continually in numbers, equipment, mobility and training, must be maintained all through the winter, not only along the beaches but in reserve, as the majority are, like leopards crouching to spring at the invader's throat. The enemy has certainly got prepared enough shipping and barges to throw half a million men in a single night onto salt water—or into it. The Home Guard, which now amounts to 1,700,000 men, must nurse their weapons and sharpen their bayonets. [Interruption.] I have taken the trouble to find out very carefully how many hundred thousands of bayonets are at this time in their possession before I uttered such an adjuration; and for those who have not bayonets at the moment, I have provided for them by the phrase: "They must nurse their weapons." During the winter training must proceed, and the building of a great well-equipped army, not necessarily always to be confined to these Islands, must go forward in a hardy and rigorous manner. My right hon. Friend the Secretary of State for War will, in the course of the next few weeks, give a further account in private Session of the tremendous strides which under his guidance our military organization is making in all its branches. He will also announce in public the improvements which we have found it possible to make in the allowances for the dependents of the Fighting Services to meet the increased cost of living and to secure the proper nourishment and care of the wives and children of our fighting men. I shall not anticipate my right hon. Friend this afternoon.

But, after all, the main reason why the invasion has not been attempted up to the present is, of course, the succession of brilliant victories gained by our fighter aircraft, and gained by them over the largely superior numbers which the enemy have launched against us. The three great days of 15th August, 15th September and 27th September have proved to all the world that here at home over our own Island we have the mastery of the air. That is a tremendous fact. It marks the laying down of the office [3] which he has held with so much distinction for the last three years by Sir Cyril Newall, and it enables us to record our admiration to him for the services he has rendered. It also marks the assumption of new and immense responsibilities by Sir Charles Portal, an officer who, I have heard from every source and every side, commands the enthusiastic support and confidence of the Royal Air Force. These victories of our Air Force enable the Navy, which is now receiving very great reinforcements, apart altogether from the American destroyers now coming rapidly into service, to assert, on the basis of the air victories, its sure and well-tried power. It is satisfactory for me to be able to announce that both in fighters and in bombers we are at this moment and after all these months of battle substantially stronger actually and relatively than we were in May when the heavy fighting began, and also to announce that the pilot situation is rapidly improving and that in many weeks our repaired aircraft alone, such is the efficiency of this organization for repair, exceed by themselves or make good the losses which are suffered; so that in many weeks the new construction is a clear gain. No one has ever pretended that we should overtake the Germans, with their immense lead, in the first year or so of war. We must give ourselves a chance. Perhaps it will be possible to make a more satisfactory statement on this subject this time next year. But do not forget that the resources of the enemy will also be substantially increased by their exploitation of the wealth, of the plants and to some extent of the skilled labor of captive countries. If it were not for the resources of the New World, which are becoming increasingly available, it would be a long time before we should be able to do much more than hold our own.

Although we have had to face this continual, imminent threat of invasion by a military Power which has stationed 80 of its best divisions in northern France, we have not failed to reinforce our Armies in the Middle East and elsewhere. All the while the great convoys have been passing steadily and safely on their course through the unknown wastes

[3] Chief of the Air Staff.

of the oceans, drawing from all parts of the Empire the forces which will, I trust, enable us to fill in time the terrible gap in our defenses which was opened by the Vichy French desertion. I shall certainly not make any prophecies about what will happen when British, Australian, New Zealand, Indian, and Egyptian troops come to close grips with the Italian invaders who are now making their way across the deserts towards them. All I will say is that we are doing our best and that there as here we feel a good deal better than we did some time ago.

I do not propose to give the House a detailed account of the episode at Dakar. I could easily do so in private, but it would be out of proportion to the scale of events. Moreover, I do not relish laying bare to the enemy all our internal processes. This operation was primarily French, and, although we were ready to give it a measure of support which in certain circumstances might have been decisive, we were no more anxious than was General de Gaulle to get involved in a lengthy or sanguinary conflict with the Vichy French. That General de Gaulle was right in believing that the majority of Frenchmen in Dakar was favorable to the Free French movement, I have no doubt; indeed, I think his judgment has been found extremely surefooted, and our opinion of him has been enhanced by everything we have seen of his conduct in circumstances of peculiar and perplexing difficulty. His Majesty's Government have no intention whatever of abandoning the cause of General de Gaulle until it is merged, as merged it will be, in the larger cause of France.

There is, however, one part of this story on which I should like to reassure the House, as it concerns His Majesty's Government alone and does not affect those with whom we have been working. The whole situation at Dakar was transformed in a most unfavorable manner by the arrival there of three French cruisers and three destroyers which carried with them a number of Vichy partisans, evidently of a most bitter type. These partisans were sent to overawe the population, to grip the defenses and to see to the efficient manning of the powerful shore batteries. The policy which His Majesty's Government had been pursuing towards the Vichy French warships was not to interfere with them unless they appeared to be proceeding to enemy-controlled ports. Obviously, however, while General de Gaulle's enterprise was proceeding it was specially important to prevent any of them reaching Dakar. By a series of accidents, and some errors which have been made the subject of disciplinary action or are now subject to formal inquiry, neither the First Sea Lord nor the Cabinet was informed of the approach of these ships to the Straits of

Gibraltar until it was too late to stop them passing through. Orders were instantly given to stop them at Casablanca, or if that failed, to prevent them entering Dakar. If we could not cork them in, we could at least, we hoped, have corked them out, but, although every effort was made to execute these orders, these efforts failed. The Vichy cruisers were, however, prevented from carrying out their further purpose of attacking the Free French Colony of Duala, and of the four French vessels concerned, two succeeded in regaining Dakar, while two were overtaken by our cruisers and were induced to return to Casablanca without any actual violence.

The House may therefore rest assured—indeed, it is the only point I am seeking to make today—that the mischievous arrival of these ships, and the men they carried, at Dakar arose in no way from any infirmity of purpose on the part of the Government; it was one of those mischances which often arise in war and especially in war at sea. The fighting which ensued between the shore batteries at Dakar, reinforced by the 16-inch guns of the damaged *Richelieu,* and the British squadron was pretty stiff. Two Vichy submarines which attacked the Fleet were sunk, the crew of one happily being saved. Two of the Vichy French destroyers were set on fire, one of the cruisers was heavily hit, and the *Richelieu* herself suffered further damage. On our part we had two ships, one a battleship and the other a large cruiser, which suffered damage—damage which, although it does not prevent their steaming and fighting, will require considerable attention when convenient.

What an irony of fate it is that this fine French Navy, which Admiral Darlan shaped for so many years to fight in the common cause against German aggression, should now be the principal obstacle to the liberation of France and her Empire from the German yoke, and should be employed as the tool of German and Italian masters whose policy contemplates not merely the defeat and mutilation of France, but her final destruction as a great nation. The Dakar incident reminds us of what often happens when a drowning man casts his arms around the strong swimmer who comes to his rescue and seeks in his agony to drag him down into the depths. Force in these circumstances has to be used to save life as well as to take life. But we never thought that what happened or might happen at Dakar was likely to lead to a declaration of war by the Vichy Government, although evidently such a step might be imposed upon them at any time by their masters. Whatever happens it is the tide and not mere eddies of events which will dominate the French people. Nothing can prevent the increasing abhorrence with which they will regard their German conquerors or the growth of the new-born hope that Great Britain will be victorious, and that the British victory will carry with it, as it must, the deliverance and restoration of France and all other captive peoples.

That is all I think it is useful to say at the present time, either about the Dakar affair or our relations with the Vichy Government, except this: We must be very careful not to allow a failure of this kind to weaken or hamper our efforts to take positive action and regain the initiative. On the contrary, we must improve our methods and redouble our efforts. We must be baffled to fight better and not baffled to fight less. Here let me say that criticism which is well-meant and well-informed and searching is often helpful, but there is a tone in certain organs of the Press, happily not numerous, a tone not only upon the Dakar episode but in other and more important issues, that is so vicious and malignant that it would be almost indecent if applied to the enemy. I know that some people's nerves are frayed by the stresses of war, and they should be especially on their guard lest in giving vent to their own feelings they weaken the national resistance and blunt our sword.

I must now ask the House to extend its view more widely and to follow me, if they can find the patience, to the other side of the globe. Three months ago we were asked by the Japanese Government to close the Burma road to certain supplies which might reach the Republic of China in its valiant struggle. We acceded to this demand because, as we told both Houses of Parliament, we tried to give an opportunity to the Governments of Japan and China to reach what is called in diplomatic language "a just and equitable settlement" of their long and deadly quarrel—there were no doubt some other reasons, but that one is enough for my argument. Unhappily this "just and equitable settlement" has not been reached. On the contrary, the protracted struggle of Japan to subjugate the Chinese race is still proceeding with all its attendant miseries. We much regret that the opportunity has been lost. In the circumstances His Majesty's Government propose to allow the agreement about closing the Burma road to run its course until 17th October, but they do not see their way to renew it after that.

Instead of reaching an agreement with China, the Japanese Government have entered into a Three-Power Pact with Germany and Italy, a pact which, in many respects, is a revival of the Anti-Comintern Pact of a few years ago, but which binds Japan to attack the United States

should the United States intervene in the war now proceeding between
Great Britain and the two European Dictators. This bargain appears so
unfavorable to Japan that we wonder whether there are not some secret
clauses. It is not easy now to see in what way Germany and Italy could
come to the aid of Japan while the British and United States Navies remain in being, as they certainly do and as they certainly will. However,
that is for the Japanese—with whom we have never wished to quarrel
—to judge for themselves. Great services have been rendered to them
by the peoples of the United States and Great Britain since their rise in
the nineteenth century. This is a matter on which they must judge for
themselves. This Three-Power Pact is, of course, aimed primarily at the
United States, but also in a secondary degree it is pointed against Russia.
Neither of the branches of the English-speaking race is accustomed to
react to threats of violence by submission, and certainly the reception
of this strange, ill-balanced declaration in the United States has not been
at all encouraging to those who are its authors. We hope, however, that
all such dangers—and the dangers can plainly be seen—will be averted
by the prudence and patience that Japan has so often shown in the gravest
situations.

There is another country much nearer home which has for some months
past seemed to hang in the balance between peace and war. We have
always wished well to the Spanish people, and in a glorious period of our
history we stood between the Spaniards and foreign domination. There
is no country in Europe that has more need of peace and food and the
opportunities of prosperous trade than Spain, which has been torn and
tormented by the devastation of a civil war, into which the Spanish nation
was drawn by a series of hideous accidents and misunderstandings, and
from the ruins of which they must now rebuild their united national life
of dignity, in mercy and in honor. Far be it from us to lap Spain and
her own economic needs in the wide compass of our blockade. All we
seek is that Spain will not become a channel of supply to our mortal
foes. Subject to this essential condition, there is no problem of blockade
that we will not study in the earnest desire to meet Spain's needs and aid
her revival. Even less do we presume to intrude on the internal affairs of
Spain or to stir the embers of what so lately were devouring fires. As in
the days of the Peninsular War, British interests and policy are based
on the independence and unity of Spain, and we look forward to seeing
her take her rightful place both as a great Mediterranean Power and as
a leading and famous member of the family of Europe and of Christen-

dom, which, though now sundered by fearful quarrels and under the obsession of grievous tyrannies, constitutes the goal towards which we are marching and will march across the battlefields of the land, the sea and the air.

Because we feel easier in ourselves and see our way more clearly through our difficulties and dangers than we did some months ago, because foreign countries, friends and foes, recognize the giant, enduring, resilient strength of Britain and the British Empire, do not let us dull for one moment the sense of the awful hazards in which we stand. Do not let us lose the conviction that it is only by supreme and superb exertions, unwearying and indomitable, that we shall save our souls alive. No one can predict, no one can even imagine, how this terrible war against German and Nazi aggression will run its course or how far it will spread or how long it will last. Long, dark months of trials and tribulations lie before us. Not only great dangers, but many more misfortunes, many shortcomings, many mistakes, many disappointments will surely be our lot. Death and sorrow will be the companions of our journey; hardship our garment; constancy and valor our only shield. We must be united, we must be undaunted, we must be inflexible. Our qualities and deeds must burn and glow through the gloom of Europe until they become the veritable beacon of its salvation.

LEADERSHIP OF THE PARTY

*Speech delivered at Caxton Hall
on Election to the Leadership of the Conservative
and Unionist Party*

October 9, 1940

1940

October 3.   For reasons of ill health Mr. Neville Chamberlain resigns from the Government and from the leadership of the Conservative Party.

LEADERSHIP OF THE PARTY

I FEEL very much honored that you have thought of calling me to assume the high and important task of leading the Conservative Party. The loss we have suffered and which I have suffered through the illness which has forced our late leader, Mr. Neville Chamberlain, to withdraw from active public life is heavy and painful. The thoughts and the wishes with which we follow him into his retirement are those of personal regard, and of respect and admiration for the courage and the integrity which have animated every action of his life.

It is now three years since I stood here and seconded the proposal that he should become our leader, and during the last thirteen months, some of which seem to count as if they were years, I was either his lieutenant or the head of the Government in which he so loyally and selflessly served. During that period our friendship, which was to some extent on both sides inherited, was welded in the fires of war into a comradeship of mutual trust and close identity of view. He has fallen out of our fighting ranks, and we must fill the gap in the Government and in the Party promptly and as best we may.

Before deciding to accept the trust and honor you wish to give me, I have asked myself two questions. The first is whether the leadership of a great Party is compatible with the position I hold from King and Parliament as Prime Minister of an Administration composed of and officially supported by all Parties. Unfortunately there are arguments both ways.

Considering, however, that I have to be in daily relations in matters of much domestic consequence with the leaders of the other two Parties who are serving in the Government, I felt that it would be more convenient that I should be able to speak for the Conservative Party with direct and first-hand knowledge of the general position which they occupy upon fundamental issues, and also to speak with their authority. It also seems to me, that, as Leader of the House of Commons at a time when the Conservative Party enjoys a very large majority over all other Parties, and when, owing to the war and the grave dangers and peculiar conditions amid which we live, no General Election is possible, I could discharge my task with less difficulty if I were in formal relation with the majority of the members of the House of Commons. If that, as I gather, Lord Halifax, from what you have said, is your opinion, I feel I need have no doubts as to either the wisdom or the propriety of the course which is now proposed.

The second question I have asked myself is much more personal. Am I by temperament and conviction able sincerely to identify myself with the main historical conceptions of Toryism, and can I do justice to them and give expression to them spontaneously in speech and action? My life, such as it has been, has been lived for forty years in the public eye, and very varying opinions are entertained about it—and about particular phases in it. I shall attempt no justification, but this I will venture most humbly to submit and also to declare, because it springs most deeply from the convictions of my heart: that at all times according to my lights and throughout the changing scenes through which we are all hurried I have always faithfully served two public causes which I think stand supreme —the maintenance of the enduring greatness of Britain and her Empire and the historical continuity of our Island life.

Alone among the nations of the world we have found the means to combine Empire and liberty. Alone among the peoples we have reconciled democracy and tradition; for long generations, nay, over several centuries, no mortal clash or religious or political gulf has opened in our midst. Alone we have found the way to carry forward the glories of the past through all the storms, domestic and foreign, that have surged about, and thus to bring the labors of our forebears as a splendid inheritance for modern progressive democracy to enjoy.

It is this interplay and interweaving of past and present which in this fearful ordeal has revealed to a wondering world the unconquerable strength of a united nation. It is that which has been the source of our strength. In that achievement, all living Parties—Conservative, Liberal, Labour, and other Parties, like the Whigs, who have passed away—all have borne a part and all today at the moment of our sorest need share the benefits which have resulted from it.

This is no time for partisanship or vaunting Party claims, but this I will say—the Conservative Party will not allow any Party to excel it in the sacrifice of Party interests and Party feelings which must be made by all if we are to emerge safely and victoriously from the perils which compass us about. In no other way can we save our lives and, what is far more precious than life, the grand human causes which we, in our generation, have the supreme honor to defend. It is because I feel that these deep conceptions lying far beneath the superficial current of Party politics and the baffling of accidental events have always been yours and have always been mine, that I accept solemnly, but also buoyantly, the trust and duty you wish now to confide in me.

TO THE FRENCH PEOPLE

An Address broadcast to France in French and English

October 21, 1940

1940

October 10. Cherbourg is bombarded by heavy and light forces of the Royal Navy, causing great damage to German shipping and stores.

October 15. H.M.S. *Ajax* sinks three Italian destroyers.

TO THE FRENCH PEOPLE

FRENCHMEN! FOR more than thirty years in peace and war I have marched with you, and I am marching still along the same road. Tonight I speak to you at your firesides wherever you may be, or whatever your fortunes are: I repeat the prayer around the *louis d'or, "Dieu protége la France."* Here at home in England, under the fire of the Boche, we do not forget the ties and links that unite us to France, and we are persevering steadfastly and in good heart in the cause of European freedom and fair dealing for the common people of all countries, for which, with you, we drew the sword. When good people get into trouble because they are attacked and heavily smitten by the vile and wicked, they must be very careful not to get at loggerheads with one another. The common enemy is always trying to bring this about, and, of course, in bad luck a lot of things happen which play into the enemy's hands. We must just make the best of things as they come along.

Here in London, which Herr Hitler says he will reduce to ashes, and which his aeroplanes are now bombarding, our people are bearing up unflinchingly. Our Air Force has more than held its own. We are waiting for the long-promised invasion. So are the fishes. But, of course, this for us is only the beginning. Now in 1940, in spite of occasional losses, we have, as ever, command of the seas. In 1941 we shall have the command of the air. Remember what that means. Herr Hitler with his tanks and other mechanical weapons, and also by Fifth Column intrigue with traitors, has managed to subjugate for the time being most of the finest races in Europe, and his little Italian accomplice is trotting along hopefully and hungrily, but rather wearily and very timidly, at his side. They both wish to carve up France and her Empire as if it were a fowl: to one a leg, to another a wing or perhaps part of the breast. Not only the French

Empire will be devoured by these two ugly customers, but Alsace-Lorraine will go once again under the German yoke, and Nice, Savoy and Corsica —Napoleon's Corsica—will be torn from the fair realm of France. But Herr Hitler is not thinking only of stealing other people's territories, or flinging gobbets of them to his little confederate. I tell you truly what you must believe when I say this evil man, this monstrous abortion of hatred and defeat, is resolved on nothing less than the complete wiping out of the French nation, and the disintegration of its whole life and future. By all kinds of sly and savage means, he is plotting and working to quench for ever the fountain of characteristic French culture and of French inspiration to the world. All Europe, if he has his way, will be reduced to one uniform Boche-land, to be exploited, pillaged, and bullied by his Nazi gangsters. You will excuse my speaking frankly because this is not a time to mince words. It is not defeat that France will now be made to suffer at German hands, but the doom of complete obliteration. Army, Navy, Air Force, religion, law, language, culture, institutions, literature, history, tradition—all are to be effaced by the brute strength of a triumphant Army and the scientific low cunning of a ruthless Police Force.

Frenchmen—rearm your spirits before it is too late. Remember how Napoleon said before one of his battles: "These same Prussians who are so boastful today were three to one at Jena, and six to one at Montmirail." Never will I believe that the soul of France is dead. Never will I believe that her place amongst the greatest nations of the world has been lost for ever! All these schemes and crimes of Herr Hitler's are bringing upon him and upon all who belong to his system a retribution which many of us will live to see. The story is not yet finished, but it will not be so long. We are on his track, and so are our friends across the Atlantic Ocean, and your friends across the Atlantic Ocean. If he cannot destroy us, we will surely destroy him and all his gang, and all their works. Therefore, have hope and faith, for all will come right.

Now, what is it we British ask of you in this present hard and bitter time? What we ask at this moment in our struggle to win the victory which we will share with you, is that if you cannot help us, at least you will not hinder us. Presently you will be able to weight the arm that strikes for you, and you ought to do so. But even now we believe that Frenchmen, wherever they may be, feel their hearts warm and a proud blood tingle in their veins when we have some success in the air or on the sea, or presently—for that will come—upon the land.

Remember we shall never stop, never weary, and never give in, and that our whole people and Empire have vowed themselves to the task of cleansing Europe from the Nazi pestilence and saving the world from the new Dark Ages. Do not imagine, as the German-controlled wireless tells you, that we English seek to take your ships and colonies. We seek to beat the life and soul out of Hitler and Hitlerism. That alone, that all the time, that to the end. We do not covet anything from any nation except their respect. Those French who are in the French Empire, and those who are in so-called unoccupied France, may see their way from time to time to useful action. I will not go into details. Hostile ears are listening. As for those to whom English hearts go out in full, because they see them under the sharp discipline, oppression, and spying of the Hun—as to those Frenchmen in the occupied regions—to them I say, when they think of the future let them remember the words which Thiers, that great Frenchman, uttered after 1870 about the future of France and what was to come: "Think of it always: speak of it never."

Good night, then: sleep to gather strength for the morning. For the morning will come. Brightly will it shine on the brave and true, kindly upon all who suffer for the cause, glorious upon the tombs of heroes. Thus will shine the dawn. *Vive la France!* Long live also the forward march of the common people in all the lands towards their just and true inheritance, and towards the broader and fuller age.

Message de M. Winston Churchill aux Français

Français! Pendant plus de 30 ans, en temps de paix comme en temps de guerre, j'ai marché avec vous et je marche encore avec vous aujourd'hui, sur la même route. Ce soir je vous parle, au sein même de vos foyers, où que vous soyiez, et quelque soit votre sort. Je répète la prière qui entourait vos Louis d'Or: "Dieu protège la France." Ici, chez nous, en Angleterre, sous le feu de Boche, nous n'oublions pas quels liens et quelles attaches nous unissent à la France: nous continuons à lutter de pied ferme et d'un cœur solide, pour que la liberté soit rétablie en Europe, pour que le peuple soit traité avec justice dans tous les pays, en un mot pour faire triompher la cause qui nous a fait ensemble tirer l'épée. Quand des honnêtes gens se trouvent déconcertés par les attaques et les coups que leur portent des coquins et des méchants, ils doivent faire bien attention de ne pas commencer à se quereller entre eux. C'est ce que l'ennemi commun essaie toujours de provoquer et naturellement quand la malchance s'y met bien des choses arrivent qui font le jeu de l'ennemi.

Je me rappelle toujours ce que dit Maître Labori il y a bien des années, après qu'il fût blessé par un assassin: "L'accident a beaucoup plus de place que l'intention dans les affaires humaines."

Ici, dans cette ville de Londres que Herr Hitler prétend réduire en cendres et que ses avions bombardent en ce moment, nos gens tiennent bon. Notre aviation a fait plus que de tenir tête à l'ennemi. Nous attendons l'invasion promise de longue date. Les poissons aussi. Mais, bien sûr, nous n'en sommes encore qu'au commencement. Aujourd'hui en 1940, comme toujours, nous avons la maîtrise des mers. En 1941, nous aurons la maîtrise de l'air. N'oubliez pas ce que cela veut dire. Herr Hitler avec ses chars d'assaut et ses autres armes mécaniques, et aussi grâce aux intrigues de sa cinquième colonne avec les traîtres, a réussi, pour le moment, à conquérir la plupart des races les plus belles de l'Europe et son petit complice italien, plein d'espoir et d'appétit, continue à trotter craintivement à son côté. Tous deux veulent découper la France et son Empire. L'un veut la cuisse, et l'autre l'aile.

Non seulement l'Empire française sera dévoré par ces deux vilains messieurs, mais l'Alsace-Lorraine va une fois encore repasser sous le joug allemand—et Nice, la Savoie et la Corse—la Corse de Napoléon—seront arrachés du beau domaine de la France. Mais Monsieur Hitler ne songe pas seulement à voler le territoire des autres peuples et à en distraire quelques morceaux pour les lancer à son petit chien. Je vous dis la vérité et il faut que vous me croyiez. Cet homme de malheur, ce monstrueux enfant de la haine et de la défaite n'est résolu à rien moins qu'à faire entièrement disparaître la nation française, qu'à désagréger sa vie même et par conséquent à ruiner son avenir. Il se prépare par toutes sortes de moyens sournois et féroces, à tarir pour toujours les sources de la culture et de l'inspiration françaises dans le monde. S'il est libre d'agir à sa guise, toute l'Europe ne sera plus qu'une Bochie uniforme, offerte à l'exploitation, au pillage et à la brutalité des gangsters nazis. Si je vous parle aussi carrément, excusez-moi, mais, ce n'est pas le moment de mâcher les mots.

Ce ne sont pas les conséquences de la défaite que la France doit aujourd'hui subir de la main des Allemands, mais toutes les étapes d'une annihilation complète. Armée, Marine, Aviation, Lois, Langue, Culture, Littérature, Histoire, Traditions, toutes vont être effacées par la force brutale d'une armée triomphante et par les ruses scientifiques et basses d'une police impitoyable.

Français! Armez vos cœurs à neuf avant qu'il ne soit trop tard. Rappelez-vous de quelle façon Napoléon disait avant une de ses victoires: "Ces mêmes Prussiens qui sont aujourd'hui si vantards étaient à 3 contre 1 à Jéna et à 9 contre 1 à Montmirail." Jamais je ne croirai que l'âme de la France soit morte, ni que sa place parmi les grandes nations du monde puisse être perdue pour toujours.

Tous les complots et tous les crimes de Herr Hitler sont en train d'attirer sur sa tête et sur la tête de ceux qui appartiennent à son régime un châtiment que beaucoup d'entre nous verrons de leur vivant. Il n'y aura pas si longtemps à attendre. L'aventure n'est pas encore finie. Nous sommes sur sa piste; et nos amis de l'autre côté de l'océan Atlantique y sont aussi. Si Herr Hitler ne peut pas nous détruire, nous, nous somme sûrs de le détruire, avec toute sa clique et tous leurs traveaux. Ayez donc espoir et confiance. Tout se rétablira.

Maintenant, nous autres Britanniques, que pouvons-nous vous demander aujourd'hui, dans un moment si âpre et si dur? Ce que nous vous demandons, au milieu de nos efforts pour remporter la victoire que nous partagerons avec vous, c'est que, si vous ne pouvez pas nous aider, au moins vous ne nous fassiez pas obstacle. En effet, vous devez renforcer le bras qui frappe pour vous. Nous croyons que les Français, où qu'ils soient, se sentiront le cœur réchauffé et que la fiérté de leur sang tressaillera dans leurs veines chaque fois que nous remporterons un succès dans les airs, sur mer, ou, plus tard—et cela viendra—sur terre. N'oubliez pas que nous ne nous arrêterons jamais, que nous ne nous lasserons jamais, que jamais nous ne céderons et que notre peuple et notre Empire tout entier se sont voués à la tâche de guérir l'Europe de la pestilence nazie et de sauver le monde d'une nouvelle barbarie. Parmi les Français, seux qui se trouvent dans l'Empire Colonial et ceux qui habitent la France soi-disant inoccupée peuvent, sans doute, de temps à autre, trouver l'occasion d'agir utilement. Je n'entre pas dans les détails. Les oreilles ennemies nous ecoutent. Les autres, vers qui l'affection anglaise se porte d'un seul mouvement, parce qu'ils vivent sous la stricte discipline, l'oppression et l'espionnage des Boches, je leur dis: Quand vous pensez à l'avenir, rappelez-vous les mots de ce grand Français que fut Thiers: Il les prononça après 1870, à propos de l'avenir: "Y penser toujours; n'en parler jamais."

Allons, bonne nuit, dormez bien, rassemblez vos forces pour l'aube—car l'aube viendra. Elle se levera brillante pour les braves, douce pour les fidèles qui auront souffert, glorieuse sur les tombeaux des héros. Vive la France! Et vive aussi la marche en avant des peuples de tous les pays qui veulent reconquérir le patrimonie qui leur appartient de plein droit.

THE WAR SITUATION V

The House of Commons

November 5, 1940

1940

October 28.   Italy invades Greece from Albania.

October 31.   Aircraft of the Bomber Command attack oil tanks and other targets in Naples.

THE WAR SITUATION V

SINCE I last addressed the House on general topics about a month ago the course of events at home has not been unexpected, nor, on the whole, unsatisfactory. Herr Hitler declared on 4th September that, as we would not bend to his will, he would wipe out our cities. I have no doubt that when he gave the order he sincerely believed that it was in his power to carry his will into effect. However, the cities of Britain are still standing. They are quite distinctive objects in the landscape, and our people are going about their tasks with the utmost activity. Fourteen thousand civilians have been killed and 20,000 seriously wounded, nearly four-fifths of them in London. That has been the loss of life and limb. As against this, scarcely 300 soldiers have been killed and 500 wounded. So much for the attack on military objectives. A great deal of house property has been destroyed or damaged, but nothing that cannot be covered by our insurance scheme. Very little damage has been done to our munitions and aircraft production, though a certain amount of time has been lost through frequent air-raid warnings. This lost time will have to be made up as we get settled down to the new conditions. None of the services upon which the life of our great cities depend—water, fuel, electricity, gas, sewage—not one, has broken down. On the contrary, although there must inevitably be local shortages, all the authorities concerned with these vital functions of a modern community feel that they are on top of their job and are feeling it increasingly as each week is passed.

Transport has been a greater difficulty, as may well be imagined when we think of the vast numbers who go in and out of our great cities every day. However, we are getting a good grip of that, and I say with some confidence that by one method or another, and probably by many methods at the same time, the problems connected with transport will be solved in a manner tolerable to the great numbers of people who are affected. Shelters are being multiplied and improved, and preparations on an extensive scale are in progress for mitigating the inevitable severities of the winter for those who are using the shelters. All this is going forward, and the House has received accounts of it from the different Ministers who are particularly concerned. In these vicissitudes the bearing of our people, not only in London, but in Birmingham, Liverpool, Manchester and other places, has gained the unstinted admiration of all classes throughout the British Empire, throughout the United States, and, so far as they have been allowed to hear about it, among the peoples of the captive countries. As I was going home the other night, I asked a group of steel-helmeted men who stood about the door what was going on, and a deep voice in the background said, "It's a grand life, if we don't weaken." There is the British watchword for the winter of 1940. We will think of something else by the winter of 1941.

There is no doubt that the full malice and power of the enemy and his bombing force have been employed against us. They have tried their best to obey Hitler's orders, but the scale of their attack has dwindled. The weekly average of the casualties killed and seriously wounded was, for September, 4,500, and for October, 3,500. In the first week of intense bombardment in September there were 6,000 casualties; in the last week of October only 2,000 casualties. This diminution in the scale of the attack is not entirely due to the weather. The weather, no doubt, has a lot to do with it, but there are other things going on which play their part besides the weather and which, I believe, will play a greater part as the months pass by. The House will not wish me to go into technical details on these points.

Meanwhile, how have the attackers fared? Two months ago I hazarded the statement—I admit it was rather a shot—that we hoped over our own country to destroy three enemy machines to one, and six pilots to one. So far it seems I was almost exactly right about the machines, taking the whole period, and I was very nearly right about the pilots, but, of course, if you count the whole of the crews of the large enemy bombers which have been brought down, all highly trained personnel, then it would be more like ten to one. So I somewhat underestimated, from that point of view, the results which have been achieved. Obviously, this process, combined with our own rapidly increasing production and the production in the Empire and in the United States of aircraft and airmen, is much the quickest road to our reaching that parity in the air which has always been considered the minimum of our safety, and thereafter reaching that superiority in the air which is the indispensable precursor of victory. Surveying the whole scene, alike in its splendor and its devastation, I see no reason to regret that Herr Hitler tried to break the British spirit by the blind bombing of our cities and our countryside.

More serious than the air raids has been the recent recrudescence of U-boat sinkings in the Atlantic approaches to our Islands. The fact that we cannot use the south and west coasts of Ireland to refuel our flotillas and aircraft and thus protect the trade by which Ireland as well as Great Britain lives, is a most heavy and grievous burden and one which should never have been placed on our shoulders, broad though they be. Moreover, we have been during the last month at the lowest point of our flotilla strength. The threat of invasion has always to be met. The great forces which we are maintaining in the Mediterranean, in addition to the escorts necessary for the protection of our innumerable convoys, have imposed on the Royal Navy a gigantic task.

However, this period of stringency is perhaps passing. The 50 American destroyers are rapidly coming into service just when they are most needed, and the main flow of new construction started at the outbreak of war is now coming on. In spite of serious losses, we have still very nearly as much shipping tonnage as we had at the outbreak of the war, and a great deal of neutral tonnage which used to trade freely with us is now under our control. Moreover, our U-boat hunting is still having its successes. Two more German U-boats have been sunk in the last two or three days on the western approaches, one of them the U-boat which sank the *Empress of Britain*. We have a number of their crews who have been saved as prisoners of war. On the other hand, when I speak of our shipping tonnage not being appreciably diminished from the beginning of the war, it must be remembered that our shipping is not so fruitful in war as in peace time because ships have to go a long way round; they have often to zig-zag and there are delays in the marshaling of convoys and sometimes delays through congestion at the ports. Therefore, it would not be wise to suppose that a greater stringency has not been brought about, although the actual volume of shipping remains practically undiminished.

I need scarcely say that intense efforts are being made by the Admiralty —my right hon. Friend the First Lord gives the whole of his life and strength and high abilities to the task, and I am confident that he is aided by the ablest officers in the Service—and also by the Ministry of Shipping to cope with these difficulties, and having lived through a lot of it in this war and the last, I, personally, cannot doubt that they will be able to cope with them and will be able to bring in all the vital supplies of food and munitions which we shall require. Dangers in the air are sudden and might have become catastrophic, but the dangers to our sea-borne traffic mature much more slowly. They are none the less formidable, however, and, if in any way neglected, they would touch the life of the State. We must expect that next year a still heavier U-boat attack will be made upon us, and we are making immense preparations to meet it.

We have to look a long way ahead on this sphere of the war. We have to think of the years 1943 and 1944 and of the tonnage programs which we shall be able to move and which we shall have to move across the oceans then. Every endeavor must be made to use the time available to produce the greatest volume of food of which this fertile Island is capable and so liberate our Navy and our merchant shipping for the movement of the considerable armies which will certainly be required in those years, if the enemy do not surrender or collapse in the meanwhile. Having dwelt upon this sea communication aspect rather openly and bluntly this morning, I should not like to leave it without assuring the House that I, personally, have no doubt whatever that we shall make our way through all right.

I turn to another of our dangers. Some of those very clever people who are sometimes wise after the event are now talking about "the invasion scare." I do not mind that, because it is true that the danger of invasion, particularly invasion by barges, has diminished with the coming of the winter months and the unpredictable uncertainty of the weather. It has also been diminished by the victories of the Royal Air Force and the ever-growing strength of the British Army. When I spoke at the end of June, I set forth in detail the well-known difficulties which would attend the invasion of these Islands and which had been forgotten in years when we had not considered the matter at all. At that time, we had only a few brigades of well-armed and well-trained troops in this Island. We had no Home Guard to deal with an invader or to deal with air-borne attacks behind the lines, and the Royal Air Force had not then proved itself master of our own air by daylight.

Very different is the scene today. We have a very large Army here, improving in equipment and training continually. The main part of that Army is now highly mobile and is being constantly imbued with the spirit of counter-attack. We have 1,700,000 men in the Home Guard, all of whom will be in uniform by the end of this year and nearly all of whom are in uniform at this moment. Nearly 1,000,000 of the Home Guard have rifles or machine guns. Nearly half of the whole Home Guard are veteran soldiers of the last war. Such a force is of the highest value and importance. A country where every street and every village bristles with loyal, resolute, armed men is a country against which the kind of tactics which destroyed Dutch resistance—tactics of parachutists or airborne troops in carriers or gliders, Fifth Column activities—if there were any over here, and I am increasingly skeptical—would prove wholly ineffective. A country so defended would not be liable to be overthrown by such tactics. Therefore, I agree with those who think that the invasion danger has for the time being diminished. But do not let us make the mistake of assuming that it has passed away, or that it may not occur in more acute form or in some other form.

What is it that has turned invasion into an invasion scare? It is the maintenance in Britain of strong forces and unremitting vigilance by sea, air and land. A mighty army crouches across the Channel and the North Sea, and substantial masses of shipping are gathered in all the harbors of the western seaboard of Europe from the North Cape to the Gironde River. We must not let our "shallow-clevers" lead us into thinking that this is all pretense, a maneuver to tie us down here and prevent our redisposing our Forces. The vital realities of their duties must be borne in on the whole of our Home Forces and the whole of our Home Guard during these winter months. There must be no relaxation except for necessary leave; but let me say this: that the plain fact that an invasion planned on so vast a scale has not been attempted in spite of the very great need of the enemy to destroy us in our citadel, and that all these anxious months when we stood alone and the whole of the world wondered have passed safely away—that fact constitutes in itself one of the historic victories of the British Isles and is a monumental milestone on our onward march.

Here let me say a word about the British Army. We are engaged in forming and training a very strong Army, and the like is being done in Canada, Australia, South Africa, New Zealand and India. We are now in the fifteenth month of the war and the British Army, of which I speak particularly now, is beginning to shape itself with precision. Although the sea and air will be the main elements of the war effort of the British Empire, we must have a strong Army, well equipped, well armed, well trained and well organized, capable of intervening as the war proceeds in

the liberation of one or the other of the many countries which are yearn-
ing to throw off the odious Nazi yoke. Without such an Army, forged,
tempered and sharpened, and the sea power which gives it so wide a
choice, the action of this war might be needlessly prolonged and might
drift towards disastrous stalemate. Nothing must be done which retards
or hinders the development of our Army. What it lacks in numbers compared with the Nazi or Fascist hosts, it must make up in quality and
equipment. This is a lengthy process, but we must persevere and not let
ourselves be drawn from the task by passing distractions or temptations.

The British Army is quite ready in any emergency to give all possible
help to Civil Defense forces in meeting local difficulties which might
arise from exceptional air attack. To some districts which are overweighted
by the burdens cast upon them they have given very great assistance and
will, where necessary, give more. But to hear some people talk, one would
think that we must begin almost immediately to draft a large portion of
our Army into the civil and A.R.P. services. One would take its lorries,
another would take its engineers and another would take its telegraphists;
yet another would use man-power on a great scale to clear away ruins.
Just as before this war it was a temptation not to make proper arrangements for Civil Defense, now there is this inclination, not unnaturally—
it appears quite reasonable and rather seductive—to trench unduly on the
efficiency of the military machine in order to meet day-by-day requirements. Let us be on our guard against this. All through this winter the
Army has got to train itself and its fighting men in all the arts and
maneuvers of war. The House of Commons, the Press and public opinion
must be active to ward off from our Army all demands and influences
which would hamper or delay the preparation of a weapon of the highest
quality. Only in this way shall we reach a position where, instead of being
forced to suffer the measureless vexations of a widespread defensive attitude, we shall regain the initiative and make the enemy wonder where
and how we are going to strike at them. I ask the House, which is the
foundation of our war-making effort, to keep a careful eye on this aspect
of our affairs.

During all this menace of invasion, so near and so deadly, we have
never failed to reinforce our armies in Egypt, almost to the limits of
our shipping capacity, not only with men but with precious weapons
which it was a wrench to take from our forces here. Scores of thousands
of troops have left this Island month after month or have been drawn
from other parts of the Empire for the Middle East. These troops have

been streaming away from this Island during the months when some of those who now talk so gaily about the invasion scare were scared stiff themselves. Several times I have told the House that I could not guarantee a favorable result in the Middle East. After all, our position there was calculated on the basis that France was our ally and that the powerful French armies that General Weygand organized would stand side by side with us in the discharge of our joint obligations. The submission of the French Government to the German conquest and to the Italian exploitation has not only deprived us of those armies in Syria, Tunis, Algeria and Morocco, but has denied us the assistance of the fine French Navy and the use of the French naval and air bases in the Mediterranean. Such a frightful desertion and loss might well have confronted us with an insoluble problem. The Italian Army in Libya, which some months ago far outnumbered the British and Imperial Forces in and around Egypt, seemed likely to roll forward irresistibly upon the Nile Valley and the Suez Canal.

I am thankful to be able to assure the House that the balance of forces on the frontiers of Egypt and in the Sudan is far less unfavorable than it was at the time of the French collapse. I can certainly not prophesy to the House about battles which have yet to be fought, but I think at the beginning of July, if we cast our minds back, the House would have been very glad to be assured that on 5th November we should still be holding in largely increased force every position of any importance. We have not had any serious collisions with the Italian forces, but we have every reason to be content with the results of the skirmishes and forays which have taken place on the ground and in the air. Up to the end of September, the Italian official published casualties for the fighting in Libya amounted to 800 killed, 1,700 wounded and 860 missing; our own casualties for the same period and in the same theater were 66 killed, 68 wounded, and 36 missing—a scale approaching something like 20 to 1. These facts speak for themselves and should be a good augury for the greater battles and engagements which will develop, perhaps in the winter, certainly in the spring.

At the same time that the Navy is keeping open the sea routes under this very dangerous U-boat attack, and endeavoring to hunt down merchant raiders in the outer seas, and maintaining a strict blockade—at the same time as it is doing that, we have ceaselessly strengthened the Fleet in the eastern Mediterranean, and we are ready at any time to engage the Italian Navy in a general action. Time after time our Fleet has moved into close proximity to the main concentration of the Italian Fleet, and we know that their presence has been detected from the air, but so far these cruises have not resulted in any decisive encounter. Still, the power of the British Fleet in the eastern Mediterranean goes a long way to restore the situation created by the collapse of France and is a great guarantee to our friend and ally, Turkey, of the unweakening power of Great Britain on the seas. Therefore, whether you look at the Home Front or at the Mediterranean theater, I do not think it can be denied that we are far better off than anyone would have ventured to predict four or five months ago.

But now a new call has suddenly been made upon us. The Italian dictator, perhaps embarrassed by the somewhat florid flirtations of M. Laval with the German conqueror, or perhaps playing his part in some new predatory design, has, in his customary cold-blooded way, fallen upon the small but famous and immortal Greek nation. Without the slightest provocation, with no pretense at parley, Signor Mussolini has invaded Greece, or tried to do so, and his aircraft have murdered an increasing number of Greek civilians, women and children, in Salonika and many other open Greek towns. The Greek King, his Government and the Greek people have resolved to fight for life and honor, and, lest the world should be too easily led in chains, France and Great Britain guaranteed to come to the aid of Greece if she were the victim of unprovoked aggression. It was a joint guarantee, and unhappily the Vichy Government is at this moment engaged in "sincere and loyal collaboration" with Herr Hitler in his schemes for establishing a so-called new order in Europe. At any rate, the Vichy Government is no longer in a position to play its expected part in the task it had accepted. We are therefore left alone.

We have most carefully abstained from any action likely to draw upon the Greeks the enmity of the criminal Dictators. For their part, the Greeks have maintained so strict a neutrality that we were unacquainted with their dispositions or their intentions. I have already been at some pains to set forth to the House the very serious preoccupations which dominate us both at home and in the Middle East. We face one gigantic army across the waters of the Channel, we face another very powerful army on the frontier of the Libyan Desert, and I must, as I say, approach the new task with a strong sense of the immense responsibilities which rest upon us both at home and in Egypt, and of the very great and continual dangers by which we are confronted. In the circumstances, there is only one thing we can do. We will do our best. We have already established a naval and air base in Crete which will enable us sensibly to extend the activities and radius of the Navy and of the Air Force. We have begun the bombing attack upon military objectives in the Italian cities and bases in the South of Italy. That will continue on an ever-growing scale. I should also say that our forces are in movement with the desire and design to help the Greeks to the utmost of our capacity, having regard to our other obligations. I hope I shall not be asked by the House to give any definite account of such measures as we are able to take. If I were to set them high, I might raise false hopes; if I set them low, I might cause undue despondency and alarm; and if I stated exactly what they were, that would be exactly what the enemy would like to know. We shall do our best. That is all I can say. To that decision and declaration, generously and faithfully interpreted, I invoke with confidence the approval of the House.

"WE WILL NEVER CEASE TO STRIKE"

The Mansion House

November 9, 1940

November 5. Franklin D. Roosevelt elected President of the United States of America for a third term of office by a popular vote of 25,956,562 against Wendell Willkie's vote of 21,591,032.

Operating from new Greek bases, the R.A.F. attack Bari and Brindisi, and bomb military objectives in Naples.

November 8. While Nazi celebrations are taking place in the famous beer cellar in Munich, the R.A.F. visit that city and drop bombs on military objectives, accidentally hitting the beer cellar in the course of the raid.

"WE WILL NEVER CEASE TO STRIKE"

I THANK you, my Lord Mayor, for the toast which you have proposed to his Majesty's Government and for what you have said about them and of the confidence felt in them. I thank you also for your reference to Mr. Chamberlain, who was so recently one of our most active colleagues, under whom so many of us have served, and whose illness causes us all the greatest sorrow today. Things happen so quickly nowadays and there are such a lot of them going on that one finds it somewhat difficult to measure evenly the march of time. For myself, I can say there are weeks which seem to pass in a flash and then again there are others which are unutterably long and slow. At times it is almost difficult to believe that so much has happened, and at another that so little time has passed.

It is now six months since the King and Parliament confided to me and to my colleagues the very grave and heavy task to which we have devoted ourselves, as I can assure you, to the best of our abilities. It is lucky that we did not make any extravagant optimistic promises or predictions, because a succession of melancholy disasters and terrible assaults and perils have fallen upon us. We have had to face these great calamities; we have come through the disasters; we have surmounted the perils so far; but the fact remains that at the present time all we have got to show is survival and increasing strength and an inflexible will to win.

The outside world, which a little while ago took only a moderate view of our prospects, now believes that Britain will survive. But between immediate survival and lasting victory there is a long road to tread. In treading it, we shall show the world the perseverance and steadfastness of the British race and the glorious resilience and flexibility of our ancient institutions.

Let me remind you that, in spite of all the blows we have endured and under all the burdens we bear, and amid so many deadly threats, we have not abandoned one jot of any of our obligations or undertakings towards the captive and enslaved countries of Europe or towards any of those countries which still act with us. On the contrary, since we have been left alone in this world struggle we have reaffirmed or defined more precisely all the causes of all the countries with whom or for whom we drew the sword—Austria, Czechoslovakia, Poland, Norway, Holland, Belgium; greatest of all, France; latest of all, Greece. For all of these we will toil and strive, and our victory will supply the liberation of them all.

The week that has now ended has brought us a message from across the ocean, a message of the highest encouragement and good cheer during the protracted tumult and controversy of the Presidential Election. Everyone in this island—Parliament, Ministers, the Press, the public—discreetly abstained from the slightest expression of opinion about the domestic, political, and Party conflicts of the great democracy of the United States.

We were deeply touched by the words of kindness and good will and the promises of material aid which were uttered by Mr. Willkie on behalf of the Republican Party, which he captained so ably. But I am sure it will give no offense, now that all is over, if I offer in the name of H.M. Government, and, if you will allow me, my Lord Mayor, in the name of the citizens of London, our most heartfelt congratulations to the illustrious American statesman who has never failed to give us a helping hand, and who now, in the supreme crisis, has achieved the unprecedented mark of American confidence of being chosen for the third time to lead his mighty people forward on their path.

The help that we have been promised by the United States takes the form at the present time of a most abundant sharing with us of the fruits of the gigantic munitions production which has now been set on foot throughout the matchless workshops, furnaces, and foundries of the United States. This has no doubt been done primarily because our stubborn and unwavering resistance here will alone gain the time needed by the United States to convert its industry to a war basis and to build up the immense naval, military, and air forces which they have set on foot for their own purposes and for their own protection.

Their interest in our successful resistance and final victory has been proclaimed by all Parties in America. But no one over here has been left in any doubt that, beyond this strong material help and foundation of common interest, there flows a tide of comprehension, of sentiment, and fierce, matchless sympathy for our cause which warms our hearts and strengthens our resolve.

People sometimes wonder why we are unable to take the offensive against the enemy, and always have to wait for some new blow which he will strike against us. The reason is that our production in munitions is now only in the early part of its second year, and that enormous factories and plants which we laid down on or shortly before the outbreak of war are only now beginning to come into production. The Germans, on the other hand, have long passed the culminating point of munitions production, which is reached usually about the fourth year.

We have, therefore, a long and arduous road to travel in which our war industries must grow up to their full stature, in which our Navy must receive the reinforcements of the hundreds of vessels which we began on the outbreak of war, and which are now coming continuously into service; in which our Army must be equipped, trained, and perfected into a strong, keen offensive weapon; and, above all, our Air Force must add superiority of numbers to that superiority of quality which, in machines, and still more in manhood, they have so signally displayed. We are straining every nerve to accelerate our production, and with the ardent, resolute aid of British labor, guided by science and improving organization, I do not doubt that we shall succeed.

But here is where the help from across the oceans is especially valuable, because in the United States, as in our great Dominions and in India, all the production of war materials and the training of pilots can proceed without any distraction or impediment. Therefore I welcome most cordially the aid which has been promised us from the United States, as I do the important contributions which have already been received. There is one other point which must, however, be borne in mind in this survey. The enemy is naturally doing his utmost to cut us from these vital supplies and, therefore, the maintenance by sea power of the ocean routes is an absolute necessity to our victory, and is of importance to all who need or who desire our victory.

It has been usual, on these occasions, for the Prime Minister to give a general survey of foreign policy and to refer to our relations with many countries in well-guarded, well-poised, and happily balanced terms. Today I need not do that. It has been obvious to all that we are striving to the utmost of our strength for the freedom of nations against the oppressor, that we are striving for the progress of peoples through the process of self-government, and for the creation of that wider brotherhood among men which alone will bring them back to prosperity and peace. We do not need to speak, therefore, of many of those nations.

But there is one small heroic country to whom our thoughts today go out in new sympathy and admiration. To the valiant Greek people and their armies—now defending their native soil from the latest Italian outrage—to them we send from the heart of old London our faithful promise that, amid all our burdens and anxieties, we will do our best to aid them in their struggle, and that we will never cease to strike at the foul aggressor in ever-increasing strength from this time forth until the crimes and treacheries which hang around the neck of Mussolini and disgrace the Italian name have been brought to condign and exemplary justice.

THE WAR SITUATION VI

The House of Commons

December 19, 1940

November 11. Planes of the Fleet Air Arm attack the Italian naval base at Taranto. Two battleships half sunk and a third severely damaged; two cruisers badly hit and other vessels put out of action, thus finally destroying Italian numerical naval superiority in the Mediterranean.

November 16. German night bombers make a concentrated attack on Coventry, causing much damage and many casualties.

November 23. The Greeks capture the important stronghold of Koriza and the Italians begin a hurried retreat through Albania.

December 11. The Italians are defeated by General Wavell at Sidi Barrani with immense losses in prisoners and matériel.

December 12. Lord Lothian, British Ambassador to the United States, dies in Washington after a short illness.

THE WAR SITUATION VI

BEFORE I come to the immediate business which this Motion suggests, I take the opportunity of expressing the grief which the House has felt in all quarters at the untimely, sudden death of our Ambassador in the United States, Lord Lothian. He was a man of the very highest character and of far-ranging intellectual scope. All his life his mind played about broad issues of human progress, and, whether at home or abroad, he animated an ardent philanthropy with the keenest and brightest intellectual powers. In India his work is much respected. His work in the last war was already important, as my right hon. Friend the Member for Carnarvon Boroughs [Mr. Lloyd George]—whom I am very glad to see here today—could no doubt remind us. But all the same, when he was appointed before the war to the Embassy in the United States, the most important of all the functions outside this country that can be discharged by any British subject, there were various opinions upon the wisdom of that choice. Very soon, however, it was seen that the new Ambassador was gaining in influence every day, that his stature rose with the greatness of the topics confided to him, and that the contacts which he established, the intimate relations which he developed, with the high personnel of the United States Administration, the friendship to which the President of the United States has himself testified—all the evidence showed the remarkable efficiency and success with which he discharged his important and extremely delicate and difficult mission.

Suddenly, he is taken from us. He passes away. But I cannot help feeling that to die at the height of a man's career, the highest moment of his effort here in this world, universally honored and admired, to die while great issues are still commanding the whole of his interest, to be taken from us at a moment when he could already see ultimate success in view—is not the most unenviable of fates. I feel that the House would have wished me to express, in these few words, the sorrow which we feel at his death, and also the very grievous and practical sense that we have of the loss we have suffered at this particular juncture in having been deprived of his invaluable services.

I should like to put rather frankly to the House a difficulty which I feel about making frequent statements on the war situation. I have to be much concerned in the conduct of the war in consequence of being called upon to occupy the offices which I do as Prime Minister and Minister of Defense, and there is a danger, if one gives full and frank and frequent statements revealing one's own point of view, or the point of view of the Government or of those who are charged with the strategical and tactical decisions, that the enemy may gain an advantage. Certainly it would be very convenient if Herr Hitler or the important chiefs in Germany were to give us, every fortnight or so, an honest-to-God—if they were capable of it—statement. I am sure we should immediately set a dozen active and agile Intelligence Officers to study not only what was said but what was not said, and to read not only the lines but between the lines, and to collate any stray words with the other information which might perhaps afford a clew. Therefore, I hope the House will be indulgent to me if, although always at their service, I choose the occasions somewhat rarely; and, in the event of their desiring information at some period which I do not feel convenient, I hope the House will allow me to impart it to them as far as possible in secret Session.

With this prelude, let me remind the House, in reinforcement of my plea for not making too many speeches, that I did say when we opened the Session, in a speech which I made on the Motion in reply to the Gracious Speech, that what was wanted was deeds, not words. Well, I do not think we have wholly failed to make good that hope. The Battle of the Libyan Desert is still proceeding, and I have no later news than that which is contained in the public Press at the moment. We are attacking the fort and town of Bardia with strong and increasing forces, and the situation there is not such that I can make any decided statement upon it. But I will go so far as to say that I have reason to believe it is developing favorably. Of course, of this memorable battle spread over this vast extent of desert, with swiftly moving mechanized columns circling in and out of the camps and posts of the enemy, and with fighting taking place over an area as large, I have been told, as Yorkshire, it is not possible to give all the details at the present time. I am, however, sure that the figure of 30,000 prisoners is, even up to the present moment, a considerable understatement, and 100 serviceable guns and 50 tanks, together with a great quantity of invaluable stores, have also been gathered by our troops. At Sidi Omar, the day before yesterday, operations resulted in another 800 prisoners and a battery of artillery being captured, and on the same day at Giarabub Oasis, west of the Siwa Oasis, that was being attacked by Australian Forces, it happened that an Australian cavalry squadron charged sword in hand and gathered both guns and transport as its trophies.

One cannot say that the Italians have shown a high fighting spirit, or quality, in this battle. In other periods of Italian history, we know, they have shown great courage; and I am certainly not going to frame a charge of lack of military qualities against a people with whom up to this time we have had—and God knows we never sought it now—no quarrel. But perhaps their hearts are not in their work. Perhaps they have been so long controlled and disciplined and ruled, and so much relieved of all share in the government of their own country, that they have not felt those virile emotions which are the foundation for the actions of brave armies, and which are best nourished by discipline imposed upon freedom. At any rate, we have seen the spectacle of at least one whole Italian division laying down its arms to far inferior forces; and our Air Force, which has been contending at odds of three or four or five to one, has been fighting with continued success. The House will be anxious to know what in this fighting the cost has been in life and limb to our troops. Up to the night of the 16th, which is the latest return I have, the British Army, a considerable Army, which was moved so rapidly into the desert, having continuous fighting the whole week, lost less than 1,000 killed and wounded, of all ranks, British, Indians and Imperial troops. There no doubt have been other losses since. We must regard this event as highly satisfactory; and its reactions in other directions will be favorable, and should permit us to take bolder views than those which have been open to us before.

This is a case where risks have been well run. The risk in the desert was considerable. The movement across 70 or 80 miles of desert of this large force was open to very considerable hazards, and the assault upon Sidi Barrani had about it this cause of anxiety—with which I did not trouble the House at the time—that petrol and water were strictly limited in the attacking force, and that failure or delay would have entailed considerable curtailment of our operations. But these risks have been surmounted by the great skill of our Commander, General Wilson, who is reputed to be one of our finest tacticians; and General Wavell, whose figure grows upon the Eastern horizon, rises there to the very great pleasure and encouragement of all the people over here who look eagerly to see the arrival upon the scene of this great war of military, naval, and air figures to whom the Armies and the Fleets can give their enthusiasm. I must not forget the work which has been done in this battle by Air Chief Marshal Longmore, who at the most critical moment in their preparations had to have a very large part of his force taken away from him for Greece, but who nevertheless persevered, running additional risks, and whose handling of this situation, in co-operation with the Army, deserves the highest praise. It is, indeed, a pleasure to me personally, because when I was at the Admiralty in 1912, forming the Royal Naval Air Service, he was one of the first few fliers there, and in those days of very dubious machines he several times used to fly me about. We were personal friends as long ago as that.

I hope that the House will be contented with the present results achieved by this offensive. I do not consider that it is by any means at an end, but I think it will be better to let the future unfold as it will, without attempting to skip on ahead or in any way to forecast how the play may run. I have said that I considered that risks were well run there. They were also well run here by the General Staff of the British Army and by the War Cabinet and by the staffs who studied this matter; because it was not an easy thing in July and August—if we cast our minds back to that date—to send precious tanks of the best quality and cannon, of which we were then so short, on that long journey around the Cape of Good Hope, in order to enable us at first to defend ourselves, and later to assume the offensive. I can only say that those were hard decisions to take, and that my right hon. Friend the Secretary of State for War and I had many anxious days in coming to those conclusions. But you will not have any means of abridging this war, or indeed, of emerging from it safely, unless risks are run. Risks do imply that when forfeit is exacted, as it may be when a great ship is sunk or some great attack repulsed with heavy slaughter, the House will stand by the Government and the military commanders. I have endeavored always to say that those who launch themselves against the enemy, in any action, with vigor and violence will, whatever the upshot, receive the support of His Majesty's Government and, I doubt not, also of the House of Commons.

Another reason which makes this victory gratifying to us is that the

British Army has at last had an opportunity of showing its quality. We have had hard and unfortunate experiences in this war; but in the fighting around Dunkirk all the divisions which were engaged with the enemy had the consciousness that they were fully a match for their German opponents. Several battles fought on a front of one or two divisions showed that we had not the slightest reason to shrink from contact on anything like equal terms or even against a show of arms with the regular mass of the troops of the German Army. Now we have seen in Libya that our military science and staff officers are capable of planning and executing extremely complex and daring operations with efficiency— and it is not there only that we have such officers. Therefore, I renew my advice to the House to do all possible to cultivate and develop the strength and efficiency of the great British Army now building up at home. Certainly, it will give its help in any emergency where air-raid damage occurs, but we must have here an Army on a large scale—I carefully avoid saying what the numbers should be, but on a large scale—not only to defend this Island, but for action in other theaters should they suggest themselves at any time. We must have a large Army, well found, equipped with the very best weapons, and drilled, trained and practiced in what I have ventured to call all the arts and maneuvers of war.

I am sure the House will feel that is a wise and provident provision for the year 1941, in which we shall, I trust, find opportunities of using our Forces, if not in defense of this Island, in other theaters, where we may hope that they will be able to contend with their opponents on terms of a moderate equality in numbers and, I trust, in terms of equality of equipment. This is the first time that we have had equal equipment. As I have said, we are still only half armed. It is no good hoping and asking for immediate conclusions. We are still a half-armed nation fighting a well-armed nation, a fully-armed nation, a nation which has already passed the saturation point in its armaments. But in the course of 1941 we shall become a well-armed nation too, and that will open possibilities to us which have not been opened up to the present. As my right hon. Friend the Member for Carnarvon Boroughs knows so well, it takes three or four years to put the industries of a country onto a war basis. The Germans reached the saturation point, the culmination point, certainly at the end of last year, and now we ourselves are still only in the second year; but by the efforts which are being made and by the great supplies which are reaching us and will reach us from the United States, we hope that we shall become well armed during the course of 1941. It

is essential that every effort should be made in the armaments and munitions factories to improve the supplies not only of the Air Force but of
the Army, and every risk well run there under the fire of the enemy,
every loyal endeavor which our united nation can procure from the
workmen in those factories, who themselves are whole-hearted in the
vigorous prosecution of the war, everything that can be done to accelerate
and to make a more abundant production, will be a step towards victory,
and towards an earlier victory than would otherwise be possible.

The House is now separating. Hon. Members will be in their constituencies in many cases. Let them use their influence wherever they can
to speed the good work, to sustain the morale, if ever it were necessary,
and to speed the work of production in every way they possibly can.
When we come back we can indeed debate these issues of man-power and
production. We are not by any means content with the results, but they
are certainly on a very great and very substantial scale. We must never
be content. We must continue the drive to our utmost in order to see
that our men have weapons placed in their hands worthy of the task that
they have to perform and worthy of the qualities and sacrifice that they
bring to the discharge of that task. What I have said in respect of munitions applies with equal force to food production in all its forms. When
I spoke the other day of the years 1943 and 1944, I did not mean that
I believed the war would go on then, but in matters like agriculture
and shipbuilding you have to get onto steady grooves. You have to look
ahead. If you do not make plans on that scale, you will not even get the
first fruits in good time. Anything that can be done to increase the
volume of our food production will be the wisest insurance for the later
years of this war, assuming it should unhappily be prolonged to such a
period, which is by no means certain.

We are separating for a short Recess, and we may, I think, look with
some sense of composure and even satisfaction at the progress which has
been made and at the state of our affairs; but it would be a disaster if
anyone supposed that the supreme dangers, the mortal dangers, are past.
They are not. There are the dangers of prolonged deadlock, but there
may be also more immediate dangers. The winter season offers some
advantages to an invader to counterbalance those which belong to the
summer season. It would be a very great lack of prudence, a lack of
prudence amounting to a crime, if vigilance were relaxed in our Armies
here at home, or if in any way it was assumed that the dangers of invasion
had passed. Most careful preparations must continue to be made, and

although it has been for some time past possible to give a proportion of leave to our troops to their homes which are close at hand, which are in this small Island, yet that should not in any way be taken as the slightest justification for supposing that we must not watch from hour to hour the dangerous menace which still exists in full force at so very short a distance away. I may say that, of course, our defense of the beaches is complete. From the North of Scotland right round the Island enormous masses of guns and machine guns and fortified posts, with every device of defense, have been erected and are guarded by large numbers of ardent and well-trained men.

But we are not making the mistake which was made by the French General Staff when they thought that holding the Maginot Line was all that was necessary. I remember well going to Paris at that dark moment after the first defeat and asking immediately, "What are you going to do with your mass of maneuver or general reserve?" It was with the greatest sorrow that I learned that a general reserve did not exist and had to be drawn from different parts of the line. Well, we have now got a very large Army behind in this country which is capable of moving to any place with great rapidity and going into action in the strongest counter-offensive, and, therefore, one may have good confidence in our power to beat the enemy, even supposing he should succeed in setting foot in any strength on these shores.

Nevertheless the watchword which we must carry must be that vigilance must be unceasing. We must remember that Herr Hitler—and I certainly deprecate any comparison between Herr Hitler and Napoleon; I do not wish to insult the dead—who wields gigantic power and is capable of wielding it in a ruthless manner, has great need of doing something now, or soon, at any rate, in the next few months. When the war began he had his plans all ready for Poland, and he doubted whether Britain and France would come in, or if they came in, would persist. When he had destroyed Poland, he found himself faced with the war effort of Britain and France. He waited a long time in complete quiescence, as it seemed, and then struck those terrible series of blows which shattered France. He then thought that in the fall of France would be involved the fall of Britain, but it did not turn out that way; it turned out differently, and one must suppose that he is making other plans which will be particularly directed to our benefit and our address. Therefore, I am using this opportunity of addressing the House to urge not only increasing vigilance but the increasing effort of all, wherever they may be.

We are not afraid of any blow which may be struck against us, but we must make increasing preparations. The attacks in the air have slackened somewhat because of the weather, but they might easily have slackened in preparation for some other form of activity. I need hardly say, however, that the method of dealing with them and fighting by night is being studied with passion and zeal by a very large number of extremely able and brilliant scientists and officers. So far we have been no more successful in stopping the German night raider than Germans have been successful in stopping our aeroplanes, which have ranged freely over Germany. We have struck very heavy blows; the blows at Mannheim appeared to be of a very heavy character, and the enemy have not found any means of preventing them. So far we have not reached any satisfactory remedy, although we have noticed a considerable improvement in various directions. We must expect a continuance of these attacks and must bear them. The organization of shelters, the improvement of sanitation, and the endeavor to mitigate the extremely painful conditions under which many people have to get their night's rest—that is the first task of the Government at home. The Air-Raid Precautions, the Home Office, and the Ministry of Health are just as much in the front line of the battlefield as are the armored columns which are chasing the Italian columns about the Libyan desert. I hope and trust, indeed, that we shall succeed in mitigating increasingly the conditions which prevail in shelters. It will not be for the want of trying or for the lack of spending money. But the difficulties of handling such great numbers of people under conditions where materials are short and labor is so fully employed on this or that other task are very great. It is a matter in which we welcome the assistance of Parliament, in either public or secret Session. Complaints can be made, and should be brought to the notice of Ministers in order that everything possible may be done.

The only other point I would mention is the sinkings in the Atlantic. They still continue at a very disquieting level; not so bad as in the critical period of 1917, but still we must recognize the recrudescence of the danger which, a year ago, we seemed to have mastered. We shall steadily increase, from now on, our resources in flotillas and other methods of defense, but we must regard the keeping open of this channel to the world against submarines and the long-distance aircraft which are now attacking as the first of the military tasks which lie before us at the present time.

I have spoken rather longer than I had intended, but the interest of these topics is such that one is bound to refer to them. All I can say now

is that if we look back to where we were in May and June, there is not
one of us who cannot go away for Christmas—I would not say for holidays, because, so far as Ministers are concerned, any relaxation must only
be the opportunity for making up arrears—or separate for the time being
without a feeling of thankfulness that we have been preserved so far
and that we have made progress after a moment when many in the
world, including our best friends abroad, despaired of our continued
power of resistance, that we have maintained ourselves, that our resistance
has grown, that we have preserved ourselves secure in our Island home
and reached out long and strong hands across the seas to discharge the
obligations which we have undertaken to countries which have put their
faith in us.

TO THE PEOPLE OF ITALY

An Address broadcast to Italy in English and Italian

December 23, 1940

TO THE PEOPLE OF ITALY

TONIGHT I speak to the Italian people and I speak to you from London, the heart of the British Islands and of the British Commonwealth and Empire. I speak to you what the diplomatists call words of great truth and respect. We are at war—that is a very strange and terrible thought. Whoever imagined until the last few melancholy years that the British and Italian nations would be trying to destroy one another? We have always been such friends. We were the champions of the Italian Risorgimento. We were the partisans of Garibaldi, the admirers of Mazzini and Cavour. All that great movement towards the unity of the Italian nation which lighted the nineteenth century was aided and was hailed by the British Parliament and public. Our fathers and our grandfathers longed to see Italy freed from the Austrian yoke, and to see all minor barriers in Italy swept away, so that the Italian people and their fair land might take an honored place as one of the leading Powers upon the Continent and as a brilliant and gifted member of the family of Europe and of Christendom. We have never been your foes till now.

In the last war against the barbarous Huns we were your comrades. For fifteen years after that war we were your friends. Although the institutions which you adopted after that war were not akin to ours, and diverged, as we think, from the sovereign impulses which had commanded the unity of Italy, we could still walk together in peace and good will. Many thousands of our people dwelt with you in Italy. We liked each other; we got on well together. There were reciprocal services; there was amity; there was esteem. And now we are at war; now we are condemned to work each other's ruin. Your aviators have tried to cast their bombs upon London; our armies are tearing and will tear your African Empire to shreds and tatters. We are only now at the beginning

of this somber tale. Who can say where it will end? Presently we shall
be forced to come to closer grips.

How has all this come about, and what is it all for? Italians, I will tell
you the truth. It is all because of one man. One man and one man alone
has ranged the Italian people in deadly struggle against the British
Empire, and has deprived Italy of the sympathy and intimacy of
the United States of America. That he is a great man I do not deny,
but that after eighteen years of unbridled power he has led your country
to the horrid verge of ruin, can be denied by none. It is all one, one man,
who, against the Crown and Royal Family of Italy, against the Pope and
all the authority of the Vatican and of the Roman Catholic Church,
against the wishes of the Italian people who had no lust for this war—
one man has arrayed the trustees and inheritors of ancient Rome upon
the side of the ferocious, pagan barbarians. *There* lies the tragedy of
Italian history, and *there* stands the criminal who has wrought the deed
of folly and of shame. What is the defense that is put forward for his
action? It is, of course, the quarrel about Sanctions and Abyssinia. Let
us look at that. Together, after the last war, Italy and Britain both signed
the Covenant of the League of Nations, which forbade all parties to that
Covenant to make war upon each other, or upon fellow members of the
League, and bound all signatories to come to the aid of any member
attacked by another. Presently Abyssinia came knocking at the door,
asking to be a member. We British advised against it. We doubted whether
they had reached a stage in their development which warranted their
inclusion in so solemn a pact. But it was Signor Mussolini who insisted
that Abyssinia should become a member of the League, and who therefore bound himself, and bound you and us, to respect their Covenanted
rights.

Thus the quarrel arose, it was out of this that it sprang; and thus, although no blood was shed between us, old friendships were forgotten. But
what is the proportion of this Abyssinian dispute, arising out of the Covenant of the League of Nations, to which we had both pledged our word—
what is it in proportion compared to the death-grapple in which Italy and
Britain have now been engaged? I declare—and my words will go far
—that nothing that happened in that Abyssinian quarrel can account
for or justify the deadly strife which has now broken out between us.

Then the great war between the British and French democracies and
Prussian militarism or Nazi overlordship began again. Where was the
need for Italy to intervene? Where was the need to strike at prostrate

France? Where was the need to declare war on Britain? Where was the need to invade Egypt, which is under British protection? We were content with Italian neutrality. During the first eight months of the war, we paid great deference to Italian interests. But this was all put down to fear. We were told we were effete, worn out, an old chatterbox people mouthing outworn shibboleths of nineteenth-century Liberalism. But it was not due to fear. It was not due to weakness. The French Republic for the moment is stunned. France will rise again, but the British nation and Commonwealth of Nations across the globe, and indeed I may say the English-speaking world, are now aroused. They are on the march or on the move, and all the forces of modern progress and of ancient culture are ranged behind them.

Why have you placed yourselves, you who were our friends and might have been our brothers—why have you placed yourselves in the path of this avalanche, now only just started from its base to roll forward on its predestined track? Why, after all this, were you made to attack and invade Greece? I ask why—but you may ask too, because you were never consulted. The people of Italy were never consulted, the Army of Italy was never consulted. No one was consulted. One man, and one man alone ordered Italian soldiers to ravage their neighbor's vineyard. Surely the time has come when the Italian monarchy and people, who guard the sacred center of Christendom, should have a word to say upon these awe-inspiring issues? Surely the Italian Army, which has fought so bravely on many occasions in the past, but now evidently has no heart for the job, should take some care of the life and future of Italy? I can only tell you that I, Churchill, have done my best to prevent this war between Italy and the British Empire; and to prove my words I will read you the message which I sent to Signor Mussolini in the fateful days before it began. Cast your minds back to the 16th of May of this year, 1940. The French front had been broken; the French Army was not yet defeated; the great battle in France was still raging. Here is the message which I sent to Signor Mussolini:

"Now that I have taken up my office as Prime Minister and Minister of Defense, I look back to our meeting in Rome and feel a desire to speak words of good will to you as chief of the Italian nation across what seems to be a swiftly widening gulf. Is it too late to stop a river of blood from flowing between the British and Italian peoples? We can no doubt inflict injuries upon one another and maul each other cruelly, and darken the Mediterranean with our strife. If you so decree, it must be so; but I declare that I have never been the enemy of Italian greatness, nor ever at heart the foe of the Italian law-giver. It is idle to predict the course of the great battles now raging in Europe; but I am sure that, whatever may happen on the Continent, England will go on to the end, even quite alone, as we have done before; and I believe with some assurance that we shall be aided in increasing measure by the United States and indeed by all the Americans. I beg you to believe that it is in no spirit of weakness or of fear that I make this solemn appeal which will remain on record. Down the ages above all other calls comes the cry that the joint heirs of Latin and Christian civilization must not be ranged against one another in mortal strife. Hearken to it, I beseech you in all honor and respect, before the dread signal is given. It will never be given by us."

And this is the reply which I received:

"I reply to the message which you have sent me in order to tell you that you are certainly aware of grave reasons of a historical and contingent character which have ranged our two countries in opposite camps. Without going back very far in time I remind you of the initiative taken in 1935 by your Government to organize at Geneva Sanctions against Italy engaged in securing for herself a small space in the African sun, without causing the slightest injury to your interests and territories, or those of others. I remind you also of the real and actual state of servitude in which Italy finds herself in her own sea. If it was to honor your signature that your Government declared war on Germany, you will understand that the same sense of honor and of respect for engagements assumed in the Italian-German Treaty guides Italian policy today and tomorrow in the face of any event whatsoever."

This is the answer. I make no comment upon it. It was a dusty answer. It speaks for itself. Anyone can see who it was wanted peace, and who it was that meant to have war. One man, and one man only, was resolved to plunge Italy after all these years of strain and effort into the whirlpool of war. And what is the position of Italy today? Where is it that the Duce has led his trusting people after eighteen years of dictatorial power? What hard choice is open to him now? It is to stand up to the battery of the whole British Empire on sea, in the air, and in Africa, and the vigorous counter-attack of the Greek nation; or, on the other hand, to call in Attila over the Brenner Pass with his hordes of ravenous soldiery and his gangs of Gestapo policemen to occupy, hold down and protect the Italian people, for whom he and his Nazi followers cherish the most bitter and outspoken contempt that is on record between races.

There is where one man, and one man only, has led you; and there I leave this unfolding story until the day comes—as come it will—when the Italian nation will once more take a hand in shaping its own fortunes.

UNITED STATES CO-OPERATION

A Talk at a Pilgrims' Luncheon given in honor of Lord Halifax

January 9, 1941

UNITED STATES CO-OPERATION

It is no exaggeration to say that the future of the whole world and the hopes of a broadening civilization founded upon Christian ethics depend upon the relations between the British Empire or Commonwealth of Nations and the U.S.A.

The identity of purpose and persistence of resolve prevailing throughout the English-speaking world will, more than any other single fact, determine the way of life which will be open to the generations, and perhaps to the centuries, which follow our own.

If the co-operation between the United States and the British Empire in the task of extirpating the spirit and regime of totalitarian intolerance, wherever it may be found, were to fail, the British Empire, rugged and embattled, might indeed hew its way through and preserve the life and strength of our own country and our own Empire for the inevitable renewal of the conflict on worse terms, after an uneasy truce.

But the chance of setting the march of mankind clearly and surely along the highroads of human progress would be lost and might never return.

Therefore we stand, all of us, upon the watch towers of history, and have offered to us the glory of making the supreme sacrifices and exertions needed by a cause which it may not be irreverent to call sublime.

I have always taken the view that the fortunes of mankind in its tremendous journey are principally decided for good or ill—but mainly for good, for the path is upward—by its greatest men and its greatest episodes.

I therefore hail it as a most fortunate occurrence that at this awe-striking climax in world affairs there should stand at the head of the American Republic a famous statesman, long versed and experienced in the work of government and administration, in whose heart there burns the fire of resistance to aggression and oppression, and whose sympathies and nature make him the sincere and undoubted champion of justice and of freedom, and of the victims of wrongdoing wherever they may dwell.

And not less—for I may say it now that the party struggle in the United States is over—do I rejoice that this pre-eminent figure should newly have received the unprecedented honor of being called for the third time to lead the American democracies in days of stress and storm.

His Majesty's Government had placed in Washington an Ambassador, Lord Lothian, whose character and qualities were outstanding and had gained him the trust and friendship of President Roosevelt. Suddenly and unexpectedly Lord Lothian was struck down by death.

A link was broken, a gap was opened, and a loss of the highest consequence was sustained at a very grave moment in the annals of the British and American peoples, and for those generous and wide causes which they have in their different ways and in their different situations so resolutely espoused.

We therefore thought it our duty to restore this link, to fill this gap, to repair this loss, by sending, without regard to the derangement of our forces and circle here, the best we could find, without regard to any other consideration whatsoever.

We chose our Foreign Secretary, who had himself chosen Lord Lothian, to fill Lord Lothian's place. Our choice was most agreeable to the President, and it commands the full confidence of nearly all of those in this country who mean to persevere in our righteous cause until its certain victorious end is reached.

In Edward Halifax we have a man of light and leading, whose company is a treat and whose friendship it is an honor to enjoy.

I have often disagreed with him in the twenty years I have known him in the rough and tumble of British politics, but I have always respected him and his actions, because I know that courage and fidelity are the essence of his being, and that, whether as a soldier with his regiment in the last war, or as the ruler of, and trustee for, four hundred millions in India, he has never swerved from the path of duty as he saw it shining out before him.

As a man of deep but unparaded and unaffected religious convictions, and as for many years an ardent lover of the chase, he has known how to get the best out of both worlds.

Like all members of the present National Government in Great Britain, most of whom seem to be gathered around this board today, he has vowed himself to prosecute this war against the Nazi tyranny at whatever cost until its last vestiges are destroyed.

We send the United States an envoy who comes from the very center of our counsels and knows all our secrets.

Although, while Lord Halifax is serving as Ambassador out of this country he cannot be a member of the War Cabinet, he will be, if I may borrow a military term not wholly inappropriate to the times in which we live, as it were seconded from it.

He still attends all our meetings, and will continue to do so during the weeks before his departure, and should he be able to return here for consultation at any time in the summer, as I hope may be possible, he will resume his full functions and responsibilities as a Minister of the Crown.

We now bid him, and his brilliant and devoted wife, God-speed and all good fortune, and it is our fervent hope that he may prosper in a mission as momentous as any that the Monarchy has entrusted to an Englishman in the lifetime of the oldest of us here.

"PUT YOUR CONFIDENCE IN US"

An Address Broadcast

February 9, 1941

"PUT YOUR CONFIDENCE IN US"

FIVE MONTHS have passed since I spoke to the British nation and the Empire on the broadcast. In wartime there is a lot to be said for the motto: "Deeds, not words." All the same, it is a good thing to look around from time to time and take stock, and certainly our affairs have prospered in several directions during these last four or five months, far better than most of us would have ventured to hope.

We stood our ground and faced the two Dictators in the hour of what seemed their overwhelming triumph, and we have shown ourselves capable, so far, of standing up against them alone. After the heavy defeats of the German air force by our fighters in August and September, Herr Hitler did not dare attempt the invasion of this Island, although he had every need to do so and although he had made vast preparations. Baffled in this mighty project, he sought to break the spirit of the British nation by the bombing, first of London, and afterwards of our great cities. It has now been proved, to the admiration of the world, and of our friends in the United States, that this form of blackmail by murder and terrorism, so far from weakening the spirit of the British nation, has only roused it to a more intense and universal flame than was ever seen before in any modern community.

The whole British Empire has been proud of the Mother Country, and they long to be with us over here in even larger numbers. We have been deeply conscious of the love for us which has flowed from the Dominions of the Crown across the broad ocean spaces. *There* is the first of our war aims: to be worthy of that love, and to preserve it.

All through these dark winter months the enemy has had the power to drop three or four tons of bombs upon us for every ton we could send to Germany in return. We are arranging so that presently this will be rather the other way round; but, meanwhile, London and our big cities have had to stand their pounding. They remind me of the British squares at Waterloo. They are not squares of soldiers; they do not wear scarlet coats. They are just ordinary English, Scottish and Welsh folk—men, women and children—standing steadfastly together. But their spirit is the same, their glory is the same; and, in the end, their victory will be greater than far-famed Waterloo.

All honor to the Civil Defense Services of all kinds—emergency and regular, volunteer and professional—who have helped our people through this formidable ordeal, the like of which no civilized community has ever been called upon to undergo. If I mention only one of these services here, namely the Police, it is because many tributes have been paid already to the others. But the Police have been in it everywhere, all the time, and as a working woman wrote to me: "What gentlemen they are!"

More than two-thirds of the winter has now gone, and so far we have had no serious epidemic; indeed, there is no increase of illness in spite of the improvised conditions of the shelters. That is most creditable to our local, medical and sanitary authorities, to our devoted nursing staff, and to the Ministry of Health, whose head, Mr. Malcolmn MacDonald, is now going to Canada in the important office of High Commissioner.

There is another thing which surprised me when I asked about it. In spite of all these new war-time offenses and prosecutions of all kinds; in spite of all the opportunities for looting and disorder, there has been less crime this winter and there are now fewer prisoners in our jails than in the years of peace.

We have broken the back of the winter. The daylight grows. The Royal Air Force grows, and is already certainly master of the daylight air. The attacks may be sharper, but they will be shorter; there will be more opportunities for work and service of all kinds; more opportunities for life. So, if our first victory was the repulse of the invader, our second was the frustration of his acts of terror and torture against our people at home.

Meanwhile, abroad, in October, a wonderful thing happened. One of the two Dictators—the crafty, cold-blooded, blackhearted Italian, who had thought to gain an Empire on the cheap by stabbing fallen France in the back—got into trouble. Without the slightest provocation, spurred on by lust of power and brutish greed, Mussolini attacked and invaded Greece, only to be hurled back ignominiously by the heroic Greek Army; who, I will say, with your consent, have revived before our eyes the glories which, from the classic age, gild their native land. While Signor Mussolini was writhing and smarting under the Greek lash in Albania, Generals Wavell and Wilson, who were charged with the defense of Egypt and of the Suez Canal in accordance with our treaty obligations, whose task seemed at one time so difficult, had received very powerful reinforcements of men, cannon, equipment and, above all, tanks, which we had sent from our Island in spite of the invasion threat. Large numbers of troops from India, Australia and New Zealand had also reached them. Forthwith began that series of victories in Libya which have broken irretrievably the Italian military power on the African Continent. We have all been entertained, and I trust edified, by the exposure and humiliation of another of what Byron called

> "Those Pagod things of sabre sway
> With fronts of brass and feet of clay."

Here then, in Libya, is the third considerable event upon which we may dwell with some satisfaction. It is just exactly two months ago, to a day, that I was waiting anxiously, but also eagerly, for the news of the great counter-stroke which had been planned against the Italian invaders of Egypt. The secret had been well kept. The preparations had been well made. But to leap across those seventy miles of desert, and attack an army of ten or eleven divisions, equipped with all the appliances of modern war, who had been fortifying themselves for three months—that was a most hazardous adventure.

When the brilliant decisive victory at Sidi Barrani, with its tens of thousands of prisoners, proved that we had quality, maneuvering power and weapons superior to the enemy, who had boasted so much of his virility and his military virtues, it was evident that all the other Italian forces in eastern Libya were in great danger. They could not easily beat a retreat along the coastal road without running the risk of being caught in the open by our armored divisions and brigades ranging far out into the desert in tremendous swoops and scoops. They had to expose themselves to being attacked piecemeal.

General Wavell—nay, all our leaders, and all their lithe, active, ardent men, British, Australian, Indian, in the Imperial Army—saw their opportunity. At that time I ventured to draw General Wavell's attention to the seventh chapter of the Gospel of St. Matthew, at the seventh verse, where, as you all know—or ought to know—it is written: "Ask, and it shall be given; seek, and ye shall find; knock, and it shall be opened unto you."

The Army of the Nile has asked, and it was given; they sought, and they have found; they knocked, and it has been opened unto them. In barely eight weeks, by a campaign which will long be studied as a model of the military art, an advance of over 400 miles has been made. The whole Italian Army in the east of Libya, which was reputed to exceed 150,000 men, has been captured or destroyed. The entire province of Cyrenaica— nearly as big as England and Wales—has been conquered. The unhappy Arab tribes, who have for thirty years suffered from the cruelty of Italian rule, carried in some cases to the point of methodical extermination, these Bedouin survivors have at last seen their oppressors in disorderly flight, or led off in endless droves as prisoners of war.

Egypt and the Suez Canal are safe, and the port, the base and the air-fields of Benghazi constitute a strategic point of high consequence to the whole of the war in the Eastern Mediterranean.

This is the time, I think, to speak of the leaders who, at the head of their brave troops, have rendered this distinguished service to the King. The first and foremost, General Wavell, Commander-in-Chief of all the Armies of the Middle East, has proved himself a master of war, sage, painstaking, daring and tireless. But General Wavell has repeatedly asked that others should share his fame.

General Wilson, who actually commands the Army of the Nile, was reputed to be one of our finest tacticians—and few will now deny that quality. General O'Connor, commanding the 13th Corps, with General Mackay, commanding the splendid Australians, and General Creagh, who trained and commanded the various armored divisions which were employed—these three men executed the complicated and astoundingly rapid movements which were made, and fought the actions which occurred. I have just seen a telegram from General Wavell in which he says that the success at Benghazi was due to the outstanding leadership and resolution of O'Connor and Creagh, ably backed by Wilson.

I must not forget here to point out the amazing mechanical feats of the British tanks, whose design and workmanship have beaten all records and stood up to all trials; and show us how closely and directly the work in the factories at home is linked with the victories abroad.

Of course, none of our plans would have succeeded had not our pilots, under Air Chief Marshal Longmore, wrested the control of the air from a far more numerous enemy. Nor would the campaign itself have been possible if the British Mediterranean Fleet, under Admiral Cunningham, had not chased the Italian Navy into its harbors and sustained every forward surge of the Army with all the flexible resources of sea power. How far-reaching these resources are we can see from what happened at dawn this morning, when our Western Mediterranean Fleet, under Admiral Somerville, entered the Gulf of Genoa and bombarded in a shattering manner the naval base from which perhaps a Nazi German expedition might soon have sailed to attack General Weygand in Algeria or Tunis. It is right that the Italian people should be made to feel the sorry plight into which they have been dragged by Dictator Mussolini; and if the cannonade of Genoa, rolling along the coast, reverberating in the mountains, reached the ears of our French comrades in their grief and misery, it might cheer them with the feeling that friends—active friends—are near and that Britannia rules the waves.

The events in Libya are only part of the story: they are only part of the story of the decline and fall of the Italian Empire, that will not take a future Gibbon so long to write as the original work. Fifteen hundred miles away to the southward a strong British and Indian army, having driven the invaders out of the Sudan, is marching steadily forward through the Italian Colony of Eritrea, thus seeking to complete the isolation of all the Italian troops in Abyssinia. Other British forces are entering Abyssinia from the west, while the army gathered in Kenya—in the van of which we may discern the powerful forces of the Union of South Africa, organized by General Smuts—is striking northward along the whole enormous front. Lastly, the Ethiopian patriots, whose independence was stolen five years ago, have risen in arms; and their Emperor, so recently an exile in England, is in their midst to fight for their freedom and his throne. Here, then, we see the beginnings of a process of reparation, and of the chastisement of wrongdoing, which reminds us that, though the mills of God grind slowly, they grind exceeding small.

While these auspicious events have been carrying us stride by stride from what many people thought a forlorn position, and was certainly a very grave position in May and June, to one which permits us to speak with sober confidence of our power to discharge our duty, heavy though it be in the future—while this has been happening, a mighty tide of sympathy, of good will and of effective aid, has begun to flow across the Atlantic in support of the world cause which is at stake. Distinguished Americans have come over to see things here at the front, and to find out how the United States can help us best and soonest. In Mr. Hopkins, who has been my frequent companion during the last three weeks, we have the Envoy of the President, a President who has been newly re-elected to his august office. In Mr. Wendell Willkie we have welcomed the champion of the great Republican Party. We may be sure that they will both tell the truth about what they have seen over here, and more than that we do not ask. The rest we leave with good confidence to the judgment of the President, the Congress and the people of the United States.

I have been so very careful, since I have been Prime Minister, not to encourage false hopes or prophesy smooth and easy things, and yet the tale that I have to tell today is one which must justly and rightly give us cause for deep thankfulness, and also, I think, for strong comfort and even rejoicing. But now I must dwell upon the more serious, darker and more dangerous aspects of the vast scene of the war. We must all of us have been asking ourselves: What has that wicked man whose crime-stained regime and system are at bay and in the toils—what has he been preparing during these winter months? What new devilry is he planning? What new small country will he overrun or strike down? What fresh form of assault will he make upon our Island home and fortress; which— let there be no mistake about it—is all that stands between him and the dominion of the world?

We may be sure that the war is soon going to enter upon a phase of greater violence. Hitler's confederate, Mussolini, has reeled back in Albania; but the Nazis—having absorbed Hungary and driven Rumania into a frightful internal convulsion—are now already upon the Black Sea. A considerable Nazi German army and air force is being built up in Rumania, and its forward tentacles have already penetrated Bulgaria. With—we must suppose—the acquiescence of the Bulgarian Government, airfields are being occupied by German ground personnel numbering thousands, so as to enable the German air force to come into action from Bulgaria. Many preparations have been made for the movement of German troops into or through Bulgaria, and perhaps this southward movement has already begun.

We saw what happened last May in the Low Countries; how they hoped for the best; how they clung to their neutrality; how woefully they were deceived, overwhelmed, plundered, enslaved and since starved. We know how we and the French suffered when, at the last moment, at the urgent belated appeal of the King of the Belgians, we went to his aid. Of course, if all the Balkan people stood together and acted together, aided by Britain and Turkey, it would be many months before a German army and air force of sufficient strength to overcome them could be assembled in the southeast of Europe. And in those months much might happen. Much will certainly happen as American aid becomes effective, as our air power grows, as we become a well-armed nation, and as our armies in the East increase in strength. But nothing is more certain than that, if the countries of southeastern Europe allow themselves to be pulled to pieces one by one, they will share the fate of Denmark, Holland and Belgium. And none can tell how long it will be before the hour of their deliverance strikes.

One of our difficulties is to convince some of these neutral countries in Europe that we are going to win. We think it astonishing that they should be so dense as not to see it as clearly as we do ourselves. I remember in the last war, in July, 1915, we began to think that Bulgaria was going wrong, so Mr. Lloyd George, Mr. Bonar Law, Sir F. E. Smith and I asked the Bulgarian Minister to dinner to explain to him what a fool King Ferdinand would make of himself if he were to go in on the losing side. It was no use. The poor man simply could not believe it, or could not make his Government believe it. So Bulgaria, against the wishes of her peasant population, against all her interests, fell in at the Kaiser's tail and got sadly carved up and punished when the victory was won. I trust that Bulgaria is not going to make the same mistake again. If they do, the Bulgarian peasantry and people, for whom there has been much regard, both in Great Britain and in the United States, will for the third time in thirty years have been made to embark upon a needless and disastrous war.

In the Central Mediterranean the Italian Quisling, who is called Mussolini, and the French Quisling, commonly called Laval, are both in their different ways trying to make their countries into doormats for Hitler and his New Order, in the hope of being able to keep, or get the Nazi Gestapo and Prussian bayonets to enforce, their rule upon their fellow countrymen. I cannot tell how the matter will go, but at any rate we shall do our best to fight for the Central Mediterranean.

I dare say you will have noticed the very significant air action which was fought over Malta a fortnight ago. The Germans sent an entire *Geschwader* of dive-bombers to Sicily. They seriously injured our new aircraft-carrier *Illustrious,* and then, as this wounded ship was sheltering in Malta harbor, they concentrated upon her all their force so as to beat her to pieces. But they were met by the batteries of Malta, which is one of the strongest defended fortresses in the world against air attack; they were met by the Fleet Air Arm and by the Royal Air Force, and, in two or three days, they had lost, out of a hundred and fifty dive-bombers, upwards of ninety, fifty of which were destroyed in the air and forty on the ground. Although the *Illustrious,* in her damaged condition, was one of the great prizes of the air and naval war, the German *Geschwader* accepted the defeat; they would not come any more. All the necessary repairs were made to the *Illustrious* in Malta harbor, and she steamed safely off to Alexandria under her own power at 23 knots. I dwell upon this incident, not at all because I think it disposes of the danger in the Central Mediterranean, but in order to show you that there, as elsewhere, we intend to give a good account of ourselves.

But after all, the fate of this war is going to be settled by what happens on the oceans, in the air, and—above all—in this Island. It seems now to be certain that the Government and people of the United States intend to supply us with all that is necessary for victory. In the last war the United States sent two million men across the Atlantic. But this is not a war of vast armies, firing immense masses of shells at one another. We do not need the gallant armies which are forming throughout the American Union. We do not need them this year, nor next year; nor any year that I can foresee. But we do need most urgently an immense and continuous supply of war materials and technical apparatus of all kinds. We need them here and we need to bring them here. We shall need a great mass of shipping in 1942, far more than we can build ourselves, if we are to maintain and augment our war effort in the West and in the East.

These facts are, of course, all well known to the enemy, and we must therefore expect that Herr Hitler will do his utmost to prey upon our shipping and to reduce the volume of American supplies entering these Islands. Having conquered France and Norway, his clutching fingers reach out on both sides of us into the ocean. I have never underrated this danger, and you know I have never concealed it from you. Therefore, I hope you will believe me when I say that I have complete confidence in the Royal Navy, aided by the Air Force of the Coastal Command, and that in one way or another I am sure they will be able to meet every changing phase of this truly mortal struggle, and that sustained by the courage of our merchant seamen, and of the dockers and workmen of all our ports, we shall outwit, outmaneuver, outfight and outlast the worst that the enemy's malice and ingenuity can contrive.

I have left the greatest issue to the end. You will have seen that Sir John Dill, our principal military adviser, the Chief of the Imperial General

Staff, has warned us all that Hitler may be forced, by the strategic, economic and political stresses in Europe, to try to invade these Islands in the near future. That is a warning which no one should disregard. Naturally, we are working night and day to have everything ready. Of course, we are far stronger than we ever were before, incomparably stronger than we were in July, August and September. Our Navy is more powerful, our flotillas are more numerous; we are far stronger, actually and relatively, in the air above these Islands, than we were when our Fighter Command beat off and beat down the Nazi attack last autumn. Our Army is more numerous, more mobile and far better equipped and trained than in September, and still more than in July.

I have the greatest confidence in our Commander-in-Chief, General Brooke, and in the generals of proved ability who, under him, guard the different quarters of our land. But most of all I put my faith in the simple unaffected resolve to conquer or die which will animate and inspire nearly four million Britons with serviceable weapons in their hands. It is not an easy military operation to invade an island like Great Britain, without the command of the sea and without the command of the air, and then to face what will be waiting for the invader here. But I must drop one word of caution; for, next to cowardice and treachery, overconfidence, leading to neglect or slothfulness, is the worst of martial crimes. Therefore, I drop one word of caution. A Nazi invasion of Great Britain last autumn would have been a more or less improvised affair. Hitler took it for granted that when France gave in we should give in; but we did not give in. And he had to think again. An invasion now will be supported by a much more carefully prepared tackle and equipment of landing craft and other apparatus, all of which will have been planned and manufactured in the winter months. We must all be prepared to meet gas attacks, parachute attacks, and glider attacks, with constancy, forethought and practiced skill.

I must again emphasize what General Dill has said, and what I pointed out myself last year. In order to win the war Hitler must destroy Great Britain. He may carry havoc into the Balkan States; he may tear great provinces out of Russia; he may march to the Caspian; he may march to the gates of India. All this will avail him nothing. It may spread his curse more widely throughout Europe and Asia, but it will not avert his doom. With every month that passes the many proud and once happy countries he is now holding down by brute force and vile intrigue are learning to hate the Prussian yoke and the Nazi name as nothing has ever been hated so fiercely and so widely among men before. And all the time, masters of the sea and air, the British Empire—nay, in a certain sense, the whole English-speaking world—will be on his track, bearing with them the swords of justice.

The other day, President Roosevelt gave his opponent in the late Presidential Election a letter of introduction to me, and in it he wrote out a verse, in his own handwriting, from Longfellow, which he said, "applies to you people as it does to us." Here is the verse:

> ... Sail on, O Ship of State!
> Sail on, O Union, strong and great!
> Humanity with all its fears,
> With all the hopes of future years,
> Is hanging breathless on thy fate!

What is the answer that I shall give, in your name, to this great man, the thrice-chosen head of a nation of a hundred and thirty millions? Here is the answer which I will give to President Roosevelt: Put your confidence in us. Give us your faith and your blessing, and, under Providence, all will be well.

We shall not fail or falter; we shall not weaken or tire. Neither the sudden shock of battle, nor the long-drawn trials of vigilance and exertion will wear us down. Give us the tools, and we will finish the job.